# www.wadsworth.com

*www.wadsworth.com* is the World Wide Web site for Thomson Wadsworth and is your direct source to dozens of online resources.

At *www.wadsworth.com* you can find out about supplements, demonstration software, and student resources. You can also send email to many of our authors and preview new publications and exciting new technologies.

**www.wadsworth.com**
Changing the way the world learns®

## Frosting

Freedom
Is just frosting
On somebody else's
Cake—
And so must be
Till we
learn how to
Bake

# Analyzing Politics

## An Introduction to Political Science

### Third Edition

**ELLEN GRIGSBY**
University of New Mexico

THOMSON

WADSWORTH

Australia • Canada • Mexico • Singapore • Spain
United Kingdom • United States

**THOMSON**

**WADSWORTH**

Political Science Executive Editor: David Tatom
Senior Development Editor: Stacey Sims
Assistant Editor: Rebecca Green
Editorial Assistant: Reena Thomas
Technology Project Manager: Michelle Vardeman
Marketing Manager: Janise Fry
Marketing Assistant: Tara Pierson
Advertising Project Manager: Kelley McAllister
Project Manager, Editorial Production: Emily
    Smith

Print/Media Buyer: Judy Inouye
Permissions Editor: Kiely Sexton
Production Service: Matrix Productions
Photo Researcher: Image Quest
Copy Editor: Dan Hays
Compositor: Laserwords
Cover Designer: Sue Hart
Cover Image: Getty Images/Peter Gridley
Text and Cover Printer: Malloy Incorporated

For more information about our products,
contact us at:
**Thomson Learning Academic
Resource Center
1-800-423-0563**

For permission to use material from this text
or product, submit a request online at
**http://www.thomsonrights.com**.
Any additional questions about permissions
can be submitted by email to
**thomsonrights@thomson.com**.

Library of Congress Control Number: 2004102715

ISBN 0-534-63077-4

**Thomson Wadsworth
10 Davis Drive
Belmont, CA 94002-3098
USA**

**Asia**
Thomson Learning
5 Shenton Way #01-01
UIC Building
Singapore 068808

**Australia/New Zealand**
Thomson Learning
102 Dodds Street
Southbank, Victoria 3006
Australia

**Canada**
Nelson
1120 Birchmount Road
Toronto, Ontario M1K 5G4
Canada

**Europe/Middle East/Africa**
Thomson Learning
High Holborn House
50/51 Bedford Row
London WC1R 4LR
United Kingdom

**Latin America**
Thomson Learning
Seneca, 53
Colonia Polanco
11560 Mexico D.F.
Mexico

**Spain/Portugal**
Paraninfo
Calle Magallanes, 25
28015 Madrid, Spain

# Contents

# Preface

This text seeks to introduce students to some analytical dimensions of political science through discussions of research, theory, comparative, U.S., and international questions within the discipline. As discussed in greater detail in Chapter 1, this text includes chapters on political science and scientific research approaches, key concepts in political science, political theory and political ideology, comparative politics and U.S. politics, and international relations.

The text draws on academic and applied contributions to political discourse in an effort to show students that political science is a field of inquiry with many practical uses. Specifically, in this text I try to introduce basic political science concepts, demonstrate their significance in understanding contemporary political issues, and connect the concepts to larger theoretical models of analysis. The goal of encouraging students to think critically about the questions discussed in this text has also motivated every substantive decision throughout the composition process. *Analyzing Politics* is written to instruct, but also to provoke, to challenge, and sometimes to unsettle readers. Furthermore, I hope the text invites students to explore a broader range of perspectives and sources than those traditionally incorporated into introductory political science classes; toward this end, I have included more advanced topics, such as postmodernism.

Many students and a few professors have accepted my invitation to e-mail me with questions and comments about any issues raised in the text. These e-mail exchanges have been among the most satisfying and enriching of my academic experiences. Students from large universities and small colleges have pushed me to think more carefully about topics and have debated with me about how concepts in the book apply to changing political circumstances. Just as my own students at UNM continue to be among the best teachers I have ever had, my "e-mail students" have helped me see politics from new perspectives and have compelled me to expand the range of questions I ask.

Students and reviewers helped me think more carefully about a number of the questions discussed in the earlier editions. This edition gives greater attention to international relations and global politics. I have included updated information on topics ranging from the U.S. approach to combating terrorism after September 11, 2001, to media politics within the context of globalization. I hope the coverage in the third edition helps students understand that recent political events should be analyzed with the depth afforded by an intellectual engagement with core disciplinary concepts.

A revised Instructor's Manual accompanies this third edition. The manual offers suggestions for class discussions, writing assignments, Internet and research projects, and exam questions. The manual also identifies articles in InfoTrac College Edition that instructors can assign to provide additional readings on topics covered in each chapter of the text. InfoTrac is a searchable online library that gives students access to full-text articles from more than 700 popular and scholarly periodicals. Instructors may obtain passwords for the InfoTrac database from Wadsworth Publishing Company representatives; students receive passwords on purchase of the text.

I owe a number of outstanding individuals a great many thanks for their work in producing this third edition: Clark Baxter, publisher; David Tatom, executive editor; Stacey Sims, senior development editor; Janise Fry, marketing manager; Rebecca Green, assistant editor; and Reena Thomas, editorial assistant. As the book approached and entered production, Emily Smith and Aaron Downey made everything work well and seem easy.

I also thank reviewers Martin Bookbinder, Passaic County Community College; David Carleton, Middle Tennessee State University; Carolyn J. Kadel, Johnson County Community College; Jody Neathery-Castro, University of Nebraska at Omaha; Kristen Parris, Western Washington University; Brett S. Sharp, University of Central Oklahoma; Jonathan R. Strand, Niagara University; Rolf Theen, Purdue University; and James Wagman, Michigan State University, for helpful critiques and suggestions. Thanks also to Gordon A. Babst for insightful analyses. Ultimate thanks go to Tracie Bartlett.

# 1

# Introduction

Studying politics can feel like walking through a maze. It is something that demands considerable time and often leaves you unsure of where to step next. At any one point, you may not know how far you have traveled. Yet you hope, at the end, to have gained some insight. You may stop equating insight with clarity, however. You may also be disinclined to regard insight as finality because the world of politics can be full of surprises, challenges, and interpretative dilemmas. The ambiguities of international politics in the aftermath of September 11, 2001, the war in Afghanistan, and the war in Iraq illustrate as much, as do recent controversies over campaign finance reform and presidential electioneering.

Indeed, complexity seems inescapably attached to politics itself. While many ponder the future of Iraq after the capture of Saddam Hussein, UN General Secretary Kofi Annan wonders why the world cannot seem to see HIV/AIDS as a weapon of mass destruction. In the United States, the political party that prides itself on electing conservative "small government," "anti-government-spending" leaders is also the party of Nevada Representative Jim Gibbons who, at the end of 2003, maneuvered Congress to spend more than $200,000 of taxpayers' money on repairing a swimming pool in Sparks, Nevada, that he had vandalized when he was a 10-year-old.[1]

How can we begin to analyze these varied political currents? The difficulty of this question has, at times, threatened to overwhelm the most respected of political scientists.[2] As we confront the enormity of the task and search for insights, it is useful to keep in mind what political scientist David Easton has observed: Politics involves *change*.[3] Politics is a world of flux, tensions, and transitions. Change can be global in its consequences, as in the rise and fall of world powers such as the Soviet Union. Change can be primarily domestic, as when one political party defeats another in a country's elections. In an increasingly interdependent world, however, even those changes that appear essentially domestic in nature may resonate with international significance.[4]

---

**BOX 1.1   Change and Politics**

### What Were U.S. Citizens Concerned About 100 Years Ago?

Studying politics involves studying change—change in governments, laws, and political–social attitudes and opinions. An examination of public attitudes held by U.S. citizens 100 years ago reveals that our counterparts 100 years ago had much to worry about:

- *Air pollution.* Filthy air seemed an inevitable part of city living. In 1881, New York's State Board of Health found that air quality was compromised by fumes from sulfur, kerosene, manure, ammonia, and other smells, producing "an inclination to vomit." The term smog was coined soon after the turn of the century, in 1905.
- *Crowding.* Busy city streets were hazardous. Pedestrians risked injury from trolleys and carriages. Indeed, Brooklyn's beloved baseball team (the Trolley Dodgers) took its name from a dangerous, but unavoidable, urban practice of competing for scarce space with speeding trolleys.
- *Food impurities.* Americans of the late nineteenth century often found interesting additives in their basic foodstuffs. Milk, for example, was likely to contain chalk or plaster of Paris, in that both items could improve the appearance of milk produced from diseased cattle. Drunk cows were another problem. Distilleries often used waste products from whiskey production as cattle feed; milk from these cows could

contain enough alcohol to intoxicate babies who consumed the milk.
- *Epidemics.* Smallpox and malaria were two diseases threatening Americans at the turn of the twentieth century. Women and men were vulnerable to these predators and were often fearful of losing their lives to diseases they could neither understand nor be assured of protection against.
- *Race relations.* Racism was pervasive as the twentieth century approached. Violence against African-Americans was widespread. Lynchings of African-Americans reached record numbers in the 1890s and declined with the turn of the century; from 1882 to 1968, however, 4,743 (of whom 3,446 were African-American) Americans were murdered by lynching.
- *Family stability.* In the years around 1900, approximately 20 percent of American children lived in orphanages because their parents were too poor to provide for them. In other families, children worked in factories and mines to supplement unstable family incomes. At the beginning of the twentieth century, approximately one-fourth of the employees in textile mills in the southern United States were children.
- *Household budgets.* Some historians have described the last half of the nineteenth century as the age of the "robber barons," as millionaires such as Cornelius Vanderbilt, Andrew Carnegie, and John D. Rockefeller assumed positions of power and

---

**BOX 1.1**  *Continued*

influence. As the nineteenth century closed, the gap between rich and poor was vast, as average Americans struggled and saved to pay their bills. Indeed, more than 80 percent of the country's wealth was controlled by just over 10 percent of the nation's households in 1890.

- *Progress.* X-rays, telephones, record players, electric lighting, combustible engines—these and other inventions from the late nineteenth century promised to change life in the twentieth century. Americans had hopes that the changes would be for the good, as seen, for instance, in the optimism surrounding the World Fairs at which many of these inventions were showcased. At the same time, the new inventions could shock and frighten. One wonders, for instance,

how many Americans could identify with the character in Thomas Mann's *The Magic Mountain* when he remarked that looking at an X-ray was like looking into the grave.

SOURCES: Otto Bettmann, *The Good Old Days—They Were Terrible* (New York: Random House, 1974); Stephen Kern, *The Culture of Time and Space, 1880–1918* (Cambridge, MA: Harvard University Press, 1983); Cynthia Enloe, *Bananas, Beaches, & Bases: Making Feminist Sense of International Politics* (Berkeley: University of California Press, 1989); Stephanie Coontz, *The Way We Never Were: American Families and the Nostalgia Trap* (New York: Basic Books, 1992); Benjamin Schwarz, "American Inequality: Its History and Scary Future," *The New York Times* (19 December 1995): A19; Robert L. Zangrando, "Lynching," pp. 684–686 in *The Reader's Companion to American History*, eds. Eric Foner and John Garraty (Boston: Houghton Mifflin, 1991); Frederick Lewis Allen, *The Big Change, 1900–1950* (New York: Bantam, 1965), especially Chapters 1–4; Geoffrey C. Ward and Ken Burns, *Baseball: An Illustrated History* (New York: Knopf, 1994), p. xvii.

---

Politics also involves decision making over the world's *resources*. Whereas we can look to Easton's comments to appreciate the concept of change as central to politics, we can also draw on the teachings of political scientist Harold Lasswell to consider that politics is about deciding who does and does not get access to what the world has to offer.[5] Lasswell's insights are important for us to reflect on as we begin studying politics because they point us in the direction of questions both intriguing and disturbing in their complexity, such as, Why is an American citizen likely to live longer than a Liberian citizen? Politics, Lasswell's insights would tell us, has a lot to do with it. Life expectancy, access to safe water sources, and opportunities for jobs paying livable wages are all areas of our lives affected enormously by political decisions of the world's governments, as those governments make choices about how the world's resources are to be distributed and how conflict is to be resolved. According to the perspectives of political science, cosmic ordination and natural predetermination do not control who lives a life of relative security and who does not. Peace, war, medicine, water, food, housing, and jobs are not phenomena over which women and men have no control. To the contrary, the world of politics consists of those governmental decisions that extend life expectancies or shorten them, enhance or reduce access to basic necessities, implement a rule of law or violate it. In other words, politics involves the choices governments and citizens (in societies in which this freedom is observed) make in shaping the process whereby medicine, water, food, housing, and jobs are made available or unavailable to the world's people.

Indeed, politics encompasses all those decisions regarding how we make rules that govern our *common* life. These rules may be made in a democratic or authoritarian manner, may sanction peace or violence, and may empower state or nonstate actors (such as trade associations, media representatives, and multinational corporations). Whatever the rules, however, politics is based on the recognition that our lives are shared, as long as we live in common, public spaces such as state territories. If you have traversed a public road, used books at a public library, stopped at a public street sign, or walked across a public university campus today, you have shared space and resources governed by politically made rules implemented by states. Thus, whether you are conscious of it or not, as you go about your days, you are immersed in politics. As the ancient Greek philosopher Aristotle taught, in essence, we are political creatures, inhabiting a world of shared problems and possibilities. Indeed, Aristotle contended, to try to remove ourselves from politics would be to remove ourselves from the world of our common humanity.[6]

In short, as you analyze politics, you will see that politics touches everything, as political scientist Robert Dahl once suggested.[7] If you doubt Dahl's point, take a moment to think of an issue or topic that seems to have nothing to do with politics—it could be art, love, emotion, or a myriad of topics seemingly personal and apolitical. If Dahl's observations are borne out, by the end of this text you may well see politics enveloping even these aspects of your life.

Artist Renee Cox has challenged political and cultural sensibilities through her art. In this photo, she is standing beside her work "Yo Mama's Last Supper." New York City Mayor Rudolph Giuliani responded to Cox's work by raising questions about whether it should be displayed in a publicly funded arena. By articulating such questions, Mayor Giuliani suggested that the scope of politics—and the jurisdiction of government—includes setting boundaries on creative expression.

## BOX 1.2 What Is Political About That?

Many parts of our lives may, at first, appear apolitical. Very rarely is this true, however. Political decision making can include almost everything in its reach. Consider how politics touches the following ostensibly "nonpolitical" issues:

- *Art.* Robert Mapplethorpe is one of several artists whose work has elicited debate between conservatives and liberals. Mapplethorpe's portfolio includes photographs of gay men. Critics have often described these works as pornographic, whereas many supporters have countered that they are representations of gay erotica. Should public dollars be used to subsidize and promote such art? Politics involves making such decisions.
- *Love.* Two people in love may not believe that politics has anything to do with their relationship. However, politics greatly influences the ways in which love may be expressed. At what age may couples get married, for instance? Why can some couples (heterosexual) get married, whereas others (gay) cannot? Governments answer such political questions.
- *Emotion.* What could be more personal than emotions? How can your emotions have anything to do with politics? Your emotions are very political if, for instance, you are accused of committing what the government defines as a crime. A person's "state of mind" may be one of the variables considered when the state brings charges and makes recommendations for sentencing in criminal cases.

This text seeks to introduce to you some of the ways in which political science analyzes politics by exploring different subfields of political science. This brief opening chapter introduces political science as a field of inquiry seeking to examine political processes in a manner that offers information without denying complexity and nuance. Chapter 2 looks at the ways in which political scientists collect political data. Chapter 2 encourages readers to think about the process of thinking itself and to reflect on the proposition that the perspective from which you choose to view politics influences what you see; for example, traditionalists, behavioralists, and postbehavioralists may study the same political phenomenon but see different things. Chapter 3 examines key concepts used in political science to classify and analyze political processes. Concepts such as power, states, and nations are assessed.

Chapter 4 explores a number of theoretical debates that have intrigued students of politics. For example, we will examine debates about whether governments should try to promote equality, and we will evaluate philosophical disagreements over whether governments should try to enforce a public morality. In Chapters 5–7, we will analyze different political ideologies and see how liberalism, conservatism, socialism, fascism, feminism, and environmentalism differ in their views of politics, government, and citizenship.

Chapter 8 looks at variations in democratic and nondemocratic governments. Chapters 9 and 10 focus on comparisons of different aspects of citizen participation (such as voting) and government decision making (such as judicial review). These

AP/Wide World Photos

Should government have the power to deny inter-racial couples the right to marry? Should it have the power to deny this right to same-sex couples? In 1967, the U.S. Supreme Court overturned a Virginia law prohibiting marriage between African-Americans and whites. Mildred and Richard Loving, the couple who challenged the interracial ban, are shown above. Currently, in the United States, marriage rights are still denied to same-sex couples, although the State of Vermont recently gave legal sanction to same-sex civil unions. The topic of gay marriage proves to be controversial during the 2004 presidential election, and it continues to prompt debates in state legislatures and courts. Lois Burnham and

© Paul Boisvert/NYT Pictures

Holly Puterbaugh (shown to the right, along with an official who "civil unioned" them) had been in a relationship for 28 years by the time their government granted same-sex couples the option of a legally valid civil union ceremony. One of the songs performed at their service was "The Impossible Dream." Could it be that these cases illustrate that falling in love can be very political indeed?

chapters discuss U.S. politics and government within the context of comparative analysis. By thinking about U.S. political issues from a comparative perspective, you can, perhaps, better view the United States as other countries might. You can assess U.S. government and political decision making as part of the larger political world, not in isolation from this world. For example, you can view U.S. election laws as but one of many legal alternatives for societies. By comparing how the United States and other countries make governing choices, you can begin to see, for instance, that U.S. executive–legislative relations are anything but the most obvious way to set up government offices. Our comparative analysis will examine how the U.S. governing system is but one choice among many possibilities.

In Chapters 11 and 12, issues in international politics are examined. Realist and idealist debates on the nature of international affairs are scrutinized, as are questions concerning the place of the United Nations and NATO. Globalization, media relations, and international economics are also discussed. For example, we will explore some of the dynamics by which the World Bank and other international financial institutions have become focal points for citizen groups wishing to discuss the connections among politics, change, resources, and public decision making. Indeed, protesters in the streets are asking questions similar to the ones posed by Dahl and Lasswell: Who is to have the power to shape the political decisions over who gets a lot (in terms of civil rights, economic resources, or life expectancies) and who gets a little?

At the end of each chapter, related Internet sites are listed. As readers of this text are probably well aware, the Internet is an invaluable resource for political data, and I hope you will use this text as a starting point for your own investigations of politics through the Internet and other sources. As you explore the questions in this text, feel free to e-mail me directly with comments and/or questions; I will respond, and we can engage in a dialogue about the political issues raised in the pages that follow. Who knows where your questions and our discussions may take us? My e-mail address is egrigsby@unm.edu.

# Political Science
# and Scientific Methods
# in Studying Politics

D uring World War I, scientists associated with the American Chemical Society and the U.S. Bureau of Mines lobbied in favor of the development and use of poison gas as an instrument of warfare. In this case, two important issues emerged. First, neither science nor the results of scientific research proved politically neutral. Second, scientists claimed an authority based, in part, on the possession of disinterested neutrality grounded in expertise. In short, chemists claimed to understand chemical warfare at a level far superior to that of ordinary citizens. Did it not, therefore, follow logically, they proceeded to ask, that chemists should have a special voice in shaping U.S. weapons policy?[1]

If political science can provide information more trustworthy than the viewpoints held by the general public, does that mean that those who study political science should have a special voice on matters pertaining to politics? If, like the chemists just mentioned, political scientists made claims to having a reliable and disinterested expertise, should you believe them?

This Chapter seeks to help you sort through such questions by exploring what political scientists mean when they present their findings as scientific. Chapter 2 points out that political science has developed and changed over the centuries; the chapter further analyzes relationships between political science and science, scientific processes, the use of scientific processes in analyzing political data, and limitations of science.

# THE RANGE OF POLITICAL SCIENCE:
## HISTORICAL DEVELOPMENTS

Political science often traces its beginnings to ancient Greece and the teachings of political thinkers such as Socrates, Plato, and Aristotle.[2] Political science as an academic field, however, is much newer. In the United States, the first political science department was organized at Columbia University in 1880, and in 1903 the American Political Science Association was formed. At the turn of the twentieth century, probably no more than a couple of hundred people in the entire United States thought of themselves as political scientists.[3] In fact, fewer than 500 doctoral degrees in political science were awarded between 1936 and 1942.[4]

From these beginnings, political science has developed different subfields (areas of specialization) and research methods, and the discipline has grown to include more than 14,000 political scientists in the American Political Science Association alone.[5] Some political scientists focus on studying **normative** issues (issues involving value judgments and ethics), others concentrate on **empirical** (observable and factual) investigations, and still others study both. Whatever the focus, political science begins by asking questions. Why do people vote as they do? Why are some people conservative and others not? Why are some interest groups more successful than others? Does money buy elections? Are U.S. elections fair? The

---

**BOX 2.1   Some of the Subfields in Political Science**

Political science has a variety of subfields. Each subfield focuses on a particular set of questions. The major subfields include

- *Comparative politics,* focusing on examining how different political systems operate. It can include comparisons of systems at a macro or micro level, that is, comparing general political structures or focusing on individual elements of political systems. For example, comparative politics can include a comparison of how democratic and authoritarian political structures differ, as well as a comparison of how specific rules governing campaign contributions differ from one country to the next.
- *American politics,* consisting of an analysis of government and politics in the United States. This subfield encompasses studies of federal, as

well as state and local, politics and government. Some political scientists view it as an element of comparative politics.

- *International relations,* focusing on relationships between and among states. Unlike comparative politics, which zeroes in on how government or politics operates within a country, international relations studies what transpires between states. Its subject matter includes war, regional integration, international organizations, military alliances, economic pacts, and so on.
- *Public policy,* studying how laws, regulations, and other policies are formulated, implemented, and evaluated. This subfield looks closely at such questions as, What makes a new policy necessary? How can

---

**BOX 2.1** *Continued*

policies be designed to meet specific needs effectively? What contributes to a policy's effectiveness? Why are ineffective policies sometimes continued rather than discontinued? What should be the standards for evaluating policies?

- *Political research methods,* focusing on a study of the many details of empirical social science. Data collection, measurement, and analysis are key areas of inquiry in this subfield. Political methods study seeks to understand the empirical research process in all its complexity and to develop means of achieving scientific rigor in the collection and interpretation of data.
- *Political theory,* in some ways unique among the subfields of political science insofar as it is concerned with normative questions. Political theory includes the study of the history of political philosophy, philosophies of explanation or science, and philosophical inquiries into the ethical dimensions of politics.

In addition to these historical subfields, political science is organized into a number of more specialized groups. For instance, the American Political Science Association provides the following specialized sections that members may join:

- Federalism/Intergovernmental Relations

- Law/Courts
- Legislative Studies
- Public Policy
- Political Organizations/Parties
- Public Administration
- Conflict
- Representation/Election Systems
- Presidency
- Political Methodology
- Religion/Politics
- Politics/Technology/Environment
- Urban Politics
- Women/Politics
- Political Theory
- Computers/Multimedia
- International Security/Arms Control
- Comparative Politics
- Politics/Society Western Europe
- State Politics
- Political Communication
- Politics/History
- Political Economy
- Transformational Politics
- New Political Science
- Political Psychology
- Undergraduate Education
- Politics/Literature
- Foreign Policy Domestic Sources
- Elections/Opinion/Voting
- Race, Ethnicity, and Politics

SOURCES: APSA Executive Director's Report, Reported 12 July 2000, Catherine E. Rudder, *PS Online* (http://www.apsanet.org/PS/sept00/rudder.cfm); David M. Ricci, *The Tragedy of Political Science: Politics, Scholarship, and Democracy* (New Haven, CT: Yale University Press, 1984), p. 9.

---

subject matter of politics is varied and complex, and political science is no less so. In this chapter, we will see that political scientists use a wide range of research methods and analytical approaches.

In its early years, political science generally involved the analysis of the formal, legal, official side of political life.[6] This approach is known as **traditionalism.** Traditionalists tried to understand politics by examining laws, governmental offices, constitutions, and other official institutions associated with politics; they tried to describe how institutions operated by formal rules and publicly sanctioned procedures. A traditionalist, for example, who wished to understand the U.S. Supreme Court might study the official rules the Court followed in making judicial decisions, or, perhaps, the formal/legal basis of the Court's authority as spelled out in the U.S. Constitution.

Traditionalists often tended to focus on what was going on inside government as opposed to looking at social and economic processes in the country.[7] Traditionalist approaches were often both historical and normative: historical in outlining the processes by which the formal rules of politics were modified over time through court decisions, laws, executive orders, and the like, and normative in the sense of hoping to provide information for improving these rules.[8] Although traditionalist approaches are still present in political science research, additional approaches have supplemented traditionalism.

**Behavioralism** is one alternative to traditionalism. Behavioralism became popular in political science after World War II. The roots of behavioralist political science have been traced back to the 1920s and the works of political scientists such as Charles Merriam. Merriam asserted the usefulness of looking at the actual *behavior* of politically involved individuals and groups, not only the formal/legal rules by which those individuals and groups were supposed to abide.[9] Thus, a behavioralist approach to the study of Congress might include an examination of how members of Congress actually behave in their positions. For example, a behavioralist might ask the following type of question: How much time is devoted by members of Congress to such tasks as writing laws, interacting with lobbyists, raising money for reelection, giving speeches, studying domestic issues, attending committee and subcommittee meetings, casting votes, meeting with foreign dignitaries, and the like? The behavioralist, therefore, is less interested in how Congress looks officially "on paper" (for example, what the U.S. Constitution says about Congress) and more interested in how Congress becomes an arena of actions, the origins and motivations of which may be found outside the formal sphere of government. That is, a behavioralist may look for informal sources of power emanating from economics, ethnic cleavages, and social relationships.[10] Thus, to a behavioralist, traditionalist approaches, focused so exclusively on government per se, were inadequate for understanding the larger context of political life.[11]

Behavioralist approaches stress the importance of empirical analysis. Behavioralists ask: How better to study behavior than through careful observation of specific actions? Indeed, behavioralism is almost synonymous with empiricism, according to many political scientists.[12] Empiricism is a means of collecting data based on observation. From an empirical standpoint, $X$ is a fact if $X$ is observed.[13] Behavioralists often favor statistical, mathematical, and economic models of analysis, insofar as they allow for a more minute empirical investigation of phenomena than would be provided by assessing the content of constitutions, laws, and governmental procedures. Given its focus on empiricism, behavioralism tends to reject historical analysis, finding little reason to explore the past (for interpretations, insights, and opinions on matters of politics) when observation is viewed as the most reliable route to knowledge.[14] The empirical orientation toward the analysis of what *is* (observable) also stands in contrast to an orientation that asks what *should be*. Indeed, one of the defining attributes of behavioralism is its rejection of the normative questions associated with traditionalism.[15] A behavioralist studying Congress does not ask how a senator or representative *should* act. Rather, a behavioralist examines how a senator or representative *does* act.

**Postbehavioralism** is an alternative to both traditionalism and behavioralism. In 1969, David Easton announced that a postbehavioral orientation had arrived in political science.[16] What had inspired it? Easton was very explicit in his answer: Postbehavioralism emerged as a reaction against the empirical orientation of behavioralism by political scientists who found such an orientation excessive and irresponsible. Empiricism, if taken to the extremes of denying the importance of values and ethics and encouraging a narrowing of research questions to only those matters self-evidently observable, could undermine political science. In such cases, postbehavioralists warned, political science would produce data that were scientifically reliable (empirically observed) but irrelevant. Moreover, postbehavioralists asserted that behavioralism is not *truly* value free because it implicitly affirms that understanding comes from observation, not ethical assessments. Behavioralism is not in opposition to values, but is itself a value statement, insofar as it upholds as reliable what is observable and distrusts as unreliable what is intuited as ethical or moral. In other words, behavioralism values the observable and devalues the unobservable. Thus, if the postbehavioralists are correct, behavioralism is as normative as traditionalism.[17]

Postbehavioralists argue that political science should be relevant as well as empirically reliable, and that the information produced by political science has ethical implications. Easton tried to remind political scientists that political phenomena were often matters of life and death—matters pertaining to war, population growth, environmental degradation, and racial and ethnic conflict. Political scientists have a responsibility to acknowledge that what they *choose* to investigate through the empirical methods of political science and what they *discover* by means of these methods affect the lives of women and men.[18]

We can see the influence of postbehavioralism in Lucius J. Barker's presidential address to the American Political Science Association in 1993. Barker challenged political scientists to be engaged citizens, actively taking part in reforming their own societies. Barker specifically recommended that political scientists promote civil rights for all citizens through such measures as the recruitment of African-Americans into the discipline of political science.[19] Note the remarkable difference between Barker's view of the responsibilities of the political scientist and the view of the behavioralists who rejected normative judgments.

The debates among traditionalists, behavioralists, and postbehavioralists are important not only for illustrating the tensions and conflicts within the discipline of political science as it evolved. These debates are also important in raising questions at the center of political science today:

- What is the nature of scientific inquiry? How is science different from ethical and/or religious perspectives on truth?
- How can political science be scientific? How can anyone study complex political phenomena in a scientific manner? What are the methods of the scientific study of politics?
- Should science be value free? Will science be corrupted by bias if it is not value free?
- How relevant is political science? What are other sources of knowledge about politics?

The questions are difficult ones, and political scientists often disagree on how best to answer them. In fact, one student of the discipline of political science has suggested that the discipline's history has been tragic: Political scientists have often failed to integrate the demands of science and humanity, falling short of Easton's plea for relevance and reliability, even as the discipline has opened up to include multiple research and analytical approaches.[20] It seems that the historical debates refuse to die, as we will see as we examine the preceding questions in greater detail.

## THINKING SCIENTIFICALLY: SOME FOUNDATIONS OF SCIENTIFIC INQUIRY

Albert Einstein believed that science creates concepts for elucidating reality.[21] Scientists search for ways to identify, define, analyze, clarify, and understand the world. Religion, art, and philosophy also seek to produce languages and models to make the universe comprehensible.[22] Each of these pursuits—science, spirituality, religion, art, and philosophy—may be conceptualized as ways of coming up with names and categories for what is considered to be real. Spirituality may name as real what is known by faith; some philosophies may name as real what is known through reason. Science differs from these two endeavors in terms of *what* and *how* it goes about naming phenomena as real, but, like spirituality and philosophy, science can be thought of as a type of naming system connecting what we think of as mind and world.[23]

To illustrate this point, we can look to the writings of Phillip Converse. Converse was president of the American Political Science Association in the early 1980s. According to Converse, science uses names to point to what it sees as truth. That is, science tells us that its names truly correspond to reality. However, science by its very nature is a process of continuously *renaming* and improving on older naming schema. Science is therefore premised on the understanding that truth, at any particular time, is incompletely named (and incompletely known). Religion, according to Converse, is premised on an understanding that there is a truth outside that is capable of being named by science, even by a science so rigorous as to overcome its own errors of naming. Converse's discussion is valuable in highlighting the similarities of science and religion (both are naming systems), as well as their dissimilarities (they name different phenomena as real, and they rest on different understandings of the nature of truth).[24]

Science names reality by means of a **scientific method,** a set of procedures (for gathering information) resting on certain epistemological assumptions. **Epistemology** is a branch of philosophy that examines evaluations of what constitutes truth; thus, epistemological assumptions are assumptions about the essence of truth. Scientific method is characterized by epistemological *empiricism* (insofar as it is based on the assumption that what is true is what is observable). Its procedures reflect this epistemological assumption, for pursuing truth by means of the scientific method entails the collection of data. The data selected for collection are the set of data observed (not what is assumed, intuited, revealed by faith, or judged to be good or bad on normative grounds). In this manner, scientific method's epistemological empiricism is reflected in its methodological (procedural) empiricism.

Once collected, the sets of data are analyzed, and when the analysis leads to assertions concerning the nature of the data, these assertions are subject to *testing*. The testing of assertions provides verification (acceptance of the assertions) or falsification (rejection of the assertions). Through these steps of data collection, analysis, testing, verification, and falsification, the scientific method offers explanations of reality. Science's explanations are necessarily incomplete and tentative, insofar as they are always subject to falsification at a later time.

Political scientists use science's methods to study questions as diverse as the causes of war and the origins of public opinions. Studying political questions in a scientific manner often involves the following:

- Formulating hypotheses
- Operationalizing concepts
- Identifying independent and dependent variables
- Clarifying measurement criteria
- Distinguishing between causation and correlation
- Developing scientific theories

Formulating a **hypothesis** can be a key step in the application of the scientific method to the study of politics. A hypothesis is a statement proposing a specific relationship between phenomena.[25] A hypothesis puts forward an idea that $X$ and $Y$ are connected in a certain, identifiable way.[26] An example can help illustrate the different dimensions of hypothesis formulation. A political scientist may be intrigued by the following question: Is voting in U.S. elections related to age? The political scientist may suspect that younger adults are less likely to vote than are middle-aged adults. This suspicion may be articulated as a hypothetical statement such as, "U.S. citizens 18–24 years of age will vote in lower numbers than will U.S. citizens 45–55 years of age." This hypothesis exemplifies the definition just noted—two phenomena (age and voting) are posited as having a specific relationship.

Once formulated, hypotheses are tested. Data collection proceeds according to the logic of the **operational definitions** contained in the hypothesis. An operational definition is a definition so precise that it allows for empirical testing.[27] Unless a hypothesis defines the phenomenon in question precisely enough to measure that phenomenon, the hypothesis cannot be tested empirically. We cannot confirm/verify or falsify if we cannot measure degrees of correspondence between what a hypothesis states as a relationship and what we observe as actual facts. This is very important because verification often involves multiple tests of a hypothesis.[28]

For example, "youth" is a general concept. We turn the concept into an operational definition when we define youth as "those who are 18–24 years of age." Once we have thus operationalized "youth," youth is something that we can observe with clarity and specificity. We can measure the correspondence between what we expect to see this group doing (as stated in our hypothesis) and what we actually see it doing.

Scientists often refer to the phenomena linked together in a hypothesis as **variables.** In our example, age is one variable and voting is a second variable. A variable is something that varies, changes, or manifests itself differently from one case to another. **Independent variables** are presented as those that act on or affect something. **Dependent variables** are what the hypothesis presents as being acted on by the independent variable. Which is the independent variable and which is the dependent in our example? Age is put forth as having an impact on voting. Age, therefore, is the independent variable, which has an effect on levels of voting (the dependent variable).[29]

As scientists proceed to test hypotheses (with the operationalized variables), they must clarify their means of testing, or measuring the correspondence between hypothetical relationships and what is observable empirically. This clarification involves specifying what is taken as an *indicator* of the variable. An indicator is evidence. How could we obtain evidence regarding our variable of voting? We could poll individuals and ask about their voting behavior. Their responses would provide evidence. As noted, operationalizing concepts and determining measurement (indicator) criteria are closely related. In our example, we could change our dependent variable from voting to political participation; our operationalizations and indicators would also change. How could we operationalize and identify indicators for political participation? We could poll individuals and inquire about not only such activities as voting, but also joining interest groups, identifying with a political party, writing petitions, attending demonstrations, debating political issues, and the like.

In addition to testing hypothetical relationships, political science also points to the importance of understanding the difference between correlation and causation. **Correlation** is a relationship in which changes in one variable appear when there are changes in another variable (for example, lower voting appears with younger age groups). Correlation is not the same as ultimate, indisputable causation (one variable absolutely causing or creating the other). Were we to confirm our hypothesis on age and voting, for instance, we could not say that we have *proven* that being age 20 absolutely determines whether someone will vote. Perhaps additional variables (income, educational level, or mobility) are associated with this person's voting behavior. As political scientist Duncan MacRae, Jr., has noted, there is often an alternative explanation for what we think we have confirmed.[30] MacRae's insight points back to the usefulness of Converse's assertion—that science can name reality, but only in an incomplete, conditional, partial, and tentative manner.

Scientific research often involves the construction of scientific theories based on empirically verified hypotheses. Although based on observable data, scientific theory attempts to transcend the limits of the observable. Scientific theories seek to offer explanations about *why* and *how* correlations occur. In this manner, scientific theory also seeks to predict.[31] For example, after having found a relationship between age and voting, the political scientist might theorize that this relationship is related to different mobility patterns among groups. Perhaps younger people move more often than other groups and do not always register to vote after moving to new cities.

Theory building can be one of the most interesting aspects of science because it takes the political scientist beyond the task of merely describing and observing. Descriptions alone may offer little in the way of meaningful additions to our understanding of politics. Explanations delving into the why and how of politics seek a more profound level of understanding. In fact, the search for such explanations can be one of the most productive sources for generating new hypotheses.

The processes associated with different usages of the scientific method—hypothesis formulation, operationalization, and so on—can be fascinating. Political scientist James Rosenau has described his own experience with the excitement of scientific research by noting the intense anticipation, curiosity, and expectation one feels while testing hypotheses and seeking out correlations.[32] Moreover, although the method of science is orderly, often the actual practice of science is not. The lack of regimentation can be part of the fun. Political scientist Thomas Dye has described the scientific method as something of an adventure.[33] Science is not so boring as to be thoroughly predictable because scientists often encounter the unexpected and the unusual.[34]

Rosenau and Dye are not alone in being surprised by the direction in which science sometimes takes them. Indeed, one offering of science is the promise of seeing the world differently, of coming to name and interpret perceptions in ways that may depart radically from our commonplace assumptions. In the 1600s, Francis Bacon pointed to this dimension of science by arguing that science can free us from various "idols" (errors, misconceptions, and distorted views). Bacon categorized these misconceptions:

- *Idols of the marketplace:* Errors based on misunderstanding and faulty communications; errors related to our inexact use of language.
- *Idols of the tribe:* Errors related to the flaws of human nature; errors caused by the human tendency to be quick to judge and to be superficial in our assessments.
- *Idols of the den:* Errors caused by our inability to see beyond our own particular surroundings; errors related to our near-sightedness and proclivity for viewing our particular way of life as the standard for judging all others.
- *Idols of the theater:* Errors based on our beliefs in dogmatic teachings; errors caused by believing in systems of thought characterized by inflexibility and closed off to questioning and critical analysis.[35]

Bacon's insights have remained relevant over the centuries. Consider the following examples of misconceptions assumed by many at the time to be "facts." In the 1800s, U.S. women who demanded the right to vote were not infrequently described as abnormal. In short, such women were likely to be seen as freaks. For example, opponents of women's suffrage sometimes charged that because such women were acting like men in terms of wanting to vote, they must be like men in other ways; they must be, the argument continued, hermaphroditic (half female and half male).[36] In the same century, a number of scholars misused Charles Darwin's theories of evolution to claim that some races were superior to others. Ernst Haeckel, for one, argued that white Europeans were superior to other peoples.[37]

These examples illustrate the significance of Bacon's teachings. Idols can be powerful—seductive to those who use them in a self-justifying manner and oppressive to those whose lives are circumscribed by their claims. Idols can form the basis of a society's discriminatory treatment of groups deemed unworthy of equal rights. Idols come in many forms—stereotypes, prejudices, and biases among them. In contrast, science, with its empiricism and logical methods of data analysis, can offer an alternative to such distortions.

## THINKING SCIENTIFICALLY ABOUT POLITICS

Political scientists use the scientific method in a variety of ways. A political scientist interested in international politics may wish to find out how countries become democratic. Or a political scientist may be curious about how U.S. presidents develop strategies for managing unruly press conferences, or how a member of Congress can sabotage a bill he or she despises. How could these questions be answered? Case studies, survey research, experiments, quasi-experiments, and indirect quantitative analysis are five ways in which political scientists may investigate and answer these questions.

### Case Studies

A **case study** is an investigation of a specific phenomenon or entity. A case study might examine a single country, law, governmental office, war, riot, president, political decision, or other phenomenon. Case studies have a major benefit over other research approaches: They allow for in-depth examination of the phenomenon selected. Because the research focuses on a narrowly defined topic, the research can be thoroughly detailed in bringing to light all kinds of information pertaining to that

---

**BOX 2.2  Case Studies**

Suppose you are a political scientist wishing to describe the impact of poverty on individuals. Surveys, indirect quantitative analysis, experiments, and case studies could be used. How would you select among these approaches? If you wish to show depth and intensity, a case study approach might be the logical choice.

Consider the picture Barbara Robinette Moss presents. In her autobiography, she describes the following event from her childhood. It was 1962, and she was living with her mother and six siblings in Eastaboga, Alabama. Her father had traveled to another town in search of work. Everyday, she and her family watched for the mail and hoped that money from her father would be delivered.

As days passed and the family's food and money were used up, her mother became desperate. At one point, the only food left in the home was a container of corn and beans. The problem, however, was that this food had been soaked with pesticides so that the beans and kernels of corn could be planted as seeds the following spring. The pesticides were highly toxic. The

mother faced a very difficult decision: Should she feed her children poisoned food or let them continue to go hungry? She decided to use herself as a test subject. She washed and cooked the beans and corn, ate a portion of them, and informed her children that they were to observe her for two hours and, if she turned out to be still alive and well, they too could eat the poisoned food. In the event that she lost consciousness, they were to call a relative living in Birmingham and explain what had happened. At the end of two hours, she felt well, so she offered her kids the remaining beans and corn. Moss recalls that she and her sisters and brothers took the food gratefully. Their hunger pains were stronger than their fears of the poison. Their mother read them a fairy tale while they had the best meal they had eaten in days.

Could impersonal statistics and poll results describe poverty in such vivid terms? Sometimes case studies not only instruct. They haunt.

SOURCE: Barbara Robinette Moss, *Change Me into Zeus's Daughter* (New York: Scribner's, 2000), pp. 19–34.

topic. Imagine, for example, the difference between doing research on a single country as opposed to conducting research on 50 or 100 countries; using the former method, all the researcher's time, energy, and creativity are devoted to a single case and this facilitates uncovering minute, specific facts, which might be overlooked in the second approach of dividing the researcher's efforts across so many countries.

Case studies are not without problems, however. First, a case study alone does not allow for empirically verified generalizations beyond the entity studied. It tells us about the particular entity comprising the case but not about other entities. For example, research about one country may produce information that does not apply beyond that country. Second, case studies typically examine an entity or event in a given time period but do not provide data beyond that time period. In other words, case studies often have a time-bound limitation. For these reasons, it is difficult to construct scientific theories and to make predictions on the basis of single case studies.[38]

Still, case studies can provide fascinating information. For example, case studies of Spanish politics have provided data on the process of building a democratic society in the aftermath of authoritarianism. Spain had an authoritarian government, headed by Francisco Franco, from 1939 to 1975. Since 1975, Spain has democratized its society, replacing the previous dictatorship with political parties and elections. What makes such an astounding transition possible? Studies focusing on Spain have pointed to a number of factors crucial to the democratization process: Franco's withdrawal from politics prior to his death (which made possible the entry into politics of competing political groups), the existence of a growth-oriented economic structure, the existence of a stable middle class supportive of democratic processes, and the forging of cross-class alliances for democratization (such as support for democracy from labor and management groups in Spanish society).[39] A case study of Spain alone cannot, however, determine how many of these factors are also associated with democratization in other countries at other times and how many are unique to Spain's democratization.

Case studies have also provided a much deeper understanding of the legislative process and the civil rights movement in the United States. For instance, case studies of the U.S. Civil Rights Act of 1964 have pointed out the lengths to which politicians were willing to go in trying to kill proposed civil rights laws in the 1960s. As originally written, the Civil Rights Act of 1964 called for federal protection against discrimination directed toward minority groups. Opponents of the measure fought hard against it. When it appeared that passage was inevitable, opponents scrambled to find a way to stop this bill. An ingenious strategy struck them. What if the law were rewritten to include a provision calling for protection against discriminatory treatment directed toward women as well as minorities? Wouldn't that be so outrageous as to ensure defeat for the entire law? Assuming the answer to that question was yes, opponents introduced such a provision. The act passed, however. With its passage, civil rights for minorities and women were upheld, and although the opponents failed to achieve their goal of sabotaging the Civil Rights Act, their actions revealed volumes of information relating to U.S. cultural assumptions. A great irony stems from this episode: A measure that has subsequently served to uphold the legal rights of women was introduced by opponents of *both* the women's movement and the civil rights movement. Although it is clear that we cannot generalize beyond this study without stretching the scientific method too far, it is also obvious that a case study approach uncovering such counterintuitive facts pertaining to this particular legislation broadens our understanding of recent American politics.[40]

Case study information has also enriched our understanding of presidential politics. By looking at individual presidents, political scientists have learned of astoundingly clever ways used by presidents to maneuver through press conferences. Looking to the right rather than the left sounds harmless, doesn't it? In fact, it was a strategy employed by the Reagan administration to manipulate press conferences. Although the television-viewing public watched President Reagan answer questions from reporters in an apparently unorchestrated fashion, a very meticulously thought-out orchestration program was in effect. What was hidden from the viewers watching television? The fact that Reagan's staff had consciously and carefully seated pro-Reagan press representatives in the front of the presidential podium and to Reagan's immediate right. If questioning from hostile reporters raised difficult or embarrassing issues, Reagan knew he could halt these questions by calling on reporters seated to the right in the "easy" section of the audience.[41] Of course, case study materials delving into the dynamics of press conferences of a single president do not generate data sufficient for constructing a scientific theory about all presidents, but these materials disclose a reality the president himself tried to conceal. From the standpoint of democracy, that alone makes this information relevant.

## Survey Research

Political scientists often conduct **survey research** (questionnaires and/or interviews) to gather data. Surveys usually consist of closed questions (questions with a range of optional answers provided). Survey research is one of the most popular research approaches in political science, in part because survey questions may be administered to large numbers of people and the results may be tabulated by means of precise statistical measurements.[42] In other words, surveys are useful because they make it possible to study larger populations than one can examine using the case study approach. In this manner, survey research provides greater *breadth* than that presented in single case studies. Insofar as surveys provide data that can be measured mathematically, they allow researchers to test their findings for *statistical significance* (testing to determine if a finding is likely to have occurred randomly or by chance; if the finding is not likely to have occurred by chance, then the finding is considered statistically significant).

Survey research is invaluable but complex. In using survey findings, it is important to understand the limitations of this approach. First, surveys are not designed to provide detailed probing of *individual* entities. Surveys identify *patterns* pertaining to large numbers of individuals, but not the idiosyncratic, unique, quirky details associated with single case studies. Second, *when surveys identify patterns they are not necessarily identifying individuals organized into groups.* However, survey findings are sometimes (mis)read so that patterns are assumed to be identical to

## BOX 2.3　Are Surveys Good for Democracy?

Survey research is a subject that can elicit strong emotions. Critics can point to fiascos, such as instances in which two polls trying to figure out the same thing produce absolutely opposite results. This happened with a poll conducted in 1992 by Ross Perot, whose presidential campaign of that year caused major headaches for both Bill Clinton and George Bush. Perot was spearheading an effort to organize popular support for tax and spending reform. His poll contained a question about whether respondents wanted to see reductions in government spending. Ninety-seven percent of respondents answered yes. The results looked unambiguous.

However, polling expert Daniel Yankelovich and associates repeated the question, worded in what they considered a more neutral fashion and administered to a more representative sample, and found the opposite. The Yankelovich question asked whether respondents wanted to see government spending reductions even if such reductions meant curtailing popular programs such as Social Security. Sixty-one percent of respondents answered no. The results suggested that the American public opposed such cuts in spending.

This example illustrates the dangers of survey results. Wording a question differently and administering a survey to populations chosen by means of different selection criteria produce different sets of answers. This raises the possibility that polls can be used to confuse and mislead. Such instances raise the specter of polls being devised to produce whatever results the pollster wants and then passed off as what the public wants. Thus, critics fear that polls could subvert the democratic process. If surveys are used in a manipulative way, how can we tell the difference between what the people truly want and what the bogus poll results say they want? "The wishes of the people" are a commodity that can be manufactured by anyone who can hire the services of a polling firm.

Political scientist Sidney Verba offers a very different view of polls. Aware of the potential abuses of surveys, Verba, nonetheless, insists that polls can promote democracy. Consider, Verba tells us, the difference between elections and surveys. Both are means of expressing the popular will. In elections, people vote and the most popular candidate wins. In polls, people express their will by answering questions administered in the survey; the results are tabulated and the most popular response is noted as such. In elections, however, an unrepresentative sample participates. As we will see in later chapters, some people are more likely to vote than others. Therefore, the results of an election are skewed in favor of the opinions of the people most likely to vote. Elections do not truly reflect the *people's will*. They reflect the *voters' will*. However, a well-administered survey does not produce skewed results. Because the survey is administered to a random sample of people—with no group having a greater or lesser likelihood of participation than any other group—it reflects the will of the *entire* people. Therefore, surveys are more accurate reflections of the popular will than are elections.

Verba's comments are intriguing. Would it be more democratic to decide key debates—abortion, gun control, taxes, affirmative action, and so on—by basing our laws on public opinion surveys rather than the decisions of politicians selected through elections?

SOURCES: Daniel Goleman, "Pollsters Enlist Psychologists in Quest for Unbiased Results," *New York Times* (7 September 1993): B5, B8; Christopher Hitchens, "Voting in the Passive Voice," *Harper's* (April 1992): 45–52; Sidney Verba, "The Citizen as Respondent: Sample Surveys and American Democracy. Presidential Address, American Political Science Association, 1995," *American Political Science Review* 90 (March 1996): 1–7.

groups. An example can help clarify this distinction. Imagine that a survey reveals that individuals with traits *X, Y,* and *Z* tend to feel favorably toward Candidate N. This survey has revealed a *pattern* involving individuals exhibiting *X, Y,* and *Z,* but these individuals may or may not represent an actual self-identified group (a group of people connected together in an organized manner at some point in space and aware of themselves as group members).[43] That is, a hypothetical survey might suggest that women earning more than $100,000 and living in urban areas strongly support candidate Mary Smith. If these women earning more than $100,000 and living in urban areas do not consciously associate among themselves in an organization with membership reflecting these traits (female, earning more than $100,000, and living in urban areas), then this hypothetical survey has identified a pattern but not a group. This is important because if the pattern is not present in an organized group, the pattern may be short term (not sustained over time by an ongoing organization). In this manner, survey research findings may be as time bound as single case studies.[44]

In addition, a number of specific difficulties may arise as the researcher is developing the questions for the survey, selecting the population to whom the survey will be administered, and carrying out the survey. First, if the population chosen to participate in the survey is not randomly selected, the findings of the survey will be unreliable. Random selection requires that each person in the population to be studied must have an equal chance (compared to all others in the population) of being selected. Thus, if a political scientist wishes to study the population of registered Republicans, he or she must ensure that each registered Republican has an equal chance of being chosen to participate in the survey. Because it is difficult (and expensive) to get a random sample of a very large group (such as Republicans), researchers often use a variant of random sampling—either stratified sampling (random samples of demographic subgroups within the population to be studied) or cluster sampling (random samples of geographic subgroups within the population to be studied). In our example, a stratified random sample would randomly select Republicans in various age, sex, ethnic, occupational, religious, and other demographic categories, whereas a cluster sample would obtain random samples from various geographic communities of Republicans.[45]

Sometimes even the most conscientious efforts to ensure randomness can fall short and create erroneous results. For example, in the 1984 presidential election, Republican pollsters experienced mild panic when their polling began to suggest that Reagan was beginning to trail behind Democratic candidate Walter Mondale. Republicans had been confident of Reagan's lead over Mondale until polling data signaled Mondale gains. Interestingly, they noticed that they tended to pick up this Mondale surge in surveys conducted on Friday nights. Then it occurred to them to ask, What if Republicans are more likely to go out on Friday nights than are Democrats? If so, polling on Friday nights is not truly random (it is skewed in favor of finding more Democrats than Republicans at home to answer survey questions, so it is not an accurate sample of the population—voters—it is seeking to study).[46]

Second, if questions in a survey are leading or ambiguous, this compromises the reliability of survey research. Researchers have found, for instance, that a word such as "few" is very ambiguous. Different people have different notions of what a "few" consists of, so survey researchers must be careful in wording questions. Third, responses to questions in a survey can be affected by the organization of the questions in a survey. Both the order of questions and the possible answers to a question can affect how people answer the questions. Why would this be so? In terms of the order of questions, one question can trigger a thought or idea that influences the way someone thinks about another question. "Should governments provide health care benefits to poor residents?" Consider how you might answer that question differently if it is preceded by either of the following questions: "Do you support raising taxes to fund health care programs for the poor?" or "If you had a sick relative who lacked money for health care, would you hope to see a state program in place to provide health care for the poor?" Moreover, if people are given the option of answering "I don't know" to a question, this can lead to different responses from when they are given only "yes" or "no" options.[47]

The information levels of respondents can also seriously affect the results of a survey. Political scientists have long known that a respondent may give an opinion on a subject whether or not that respondent actually has any information on that subject. Studies asking respondents about their opinions on bogus laws often elicit opinions on the laws, even though the laws do not exist. Similarly, surveys asking for opinions about imaginary ethnic groups have produced answers giving detailed opinions on these groups even though the groups were nonexistent.[48] In fact, it is sometimes startling to consider how serious a potential problem this lack of information can be. After the 1992 election to the U.S. Congress, a group of freshmen representatives were asked their opinions on the conflict in Fredonia. They gave various opinions, including support for U.S. involvement in the country's internal affairs. Where is Fredonia? It does not exist. None of these newly elected representatives knew that, however. Whether you consider these results amusing or frightening, they illustrate the limitations of the survey method.[49] When presented with survey results, political scientists must always be aware that the opinions recorded may reflect low levels of knowledge.

Finally, survey findings may be compromised by the comfort level of respondents. In short, people may not be comfortable answering a question honestly. They may lie. Burns W. Roper, former chair of the public opinion polling firm Roper Starch, has commented on this problem. His experience has suggested that Roper survey results were affected by dishonest answers on more than one occasion. For example, he believes that white respondents may be less than candid when surveyed about issues pertaining to race. In addition, he suspects that survey questions about AIDS have sometimes elicited dishonest answers because the people in the survey were uncomfortable talking about certain sexual practices.[50]

Despite such limitations, survey research has provided enormously useful data to political scientists. Presidential politics is one area in which survey research has been highly successful in increasing our knowledge. For example, surveys of U.S. voters have shown that presidential popularity tends to decline over a president's first year in office. This drop in popularity holds true for Republicans and Democrats and seems to occur regardless of the personal decisions, management styles, and policy proposals of presidents. In fact, public opinion research has indicated that presidents can expect to see their support levels diminish by approximately 15 percent by the end of their first year. This finding is very significant—it suggests that we should be cautious in predicting doom for new presidents whose popularity slips. The slippage may not mean the president is a definite one-termer; rather, it may mean business as usual in American politics. To illustrate, one-term president Jimmy Carter's approval rating (45.5 percent) in his second year is only slightly different from two-term president Ronald Reagan's approval rating (43.7 percent) in Reagan's second year. As you can see, the actual numbers captured by the survey research are virtually identical, although the general assumption (the idol, in Bacon's terminology) is typically that Reagan was one of the most enduringly popular presidents in recent history and Carter was one of the most enduringly unpopular ones.[51]

In addition, survey research has shown that presidential popularity is correlated with certain types of events. For example, a president's approval rating is likely to rise if the United States becomes involved in a short-term military conflict. Bush enjoyed higher than usual approval ratings during the Gulf War, as did Clinton during U.S. intervention in Haiti. In fact, presidential popularity may increase when presidents get involved with international affairs, even in the absence of military conflict. Some studies have suggested that presidents benefit from higher approval ratings simply by traveling abroad.[52]

## Experiments and Quasi-Experiments

An **experiment** investigates a hypothesis by using a test group and a control group. The test group is exposed to a variable, whereas the control group is not. The researcher then observes whether the variable produces the hypothesized effect. In medicine, for example, researchers may test the effects of an experimental drug by comparing the progress of a test group (taking the drug) with that of a control group (not taking the drug). Clearly, the control group is a vital element in the experiment; used as a reference point, it allows the researcher to more accurately examine the effects of a variable (such as a drug). In the social sciences, experiments have been used to test a variety of hypotheses, ranging from ones postulating the negative effects of authoritarianism on emotional health (confirmed in the Zimbardo Prison Study, 1971) to the examination of the tendency of negative campaign advertising to reduce voter turnout (confirmed by Stephen Ansolabehere et al.).[53]

In medicine and social science, experiments can go awry. The **Hawthorne effect** is one danger that researchers must avoid. Named after a series of experiments involving the Hawthorne Works of the Western Electric Company, this effect appears when members of a test group modify their behavior because they know they are in an experiment. Subjects who know they are being observed may not act according to their usual behavioral mode. The **Rosenthal effect** can also undermine an experiment's integrity. This effect is produced when investigators unwittingly convey their expectations to the subjects in the experiment. Double-blind experiments (in which neither researcher nor subject knows pertinent details relating to the experiment) can protect against these effects.[54]

**Quasi-experiments** are also known as *field experiments*. Quasi-experiments are investigations in which the effect of a variable is studied by comparing different groups, even though the investigator knows that neither group completely meets the criteria of a control group, or in which an investigator studies a group before and after an occurrence to observe the effects of the occurrence, although the "before" group fails to fully meet the criteria of a control group. That is, quasi-experiments are experiments "in the real world," in which laboratory conditions and perfect control groups do not exist. The quasi-experiment replicates the logic of the experiment, but only imperfectly.

Sometimes quasi-experiments are the most obvious way to study certain questions. Suppose a political scientist wished to determine whether local immunization programs help contain the spread of infectious diseases. The political scientist could conduct a quasi-experiment to compare infection rates of "before groups" (preimmunization populations) and "after groups" (postimmunization populations).[55] Data based on these studies could help confirm or falsify hypotheses concerning the effectiveness of immunization policies, even though no perfectly defined control group existed.

## Indirect Quantitative Analysis

**Indirect quantitative analysis** is a research approach that is indirect in the sense that it uses data already compiled by others (as opposed to original survey research, for example, which collects data directly through questionnaires).[56] It assesses quantitative (that is, mathematical and statistical) information to discover empirically verifiable patterns. For example, political scientists and other researchers might study statistics compiled by the World Bank and other international organizations to find patterns on life expectancy, infant morality, and literacy levels in different countries. This approach formed the basis of many of the findings in the study titled *The Material World: A Global Family Portrait*. In this study, investigator Peter Menzel compared statistics on population density, population growth, energy consumption, income levels, daily caloric consumption, life expectancy, major causes of death, and other variables across 30 countries to provide an overview of family well-being in the late twentieth century. The indirect quantitative analysis in this study shows that high-income societies tend to have certain types of families (for example, having low birth rates), whereas low-income societies tend to have other types (characterized by high birth rates and low status for women relative to men).[57]

Indirect quantitative analysis is a very useful research strategy providing means of interpreting information on a variety of political topics. This research is especially important given the possibilities for data maintenance and transmissions through computers. With the Internet, it is increasingly possible to use data already collected and stored by previous investigators. However, political scientist Frank L. Wilson has noted that this research strategy has its drawbacks. Indirect quantitative analysis of international politics can be problematic insofar as political scientists often depend on data collected by a variety of investigators who may be using different standards of collection and measurement. That is, it is sometimes difficult to compare the data when they have been collected under vastly different conditions from one country to the next and when the data may connote very different political realities from one country to the next. Comparing statistical measurements across radically different

---

**BOX 2.4  Choosing Research Strategies in the Study of Politics**

*Case Studies*

- *Strength:* Allows for in-depth study of people, events, countries, elections, or other political questions.
- *Weakness:* Information may not apply to other cases.

*Survey Research*

- *Strengths:* Large amounts of information can be gathered and quantitatively assessed; information is more general in application than in case studies.
- *Weaknesses:* Wording, sampling, and other problems with surveys may compromise results; survey does not provide up-close, in-depth details of a case study.

*Experiments and Quasi-Experiments*

- *Strength:* Experimental conditions allow researchers to carefully test hypotheses.

- *Weaknesses:* Participants may alter their behavior because of the conditions of the experiment; many questions cannot be tested by experiments; in quasi-experiments, researchers lack perfect control groups.

*Indirect Quantitative Analysis*

- *Strength:* Researcher builds on findings of others and extends and applies large amounts of quantitatively tested data.
- *Weakness:* It is often difficult to compare findings collected in different research projects under different conditions and through studies asking different questions.

---

cultures, communities, and nations may produce misleading conclusions. Wilson offers the example of voter turnout. If we compare 20 countries on the issue of voter turnout, we can discover how they rank in terms of high or low turnout relative to one another; however, low turnout in one country may be suggestive of something entirely unrelated to low turnout in another country. Thus, merely comparing existing quantitative figures on voting levels provides an ultimately limited picture of comparative patterns of voting.[58]

What do each of these research approaches have in common? Each approach—from case studies to indirect quantitative analysis—proposes to use science to help us better understand politics, with its manifold changes and its fluctuating resources (as discussed in the introductory chapter). However, how much can any of these approaches tell us? How far can political science extend our understanding? Science cannot transcend its own limitations. As a result, thinking scientifically about politics involves knowing the limits of science. It involves realizing how much we do not know.

## SCIENCE: LIMITATIONS

In science, the decade of the 1990s offers an interesting period for reflection and analysis. During this decade, 90 percent of the cosmos remained unclassified and unknown.[59] A new life-form unlike any other species—the tiny Cycliophora—was discovered.[60] A professor at Harvard Medical School came under attack for studying humans who claimed to have had sex with aliens from outer space,[61] and psychologists published findings suggesting that human brains apparently cannot operate without bias.[62]

Yet the 1990s were not particularly strange years, as far as the history of science is concerned. The previously noted events are important not because of their oddness value but because they point to important aspects of science itself. Science is sometimes routine and sometimes amazing. What is bizarre to one person is a perfectly logical research question to another person. Science has limits, both in terms of what it has produced in the way of knowledge and in terms of the logic by which it operates. Some of these limits are more obvious in political science (and the social sciences generally) than in the natural sciences (for example, biology, chemistry, and physics), whereas others apply to all sciences. We can begin thinking about these limits by considering a number of questions.

## How Can We Have a Science of Human Behavior When Human Behavior Is Often Unique?

What if behavior does not repeat itself? If behavior does not repeat, it is difficult, if not impossible, to observe empirically a sufficient number of instances of a particular behavior to provide confirmation or falsification of that behavior. This would imply that an empirically based science of politics is limited by the essence (nonrepeatability, or low levels of repeatability) of the subject matter (human behavior) under observation. Social scientists and philosophers have often pointed to this problem.[63] For example, comparative studies of democracy find that a particular type of democracy rarely "repeats" itself cross-culturally, and consequently our understandings of the nature of democracy are not as clear as they might be were political life less varied and nuanced. As you will see in later chapters, democracies can have parliamentary or presidential structures, two political parties or multiple political parties, a written constitution or no written constitution, and judicial review or the absence of judicial review. Democracy does not "repeat" perfectly from one system to the next. This makes a science of democracy more tentative than sciences of matter, which can be studied under laboratory conditions.

A similar problem of limited repeatability plagues political science studies that attempt to make precise predictions of political outcomes. For example, political scientists have struggled for years to develop a means of predicting the winners of presidential elections. Some have looked for correlations with economic indicators; others have labored over public opinion polls searching for the key variable that would allow us to know ahead of time who would be the next president. Although numerous formulas have been put forth (with varying ranges of error), a review of these attempts at forecasting presidential election winners left its readers with this question: Can science offer better predictions than provided by hunches, reading the stars, interpreting Tarot cards, or consulting fortune tellers? The basic question is reasonable, in that presidential elections are often complicated by many factors specific to a single election. Like democratic governments, presidential elections do not perfectly repeat. By the way, the review found that political scientists and psychics were similarly divided on who would win the next presidential election.[64]

## How Do We Know Our Findings Are Correct?

We have seen that science is based on empiricism, that science does not accept as correct what is not observable, and that science rejects what has been falsified. Such is the very logic of science itself. However, a number of problems may complicate this logic. Specifically, observation implies some degree of interpretation. Observation is never "purely" observation. Even as we observe and mentally record data, we are imposing meaning on it (that is, interpreting it). Observation rests on our ability to put facts together, to make sense of them, to interpret them.[65] Because interpretation is an inevitable part of observation, personal bias or opinion in the process of interpreting may be unavoidable.

Thus, no matter how hard we try to be scientific, we may be viewing the world in a biased manner. As a consequence, falsification is a complex matter. If we fail to falsify our hypothesis, our failure may not indicate the ultimate falsifiability of the matter in question; it may be caused by our interpretation of the facts we are recording. Our interpretative mode may conceal the means of falsification from us.[66] We may be victims of the Baconian idols, viewing the world in terms of misconceptions, prejudices, and stereotypes; the means of falsification may exist, but they may be outside our field of vision and imagination. Consider the Harvard scientist studying human–alien sex contacts. Perhaps this scientist has escaped our interpreting biases (which, for some of us, would deny outright the existence of aliens). Maybe aliens do exist and do enjoy sex with human beings, but our bias makes us interpret away all the empirical evidence pointing to such "facts." Or maybe it is thoroughly ludicrous to talk about aliens from outer space. How do we ever know? We return to what has been a recurring theme of this chapter: the tentative nature of scientific knowledge.

## Does the Pursuit of Science Lead Us to Ignore Important Questions?

If the scientific method of empirical-based data collection and analysis is to be our means of pursuing knowledge, we are limited in terms of what we can study. What is unobservable is outside our range of inquiry. For political scientists comfortable with the scientific method, this is not a problem. Dye, for one, believes that this is in fact a strength of political science.[67] However, other political scientists have suggested that what is *most* important to most citizens is exactly what science finds it difficult to measure. What about a good life, fairness, justice, decency, political parties that serve the public good, and politicians interested in the welfare of all citizens? These are things that are difficult to operationalize, turn into hypotheses with independent and dependent variables, test for correlations, and use as a basis for scientific theory construction. Yet these questions may be more interesting to citizens than any hypotheses tested in any single issue of the *American Political Science Review*. If we avoid such questions—preferring others that are easier to operationalize and study empirically—we may be upholding scientific canons but removing ourselves from a discussion of what people actually find important. As you will recall, this worry inspired the postbehavioralist critique of pure behavioralism.[68] This worry seems to haunt successive generations of political scientists.[69]

## BOX 2.5  Science Redraws Its Boundaries as It Responds to Its Rivals: The Scopes and Creationist Cases

From the 1920s to the 1980s, many scientists participated in refining the definition of their practice in response to what was perceived as an assault on science by religious authorities upholding a literalist reading of the Christian Bible. A close look at this process of refinement reveals how science can redefine itself in order to better compete with alternative naming systems (as Converse might call them) or myths (as Spence might suggest).

In 1925, Tennessee biology teacher John Scopes was brought to trial for teaching evolutionary science in violation of a state law prohibiting instruction in any doctrine contrary to the Christian Bible. The case became a forum for discussing the nature of science itself. Scientists came forward in defense of Scopes and explained their view that science was a discipline thoroughly distinct from religion but entirely compatible with it; they said science was a discipline dealing with the domain of here-and-now facts, whereas religion consisted of faith and spirituality. Neither should be construed as precluding the need for the other, according to the scientists giving testimony.

In 1981, court challenges to an Arkansas law mandating the teaching of creationism in the state's public schools brought scientists forward again to defend science. Interestingly,

in this case scientists emphasized that science and religion were *contradictory*, not compatible. They defined science as a profession confined to experts who, unlike religiously minded folk, were trained to distrust any perspective grounded in concepts of eternal truth. They presented science as consisting of "facts" proven by meticulous research methods and put forth these facts as superior to the untenable claims of religious authorities.

Why did the definition of science change? Some scholars believe it was a matter of politics. In the 1920s, religious authorities were too influential to challenge directly, so scientists claimed that science could coexist with religion. In contrast, the 1980s scientific establishment was more powerful than its 1920s counterpart, so scientists did not need to defer to religious authority on the matter of scientific education.

If science's definition is as contextually influenced as these two examples suggest, what does this imply about the logic of scientific processes? Is science defined by its search for empirical data, its competition with its rivals (such as religion), or both?

SOURCE: Thomas Gieryn et al., "Professionalization of American Scientists: Public Science in the Creation/Evolution Trials," *American Sociological Review* 50 (June 1985): 392–409.

## Does Science Contradict Its Own Logic?

Scholars studying the history of science have sometimes raised this question in relation to two issues. First, does science really operate according to the scientific method? For instance, history holds many examples of scientists who were unorthodox to the point of being unscientific in their methods. Louis Pasteur, the developer of the rabies vaccine, apparently failed to specify his data collection methods (making verification extremely problematic) and made false claims about his anthrax vaccine.[70] Second, does science truly differ from dogmatic beliefs? Is science a closed system of thought?

Thomas S. Kuhn's work is considered a classic in terms of addressing the first question. In *The Structure of Scientific Revolutions*, Kuhn points out that scientists have often violated the canons of empiricism. Scientists have often been slow to accept empirical data capable of falsifying scientific hypotheses and theories. Rather than rejecting a theory that some newly discovered observable facts would disprove, scientists have been more likely to come up with exceptions explaining away such facts. The inconvenient facts are judged to be exceptions, not falsifications. In such cases, Kuhn points out, scientists make judgments having nothing to do with scientific methods of empiricism. Generally not until a competing theory (what Kuhn terms a *paradigm*) is conceptualized to make sense of such facts are the facts judged as valid (rather than as exceptions).[71]

This consideration leads to the second question. Is science dogmatic? That is, is science closed, inflexible, and hostile to competing ways of naming reality? Paul Feyerabend has suggested that science does have this tendency. Feyerabend has asked us to consider the possibility that science can be as closed to nonscientific explanations of reality as religion can be closed to nonspiritual explanations of reality. As some religions would deny scientific narratives of what is real (for example, the origins of the earth and what happens after death), so science rejects spiritual narratives. What is important to keep in mind is that science is not generally viewed this way. Science is often seen as being more open, less rigid, and more progressive than religion. Suppose, however, that a freshman college student went into an astronomy class on the first day of the semester and, when the professor began discussing planetary and galaxy formations, he or she raised a hand and stated that Earth was created in so many days by God Almighty. Would that student fare better—in terms of being given serious consideration and intellectual respect—than a Darwinist raising issues of evolution in a Sunday school class at a fundamentalist church? Is science truly open to any possibility?[72] Would you want to be the student in this example?

Pondering similar questions, Larry Spence has argued that social science is, in many cases, little different from myth: It is closed, idiosyncratic in its selection of "facts," and unempirical. Only the naive and the uninitiated really believe its tales of empiricism, careful operationalization, and falsifiability. Those close to it know better because social science is replete with instances in which it summarily dismisses what it does not wish to admit as fact. The dismissals are not based on empiricism but on the upholding of Baconian idols. It has become an idol of social science, Spence teaches, that hierarchy and power are inevitable in human society. Evidence to the contrary (altruism, relationships of affection rather than power, and so on) is dismissed as trivial and irrelevant. Thus, Spence charges, social science is not really a narrative of observable facts but rather a set of myths proffering supports for socially held maxims and competing with what it regards as rival myths.[73]

## Can Science Avoid Coming into Conflict with Ethics?

Insofar as the scientific method upholds the distinction between normative and empirical issues and calls on scientists to avoid making judgments about facts (pronouncing that the facts are good or bad), science proclaims the importance of value neutrality. However, a growing number of scholars have raised questions about this aspect of scientific inquiry. Two issues are involved. First, science often affects our lives; therefore, do scientists not have an ethical obligation to weigh the consequences of these effects and determine whether the effects serve the common good? How is the common good to be understood, and how are our conceptions of the common good affected by our circumstances as members of powerful or powerless constituencies? Second, science seeks knowledge, but what if the pursuit of knowledge causes suffering? In such instances, is the pursuit of knowledge unethical?[74]

---

### BOX 2.6    Should Smallpox Be Destroyed?

A fascinating example of how science, the pursuit of knowledge, ethics, and the concern for helping humanity can run counter to one another is provided by the case of the smallpox virus. This virus is disfiguring and potentially deadly. As recently as the 1960s, smallpox was infecting up to 15 million people in approximately 30 countries per year. As many as 2 million of those infected by the virus were dying from it. An extensive vaccination effort brought smallpox under control by the late 1970s. The World Health Organization (WHO) pronounced it eradicated from the world population in 1980. This was cause for jubilation and for laudatory comments regarding the power of medical science to better the lives of people throughout the world. Science could work wonders, this example proved. Disturbing questions about the nature of science would soon follow, however.

Although smallpox, as a viral agent occurring naturally within human populations, was wiped out by 1980, the virus itself was not destroyed. Samples of the virus remained in scientific laboratories in the United States and Russia. The obvious question arose, Should these samples be preserved or destroyed? Scientists and policymakers were divided. The task of weighing the consequences of killing or saving the laboratory samples was potentially overwhelming to even the most knowledgeable of decision makers. What was there to consider? Nobody could afford to forget how deadly this virus was. Smallpox would once again pose a danger to public health if it were somehow re-released into the human population. Terrorists who could access the virus would have a frightening weapon capable of threatening millions of people. Yet destroying smallpox was not to be done in a cavalier manner; were it destroyed, its demise would constitute the first deliberate extinction of a species of life. Should humans consciously and intentionally cause an entire species to die? Moreover, destroying the virus would mean its permanent removal from the laboratory studies of scientists. Some scholars believed this virus should be saved in hopes that it could be studied as part of a process of more fully understanding other viruses (such as HIV).

What should be done? Could the quest for scientific knowledge be reconciled with the ethical claims of protecting public health? In January 1996, WHO voted to support the position of killing the laboratory samples by June 30, 1999. In May 1999, WHO representatives and affiliates upheld the decision in favor of eventual destruction of the stock but determined that the virus supply should be retained until 2002 so that further research could take place. In March 2003, WHO again determined to delay the destruction of the smallpox samples to provide additional time for study and analysis. Did WHO make the correct decision?

SOURCES: WHO, "Future Research on Smallpox Virus Recommended," Press Release 10 December 1999 (http://www.who.int); Charles Siebert, "Smallpox Is Dead, Long Live Smallpox," *New York Times Magazine* (21 August, 1994), Section 6: 31–37, 44, 52, 55; Lawrence K. Altman, "Stocks of Smallpox Virus Edge Nearer to Extinction," *New York Times* (25 January 1996): A1, A5; WHO 56th World Health Assembly, Provisional Agenda Item 14.6, 13 March 2003, "Smallpox Eradication: Destruction of Variola Virus Stocks. Report by the Secretariat."

Political scientists cannot escape these questions. It is clear to traditionalists, behavioralists, and postbehavioralists that political science is a discipline with the potential to change lives even as it searches for knowledge. We can consider the example of survey research. As discussed previously, survey research is one of the most popular information-gathering tools of political science, in part because it can provide statistically significant scientific data. Surveys can also influence elections. Indeed, they have the power to alter reality. Burns Roper believes that polling results made available prior to the 1948 presidential election between Republican Thomas Dewey and Democrat Harry Truman helped swing the election to Truman. Why? Roper explains that polling results showed Dewey beating Truman; seeing these results, Republicans became overconfident and Democrats grew scared and went into a frenzy of activity to get out the vote. The surveys shaped the actual voting behavior, as Roper sees it.[75] Working especially hard because they feared defeat, the Democrats mobilized their supporters and ended up with the victory.

More recently, surveys have been used to decide elections, according to Patrick Caddell. In 1988, Caddell was a polling expert for Alan Cranston, Democratic senator from California. Cranston was in a close race with Republican Ed Zschau. Caddell and colleagues studied surveys of California voters and discovered an intriguing bit of data: Voters were tiring of negative campaign ads and were ready to ignore the election altogether if the ads continued. This bit of data became the basis for devising a successful reelection strategy for Cranston. Cranston's team decided to run negative ads to annoy people so much that they would become sickened by the very thought of politics. This would have the effect of reducing the voter turnout in the election. Lower turnout would help Cranston because as the incumbent senator he had higher name recognition than Zschau. It worked. Turnout dropped, and Cranston edged out the lesser known Zschau.[76]

These uses of survey results represent possible harm to the principles of democratic decision making and fair competition in elections. But what of actual harm to human lives? Political scientists have also been forced to confront this question. The Tuskegee study and the Cincinnati study illustrate issues pertaining to science and ethics. Both studies deal with policies that were designed to provide knowledge but pursued knowledge through a process involving physical pain and death.

The Tuskegee study began in the 1930s, when medical researchers, under the sponsorship of the U.S. Public Health Service, carried out an experiment for observing the effects of untreated syphilis. Syphilis is a contagious disease that produces very painful ailments, such as skin ulcers, bone deterioration, liver failure, intestinal failure, aneurysms, dementia, and eventual death. When the study began, safe and effective treatments for syphilis were unavailable. This study recruited syphilis-infected men from rural areas in eastern Alabama. Researchers offered the participants free meals, free transportation, free medical care (although the care would not extend to treating the syphilis itself), and burial funds. The recruitment process produced a group of 399 syphilis-infected men who agreed to participate in the study. These participants were very poor, and

---

**BOX 2.7    Science and the Public Good: Who Decides What the Public Good Is?**

Dr. Marion Sims is generally regarded as a scientist whose research has promoted human betterment and public health. He practiced medicine in a number of states, including South Carolina, Alabama, and New York, in the nineteenth century. Much of his research took place in the South in the years before the Civil War. Sims developed surgical techniques that advanced the field of modern gynecological science. In fact, he is regarded by some as a founder of this medical subfield.

However, Sims' research agenda was carried out at the expense of the slave women who served as his experimental subjects. To obtain subjects, he sought out slave owners who would allow him to operate on their slaves as long as he promised not to undertake any procedure so dangerous as to risk a slave's life. He also entered into financial agreements with the owners to pay for the upkeep of the slave women

in his experiments, as long as the owners provided clothing and paid all state taxes on the slave subjects. Records indicate that some slave women were successfully treated for vaginal ailments and returned to their owners, whereas others remained with Dr. Sims for extensive periods. One slave woman named Anarcha endured 30 surgical procedures and numerous public displays of her body during lectures and surgical demonstrations given by Sims. At least one woman died from his experiments.

Sims considered himself a scientist contributing to the public's storehouse of knowledge. It would be instructive to have a record of Anarcha's candid assessment of the doctor's work.

SOURCE: John Langone, "Trying to Bridge the 'Death Gap' Confronting Minority Groups," *New York Times* (19 December 2000): D7; Todd L. Savitt, "The Use of Blacks for Medical Experimentation and Demonstration in the Old South," *Journal of Southern History* 48 (August 1982): 344–346.

---

most were illiterate. For the most part, they had never received medical treatment of any kind at any time in their lives. They were also African–American.

As the study progressed in the 1940s, an important ethical issue arose: Penicillin became available as a safe and effective treatment for syphilis. The question confronting the researchers at that point was, Should they give the men in the study penicillin, or should they withhold the penicillin so that the study could continue? The researchers chose to pursue knowledge. They reasoned that given penicillin's effectiveness, syphilis would soon be eradicated, and therefore the Tuskegee test group was likely to be the last group of known syphilitics; to the researchers, this meant that the study was too important to discontinue. Thus, they withheld the treatment, the men continued to suffer and die, and the researchers studied sufferings and deaths empirically. Did the pursuit of science conflict with the values of humanity? Had the scientists been more concerned with ethics, would they have chosen to treat the men and end their suffering even at the cost of knowledge?[77] These questions prompted President Clinton to offer an official apology for the government's participation in the Tuskegee study in May 1997.[78]

These questions reappear in the radiation experiments conducted at the University of Cincinnati during the Cold War. Between 1960 and 1971, in this study 88 cancer patients were exposed to high doses of full-body radiation. The Pentagon sponsored the study to collect information on the probable effects of exposing military personnel to areas contaminated by radiation. Cancer patients became the test group for satisfying the Pentagon's curiosity. The researchers presented full-body radiation to these patients as an experimental treatment for controlling their cancer. They did not tell the patients that the study was funded by the Pentagon, that the levels of radiation put them in danger, or that the type of radiation they were receiving was not generally seen as effective for treating their forms of cancer. A 1972 study of the patients revealed that as many as one-fourth of the patients died from the radiation, not the cancer.[79]

Did the Pentagon and the researchers violate basic values associated with a society's obligation to promote public health? Did science contradict ethics? Political scientists may see in these two cases the difficulties of separating science and ethics. In fact, the individual questions we have explored in this section are interrelated, highlighting similar concerns about the costs associated with science as a method of inquiry. Some readers may conclude that although limited, science is still the most reliable route to knowledge. Others may adopt a different opinion, seeing the scientific method as insufficient, believing that science can help us gather data, but feeling, perhaps, that we need something beyond science—empathy, ethics, religion, humanism, and so on—to teach us how to use those data responsibly. As you examine some of the key concepts in political science in the next chapter, you will continue to see the difficulties and challenges of answering these questions. You will continue to see the possibilities and the limits of political science as you investigate power, nations, states, sovereignty, legitimacy, and other vital areas of political life.

## SUMMING UP

- Political science is an academic discipline that seeks to study politics scientifically and to address **empirical** (factual) and **normative** (ethical) questions about politics. Political scientists have disagreed over the years as to how to best study politics; hence, disputes among **traditionalists, behavioralists,** and **postbehavioralists** have divided the discipline.

- Political scientists use the **scientific method** of empirical data collection in a number of ways—**case studies, survey research, experiments, quasi-experiments,** and **indirect quantitative analysis**.

- Although the scientific collection of data has enriched human understanding of many aspects of politics—by providing an approach to study that emphasizes **hypothesis** formation, clear **operational definitions** of **independent** and **dependent variables**, careful analyses of indicators, and strict attention to the difference between ultimate causation and **correlation**—science is not without limits. Human behavior is sometimes unique and not entirely susceptible to scientific classification. Science is difficult to practice in a manner that is thoroughly untouched by bias and interpretative assumptions. Not all questions about politics can be answered scientifically. Moreover, when science investigates humans, as in the Tuskegee and Cincinnati studies, it conceptualizes humans as subjects—that is, as testable "objects"—and, as such, runs the risk of violating ethical principles. After all, when you use humans as test subjects, you may well change their lives in ways they cannot imagine and might not choose for themselves. Should science (and political scientists) have that power?

## STUDY QUESTIONS

1. What are the differences separating traditionalists, behavioralists, and post-behavioralists? How would these groups differ in their strategies for analyzing the following question: How does the U.S. Congress operate?

2. Discuss hypothesis formation, operationalization, independent variables, dependent variables, and indicators as elements of the process of studying politics scientifically.

3. What differentiates correlation from causation?

4. What are the different "idols" Francis Bacon identified, and how can the use of scientific procedures help free people from such idols?

5. What is a case study? What are the strengths and weaknesses of case studies?

6. What is survey research? What potential problems are associated with surveys? What have surveys suggested about U.S. presidential popularity patterns?

7. Discuss experiments and quasi-experiments, including any difficulties or limitations.

8. What is indirect quantitative analysis? What are its strengths and weaknesses?

9. In what ways is science as a process of inquiry limited in terms of its contributions to our intellectual and civic lives?

## FOLLOWING UP THROUGH
## INTERNET SOURCES

*Political Science as a Scientific, Academic Discipline*

- American Political Science Association (APSA) (http://www.apsanet.org). An overview of the organization's activities, schedules, and a brief selection of historical material.

*Science as a Method of Inquiry*

- The National Science Foundation (http://www.nsf.gov). Press releases, speeches, documents on science, science's societal applications, the potential conflict between science and ethics, and other questions pertaining to scientific study and data collection.

*Public Opinion Polls and the Scientific Study of Attitudes*

- The Gallup Organization (http://www.gallup.com). Provides links to actual poll results, including an overview of methodological issues raised by actual polls (for example, size of sampling error and issues raised by the wording of questions).

*Human Radiation Experiments*

- Department of Energy Openness, *Human Radiation Experiments* (http://tis.eh.doe.gov/ohre/). Information on human radiation experiments funded by the U.S. government from the 1940s through the 1970s.

- The National Security Archive/ Advisory Committee on Human Radiation Experiments (ACHRE) (http://www.gwu.edu/~nsarchiv/ radiation). Interim and final reports on human radiation experiments funded by the U.S. government, as well as background and organizational information.

*The Tuskegee Study*

- Centers for Disease Control and Prevention (CDC). *The Tuskegee Syphilis Study: A Hard Lesson Learned.* (http://www.cdc.gov/hchstp/od/ tuskegee/time). Overview of the Tuskegee study, what was unethical, and what was learned from the standpoint of the CDC.

- The Tuskegee Study Legacy Committee Report. *A Request for Redress of the Wrongs of Tuskegee* (http:// www.med.virginia.edu/hs-library/ historical/apology/report.html). Report of the Tuskegee Syphilis Study Legacy Committee, established in January 1996, on the history of the study and on contemporary reactions to the study.

# 3

❖

# Key Concepts in Political Science

In the seventeenth century, hundreds of U'wa people committed suicide as a means of resisting Spanish colonizers. Rather than submit to occupying powers, they threw themselves off a mountain.

In the late twentieth century, the U'wa people were once again talking about suicide—this time in opposition to their government (Colombia) and a multinational oil company (Occidental Petroleum). In 1995, Occidental obtained exploration rights from the Colombian government to develop petroleum resources in land historically claimed by the U'wa. The U'wa regarded Occidental as the new occupier. They used public appeals, demonstrations, pickets, blockades, and international pressure in their efforts to oust Occidental. Knowing their own history, the U'wa understood that, when it looks as if there is nothing else left to do, people can sometimes find a source of power more compelling than the militaries of governments and the riches of private interests. The threat of ritual mass suicide slowed Occidental's project, and, in May 2002, Occidental announced plans to terminate its operations in U'wa territory.

This chapter examines how individuals, groups, and organizations use power; how states and nations define themselves; and how complex interactions among states, nations, cultures, and groups can be assessed by using some of the scientific tools of analysis discussed in Chapter 2. The chapter focuses on an examination of basic political concepts, such as power, state, and nation. Although no discipline as large and varied as political science exhibits unanimity in terms of defining these

---

**BOX 3.1    Power: Definition and Characteristics**

- Power is the ability to influence an outcome to achieve an objective or the ability to influence someone to act in a way contrary to the way he or she would choose to act.
- Power involves the exercise of volition (will).

- Power over someone else involves altering his or her volition (will).
- Power can be latent or manifest.
- Different types of power are generally blended together when power is made manifest.

---

concepts, certain definitions are widely accepted. As the U'wa struggle in Colombia suggests, power struggles often raise normative and empirical questions and often involve multiple governmental and nongovernmental participants.[1]

## POWER

Power is one of the most important concepts in political science. In fact, some political scientists see it as a defining element of the discipline.[2] Power affects how resources are distributed, how countries interact, whether peace or war prevails, and how groups and individuals pursue their interests; that is, power affects the myriad of topics studied by political scientists. Ironically, however, power is one of the most difficult concepts to define.[3]

What is power? At its most fundamental level, **power** is an ability to influence an event or outcome that allows the agent to achieve an objective and/or to influence another agent to act in a manner in which the second agent, on its own, would not choose to act.[4] In terms of the first meaning, an interest group, for example, could be said to have power if it succeeded in reaching its financial goals. The interest group, in this case, would have achieved its objective if its assets increased to meet its stated aims. Significantly, this type of power may or may not involve exercising power over another agent. Conceivably, the interest group could use its assets wisely and build up its revenues without enacting power over any other interest group, political party, politician, and so forth. However, in regard to the second meaning, having power means having power over another agent.[5] For example, one country can be viewed as exercising power over another if it can influence the second country to act in a manner favored by the first country but not favored by the second country.

These meanings become clearer when you recognize that the word *power* stems from the older Latin term *potere,* defined as an ability to affect something else.[6] Thus, for example, a person was said to possess *potere* if that person had some attribute allowing him or her to cause an effect on someone else. The word *power,* with its present spelling, has been in use since the fourteenth century.[7] In our two examples, one agent (an interest group or a country) has acted to bring about an effect; thus, both have wielded *potere*/power, with the interest group affecting its own financial well-being and the country affecting a second country.

A closer examination of power reveals that its exercise by an agent involves **volition** (will or choice). In terms of power as the achievement of an objective, clearly the objective attained must be one that the agent wills or desires; otherwise, the agent is not said to possess power. If, for example, an interest group obtains a benefit but has not sought out this benefit, we would not attribute attaining benefit to the interest group's power. We might attribute it to luck, chance, randomness, charity, or some other fluke. Volition is also central to the second meaning of power, as influence over another agent. For instance, we would not view an interest group as exercising power over a politician if the interest group does not compel the politician to act contrary to the politician's own volition or desire. Similarly, if one country ordered another country to perform an act the second country wanted to do anyway, this would not represent an act of power because the first country has not actually influenced the second country.[8] Clearly, will, desire, and choice enter into the exercise of power when it is exercised by an agent or over an agent.

Power can either be held in reserve or deployed. That is, it can be *latent* (inactive) or *manifest* (active). You can imagine how the possession of latent power by one agent can be highly effective in producing changes in a second agent. In such cases, the mere possibility that the first agent will activate power can be feared by the second agent and elicit changes in the second agent's actions. Indeed, this is the idea behind military deterrence: A country's stockpile of weapons may be enough to preclude aggression by its enemies, who know that the weapons can be changed from a latent power to a manifest power at any time.[9]

Political scientists have often tried to sort out the many different forms power can assume. This is useful in allowing us to analyze the implications of using one type of power rather than another. However, in actual political relationships one type of power is rarely found in isolation from other types. In practice, power generally possesses a *blended* quality, with one type of power blending into another. This concept of blending will be clearer as we begin looking at the actual types of power.[10]

## Types of Power

**Force** is the exercise of power by *physical means*.[11] Force can include acts of physical violence and acts of physical obstruction. For example, one agent can use power over another by restraining, assaulting, assassinating, impeding access to an

---

**BOX 3.2   Types of Power**

- Force is power involving *physical means.*
- Persuasion is nonphysical power in which the agent using power makes its use of power *clear and known* to the agent over whom power is exercised.

- Manipulation is nonphysical power in which the agent using power *conceals* the use of power.
- Exchange is the use of power through *incentives.*

object, or other types of physical activity. Force can include physical sabotage of resources, as well as conducting war. It can be carried out in the form of embargoes and boycotts (which deny physical access to resources), blockades and barricades (which deny physical access to a place), or revolutions and riots (which physically mobilize groups in support of or opposition to a government or policy). It can involve physically blocking access to a courthouse, voting booth, public school, or abortion facility. It can entail physically incapacitating a machine or, by introducing steel spikes, physically rendering a tree too dangerous to cut down. It can involve no violence (a boycott) or extreme levels of violence (a bombing). In sum, whenever people use physical means to pursue power, *force* is the term that designates this display of power.

---

### BOX 3.3   Violent Force: Assassination

In September 1980, a small group of individuals associated with the Argentinian Revolutionary Workers' Party (PRT) assassinated Anastasio Somoza, who had relinquished the presidency of Nicaragua in July 1979. Somoza's tenure as Nicaraguan president had been characterized by human rights abuses, the denial of civil liberties, political repression, and economic corruption. A broad-based opposition movement had forced him from power, and when the Sandinista revolutionary leaders who had struggled against the Somoza regime for years marched triumphantly into the country's capital in the summer of 1979, many observers looked with hope to Nicaragua's post-Somoza future. Somoza himself fled the country—first to Miami and later to Asuncion, Paraguay.

Why did PRT activists decide to assassinate Somoza? Among their reasons was the belief that Somoza would finance a counterrevolution against the new Nicaraguan leaders as part of a plan to restore his own power. Thus, the PRT activists began a long, arduous process of planning for Somoza's execution as a means of supporting the new Nicaragua. An examination of the details of their preparation reveals a fascinating—some would say blood chilling—example of calculated, deliberate violent force as a type of political power.

The assassins began schooling themselves on Somoza as an individual. They had to learn his habits, his likes, and his dislikes. They read newspaper articles and did research on Somoza at public libraries. Then they traveled to his new home country of Paraguay. Knowing his neighborhood but not his actual house, one of the activists devised an ingenious plan to discover his address. She booked a hair/manicure appointment at a plush beauty parlor in the neighborhood known to be Somoza's. Afterward she hailed a cab and, during the ride, casually asked the driver if he knew the Somoza residence. The driver responded with the address.

The assassins proceeded to rent a house conveniently located for the execution. However, they needed a cover story to ensure that the owner did not appear unexpectedly or reveal too much about her new tenants. So they concocted the story that they were renting the house on behalf of the singer Julio Iglesias, who would soon be visiting Paraguay. Iglesias, they explained, needed his privacy and preferred that his whereabouts remain hush-hush. At the time, Julio Iglesias was a major celebrity and the owner was beside herself with excitement at the thought of Iglesias staying in *her* house. Yes, she assured the assassins, she would be discrete about their presence.

---

BOX 3.3 *Continued*

With these steps taken, the activists were ready to carry out their task. They had skilled themselves in maneuvers involving secret communications, explosives and weapons use, surveillance, disguises, and document forgery. They were ready to defend Nicaragua's future. On September 16, 1980, they executed Nicaragua's former president.

As you think about this historical example, reflect on the public's demand for bin Laden "dead or alive" after September 11, 2001. In your estimation, could political assassination ever be justified?

SOURCE: Claribel Alegria and Darwin Flakoll, *Death of Somoza: The First Person Story of the Guerrillas Who Assassinated the Nicaraguan Dictator* (Willimantic, CT: Curbstone Press, 1996).

---

Perhaps for many U.S. readers of this text, in the period following September 11, 2001 (9/11), to read about force in relation to politics is to find one's thoughts going immediately to Osama bin Laden and Al Qaeda, just as previous readers may have thought instantaneously of Oklahoma City bomber Timothy McVeigh. In April 1995, Timothy McVeigh killed more than 160 people in the Oklahoma City bombing as a statement against the U.S. government. The 9/11 attacks by Al Qaeda killed thousands of people in another political statement against the U.S. government.

In radical contrast to the previous examples of violent force, there exist long-standing traditions affirming that force is used most effectively as a nonviolent approach to power. Martin Luther King, Jr., Cesar Chavez, and Dolores Huerta have championed such uses of force. For King, force was a legitimate form of power only when certain conditions were met. First, force was never to be used violently. For King, acceptable examples of force included boycotts, marches, demonstrations, sit-ins, and other peaceful instances in which people used their bodies physically to try to obtain objectives (civil rights reform) and to make other

---

**BOX 3.4   Martin Luther King, Jr. (1929–1968)**

- Civil rights activist, minister, and political theorist
- Influenced by the civil disobedience philosophies of Henry David Thoreau and Mohandas K. Gandhi
- Leader in organizations and movements promoting civil rights and economic justice, including the Montgomery Improvement Association, which fought against segregated buses in the mid-1950s; the Southern Christian Leadership Conference (SCLC), which advanced desegregation and civil rights in the 1950s and 1960s; the opposition to the Vietnam War in the 1960s; and the 1968 Poor People's Campaign, which advanced the interests of the impoverished

- Major writings include *Stride Toward Freedom* (1958), *Strength to Love* (1963), "Letter from a Birmingham Jail" (1963), *Why We Can't Wait* (1964), and *Where Do We Go from Here?* (1967)
- Awarded the Nobel Peace Prize in 1964, named as posthumous recipient of the Presidential Medal of Freedom in 1977, and had a U.S. national holiday proclaimed in his honor in 1986

agents act in ways they would not, on their own, otherwise choose to act (enact desegregation policies). Second, King upheld force as legitimate only when verbal negotiations with authorities failed to end segregation and discrimination. Third, force was acceptable only if conducted after a process of self-scrutiny, in which the individuals designated to carry out the force examined their motives and ensured that their use of force would not be motivated by anger, revenge, or other self-gratifying (as opposed to just) motives. Finally, force was acceptable only when employed to alter discriminatory laws, not laws generally; King insisted that this distinction between discriminatory laws and nondiscriminatory (fair) laws was vital in maintaining the distinction between force as he justified it, on the one hand, and common crime, on the other hand.[12]

Cesar Chavez and Dolores Huerta have been key activists in the United Farm Workers (UFW) movement. The UFW has pressured agribusiness and political leaders to improve the safety and working conditions surrounding farm labor; specifically, the UFW has sought higher wages, collective bargaining rights, and humane working conditions (such as worker access to sanitary facilities on the job), among other demands. Like King, Chavez and Huerta have insisted that using force to achieve the UFW's objectives was legitimate only so long as force remained nonviolent. A strategy of boycotting key agricultural products fit their criteria for force with nonviolence. During the 1970s, they called for a national boycott of grapes, lettuce, and Gallo wine. The boycott sought to physically re-move buyers and dollars from the market for these products, thereby penalizing the affected industries for failing to accede to workers' demands. It was under-taken as a strategy for involving massive groups of people (consumers at the na-tional level) in a physical activity designed to pressure agricultural interests to an extent that farm workers alone could not.[13] The boycott was highly effective and helped to bring about passage of the Agricultural Labor Relations Act in 1975, an act upholding collective bargaining rights. Although Chavez is deceased, Huerta continues to serve as a leader in the UFW.[14]

---

**BOX 3.5   Dolores Huerta, Cesar Chavez, and the United Farm Workers**

Dolores Huerta (born in 1930) helped establish the Community Service Organization (CSO) in Stockton, California, in 1955. The CSO was a civil rights advocacy group that led voter registration drives and other community-based efforts on behalf of nondiscrimination and racial equality. Through her work with CSO, Huerta met Cesar Chavez, and the two activists left the CSO in 1962 and went on to form the National Farm Workers Association (NFWA). The NFWA merged with another union—the Agricultural Workers Organizing Committee (AWOC)—to form the United Farm Workers Organizing Committee (UFWOC), the fore-runner of the United Farm Workers Union (UFW).

The UFW's Web page is found at http://www.ufw.org. News alerts, organizing drives, and biographical sketches of Huerta and Chavez can be accessed at this Web address.

King, Chavez, and Huerta may be thought of as heirs to a tradition of force passed along in an especially creative manner by a nineteenth-century American named Henry Brown. In the early 1800s, Henry Brown was born a slave in Louisa County, Virginia. In 1849, he mailed himself out of slavery. Literally, he enclosed himself inside a crate addressed to a location in Pennsylvania, a free state; the crate was then sent through the mail system. By mailing himself over 300 miles and more than 24 hours away, he physically—that is, forcefully—denied his "owner" access to his body as property. Nonviolent force was used to achieve his goal of liberation.[15]

In addition to the historical examples just noted, force has been central to various other key episodes of international politics in recent decades. Among the most familiar to readers will be the examples of the Bush administration's use of violent military force against both the Taliban leaders in Afghanistan and the Saddam Hussein regime in Iraq in a campaign President Bush believes to be necessary as a means of reducing U.S. vulnerability to terrorism after 9/11. In other cases, states have employed violent force against their own citizens, as was true of Nigerian ruler Sani Abacha's measures designed to silence the voice of Ken Saro-Wiwa. Saro-Wiwa was an activist seeking justice for Nigeria's Ogoni people. In recent years, the Ogoni lost control over much of their oil-rich lands, as multinational corporations, with the support of the Nigerian government, claimed their ancestral territories. Saro-Wiwa helped organize the Movement for the Survival of the Ogoni People (MOSOP) to work on behalf of Ogoni rights. He was honored with a Nobel Peace Prize nomination for his efforts. Human rights groups praised his courage but feared for his safety, given the government's opposition to MOSOP. The fears proved well founded. In November 1995, the government hanged Saro-Wiwa and other activists after prosecuting them through legal proceedings that international human rights groups condemned as farcical.[16]

Despite the international criticism that the use of force may elicit, the exercise of this type of power is often attractive to groups or individuals because it is often

---

**BOX 3.6   Ken Saro-Wiwa, MOSOP, and the Internet**

Ken Saro-Wiwa and other activists in the Movement for the Survival of the Ogoni People (MOSOP) have demanded that the Nigerian government recognize the rights of the Ogoni people to govern their own territory. MOSOP has critiqued the environmental destruction caused by the Nigerian government's support of oil drillings in Ogoniland, the lack of democracy in Nigeria, and the Nigerian government's abuse of human rights. The struggles of Ken Saro-Wiwa and MOSOP have been publicized and advanced by many groups—including the Sierra Club, Amnesty International, the Association of Concerned Africa Scholars, Earthlife Africa, and the Nigerian Democratic Movement—via the Internet. Indeed, the case of MOSOP exemplifies the use of the Internet for political advocacy by movements seeking international support and recognition. See, for example, the suggested Internet sites on MOSOP at the end of this chapter.

inexpensive, in comparison with other types of power. As writer Saul D. Alinsky has explained, groups with very limited funds can have a very big impact if they know how to mobilize comparatively cheap, and widely available, resources. Although it is important to note that Alinsky himself was not an advocate of violence, he was an astute observer who pointed out that it is often less expensive for a group with aspirations to power to use physical means to make a colossal disturbance than to employ some of the other types of power (e.g., persuasion, manipulation, or exchange) discussed later in this chapter. As an illustration, it cost Timothy McVeigh less money to blow up a building than it would have cost him to conduct a national media campaign to peacefully disseminate his views through the power of persuasion. The disturbances Alinsky studied were nonviolent examples of force (see Box 3.7), but Alinksy's teachings also provide insight into some of the violent political acts of recent years. Given the cheapness of force, even violent force, it is likely to remain a viable option in the eyes of many.[17]

**Persuasion** is a nonphysical type of power in which the agent using power makes its intentions and desires known to the agent over whom power is exercised. Person A persuades B by explaining A's desires, choices, and will and then produces a change in B in conformity with A's desires, choices, and will. B is altered from his or her preferred course (that is, power has been exercised over B), but B has not been acted on physically (restrained, assaulted, picketed, boycotted, and so on). B has been presented with A's will and has responded by consenting to follow A's will.[18]

Persuasion is a major part of politics. Lobbying, speechmaking, debating, writing letters, issuing position papers, making proclamations in the form of court decisions, executive orders, laws, and policies are examples of persuasion. In each instance, an agent spells out its will with the intention of producing a response in compliance with that will from other agents. Persuasion, like other types of power, may fail, but when it works it can be an impetus to political and social change.

For example, between 1787 and 1788 a series of articles was published in the New York press arguing in favor of the ratification of the U.S. Constitution. The articles came to be known as *The Federalist Papers*. The authors (James Madison, Alexander Hamilton, and John Jay) successfully exercised power through these essays, convincing New York delegates to the state ratifying conventions to put aside their fears of the proposed Constitution and vote for its ratification. One hundred years later, Jacob Riis published *How the Other Half Lives* (1890), a study of New York's poor; the text of the book was accompanied by photographs of the squalid living conditions of impoverished families. Theodore Roosevelt, one reader of Riis's book, described its author as highly influential in educating and shaping attitudes toward poverty. Through his photographs and text, Riis exercised power. He showed readers what many had preferred not to see as they walked the streets: the crowded, drab, tedious, dangerous lives of the poor.[19] These historical examples illustrate the persuasive power of words and images.

Shirin Ebadi understands such power. In 2003, she was awarded the Nobel Peace Prize for ability to use language in such a manner as to prompt people to rethink political and legal boundaries. Ebadi's adult life has been devoted to the

## BOX 3.7  Being Creative with the Use of Force

**Case Study One:** The Woodlawn neighborhood organization pressured the city of Chicago to honor its agreements with the organization by creating a very difficult situation for the city. Chicago is home to one of the world's busiest airports, O'Hare International Airport. Woodlawn devised a strategy of having its members go to O'Hare, form groups, enter the airport's restrooms, and then occupy all the toilet stalls. This would obviously prevent the use of such facilities by airport travelers. Such an occurrence was guaranteed to attract notice, get news coverage, and provide a means of publicizing the city's poor relations with Woodlawn. The proposed strategy was leaked to the city government, which very quickly appeased the neighborhood organization. Threatened force—physically denying access to an important facility— worked to facilitate the group's aims.

SOURCE: Saul D. Alinsky, *Rules for Radicals: A Practical Primer for Realistic Radicals* (New York: Vintage Books, 1971), pp. 141-144.

**Case Study Two:** *The Army of God* is an antiabortion book outlining various types of force that can be used to thwart the operation of abortion providers. Among the nonviolent uses of force suggested are to squirt superglue into the locks of doors at abortion clinics, climb onto the roof of an abortion clinic and drill holes in it so that the roof will leak and the clinic will have to close, put a garden hose through the mail slot in the door of a clinic and then turn on the water to flood the clinic, and dump lots of cow manure in front of the clinic. Each of these tactics can be used to shut down a clinic and thus physically cut off access to its services.

SOURCE: "Pro-Life Terrorism: A How-To," *Harper's Magazine* (January 1995): 19–20.

**Case Study Three:** *Ecodefense: A Field Guide to Monkeywrenching* (second edition) is an environmentalist manual. Its editors, Dave Foreman and Bill Haywood, highlight several ways of using force to disable vehicles used in logging, roadbuilding, or other acts seen as environmentally destructive. What does the manual suggest? Use superglue to destroy locks and ignitions, pour water into the vehicle's gas tank, pour dirt or salt into the oil line, slash the tires, or pour minute rice into the radiator. Each action should disable vehicles and thus physically neutralize them.

SOURCE: Dave Foreman and Bill Haywood, eds., *Ecodefense: A Field Guide to Monkeywrenching*, 2nd ed. (Tucson, AZ: A Ned Ludd Book, 1987), p. 117.

**Case Study Four:** Olympics Out of Cobb formed after the Atlanta Committee for the Olympic Games (ACOG) announced plans to include Cobb County as a site in the 1996 Summer Olympics in Atlanta. Cobb is a local county in the Atlanta area, and from a geographical perspective the decision to schedule Olympic events in Cobb made perfect sense. However, not long before the ACOG's announcement to include Cobb, Cobb County commissioners had officially passed a resolution against gay rights. Olympics Out of Cobb believed that the resolution was a violation of basic democratic values and that Cobb should not be rewarded with Olympic events. So, Olympics Out of Cobb proceeded to use force creatively. To show Olympic organizers just how easily Olympics Out of Cobb supporters could "monkeywrench" the summer games, Olympics Out of Cobb supporters organized car caravans to drive 40 miles per hour on the city's interstate highway system. This speed was the slowest legal speed, and it created traffic nightmares for Olympic organizers, who knew that if such caravans were formed during

| BOX 3.7 *Continued* |
| --- |

the games, transportation to and from events would be virtually impossible. Thus, by threatening to physically deny effective transportation along the highway system, Olympics Out of Cobb succeeded in convincing ACOG to move the events planned for Cobb County to nearby Athens, Georgia.

SOURCE: Detroit News Voices. Deb Price, "Gay Activists Deserve a Medal for Averting Bias at the Olympics," *The Detroit News* (http://www.detnews.com/VOICES/PRICE/0614/0614.htm, accessed 14 June 1996).

cause of using persuasion to work for human rights in her home country of Iran. A lawyer, teacher, judge, and writer, she has used persuasion to uphold the rights of women, children, and political prisoners. She has also argued the case that Islam, human rights, and democracy are compatible and reinforcing moral perspectives.

One can look to her work as an attorney to discern her persuasive acumen. In one of her most famous legal cases, Ebadi represented the mother of the late Arian Golshani. Arian was a 9-year-old girl murdered by her father and stepbrother. Under Iranian law, fathers cannot be convicted for murder in the death of their own children. Undeterred by what many would have called a hopeless venture, Ebadi called upon the public to affirm justice for Arian Golshani and to oppose the law. Go into the streets and toss white flowers onto the ground, she urged her fellow citizens, if you are persuaded that the law is wrong. The street in question became white with flowers in response to her appeal.[20] With persuasion, words matter—words can change lives and, Ebadi and her supporters hope, the Iranian legal and political system.

When persuasion is used successfully, the agent over whom power is exercised knows of the power. Persuasion is felt and experienced by the recipient of the power. Moreover, the recipient is aware not only of the act of power but also of the intentionality of the act. What if Shirin Ebadi used words to try to bring about political change but chose to do so by concealing her aims and intentions? In this case, the power employed would have been both similar and dissimilar to persuasion: Like persuasion, this power would have been *nonphysical,* but unlike persuasion it would have been exercised in a manner that disguised and cloaked the motives and will of the person using power. Such a power is known as manipulation. **Manipulation** is the nonphysical use of power in which the agent exercising power over a second agent conceals the aims and intentions motivating the exercise of power.[21] When manipulation is successful, the agent over whom power is exercised generally is unaware that power has even been used. If you are persuaded, you feel it; if you are manipulated, you do not feel it because you do not know anything has happened. The implication is disturbing: How can you resist something if you do not know it exists? Generally, social scientists who study power relations note that manipulation power is very difficult to oppose because of its cloaked quality.[22]

How could an agent cloak power in this way? An historical example can help clarify the dynamics of manipulation. During Richard Nixon's administration, White House staff members pursued an ongoing manipulation campaign involving public opinion pollsters from two leading polling firms (the Gallup and the Harris firms). President Nixon was convinced that public opinion poll results affected public attitudes of both voters and rival politicians. If his staff could devise a way to *manage* what the major polling firms published as poll results, this could allow the president to shape the polls, which shaped public attitudes. The strategy could work, however, only if the public remained unaware that the polling results were being shaped by the Nixon White House. If voters knew the results were "doctored," the results would be dismissed as useless. As a consequence, a detailed strategy of managing the Gallup and Harris polling results ensued: Pollsters informed the White House of polling results prior to publication (giving the Nixon staff time to issue press releases highlighting certain items in the poll and playing down less attractive ones), pollsters used questions written by White House staff (allowing the Nixon people to ask questions they knew would be flattering to the president and damaging to rivals), pollsters consented to White House requests to "bury" unflattering poll results (publishing the "bad" results at the very end of a long press release), and pollsters held back from publishing altogether some results perceived as harmful to Nixon. Managed by means of these tactics, polls would have a pro-Nixon effect on public attitudes, the White House hoped.[23]

Keep in mind that citizens reading these polling results had no idea any of this was happening. The polling results were presented to readers as neutral, objective, and empirically reliable. The readers were the objects over whom the White House was attempting to exercise power, but they did not know it. Had someone gone up to a randomly selected reader of these polls at some point during the Nixon administration and said, "Power is being exercised over you," the reader most probably would have regarded the accuser as mad. The power was thoroughly invisible to the agents on the receiving end of the power play. Has this happened again? To take one example, Bill Clinton's pollster, Stan Greenberg, denied that the Clinton administration tried to manipulate the public through poll management; however, Greenberg did admit that he met regularly with pollsters and even tried to influence the wording of their questions.[24] Is this a neutral action, or is it a power-seeking endeavor?

The Nixon case illustrates how one politician can try to gain an advantage over another by manipulating the public. Manipulation also came into play during the administration of Ronald Reagan. The Reagan White House pressured fellow Republican Pete Domenici to support the administration's budget. As chair of the Senate Budget Committee, Domenici was a potential rival of the Reagan staff. Domenici commanded respect for his authoritative position and his knowledge of budgetary matters. When presented with the administration's proposed budget early in Reagan's first term, Domenici thought Reagan's budget would generate unacceptable deficits. The Reagan administration knew that if Domenici campaigned against the White House budget, it could be disastrous. When persuasion failed to quiet Domenici, the White House staff turned to another strategy. They convinced journalists to publish articles critical of Domenici; indeed, one such piece appeared in the highly influential and respected *Wall Street Journal*. Domenici withdrew his opposition to the budget. This incident can be read as a classic display of manipulation: Through these articles attacking Domenici, the White House gave the appearance to the public of simply presenting information to serve the public interest, but in reality the Reagan administration had a covert agenda of defeating a budgetary rival and winning an executive-legislative conflict. The readers of these articles were presented with language suggesting the articles were about economic processes, not about an individual (Domenici); concealed from the public was the apparent power motivation behind the language.

Because manipulation by its very nature has a hidden quality, it can be difficult to pinpoint and prove. When the person exercising it is trying to be oblique and the people over whom it is exercised are unaware of it, people have difficulty being certain that manipulation has occurred. Was James Baker using manipulation when he tried to kill fellow Republican Dan Quayle's nomination for vice president in 1988 by leaking news of Quayle's impending nomination, hoping that, when word got out, a backlash against Quayle would sink his chances of being George Bush's running mate?[25] The fact that Baker used an indirect, hidden method (a leak to the press)—rather than simply trying to go public and openly persuade people to oppose Quayle—suggests manipulation. Was Clinton using manipulation in the 1992 election when, on the advice of his campaign staff, he started emphasizing the merits of hard work in his speeches? His staff told him that such a message played well with the voters and could boost his popularity, but Clinton did not begin his subsequent speeches by saying, "I'm going to talk about working hard because I'm told by the experts that doing so may make you want to vote for me." Indeed, listeners heard the language of the work ethic, not the language of power politics.[26] The existence of two layers of language and the suggestion of motives beyond those revealed to his audiences implies indirection and cloaked motives. Politicians are so adept at this power that members of some professions, most notably journalism, have outlined steps for trying to identify manipulation efforts when they are occurring to prevent being "overpowered" by them.[27]

A number of U.S. conservatives believe that manipulation is even more widespread than these examples imply. What if manipulation is operating at the level of popular culture and being exercised through the institutions of public education, they ask? The Coalition of Concerned Citizens of Clay County (Florida) and Citizens for Excellence in Education (California) have argued that such manipulation has been exercised through school systems assigning Pumsy the Dragon books. These books depict Pumsy, a young dragon with self-esteem problems rooted in her inability to breathe fire in great doses. According to these interest groups, the surface message conceals the fact that the books actually teach New Age occultism and disrespect for traditional authority. Pumsy does not solve her problems by looking to God and her own family but, rather, by looking inside herself. Insofar as these books have been used in numerous public school districts, they represent an effort to manipulate children by means of school-sanctioned propaganda against traditional values, according to critics.[28] The children may like the books, but that would not surprise students of manipulation, because manipulation is something not felt as such.

Other groups have also seen manipulation operating at the level of popular culture and exercised through mainstream U.S. institutions. Such groups include gay rights advocates who may see socially enforced heterosexuality as imposed even on those who would, of their own accord, be lesbian, gay, or bisexual were it not for manipulative efforts demonizing anything other than strict heterosexuality as deviant. Similarly, Marxists may see socially enforced capitalist ideology imposed even on those who would choose to be socialists were socialists not dismissed as irrelevant or traitorous. Also, multiculturalists may assert that minority cultures are subject to manipulation through cultural messages denying equal legitimacy to nonwhite European cultures.[29] Advocates of these positions have claimed that individuals can be influenced away from positions they might freely choose for themselves by the power of society's institutions. If your will has been altered by an institution seeking its own goal (promoting Pumsy's occultism over God, heterosexuality over homosexuality, capitalism over socialism, or ethnocentrism over multiculturalism), then power has been exercised over you. If the power is cloaked, it is manipulation. Thus, depending on the merits of the interest groups just noted, liking Pumsy, not identifying as gay, not advocating socialism, and not respecting multiculturalism may be related phenomena.

**Exchange** is a type of power involving incentives, in which one agent gives another agent an item in return for another item. One agent can obtain an objective or exercise power over another agent by giving the second agent the incentive to concur with the first agent's will; if the second agent knows that such a concurrence will be rewarded (for example, the second agent will be given a desired item), the second agent has an incentive to concur. Power has been exercised, insofar as the second agent concurred with the first agent's wishes *only* after being influenced to do so by the incentive.[30] A bribe is an example of exchange power, but so is a legally sanctioned transmission of money or other objects or outcomes in return for a second desired item/outcome/object. As we will see in Chapter 10, log-rolling is an example of exchange. The term log-rolling refers to a practice in a legislative body in which one person agrees to vote for a second person's favored bill if the second person, in exchange, will vote for the first person's favored bill. In log-rolling, votes are exchanged as a means of pursuing desired objectives and altering the behavior of others.

In international politics, one finds numerous instances of exchange as a preferred means of power. The U.S. government's policy of extending economic assistance to Colombian cocoa growers who agree to make a different crop choice is a notable example, as is a recent United Nations policy to give cash to Afghan poppy farmers who avow to substitute another non-drug-related crop. In both the Colombian and Afghan cases, it is clear that the international war on drugs has included exchange as part of its arsenal of weapons.

After 9/11, exchange was part of President Bush's strategy for building international opposition to Afghanistan's ruling Taliban, insofar as President Bush and his administration held the Taliban responsible for not immediately turning over bin Laden and Al Qaeda. U.S. economic assistance was quickly offered to various members of the so-called "Six Plus Two Group." The Six Plus Two Group included the United States, Russia, and the six states bordering Afghanistan (China, Iran, Pakistan, Tajikistan, Turkmenistan, and Uzbekistan). For example, the United States pledged to Pakistan $600 million in foreign aid and $73 million to secure the country's borders; $300 million in investment credits was also offered. In addition, Russia was promised profitable trade deals.[31]

Exchange power is central to many key developments in recent U.S. politics. Exchange, for example, helps explain some of the reasons for historical and more recent population shifts, as well as some of the intricacies of contemporary urban politics. Boom towns (with perceived economic opportunities just waiting for people to migrate and take advantage of them) arose in the American West in the nineteenth century as populations shifted west in hopes of getting cheap land, gold, or other resources. In recent years, boom towns have emerged in places such as Branson, Missouri, as populations leave older cities in hopes of finding jobs in newer cities with expanding service sectors. Many of the new jobs in these boom towns pay minimum wage or slightly above, and the boom towns often lack expansive social service agencies (such as public day care facilities), so migrating populations often find themselves experiencing life as the "working poor." The strain placed on local governments in these towns is enormous; city officials find that the demand for social support exceeds the supply of such services that can be funded by the boom town's tax base. Urban politics becomes an arena in which needs are many and the means of meeting them are often few. In such instances, exchange has fostered political and economic change: The incentive represented by a perceived plentiful supply of jobs has induced migration by populations experiencing limited job opportunities in their present markets. People have been induced to move to a boom town, a move they would not have considered without the exchange power represented by the perceived jobs.[32]

The concept of exchange provides insight not only on recent population dynamics but also on a number of conflicts in the area of environmental politics. What if a poor community needs to find a job-creating industry to recruit into its midst? How can a poor community lure an industry away from more affluent, promising environments? A poor community has a chance of doing so if it seeks out an industry that more financially secure communities do not want. For example, it can invite a toxic dump. In such a scenario, the community can gain jobs and the industry can gain support for its operations. Would such an exchange be a positive relationship, with both the community and the industry gaining power and thus benefiting from the exchange? Or would the industry be taking advantage of the desperate neediness of the community and be reaping all the benefits from the exchange?

These questions arose in Noxubee County, Mississippi. Noxubee County is poor, and jobs are scarce. Seventy percent of the county's population is African-American. The local chapter of the National Association for the Advancement of Colored People (NAACP) supported the creation of a toxic waste facility in the county; the NAACP saw the facility as a means of creating jobs and working for the betterment of Noxubee's economic future. African Americans for Environmental Justice organized opposition to the facility, viewing it as dangerous to the public health of Noxubee residents. African Americans for Environmental Justice was joined by another environmentalist group, Protect the Environment of Noxubee, in fighting the facility. The NAACP responded with severe criticisms and pointed out that opposition to a job-creating industry in a primarily African-American county raised the possibility of racism given that, for the most part, the beneficiaries of the jobs would be African-American. Ironically, a number of the environmentalists saw racism behind the industry's proposed move to Noxubee, insofar as most of those who would be placed at risk from toxins would also be African-American.[33]

The issues in this dispute are very complex, and exchange is at the core of the complexity. Noxubee has the option of pursuing power by means of exchange: recruiting an industry to a region where few industries have chosen to locate. The industry also has the option of pursuing power through exchange: giving the county the incentive to support its establishment, with full knowledge that many other counties would deem it undesirable. Exchange can be Noxubee's route to jobs and economic growth, if the NAACP is correct. Exchange can turn out to be Noxubee's path to environmental and health disaster, if the industry critics are correct.

Exchange is similar to manipulation in that it often baffles the people studying it to a degree that the other types of power do not. Although manipulation can be difficult to analyze because it operates by veiling its own use, exchange can be puzzling to assess because of the apparent reciprocity of gains it offers. In exchange, even the agent over whom power is exercised is gaining something. Indeed, it is the incentive to attain a desired object on this agent's part that makes exchange work. Because of this reciprocity, some writers have seen exchange as conducive to freedom in ways that other forms of power are not. Yet at the same time, insofar as individuals, groups, or communities may be very needy of what is held out as an incentive, other analysts have contended that exchange is fully as coercive as other forms of power.[34] Think of Noxubee. Is exchange a more mellow and less heavy-handed form of power than force, manipulation, or persuasion because it offers benefits to those on the receiving end of power?

## Debates in the Study of Power

**Are Some Forms of Power Unethical?** Is violence an acceptable means of force? Does the violence of 9/11 differ from less lethal uses of violence, or is all violence to be viewed similarly? Is violence ethical if undertaken by a state's military but not by a nonstate organization? Shifting one's focus from violent force, one might also consider the following: Is manipulation unethical insofar as the power involved is disguised? Is exchange more ethical than other forms of power because it offers desired items to those having power exercised over them? These questions have divided students of politics for centuries and have, to some extent, polarized states, nations, and individuals in the aftermath of 9/11.

**If Power Is So Complicated, How Can We Identify It Clearly Enough to Study It Scientifically?** As previously noted, empirical manifestations of power are often blended. An interest group can use a combination of force and persuasion over its members; a public official can blend manipulation and persuasion in his or her campaign. This complicates the study of power because it makes it very difficult to operationalize exactly which type of power is in use at any given time during which power types are blended. In addition, power is difficult to study because amounts of power are difficult to measure with the precision of science. If one country changes the will of a second country using exchange and persuasion, how much power was represented by exchange and how much by persuasion? What if country A has a large military (high reserves of force) but a weak economy (low reserves of exchange), whereas country B has the opposite? Which country is more powerful? Such measurements are often very difficult to determine.

**Is Power Escapable?** Imagine all the ways in which power can be exercised over you. Force, persuasion, manipulation, and exchange are ever-present options for individuals, groups, and the government to use over you. Have you ever been free of power? Such questions have prompted some social scientists and philosophers to assert that power may be so pervasive that it is virtually inescapable. Other scholars have argued that power *is* escapable, in that we can select how we respond to different power relations. We can choose resistance or compliance. This possibility of choice makes us free, it is argued; if not free of encountering power, at least, free in taking responsibility for how we relate to power.[35] Indeed, you could argue that the pervasiveness of power contributes to freedom in that each power type can be used for liberation as well as coercion. Force, persuasion, manipulation, and exchange can be used by the strong to overcome the weak, but each one can also be used by the weak to fend off the strong.

## STATES

Two days after the 9/11 attacks on the United States, President Bush vowed to "end" states that support terrorist acts.[36] Exactly what was President Bush making reference to? While political scientists note that states vary in size, structure, and resources, political scientists have traditionally understood all states to have certain defining characteristics. A **state** is an organization that has a number of political functions and tasks, including providing security, extracting revenues,

---

**BOX 3.8** **States: Definition and Characteristics**

- States are organizations claiming ultimate rule-setting and rule-enforcing authority within their borders.
- States may be organized as unitary, federal, or confederal systems.

- Sovereignty is the actual ability of states to act as ultimate rule-making and rule-enforcing organizations.
- Legitimacy is the belief by citizens that the state operating over them is proper.

and forming rules for resolving disputes and allocating resources within the boundaries of the territory in which it exercises jurisdiction.

That is, states consist of government offices, which have the tasks of providing the ultimate, or primary, security, extraction processes, and rule making within a territory. In providing security, states may create large military establishments or small ones, seek membership in international treaty organizations, or pursue isolationism. In funding their operations through extraction, states may create tax structures to fund expansive or limited social welfare programs. In setting the ultimate rules of conflict resolution, states may create court systems with judicial review or may reject judicial review; states may allow for or ban gun ownership by private citizens, just as states may legalize or prohibit the organization of private security forces (such as militias). In setting the rules for resource allocation, states may create distribution systems that are capitalist, socialist, or a combination of the two. In enforcing its rules over the territory within its borders, a state may rely primarily on force (physical aggression against its own population), persuasion (the issuance of decrees or laws), manipulation (propaganda), or exchange (fostering a growing economy with a high standard of living in order to "buy" acquiescence from its citizens).

States possess characteristics both similar and dissimilar to other types of organizations. For example, families and voluntary associations may also make rules, collect extractions and contributions (such as chores or dues), and offer secure environments for their members. What makes a state unique relative to other organizations are the ultimate and primary claims a state makes relative to its rules, its processes of extraction, and its procedures for security. Although a voluntary association may impose rules of membership on its members, the rules must conform to the rules (laws and policies) of the state; if not, the state can penalize the association with violent force.[37]

States may be organized in a variety of ways. **Unitary states** concentrate power at the central, or national, level. The United Kingdom, France, China, and Japan are examples of unitary states. **Federal states** create different divisions and levels of government and divide power among those divisions and levels. The United States is a federal state, with power accorded to offices at three levels: national or federal offices, state offices, and local offices. Germany, India, Canada, Brazil, and Mexico also have federal systems.

In addition to federal and unitary arrangements, states also have the option of a **confederal** type of organization, with power decentralized and held primarily or exclusively by local offices. This type of state existed briefly in the United States prior to the ratification of the U.S. Constitution. In 1781, the Articles of Confederation established a confederation in which states had supreme power and a central governing power was virtually nonexistent, in that there was no central executive, no central judiciary, and only a weak central legislature. Confederalism was replaced by federalism when the U.S. Constitution was ratified in 1788. Today, confederalism is an organizational mode found in some international organizations in which individual states are members, but it has not proven a very popular and durable means of organizing states themselves.[38]

However states organize themselves, they profoundly influence the lives of citizens. Whether travel is open or restricted, certain drugs are legal or illegal, military service is required or optional, public prayer in schools is sanctioned or disallowed, and race and ethnicity are relevant or irrelevant in university admissions, these and similarly important questions are decided by the rules administered through unitary, federal, or confederal states in the form of laws, policies, regulations, and orders. Moreover, whether you favor or oppose the present level of state power, that power has most likely affected practically every aspect of your life. If you live in the United States, for example, that power has been used to subsidize your education if you have ever attended a public school or used the resources in a public library. It has been used to subsidize your ability to travel inside the country if you have ever used public highways with public traffic lights and kept passable by public maintenance crews and public police officers. It has been used to subsidize your health and well-being if you have ever used the services of a doctor trained at a public medical school or purchased domestically produced goods and services made in conformity with consumer safety laws, or if you have ever traveled on domestic airlines subject to aviation safety guidelines. It has been used to subsidize your family's budget if you have a parent who was educated with the help of the G.I. Bill, or if your family has been compensated through farm subsidy programs or social welfare policies. Extraction, rule making, and security are not, on reflection, merely abstractions, but are, rather, ways in which states touch our lives personally and continuously.

## States: State Formation, Development, and Change

The United States and more than 180 other states comprise the international community. Many of the world's existing states are new. In fact, fewer than 30 states now in existence were independent states possessing their own governing systems over a unified territory in 1800. Argentina, Brazil, Chile, Colombia, and many other Latin American countries established self-governing states in the nineteenth century after gaining independence from Spain and Portugal. After World War II, many new states (whose populations and territories were previously under the jurisdiction of separate colonial states) were created in Africa and Asia. For example, Madagascar, a long-time colony of France, became an independent state in 1960, the same year in which Nigeria gained independence from Britain. The disintegration of the Soviet Union, Czechoslovakia, and Yugoslavia resulted in the formation of more than 20 new states within the regions previously occupied by only three.[39]

As you can see from these examples, states come and go. In addition, even the oldest of existing states evolve and undergo remarkable changes. Turkey, for example, was previously known as the Ottoman Empire and governed a vast region, including the territories now occupied by Syria, Lebanon, Iraq, Jordan, Israel, and Saudi Arabia. After defeat in World War I, its territory shrank and its state organization was transformed from a sultanate to a republic. Japan's state has evolved through transformations from administration by shoguns (military elites), rule by a divine emperor, and, since 1947, government through constitutional democracy. Germany, established as an independent and unified state in 1871, has been an empire, a democracy, a Nazi totalitarian regime, a territory divided into rival states of democracy and communism, and a unified democratic state again all in slightly more than 100 years.

The history of U.S. development as a state has been, similarly, a narrative of dramatic changes in organization and jurisdiction. Since its establishment as an independent state in the late eighteenth century, the U.S. state has been confronted by a civil war in which much of the population rejected the power of the U.S. state altogether, in which approximately one-third of all free adult males were mobilized to fight, and in which more than 600,000 people died. The U.S. state has experienced violent opposition manifest in the assassinations of four heads of state since 1865 and the attempted assassinations of others, including Presidents Truman, Ford, Reagan, and Clinton. In addition, the United States has radically enlarged its original territory of 13 states to include 50 states plus the District of Columbia. It has also evolved from a relatively limited state apparatus with meager funds into a state that by the time of the administration of Franklin D. Roosevelt in the 1930s had grown so much that it was spending $1 million per hour.[40] All this has happened in just over 200 years of state development. As noted in the Introduction, change seems to be the essence of politics.

## Debates in the Study of States

**Are States the Most Important Agents of Political Decision Making?** Although states claim ultimate power to make rules and provide security in a territory, they have major nonstate rivals with which to contend. The attack of 9/11 demonstrated the ability of a terrorist network to violate state security, and the international drug trade reveals the capacity of criminal groups to establish illicit markets that crisscross state boundaries. Beyond these examples, state power may be limited by the actions of nonstate organizations, such as **multinational corporations (MNCs), nongovernmental organizations (NGOs),** and **intergovernmental organizations (IGOs)**. Although MNCs, NGOs, and IGOs have not replaced states or taken away the power of states to govern their territories, these entities have emerged as organizations affecting the context in which states pursue power. In some cases, these organizations have limited the ability of states to be the sole decision makers on matters pertaining to their own territories.

**Multinational corporations** are international businesses with operations, transactions, and assets in the territories of different states. Some MNCs are richer than some countries, as noted in the Introduction. This gives MNCs the potential to amass enormous resources in support of their objectives. Indeed, the key markets of some MNCs constitute a larger geographic territory than the territories of history's greatest empires.[41] MNCs also have the ability to transport money, jobs, personnel, research expertise, and corporate products from one country to another. This mobility gives MNCs the power to leave the territory of a state whose taxation or labor policies, for example, it finds unattractive and relocate its operations to another state. Wal-Mart and Sears can move (and have moved) shirt-making jobs to Bangladesh, where employees work 60-hour weeks for less than $30 per month.[42] Sony has transferred jobs from Japanese workers to Thai and Malaysian employees, who work for even less.[43] In these and other ways, states can lose jobs, technology, know-how, and taxable assets; they can see the resources within their territories diminished by the decisions of MNCs.

This fact of transportability has led some observers to suggest that states are hindered in their ability to govern their own economies. States may find it difficult to make policies if they anticipate objections from MNCs. For example, if a policy would be supportive of the public interest, but not supportive of the MNC, what is a state to do?[44]

Moreover, a multinational corporation with a home base in one country may sometimes negotiate directly with foreign states in a manner inconsistent with the foreign policy aims of its home country. The MNC may go on to develop a "foreign policy" of its own against that of its home state. This happened with oil companies during the United States–Libya conflict in the 1980s, a conflict that escalated to such an extent that the United States bombed Libya. During this conflict, while U.S. intelligence forces were pinpointing Libya as a source of support for international terrorism, U.S.-based multinational oil companies lobbied the U.S. government in support of Libya and against U.S. policies calling for the removal of U.S. oil personnel from Libya.[45] The MNCs had interests in opposition to those of the U.S. state and worked to alter U.S. foreign relations with Libya because the MNCs had business interests in Libya. Instances such as these raise the intriguing question, Who is in control, the state or the MNC?

**Nongovernmental organizations** are nonstate, voluntary groups that pursue political objectives. Like MNCs, they may exercise power you would usually assume to be associated with states. Specifically, NGOs have emerged as important agents in the area of international conflict resolution. Increasingly, a conflict within or between states may be negotiated and resolved not only through the efforts of states but also through the influence of NGOs. NGOs have existed since the nineteenth century, but their numbers and their range of influence increased in the twentieth century. Examples of NGOs include the Red Cross, the International Chamber of Commerce, the American Friends Service Committee, the Lutheran World Federation, Doctors without Borders, Space Media Network, and the International Negotiation Network. NGOs have been participants in conflict resolution in the Middle East in 1955 and 1967, in Germany in the 1960s, in the India–Pakistan war in 1965, in Guatemala in 1990, and in the former Yugoslavia in the 1990s. In addition, NGOs have helped publicize environmental destruction in the former USSR (Soviet Union) at a time when the Soviet state was trying to hide such damage, and NGOs have helped publicize human rights abuses in El Salvador during periods in which the Salvadoran state was denying the existence of such abuses. These examples illustrate how the activities of NGOs can make it difficult for states to articulate rules regulating access to information, and how NGOs have entered the arena of conflict resolution so that the job of providing security over a territory is not a power states can necessarily monopolize.[46]

NGOs can also shape political processes within the territories of states by exerting direct pressures on MNCs. That is, rather than prevailing on states to regulate MNCs, NGOs may try to influence MNCs through direct contact. Three examples illustrate this type of NGO–MNC interaction. First, a number of environmental NGOs (for example, Environmental Defense Fund, Earth Action Network, and Kids against Pollution) pressured McDonald's to make its food packaging more environmentally friendly. Tactics included a "send back" movement, in which consumers mailed used McDonald's wrappers and boxes to corporate headquarters. Second, the Public Interest Research Group and other NGOs pressured Uniroyal Chemical Company to stop making Alar, a chemical used by apple growers. Third, Greenpeace, Friends of the Earth, and other NGOs organized campaigns against StarKist and Chicken of the Sea tuna companies for harvesting tuna with drift nets. These nets capture dolphins as well as tuna. What stands out about these three cases is the success of NGOs in shaping corporate policy and practice. In all three instances, NGOs successfully pressured MNCs to change policies affecting the citizens of states. In other words, citizens could thank NGOs for doing what they might traditionally have regarded as the job of the presumably more influential state.[47]

**Intergovernmental organizations** are political organizations in which membership is held exclusively by states. The United Nations (UN), the Organization of American States (OAS), the North Atlantic Treaty Organization (NATO), and the UN Conferences on Trade and Development (UNCTAD) are examples of IGOs. IGOs may have a significant impact on political relations between states. Like NGOs, IGOs may become vital participants in conflict resolution, as was the case when UN forces imposed sanctions over and committed troops during the Gulf War of 1991. IGOs may also work in conjunction with states to resolve particular problems. For instance, since sponsoring the first international conference on AIDS in 1983, the UN's World Health Organization (WHO) has assisted states in tracking HIV/AIDS infections and in developing research and public health programs.[48] Through these efforts, WHO has helped publicize the related problem of a resurgence in tuberculosis (TB) cases worldwide. In fact, WHO has pointed out that the number of TB deaths in 1995 exceeded the number of such deaths in any previous year; HIV-positive individuals are particularly susceptible to TB. WHO has assisted the states of China, Peru, and the United Republic of Tanzania in implementing effective TB treatment programs.[49] IGOs often work in cooperation with NGOs as well as states, which further indicates the extent to which states are joined by nonstate entities in making critical decisions over their own territories, as is explored further later in this text.

**Does Political Science Consider the Exercise of Power by States to Be Different from the Exercise of Power by Individuals or Groups?** You may view the exercise of power over your life differently, depending on whether that power is emanating from a state or from another person. Many political scientists would agree with you. Two terms—*sovereignty* and *legitimacy*—are often used to analyze state power. States that possess both sovereignty and legitimacy are generally viewed by political scientists as having a different type of power from that held by mere individuals and groups because such states are viewed as appropriate wielders of ultimate power.

**Sovereignty** has traditionally been understood as the attribute states have when they, in actuality, carry out the tasks of providing security, extraction, and rule making. That is, technically a state can exist (the offices can exist), but the state may or may not be effective in carrying out its tasks; in this case, we would say a state is present, but it lacks sovereignty (the ability to actually carry out the tasks of providing security and so on).[50] Insofar as states claim for themselves the ultimate power over a territory (and thus claim that individuals and groups can exercise power in that territory only as long as they do not contradict state power), states claim sovereignty for themselves and deny it to individuals and groups

---

**BOX 3.9  The Surprises of Power: How a Library's Decision Foiled an MNC**

Brown & Williamson (B&W) is a very powerful corporation. It is the third largest tobacco manufacturer in the United States. B&W earned approximately $400 million in profits in its domestic and international markets in 1993. Among its brands of cigarettes are the big sellers Kool, Lucky Strike, and Pall Mall. It is difficult to imagine that the decisions of a library could hurt a giant like this in any way. However, the University of California at San Francisco library played the role of David to B&W's Goliath. Dr. Stanton Glantz of the university's medical school received a shipment of copies of B&W documents that apparently had been photocopied and smuggled out of the company's files by an office worker. The documents made B&W look awful, according to Glantz, who found statements suggesting that tobacco manufacturers lied to the public for years about what they (the manufacturers) knew regarding smoking and health.

For a time, Dr. Glantz kept the documents in his office, but then decided to deposit them in the university's library. Placed on top of one another, the documents made a stack approximately 4 feet high. The documents were so numerous that they were difficult to manage, and library staff knew there would be great demand by re-

searchers, journalists, students, and political scientists wanting to sort through these very revealing files. The library's deputy director, Karen Butter, decided to scan the documents and place them on CD-ROM and on the Internet. This would ease pressures on library staff and allow library patrons to efficiently sort through the materials. This decision cast Butter in the role of David. Although her decision was motivated by her aim of facilitating the smooth functioning of the library, the effect of her action was to transfer these documents to the public domain (the Internet), and, as it turned out, to prevent B&W from controlling access to the information contained therein. On finding out about all this, B&W fought hard to have the documents removed from public postings, but it failed. Besides, once posted, there were no longer any secrets. During the first 5 weeks after the files were posted to the Internet, more than 4,000 users per day were logging requests for information from the files. This case suggests that technological development may not only weaken the sovereignty of the state but also limit the powers of corporations. If you want to see the files, go to http://www.library.ucsf.edu/tobacco/ bw.html.

SOURCE: Jon Wiener, "The Cigarette Papers," *The Nation* (1 January 1996): 11-18.

within their territories. Later in this text, we will see that globalization calls into question this traditional understanding of sovereignty, insofar as global exchanges of ideas, products, services, and people raise the possibility of rendering territoriality porous and penetrable and thus uncontrollable. **Legitimacy** is the attribute states possess when their citizens view their sovereignty as appropriate, proper, or acceptable. Consider the civil war in the United States: Southern leaders who joined the Confederacy were denying the legitimacy (appropriateness) of the sovereignty (actual governing ability) of the U.S. government. Such leaders asserted that the Confederate government was the legitimate sovereign over Southern territories.

Just as disputes over sovereignty and legitimacy plunged the United States into a civil war within the first 100 years of its existence, so have such disputes threatened stability in a number of newly independent African states. Indeed, in sub-Saharan Africa many states are former colonies that have achieved independence only since World War II. In these states, legitimacy and sovereignty have been very problematic, as evidenced by civil conflicts and/or wars in Sudan, Rwanda, Zaire, Ethiopia, Zanzibar, Burundi, Chad, Uganda, Nigeria, and Angola between 1956 and 1982.[51] Military coups and ethnic violence in these societies have attested to the limited legitimacy accorded to the state and, not surprisingly, to the lack of sovereignty on the part of the state, in such instances, for commanding loyalty and obedience to law within its territory.[52]

**Does Culture Shape the Decisions of States?** A number of political scientists regard culture—defined as values, ideas, beliefs, and/or attitudes held in common by a population—as a potentially crucial agent shaping state policies.[53] The potential impact of culture can be analyzed from a variety of perspectives, including those that examine the culture of (1) citizens in general and (2) decision makers within government. With respect to the first perspective, Robert Putnam has suggested that the presence or absence of widespread cultural support for popular participation and deliberation among the citizens of a country can affect that country's prospects for realizing both democracy and effective governmental institutions.[54]

Social scientist Ronald Inglehart has also suggested that the cultural dispositions of citizens can mold the types of policies citizens expect from their government and can thereby shape the decisions of states. Inglehart's work has put forward the thesis that the post-World War II period has been a time of cultural transformation within many industrialized countries. As these countries experienced increasing levels of economic prosperity, they likewise began to experience a movement away from materialist culture and toward postmaterialist culture. Inglehart describes this shift in the following terms: Younger citizens in advanced, economically prosperous countries began to displace older citizens whose formative years were spent under conditions of relative economic austerity. Compared to their elders, younger citizens have been inclined to take economic well-being for granted and have thus exhibited signs of postmaterialist cultural values. Broadly speaking, postmaterialist culture often tends to rank highly values such as emotional and psychological fulfillment, diverse opportunities for self-expression, and personal exploration with nontraditional life choices; in contrast, materialist culture places great emphasis on the achievement of economic security. Given their different cultural orientations, postmaterialists and materialists are likely to disagree on what they want from government. If choices are framed, for example, between (1) wilderness protection and (2) road construction to promote job creation, or between choosing a candidate on the basis of (1) social equality issues or (2) economic policy, postmaterialists and materialists are likely to make different choices. In these instances, postmaterialists can be expected to support policies ranging from environmental protection to women's rights to a degree unprecedented among their materialist counterparts.[55]

If Putnam, Inglehart, and other social scientists working from this perspective are correct, mass-based, citizen-level culture provides an important context for understanding state policy. However, the culture of official governmental decision makers may also be important in shaping governmental decisions. For example, studies of government policymaking during World War II have suggested that crucial military decisions were often shaped by the values, attitudes, and ideas of key security personnel. Consider the fact that Nazi Germany possessed chemical weaponry from the beginning of the fighting but opted against this form of warfare. What accounts for this seemingly restrained policy? Nazi military officials held to an organizational military culture that valued blitzkrieg offensive maneuvers. During World War II, Britain "underused" its submarine capacity, a decision that has been linked to the Royal Navy's culture, which valued battleships over submarines as primary instruments of naval warfare.[56] More recently, according to some studies of elite-level culture in the 1990s, Germany's decisions to build European security alliances and to participate in NATO operations in Bosnia have been shaped by a pronounced multilateralism component in Germany's post–World War II culture.[57]

Despite the evidence offered in the preceding studies, cultural explanations leave some political scientists unconvinced. Many critics question whether culture is not as much influenced *by* governmental policy and/or social conditions as it is an influence *on* them. In addition, critics point out that cultures may be more complex and less homogeneous than some cultural explanations imply. What if cultures have contradictory values? If cultures include internally inconsistent and opposed values, ideas, and attitudes, can't culture be employed as a variable to explain the opposite of the outcome it is said to explain as well as the outcome itself? Moreover, if culture itself is shaped by economic class, race, ethnicity, social standing, or other variables, should not these more basic influences be the focus of scrutiny?[58]

**Are States Likely to Vanish and Be Replaced by Some Other Form of Political Organization?** So far, our discussion has shown that even powerful states have rivals to their sovereignty in the form of MNCs, IGOs, and NGOs, just as newly independent states may see their sovereignty challenged by groups viewing the state as lacking legitimacy. Potentially, therefore, states are subject to forces threatening to weaken them. What if such forces are multiplying in number and intensity? This question is posed by a number of political scientists in the subfield of international relations. James Rosenau has argued that five forces have converged to threaten the state's existence as an organizational entity: (1) technological development that enhances communications and interactions across state territories; (2) global problems (AIDS, global warming, and terrorism) that make states vulnerable because states cannot keep the problems from penetrating their borders; (3) citizens' tendencies to look to entities other than states for information, leadership, and ethical guidance; (4) strengthening of the resources and appeals of groups within a state's borders, given the inability of states to keep groups from obtaining information resources; and (5) increasing know-how on the part of citizens to analyze and resist state authority.

If Rosenau's observations are correct, we are faced with an astounding possibility—that states may no longer be capable of being sovereign entities regarding much of anything within their territories. In a world in which between 5 and 10 billion telephone calls are made daily, and in which 600 million television sets and more than 1.5 billion radios are turned on, how could borders not become completely permeable and thus increasingly ungovernable?[59] Is any entity sufficiently sovereign over you so that were you to take a break from reading this book and go to a computer and access the Internet, it could stop you from communicating and sharing information with someone in virtually any place on the globe? You can communicate via e-mail, a fax, or a phone call; you can observe practically any part of the world through computers and television. You have so much technological know-how at your command that you possess arguably a greater basis for autonomous opinion formation and decision making than members of any previous generation. If you are so very sovereign over your life, how can any state be sovereign over you? If states are in decline, should we mourn or applaud the apparent passing of the state?[60] Yet if individuals can so easily access information-rich technologies, so can states, and will this not enhance state authority in the long run? Will states not, for example, be able to more fully regulate individual and group transactions with the new technologies discussed by Rosenau? These are among the intriguing questions in political science's study of states.

## NATIONS

Nations are sometimes confused with states. However, the two entities are very different.[61] A **nation** is a group of people with a sense of unity based on the importance the group attributes to a shared trait, attribute, or custom. A common language, religion, ethnicity, race, religion, and/or culture are often the foundations of national identity. Indeed, the very origins of the word *nation* attest to such foundations because *nation* is based on the older Latin word *natus* (birth), and nations generally consist of people whose sense of unity is based on something shared by virtue of the group into which they are born.[62] It is important to note, however, that not every group into which one is born becomes the basis of a nation; if, for example, you are born into the group of right-handed people, most probably you do not feel a sense of national oneness based on this shared attribute. However, if you are by birth a member of the group of Cherokees, Jews,

---

**BOX 3.10  Nations: Definition and Characteristics**

- A nation is a group with a sense of unity, and the unity is generally related to the fact that members of the group share a common language, culture, history, ethnicity, and/or religion.

- Nations may or may not have their own states.
- More than one nation may exist within a state's boundaries, in which case the state is known as a *multinational state*.

---

Lithuanians, Armenians, Serbs, or Croats, you may indeed feel a sense of national unity based on the attributes shared with others born into your "*natus*-group."[63] A nation arises when significance is attached to that which the group shares and around which a feeling of unity develops.

### States and Nations: Relations and Interactions

Nations may or may not possess their own states. National identity, or nationalism, may precede the emergence of a nation's state. Zionism (Jewish nationalism) and a community of people identifying with a Jewish nation, for example, existed before the creation of the state of Israel in 1948. Zionist arguments were advanced through the works of nationalist leaders such as Theodor Herzl (1860–1904), Chaim Wiezmann (1874–1952), and Israel Zangwill (1864–1926). The efforts of these and other pre-1948 Zionist leaders attest to the importance of maintaining the distinction between nations and states. Nations may be growing and defining themselves as such long before they gain their own states.[64]

Moreover, national identity may exist even though a nation lives within the territory of a separate state rather than within the borders of a state conforming to the nation. This describes the situation of many French residents in the Canadian province of Quebec, according to their nationalist leaders. French-speaking Canadians, like their English counterparts, are under the authority of the state of Canada. However, many French-Canadians feel a sense of national identity based on a shared language and culture. Nationalist pressures prompted the passage of the Charter of the French Language (1977), which made French the official language of Quebec. Nationalist sentiment culminated in demands for the separation of Quebec from the state of Canada and the creation of a sovereign Quebec republic. In 1980, nationalists tried but failed to win separation from Canada by means of a referendum. In 1994, Jacques Parizeau was elected premier of Quebec, in part because of his promise to support another referendum calling for Quebec's separation and independence. The referendum, held in October 1995, failed to pass by the slimmest of margins (50.56 percent of voters opposed the separation and 49.44 percent supported separation). For now, the French-Canadian nation exists without its own sovereign state (an independent Quebec) and within the territory of a separate sovereign state (Canada) whose legitimacy it rejects.[65]

Although nationalist pressures failed to alter the borders of the Canadian state, such pressures contributed to the recent redrawing of Yugoslavia's borders.

Yugoslavia was formed in 1918; its territory came primarily out of regions of the former Ottoman Empire and Austria-Hungary. From the beginning, Yugoslavia was potentially unstable because of the presence of rival nationalist groups. Serbs accounted for 36 percent of the population, whereas Croats represented 20 percent. Smaller groups included Muslims, Slovenes, Macedonians, Albanians, and Montenegrins. During the tenure of leader Josip Broz (Tito), Yugoslavia was organized as a federation and nationalist tensions were kept to a manageable level. Following Tito's death in 1980, nationalist pressures eventually led to the collapse of the state in regions within its own territory. Specifically, during 1990 a Serb nationalist, Slobodan Milosevic, won power in the province of Serbia and a Croatian nationalist, Franjo Tudjman, came to power in Croatia; meanwhile, Albanian nationalists were demanding greater control in the province of Kosovo. Divisions soon worsened. Serb nationalists were calling for the creation of a "Greater Serbia" by 1991; Croatia and Slovenia broke away from Yugoslavia and declared themselves nations in possession of their own sovereign states in 1991; Bosnia Muslims declared themselves independent in 1992; in turn, Serbs in Croatia and Bosnia declared themselves independent of the newly independent states that were not dominated by Serbs. "Ethnic cleansing" and civil war fueled by these nationalist maneuverings culminated in perhaps 200,000 deaths and the creation of a refugee population in excess of 1 million. The example of Yugoslavia shows the potential of nationalist movements to force a redrawing of state borders.[66]

Yet some nations exist without ever demanding the formation of their own states. For such nations, nationalism becomes a means of affirming a group's identity and a basis for demanding respect for a group's interest. The deaf nation represents an example of this type of nationalism. How can the deaf be a nation? Advocates of deaf nationalism and deaf culture say it is obvious: The group is united by a common language (sign language) through which common customs and a shared culture are transmitted. Behavioral indicators of the existence of such customs abound. First, members of this nation see deafness as a trait, not a disability. The trait is shared among members of the nation (just as being ethnically Irish is shared by the Irish nation). Second, members of the deaf nation tend to resist "cures" for their deafness; indeed, potential cures for deafness (such as hearing implants) are typically viewed as genocidal weapons (just as a "cure" for being Armenian so that Armenians ceased to exist as Armenians would likely be viewed by Armenians as genocidal). What is the difference between ethnic cleansing in Yugoslavia intended to remove all traces of Bosnian Muslims and the ethnic cleansing represented by implants that would remove from the world all vestiges of deafness, they ask? Third, the fact that the deaf have their own culture is evidenced by their propensity for marrying within their own group (just as other nations whose members display strong feelings of nationalism tend to exhibit a preference for intragroup marriages). For the deaf who view themselves as members of a nation, nationalism has become a means of expressing group pride and a means of promoting group acceptance, leaders explain, even though there is no movement for the creation of a separate sovereign state.[67]

In other instances of state–nation relations, the presence of a state can foster the development of nationalist sentiments or foster the weakening of nations. In terms of the former, you can look to the example of the African state of Burundi, which gained independence from Belgium in 1962. Belgians pursued a "divide and conquer" policy in Burundi whereby they favored the indigenous Tutsi over the indigenous Hutus. Belgians promoted racial myths of Tutsi superiority and Hutu inferiority. Historically, however, the Tutsis and Hutus had not existed as separate nations; in fact, they intermarried and shared common religions, language, and customs. Belgium's colonial policy of creating divisions between the two groups (as a means of serving its own interests in maintaining colonial dominance over both) had an enormous impact. Tutsi and Hutus became enemies and began thinking of themselves as two separate peoples. Since independence, assassinations, coups, and violence against civilians have threatened to overwhelm Burundi. In 1961, the prime minister designate was assassinated by individuals linked to Tutsi nationalists; in 1965, a Hutu prime minister was assassinated by Tutsis; coup attempts by Hutus and Tutsis followed; a Tutsi military government was established in 1966; and a Hutu rebellion was launched in 1972 and massive killings of Hutus followed. Hutu-Tutsi violence has continued in both Burundi and neighboring Rwanda. It is ironic and tragic that these groups, which previously comprised a common people, split into warring, separatist groups in response to state (Belgian) policies.[68]

In contrast, the colonial policies of Britain in Nigeria weakened the indigenous Ibo people, according to Nigerian writer Chinua Achebe. Far from increasing the strength of identification with the Ibo, British colonists undermined it. Colonists presented young Ibo members with choices in stark contrast to the traditions of their people. In his novel *Things Fall Apart,* Achebe depicts Ibo characters who want to be like the Europeans, who abandon the indigenous religions and customs of their nation, and who ultimately render the authority figures of that nation powerless. The significance of Achebe's work for our discussion is in its ability to portray the complexity of state–nation relations. State policies can encourage indigenous nationalist identities in one context while weakening them in another.[69]

These examples illustrate the diversity of patterns found in present state–nation relations. Perhaps no pattern is more common than that of multinational states. For most states, two or more nations exist within the territory over which the state presides. Mononational states, in which only one nation exists within the territory of a state, are extremely rare. Indeed, strictly defined, probably no state is mononational. However, Japan, Denmark, and Norway have been identified by some political scientists as approximating varying degrees of mononationalism.[70] In contrast to Japan, Denmark, and Norway, **multinational states** such as India may have within their territories numerous ethnic, language, and religious groups with varying degrees of nationalist sentiment. For example, in India, there are more than 40 language groups and there are thousands of castes (social groups). Approximately 80 percent of the population is Hindu, 11 percent is Muslim, and 2 percent is Sikh. Sikh nationalists have called for the creation of a sovereign Sikh state, Khalistan. At times, nationalism has led to violence in Indian politics. Sikh bodyguards assassinated Prime Minister Indira Gandhi in 1984, and Tamil nationalists were linked to the assassination of Rajiv Gandhi in 1991. (Tamil nationalists were angered by India's support of Sri Lanka's efforts opposing the formation of a separate Tamil state.)[71]

India represents the challenges facing all multinational states. Whether expressed violently or peacefully, nationalist feelings of unity among members of groups attaching significance to a shared language, religion, ethnicity, and/or cultural tradition may pose difficulties for state sovereignty and legitimacy. Feelings of nationalism may change, rising or falling in response to events within or outside a nation. Whatever the case, the choices made by nations will probably continue to affect the choices available to states.

## Debates in the Study of Nations

**How Do We Know Who Is a Nation and Who Is Not?** As the preceding discussion illustrates, it can be very difficult to determine the existence of nations. Is every group that calls itself a nation to be considered one? Given the definition of a nation (a feeling of oneness based on a shared language and so forth), it is possible for groups expressing a sense of oneness and sharing something such as a language to make an argument for recognition as a nation. Indeed, in addition to advocates of the deaf nation, there are writers who assert that there is a basis for viewing gays, African-Americans, and Southerners as separate nations. How could one argue that these groups are nations?

- *Gay nationalism (often called queer nationalism).* Advocates have argued that gays comprise a natus-group (gays are born gay) sharing a trait (gayness) to which great significance is attached (being gay represents being part of a shared culture transmitted through gay traditions, gay norms, gay institutions, and so on) and from which a sense of unity (standing together to oppose antigay attitudes and actions) emerges.[72]

- *African-American nationalism.* Advocates have argued that African-Americans comprise a natus-group with cultural and genealogical ties distinctive from those of the larger American culture. African-Americans are a nation, insofar as they possess their own shared language and traditions. Like gay nationalists, African-American nationalists point out that a distinctive culture is transmitted through the nation's own institutions (the African-American church or mosque, for example).[73]

- *The Southern nation.* Those who see Southerners in the United States as comprising what may be regarded as a nation tend to point out that the region has been distinctive in terms of culture (literature, food, language, music, and so on) and has passed on its traditions to those in the natus-group.[74]

Are these arguments convincing? As you study politics, you will find that political scientists are far from achieving anything like consensus on such questions. Some political scientists believe that the designation *nation* should be applied only to groups identifying with or striving for the creation of their own state. Such a view is based on the proposition that defining a nation as existing whenever a group feels a unity/oneness based on shared traits, language, or the like is to define the concept of nation so broadly that it comes to mean just about anything. What group does not, after all, feel a degree of oneness based on something it shares? Is that not a defining characteristic of any group? Girl Scouts and Rotarians, no doubt, feel some degree of oneness with their respective group members. Other political scientists believe that defining nations so narrowly (as equated with loyalty to or desire for a state) is unscientific. Which is better, they ask, having social scientists impose their opinions of the best definition of nations on people or allowing people to define themselves? The first option, they say, would have political scientists creating the parameters of nations, whereas the second would have political scientists empirically recording the parameters created by people themselves, as they live as members of self-identified nations.[75]

**Is Nationalism Ethically Problematic?** Some students of nationalism believe that nationalism leads to exclusionary and intolerant politics. Would it not be better, they ask, if we stopped thinking of ourselves in terms of our own nations and national roots and started thinking of ourselves in more cosmopolitan terms? Other analysts see nationalism as a positive force, as an expression of the desire for self-determination, and as a statement of group pride. Such analysts point out that atrocities and efforts to "cleanse" areas of various groups cannot, accurately, be used to condemn nationalism per se. Indeed, throughout history one finds campaigns to force removal of peoples from sections of a state's territory. England expelled Jews in 1290, as did France in 1306, Hungary in 1349–1360, Austria in 1421, and Portugal in 1497. Spain expelled Jews in 1492 and Muslims in 1502. England drove out most Irish Catholics from the territory of Ulster by the late seventeenth century.[76] In the United States, between 1830 and 1870, the government removed Native Americans from their homelands and, thereby, fostered homesteading by and property transmission to whites.[77] Campaigns such as these have not always been motivated by nationalism. Sometimes bigotry, territorial expansion, state rivalries, or greed motivated powerful groups to remove, attack, or slaughter weaker ones. Therefore, some social scientists point out, nationalism should not become a catchall category used to explain violence. Violence has been inspired by many sources other than nationalism. Nationalism can be used to serve humanitarian purposes or antihumanitarian purposes, they conclude.

## SUMMING UP

- Power, state, and nation are key concepts in the study of politics.
- **Power** is the ability to influence an outcome or alter the will of another agent, such as a person, a group, a state, or a nation.
- Power can be exercised in physical ways (**force**), in a manner in which the agent using power displays clear and openly acknowledged intent (**persuasion**), in a manner in which the agent using power conceals his or her intent

(**manipulation**), or in a manner involving incentives to the entity over which power is exercised (**exchange**). Generally, in the "real world" of politics, people or groups using power combine the different types of power as they pursue their political objectives.

▪ Is it possible to be free of power? Is each type of power ethical to use in pursuit of one's political goals? These normative questions invite intense debate among students of politics.

▪ **States** are offices claiming ultimate (or final) authority within their boundaries. States have numerous tasks: the provision of security to their citizens, the collection of revenues to finance their operations, and the delineation of ultimate rules. A state that actually has the ability to carry out these tasks is said to possess **sovereignty,** and if citizens view their state as proper in its execution of these tasks the state is said to possess **legitimacy.**

▪ States can be highly centralized (**unitary**), highly decentralized (**confederal**), or moderately centralized (**federal**). Whatever their degree of centralization or decentralization, states interact with and sometimes compete with **MNCs, IGOs,** and **NGOs** in their exercise of sovereignty, and states may be constrained by cultural attributes held by the citizenry or by elite decision makers.

▪ **Nations** are people bound together with a sense of oneness based, usually, on their shared language, culture, historical traditions, ethnicity, and/or religion. Because this sense of oneness is based on feelings—which are subjective—it is sometimes a controversial matter to determine who does or does not constitute a nation.

▪ Some nations possess their own states, whereas others do not. In some cases, a nation's demands for its own state can create extreme pressures on existing states, as when nations within the former Yugoslavia demanded their own separate states and prompted the reconfiguration of the Yugoslav state borders. When more than one nation resides within the boundaries of a state, such a state is termed a **multinational state.**

## STUDY QUESTIONS

1. How do the events of 9/11 influence your view of power and the ethical debates regarding how power may be used for political purposes?

2. What is power? How does the concept of power relate to the concept of volition?

3. Identify and define the different types of power. Often these types of power are blended together; what does this mean?

4. Is force always violent? Explain.

5. What is the difference between persuasion and manipulation?

6. What type of power was being resisted by African-Americans for Environmental Justice in Noxubee County, Mississippi, recently?

7. Have you ever been free of power? Explain your answer.

8. Are there some types of power you would never use because you find them ethically objectionable? If

so, what are they? Why do you find them objectionable?

9. What is a state? How does it differ from a nation? Do all nations possess their own states?

10. Compare and contrast unitary, federal, and confederal states.

11. Do you believe that states are more important than MNCs, IGOs, and NGOs in terms of political decision making? In your answer, be certain to define MNCs, IGOs, and NGOs.

12. Define *sovereignty* and *legitimacy*. Why are these concepts important to consider when analyzing states?

13. What are some examples suggesting that culture can shape states? What are some counterexamples?

14. Are American citizens a nation, or is the United States a multinational state?

# FOLLOWING UP THROUGH INTERNET SOURCES

*Power through Nonviolent Force*

- The United Farm Workers (http://www.ufw.org)

- Martin Luther King, Jr., Directory (http://www.stanford.edu/group/King)

- Martin Luther King, Jr., National Historic Site (http://www.nps.gov/malu)

*Perspectives on State–Nation Relations: Canada and Quebec*

- Government of Canada Primary Internet Site (http://canada.gc.ca/)

- Quebec Referendum on the Web—1995 Archival Information (http://www.synapse.net/~radio/refer.htm)

*Perspectives on State–Nation Relations: Yugoslavia*

- Federal Republic of Yugoslavia Official Web Site (http://www.gov.yu)

- International Criminal Tribunal for the Former Yugoslavia (http://www.un.org/icty/)

# 4

# Political Theory

## Examining the Ethical
## Foundations of Politics

At the conclusion of Chapter 3, we considered the ethics of nationalism. Is nationalism an ethical means of expressing a group's desire for self-determination, or is it an unethical posture that nurtures the tendency to exclude from fair treatment members outside the nation? Normative questions (questions involving value judgments concerning what is right and wrong) such as these are central to politics. Even when political scientists are being thoroughly empirical—recording, observing, and analyzing data—they deal with a subject matter that, by its very nature, raises ethical questions.

For example, in your political science classes, you might read various accounts of the war and postwar reconstruction efforts in Afghanistan and Iraq. You might learn of battles, leaders, national conflicts, demographic statistics, and other politically relevant details. Indeed, the authors of these studies might teach you more than you ever thought possible about the empirically documented history and politics of these two countries. Still, you might come away from these accounts with the disturbing sense that you still did not *understand* what really happened—either before or after President Bush declared the war on terrorism—in either Afghanistan or Iraq. You might suspect that you can never comprehend such complexities until you sort out for yourself the following kinds of questions: Can ethics be reconciled with politics? Is there such a thing as human nature and, if so, is it ethically neutral? Are efforts to combine religion and politics destabilizing to social relations? Is it worse for individuals to kill in the name of politics or religion than for states to do so? Is terrorism like that perpetrated on 9/11 a cowardly act? An understanding of political life that never scrutinizes the ethical dimensions and puzzles of politics is an incomplete understanding.

Political theory is a subfield in political science, focusing on the normative and ethical questions of politics. In this chapter, we will explore some of the perennial normative issues that have puzzled political theorists for centuries. Our objective will be twofold: to understand the historical and textual teachings of the theorists we study and also to take their teachings out of their own historical settings and see whether those teachings can be relevant to us as we struggle with the political, social, and economic problems of the twenty-first century. In other words, political theory involves both the study of texts and the act of critically thinking about what those texts teach us.

## ANALYZING POLITICAL THEORY: PLATO'S ALLEGORY OF THE CAVE

Plato (427–347 B.C.) was one of the leading philosophers in ancient Athens. His family included notable political leaders, and he served Athens, first, by a term in the military during Athen's war against Sparta, and, second, through his intellectual and cultural contributions. Plato formulated his philosophy during a period of intense intellectual activity in ancient Athens. He observed his teacher Socrates (470?–399 B.C.) critique the Sophists, a group of philosophers who taught the art of rhetoric and who claimed among their practitioners the philosopher Protagoras (480?–411 B.C.). The search for wisdom—not the mastery of the art of rhetorical argument—should engage the mind, according to Socrates. Socrates' philosophizing brought him into conflict with the political elites of Athens, who condemned him to death in 399 B.C. on charges of impiety and the corruption of youth.

Both Socrates and Plato lived through the Peloponnesian War between Athens and Sparta, in which Athens was finally defeated in 405 B.C. This war was chronicled by the great Athenian historian and theorist Thucydides (460?–404? B.C.). In his history of the war, Thucydides records the famous funeral oration of the Athenian leader Pericles (495?–429 B.C.), delivered during the first year (434 B.C.) of the war. In this oration, Thucydides praises Athens as a city-state devoted to intellectual and cultural excellence as well as the realization of the common good of the entire citizenry.

Plato's Academy taught students between the years 387? B.C. and A.D. 529. The Academy educated Aristotle (384–322 B.C.) and others in philosophy, law, mathematics, and logic. Plato's writings would influence scholars such as Philo of Alexandria (15 B.C.?–A.D. 50?), who integrated Platonic teachings with Judaism; St. Augustine (A.D. 354–430), whose works on Christian political theory were influential in shaping ideas on secular–religious relations during the medieval period; and Averröes (A.D. 1126–1198), an influential Islamic writer whose works have contributed to legal, religious, and political theory.

Plato uses Socrates as a major character in many of his works. In *The Republic,* Plato presents an allegory that is useful in illustrating the difficulties and rewards of critical, philosophical analysis. This allegory, the **allegory of the cave,** may be read as a parable of political theory. Like all parables and allegories, the richness of its teachings lies not in the literal details of the story but rather in the larger philosophical questions implied by the details. Just as the parable of the boy who cried wolf, for example, is not really meant to teach the mechanics of sheep herding or wolf tracking, but instead is a compelling allegory because it teaches us about issues such as honesty and human needs, so it is with Plato's allegory of the cave. It is not really about caves at all; it is about grappling with the questions we need to understand in order to become enlightened about the world.

In *The Republic,* Plato has the character of Socrates begin the allegory of the cave by telling us the allegory is supposed to illustrate the process of achieving understanding and enlightenment. This is why the allegory is so useful as a parable of political theorizing, because political theory is a history of the search for enlightenment on the normative questions of politics.

What is the human condition as it pertains to enlightenment or ignorance? In the allegory, Socrates contends that to begin answering this question, we should imagine ourselves living in an underground cave. As residents of this cave, we are unaware of the most fundamental aspects of our environment. For example, we do not know we are actually inside a cave because we assume the surroundings we observe constitute the entire universe. We have no idea that above us is a ground level, a sky, a sun, because we automatically believe all that we see is all that is real. Our vision in this cave, Socrates explains, is very limited. The cave is dimly lit, and discerning images and shapes is difficult. However, because we have always lived in this cave, we do not *feel* it is dark and blurry; to us, everything looks normal.

Things are going on in this cave that we do not know about. We are shackled so we can only look forward. Having never experienced looking backward, we do not know this is even possible, and therefore we do not realize we are shackled. Behind us are three important objects: a fire casting light on the walls of the cave, a pathway leading out of the cave, and groups of people moving objects that cast shadows on the walls of the cave. We see only the shadows in front of us and have no clue these are merely shadows being created by moving objects. Having no reason to think otherwise, we consider the shadows real.

Thus, our lives consist of watching shadows. We are mesmerized by our world, not knowing its vacuous nature. We are entertained, informed, and reassured by the mundane and the sublime in our reality, not knowing both are merely artificial constructs. We are so certain that we know reality—after all, we are empirically observing it—that our complacency has become part of our nature. All is right with the world, we feel.

Then something shatters life in the cave: A person stands and looks around. On making these unprecedented movements and looking into these new directions, the person feels intense discomfort. Standing up, turning around, seeing the fire—all these bold moves strain muscles and eyes unaccustomed to such "unnatural" things. The individual experiences confusion, as his or her vision and equilibrium have to adjust to the newness of standing and seeing light. The individual, Socrates continues, immediately considers rejecting everything he or she sees: It all looks unfamiliar, unreal, untrue, unnatural, wrong. It makes the individual feel very uncomfortable. The individual may want desperately to turn away from all these new things, but what if he or she does not? What if the individual moves up the cave's pathway and above ground? Here the individual encounters more shocks and becomes even more frightened and miserable because the light of the sun is completely overwhelming to someone who has always lived in a cave. The individual is blind and lost.

Yet slowly things begin to change. The eyes adjust, and the individual begins to see not only the sun but also the land, the sky, the world. The individual now realizes there is an entire universe beyond the underground cave. The cave is not the world, living in shackles is not living freely, watching shadows play along a wall is not knowledge of what is real—the former prisoner now knows all these things.

The enlightened individual begins to feel an urgent need to share this wonderful knowledge with the others in the cave. Thus, in the allegory, the individual goes back down the pathway, reenters the cave, and starts revealing to the others that there is a life above ground. He or she tells the cave dwellers that they are in shackles, looking backward is possible, standing up and moving around is possible, and those shadows they have been watching all their lives (and which their parents watched before them) are just images created by movements they have never seen.

How do you think the prisoners respond to these claims? In the allegory, the prisoners decide the individual is mad, dangerous, or both. They assume the individual's vision has been ruined. The individual has lost touch with reality if he or she thinks looking backward is "normal." The individual is talking nonsense, the cave dwellers conclude. If the individual persists in trying to liberate the others, Socrates is very clear on what will happen: The individual will be killed by the cave dwellers.[1]

All of us relive the journey of the individual in Plato's allegory, perhaps, when we think critically about politics. Critical thinking is difficult and sometimes unsettling, and it often produces conclusions at odds with the status quo of our "caves." Thinking critically about the purposes of the state may lead us to believe that the accepted wisdom of our society is no more real than a shadow on a wall. As a result, political theory has produced ideas that are often controversial and sometimes elicit strong opposition. Socrates himself was considered dangerous and was condemned to death by Athens. Eighteenth-century conservative theorist Edmund Burke, whom we discuss in Chapter 5, was sometimes vilified by opponents, and liberal theorists such as eighteenth-century writer Mary Wollstonecraft (discussed in Chapter 7) have been ridiculed for challenging contemporaries to throw off their shackles, to live boldly, and create a life beyond the cave. Whenever theorists ask questions about the normative issues of politics, offering paths out of the cave, they enter controversial territory, as we see in the following sections.

## SOME FUNDAMENTAL ETHICAL QUESTIONS
## IN POLITICS

### What Purpose Should the State Serve?

One of the oldest questions of political theory is, What purpose should the state serve? The range of possible answers is enormous. We can examine the teachings of Plato and Thomas Hobbes to find two vastly different approaches to confronting this issue. In *The Republic,* Plato suggests that the highest purpose of the state is the promotion of justice and that the best form of state is one that pursues justice. Justice is presented as *following nature.* Plato explains that following your nature means being true to the person you are. It is doing what is natural, honest, correct for yourself.[2] It is following your natural calling, your natural purpose.

Moreover, when each person is acting justly, the state itself is just. As Plato saw it, if each person followed his or her nature, individuals would divide themselves into three basic groups. In *The Republic,* he elaborates on these three natural groups. Some people would naturally be inclined to pursue manual labor and would become workers; others would naturally be drawn to careers involving physical danger and would become auxiliaries (military leaders); and others would naturally be interested in and good at public service and policymaking and would, therefore, enter the class of guardians (rulers). Plato believed that philosophers would be naturally suited to comprise the group of guardians, insofar as philosophers most fully pursue the life of reason. In this discussion of justice, the most important consideration, for Plato, was that each person do what is natural and therefore enter the group consistent with his or her natural inclinations, talents, and abilities.

Plato defined injustice as acting contrary to nature.[3] Thus, if someone is naturally suited to become a member of the auxiliary but seeks to move into the class of rulers, this is unjust. If someone, by nature, is fit to be a worker but wishes to rise up into the class of guardians, this is unjust. Moving out of the grouping into which nature suits you puts you at war with justice. Interestingly, we see here that Plato warns against ambition, upward or downward mobility, and doing something simply because it is popular or simply because you have the power to do it. Each of these actions can lead us away from our nature and bring unhappiness to ourselves and harm to the state.[4]

Notice that Plato's theory criticizes the very striving for advancement, the competition to best your peers in as many fields of endeavor as you physically and mentally can, and the ambition for ever-greater achievements in every area of life—all of which U.S. culture praises. If we listen to Plato, we may begin to look askance at such approaches to life. We may ask whether all avenues of pursuit are natural for all people.

Plato's writings raise fascinating possibilities and have been the subject of innumerable commentaries. Some readers have been appalled by his notion of three social classes into which individuals are placed. Plato strikes some people as hopelessly hierarchical and authoritarian in his thinking. Indeed, Plato was a critic of democracy, for he was convinced that ruling and policymaking were natural talents possessed by some people, but not by all. In making such claims, Plato has not only offended democratic sensibilities but has also struck some commentators as self-serving, insofar as he saw philosophers (like himself) as the class most naturally suited for ruling the perfect state. Yet other students of Plato have seen his criticisms of ambition, competition, and individual self-aggrandizement as compelling antidotes to U.S. culture's message that the only life worth living is the frenzied climb-the-ladder-of-success-to-the-very-top approach to life. Some commentators are moved by Plato's argument that living justly is more important than following personal ambitions. The only thing certain in these interpretations is that Plato will continue to challenge his readers, infuriating some and inspiring others.[5]

In the seventeenth century, English political theorist Thomas Hobbes (1588–1679) would equally confound his peers and readers. Hobbes's life spanned the sailing of the Spanish Armada and the outbreak of religious civil war in England. He was educated at Oxford, lived for a time in Paris and there met philosopher René Descartes, traveled to Italy and met Galileo, and served as a tutor of Charles II. The bluntness of his words sometimes astounded his contemporaries and inspired wild stories. Indeed, John Aubrey recalls that Hobbes had to live with gossip alleging that Hobbes was too paranoid to sleep alone at night in his own home and with rumors that he was a heretic.[6]

In his *Leviathan*, Hobbes tells his readers early on that he has no intention of looking to ancient philosophers such as Plato to understand politics. What is the purpose of the state? According to Hobbes, we cannot know until we have answered another question: What is human nature? To understand human nature, Hobbes concludes, look into your own psyche.[7] When you do this, you will find passion, desires, fears, aggressive impulses, and instinctive urges to acquire power. However, you will also find an element of rationality. This mixture of passion

---

**BOX 4.1    Crime in the United States: Is Hobbes Correct—Does Life Look Brutal and Violent?**

In his seventeenth-century masterpiece *Leviathan*, Thomas Hobbes depicts human nature as violent and warlike. Life is uncertain, Hobbes says, because of the human propensity to commit innumerable acts of aggression against persons and property. Thus, without a strong state to control these aggressive tendencies, violence becomes a way of life.

Does the United States look Hobbesian? Consider the following statistics provided by the U.S. Department of Justice for crime levels in 1999:

- 48% of reported murders were committed by people who knew their victims.
- 916,383 aggravated assaults were reported.
- 1.4 million violent crimes were reported.
- $14.8 million in property was reported stolen.
- 7,876 hate crimes were reported.

SOURCE: U.S. Department of Justice, Federal Bureau of Investigation, *Crime in the United States*, Press Release 15 October 2000 (http://www.fbi.gov/pressrm/presrel00).

and reason in human nature must be understood, Hobbes says, if politics is to be made comprehensible.

Hobbes proceeds with his analysis by stating that the violent and impulsive components of human nature lead to social conflict. Whenever aggressive human beings live in groups, violence is always a possibility. Moreover, Hobbes believes humans are naturally equal to one another. What leads him to this conclusion? He tells us he has observed weak humans and strong ones and has been struck by the following fact: Even the weakest of humans is capable of killing the strongest. The weak person can launch a sneak attack, wait until the strong person goes to sleep, creep up on a strong person from behind, use cunning and trickery, and manage somehow to kill the strong. Does this not, Hobbes asks, prove that—in terms of the only thing that really matters, that is, staying alive—we are all fundamentally equal?[8] The fact of our equality, coupled with our shared tendencies toward aggression, creates a human condition in which each of us is vulnerable to all others. No one is safe. The strongest can fall at the hands of the weakest.[9]

Our reason shows us the alternative to such a miserable life. Each of us can use our reason to deduce that, were we able to protect ourselves from the dangers posed by all others, we could improve our chances of having a longer and less brutish life. Reason tells us that it is in our self-interest to join with others to create a power over all of us that will have the function of deterring each individual's natural aggressiveness. We will find it rational to create a power that will function in the following manner: It is to leave us alone unless we act aggressively toward another, in which case it is to punish us severely and quickly. Knowing that such severe punishment is certain if we ever commit aggression, we will each be deterred from harming others by our fear of such punishment. At the same time, knowing that the power will leave us alone if we do not act aggressively, we will be able to live full, active, productive lives unencumbered by any unnecessary intrusions from this power.

The power Hobbes describes is the state. In spelling out its reason for being (deterrence), he has also laid the foundations for justifying its existence. Its purpose is to provide security through deterrence and thus *promote the survival of humanity*. Notice how different this argument is from Plato's advocacy of the just state. Hobbes rejects what he considers to be lofty and utopian dreams of achieving a perfectly just state (as Plato would define it) and concentrates, instead, on teaching us the importance of creating a state that can crack down on violence. Without the powerful state capable of enacting, and willing to enact, swift and severe punishment on any and all wrongdoers, each of us is vulnerable to attack from naturally aggressive human beings. Without the powerful state watching over us, we are likely victims in a world of predators.[10] Our choice is clear: We can have a powerful no-nonsense state that will protect us, or we can live desperate and terrified in a violent world in which every single person has the power to kill any of us at any moment.

If this sounds far-fetched and unduly pessimistic, Hobbes argues, think again. In a provocative anticipation of how his critics will assail his low opinions of human nature, Hobbes asks us to think about the following: When you leave your home, do you lock your doors and windows? Thinking like a Hobbesian in terms of the technology of the twenty-first century, do you do the same when you leave your car unattended? If you are at home alone in the evening, do you make certain your doors are locked? When you travel alone, are you mindful (and perhaps suspicious) of strangers you encounter? If you have a child and live close to your child's school, do you allow your child to walk alone to school? Do any of your actions implicitly affirm the violent propensities of which Hobbes writes?[11]

Just as Plato elicits strong reactions, so does Hobbes. Some writers have seen him as pathological. Some have attacked him for justifying what looks like a police state. Some have blamed him for trying to steer political theory away from questions of justice and toward more prosaic issues of law and order. Others have found in Hobbes a cogent argument that governments need to be more concerned with fighting crime and promoting safety. Some have read Hobbes and wished that we did have such a deterrence power so we could take a peaceful walk in the late evening along city streets or be away from our possessions without worrying so much about theft and vandalism.[12]

Whatever our individual interpretations of Plato and Hobbes may be, their writings convey the complexity of issues in the field of political theory. They help us to begin thinking critically about the purposes of states and about the normative dimensions of governing.

## Should States Promote Equality?

Political theorists have disagreed among themselves on many issues relating to equality. There is no agreement on how equality should be defined, nor on the question of whether equality should be actively promoted by state policies. To get a sense of how such disagreements have divided political theorists over the centuries, we can look to the teachings of Aristotle, Thomas Jefferson, Tecumseh, Chico Mendes, Friedrich Nietzsche, and Kurt Vonnegut.

As noted previously, Aristotle was a student of Plato's Academy in the fourth century B.C. Like Plato, he came from a prominent family, and he went on to make his own contributions to ancient Greek culture. Aristotle founded a school, the Lyceum, and his writings spanned the fields of politics, poetry, metaphysics, ethics, and science. Aristotle was also a teacher of Alexander the Great.

Aristotle's *Politics* offers astute insights on the issue of equality. Reading Aristotle's observations gives us an opportunity to think about what equality implies. Aristotle notes that it can imply any number of things. He advises that equality best serves human beings when equality is understood to mean *equal consideration of interests*. So defined, equality should be promoted by states. In explaining equal consideration of interests, Aristotle asks us to consider the different forms states can assume. He identifies six such forms: monarchy, aristocracy, polity, tyranny, oligarchy, and democracy. Each form is defined by two elements: who rules and whose interests are considered and served. Viewing each form of state on the basis of these two criteria, Aristotle outlines the following definitions:

- *Monarchy*: Rule by one in the interests of all
- *Aristocracy*: Rule by the few in the interests of all

- *Polity*: Rule by the many in the interests of all

- *Tyranny*: Rule by one in the interests of the ruler

- *Oligarchy*: Rule by the few in the interests of the rulers

- *Democracy*: Rule by the many in the interests of the rulers

According to Aristotle, monarchy, aristocracy, and polity are all proper forms of government because each treats all interests as meriting consideration. No interests are excluded from consideration. In these three forms of government, no matter how many people are involved in the process of ruling, the interests of all are served by the state. Aristotle considered tyranny, oligarchy, and democracy to be improper forms of government because interests were not equally considered. Under tyranny, the interest of the leader is elevated above all others. In an oligarchy, the few who hold power pursue their interests to the exclusion of the interest of the many. In democracy, the many have power, but they act like tyrants. They rule in a self-serving manner and exclude from consideration the interest of the few. That is, each of the improper forms of government violates the principle of equal consideration of interests. Each improper form discriminates against or oppresses another group.

Interestingly, for Aristotle, therefore, it is less important to have equal participation in the *process* of decision making than it is to have equality reflected in the *results* of the decision arrived at. This contrast is very striking in his comparison of monarchies and democracies. If one defined equality in terms of participation, democracies might look more ethical than monarchies. In Aristotle's definition, a democratic society is one in which most people are participating in ruling, so there is, at least, an approximation of participation on an equal basis (all people have the same or equal participation rights). However, in a monarchy equality of participation is altogether absent: One person is doing all the ruling.

Yet Aristotle favors monarchy over democracy. Does this make sense? Think about the following hypothetical scenarios. Suppose that, in your class, you and your fellow students are given the opportunity to vote on the following proposition: Every person who is right-handed gets 10 bonus points on the next exam, but only if everyone who is left-handed loses 20 points on the same exam. Suppose a majority of the class is right-handed. Suppose that most students show up to class on the day of the vote and cast a vote on the proposition. If the majority of right-handed students swings the vote in favor of the proposition benefiting them, this would represent an example of democracy, as defined as Aristotle. The majority is ruling, but it is doing so in a self-serving manner. The result of the decision made by the majority does not give equal consideration to the interests of the minority. Indeed, the decision imposes "exam points discrimination" on the minority.

Contrast this situation with one in which a single ruler is in charge of the class, makes decisions regarding point distributions on exams, and those decisions make no distinctions between right-handed and left-handed students but, rather, treat all students equally according to the same set of rules. That would represent Aristotle's understanding of monarchy: There is no equality in the process of decision making, but there is equality in the result of the decision. To Aristotle, it is obvious which is more important.[13] Note that he has not advocated equality of income, equality of power, or even equality of rights (he does not uphold equal rights of participation in politics in his definition of legitimate states). His assessment of state responsibilities in the area of equality is focused on interest. Good states serve the public's interest, not *most* of the public's interest, but the interest of the *entire* public (the interests of the many *and* the few).

Thomas Jefferson (1743–1826) offers a contrasting view of the nature of equality. Jefferson's contributions to U.S. politics are many and varied. He served in the Virginia colonial legislature, was a delegate to the Continental Congress, was governor of Virginia, served as the first secretary of state, and was elected the third president of the United States. He was also the primary author of the Declaration of Independence, which in 1776 made the argument for American independence from England. We can examine this document to find a theory that conceptualizes equality in terms of *equality of natural rights*. The Declaration's political theory is straightforward. It states that (1) individuals are created naturally equal; (2) individuals possess natural rights; (3) it is the proper role of government to protect and respect these natural rights; and (4) if governments aggress against these equal natural rights, individuals may overturn such governments.[14]

Jefferson's political theory has been the subject of much controversy. Many critics have highlighted the fact that Jefferson owned slaves and that the practice of slavery and the exclusion of political rights for other groups (women and Native Americans, for example) during this period calls into question the integrity of the Declaration. That the theory of equality in the Declaration was selectively applied and was not extended to African-Americans, Native Americans, and women is indisputable. But what was this theory that was applied so selectively?

First, we see that the theory is essentially anti-Aristotelian, in that equality is discussed not in terms of political results but in terms of human essences. If Jefferson is correct, equality is not to be viewed as an attribute of decisions but instead is to be seen as an attribute of people. People, by their very (human) nature, possess equality of natural rights. Indeed, in calling the rights *natural,* the Declaration emphasizes that they are a part of human nature itself. Having the right to life, liberty, and happiness is a fundamental part of being a human being, Jefferson's followers insist, just as much a core element of our essence as is possessing a mind, a heart, and, some would say, a soul. Insofar as each of us is equally human, none of us possess these rights to a greater or lesser extent than others. It is in this sense that the rights are equal. Because these rights are a part of our very nature, who is government to deny them or take them away? It is a fundamental duty of the state to protect these rights, Jefferson claims. Hence, the Declaration proclaims the morality of revolution against a government that would deny the existence of these naturally existing rights.

It is instructive to note that theories of equality of natural rights similar to Jefferson's have been embraced by groups that elites like Jefferson were hesitant or unwilling to accept as social and legal equals. Tecumseh (1768?–1813) was a Shawnee theorist who, in the early nineteenth century, argued for *equality of natural rights with an emphasis on property rights.* Born in Ohio, Tecumseh and his brother Ten-skwatawa founded Prophet's Town, Indiana, in 1808. As a political thinker and activist, Tecumseh argued that native lands transferred to whites through treaties negotiated with Native American leaders should be recovered by Native Americans on the basis of natural equality doctrines. Specifically, Tecumseh taught that a spiritual force placed Native Americans on their lands and that each member of the Native American community had an equal and natural right to the lands.[15]

Native American leaders, therefore, had no authority to negotiate away the land, and such negotiations as had occurred should be considered invalid. Note the similarity to Jefferson's theory. Equality, as Tecumseh conceptualizes, is an attribute (a right) of people.

Through his activism and political writings, Chico Mendes (1944–1988) articulated a concept of *equality of participation.* Mendes was a rubber-tapper and union activist in the Brazilian state of Acre. Mendes, like many other indigenous people in the Brazilian rain forest, depended on the forest's products for his life. He worked in the forest harvesting latex from rubber trees in a part of Brazil that remained largely isolated until the mid-1980s. When road construction made the area more accessible, cattle ranchers and others saw the forest as a prime target for clearing and developing. For the rubber-tappers, the threatened loss of forest spelled the end of their traditional livelihood. Mendes and others mobilized and demanded equality of participation in the decision-making process regarding the rain forest. Mendes and other rubber-tappers pointed out that no one knew the rain forest as well as the people who lived in it. Assisted by international environmentalist groups, who were interested in preventing the deforestation threatened by the cattle industry and developers, Mendes and organizations of rubber-tappers advocated the development of land set-asides; that is, land protected from development. These protected areas would remain regions in which native communities could pursue traditional means of work—such as extracting rubber and collecting native products such as brazil nuts, jute, and palm oil—while the region as a unit would be guaranteed protection from deforestation. Resources within the area would be extracted, but the area's ecological integrity would be preserved. Although Mendes was successful in contributing to the development of the forest protection, he paid dearly for his activism. He was murdered in 1988.[16]

Mendes's concept of equality, like Jefferson's and Tecumseh's, is anti–Aristotelian. According to Mendes and the rubber-tappers, equality in the *process* of decision making is the only way to ensure equality of results. If no one understands the life of the rubber-tapper as well as the rubber-tapper him- or herself, how can someone else, in Aristotelian fashion, determine, consider, and then serve the interest of the rubber-tapper? Cattle ranchers and developers could not be trusted to serve the tappers' interest, nor could environmentalists. When the developers saw the forest, they saw future roads, clearings, and concrete; when the environmentalists looked at it, they saw a near-pristine environmental utopia they wanted to set off as wild and as free of human (including tapper) traces as possible. Neither saw what Mendes saw: a forest that should neither be destroyed nor romanticized. How could either group speak for the rubber-tappers? They could not. The only legitimate solution was equality of participation by all groups speaking for themselves. Mendes's example suggests the importance of thinking critically about what interests are and who is in a position to recognize and serve interests.

As distinctive as the approaches of Aristotle, Jefferson, Tecumseh, and Mendes are, they share the position that equality is a desirable political goal for individuals and governments. However, what if the pursuit of equality were harmful? Powerful insights into this perspective are found in the writings of nineteenth-century German theorist Friedrich Nietzsche and contemporary U.S. writer Kurt Vonnegut.

German philosopher Friedrich Nietzsche (1844–1900) is perhaps one of the most controversial political theorists in the modern period. Nietzsche, a professor of classical philology at the University of Basel, was a prolific writer whose works included treatises on ancient Greece, philosophy, linguistics, religion, and politics. Nietzsche's writings continue to incite controversy, for one finds in them a provocative theory of the harmful consequences of egalitarianism, along with various commentaries on the death of God, the pettiness associated with religious beliefs, and the lies that make up the teachings of traditional morality. These arguments made by Nietzsche, whose father was a Lutheran minister, have brought him notoriety.

What is Nietzsche's argument? He maintained that equality, as a concept, is rooted in a certain type of morality. He termed this morality a *slave morality,* which he defined as a morality articulated by the weak and thus designed to serve the interests of the weak. Slave moralities are contrasted with *master moralities,* ethical codes that serve the strong and praise the attributes of strength, conquering, ruling, and dominating. Slave moralities condemn as "bad" what is called "good" by master moralities. Master moralities call "bad" what is termed "good" by slave moralities. Notice the logic of Nietzsche's assertions. Both forms of morality are self-serving in the manner in which they determine what is "good" and what is "bad." Neither morality provides a concept of good or bad that exists beyond its own context.[17]

Christianity, according to Nietzsche, is an example of a slave morality, in that it teaches forgiveness, humility, and meekness. Nietzsche introduces the concept of resentment to make the argument that advocates of slave morality seek a vengeful retribution against those who are strong. How does all this make sense? Nietzsche ties the strains of his thought together by concluding that slave morality appeals to the desire of those who are weak to bring down the strong (because the weak resent the strong) by condemning as "bad" all those things that make the strong powerful (such as the drive to conquer and dominate). For example, Christians resent the powerful, so they condemn as "sinful" the traits of the powerful and then fancy the powerful burning in hell, taking delight in the imagined torments of the powerful because Christians deeply resent the powerful and love the idea of the powerful being made to suffer.

Equality is a part of slave morality. The weak uphold equality as "good" and "ethical" because they want to destroy the privileged positions of the powerful. Equality, as Nietzsche sees it, is a buzzword for people who want to destroy those who have risen above them. Democracy, from a Nietzschean perspective, is an example of slave morality, if it preaches that none should be privileged above others. What is behind the demand for equality? If Nietzsche is correct, resentment is behind it, the drive to punish those who excel, those who rise to the top, and those who climb to powerful positions. These people are to be punished by being defined as "bad" under the terms of a slave morality. "Goodness" ensues when all are brought down to the same level because that is when all are equal.

Nietzsche's writings have horrified some readers, who see his work as an argument for elitism or perhaps domination. Insofar as his writings expose the flaws of egalitarianism, some commentators see Nietzsche as a precursor of antidemocratic movements such as Nazism, which is discussed in Chapter 6. Nietzsche's sister Elizabeth, who edited some of his works, had close ties with the Nazis. Other writers see a different meaning in Nietzsche's philosophy. They point out that when Nietzsche took pains to uncover the vengeful motives behind the slave morality, he was not doing so to glorify the master morality. Rather, he was making the logical point that both moral systems serve interests: Master morality serves the interest of those who need to legitimize their position of dominance, whereas slave morality serves the purposes of those who need to delegitimize dominance and legitimize equality.[18]

In 1961, U.S. author Kurt Vonnegut published a short story, "Harrison Bergeron," in which characters and plot twists offer a fictional laboratory for examining Nietzschean concepts. In this story, set in the United States in the year 2081, laws have made everyone thoroughly and completely equal. If one person begins to look unequal in comparison to any other, the inequality is cured swiftly. For example, people who are smarter than others are made to wear devices that impede their ability to use their intelligence to compete and do things better than anyone else. Individuals who are physically stronger than others are similarly required to wear "equalizing" gear so that they do not climb above the equal level of all others. In the story, the major character Harrison is naturally gifted in terms of intellect and physical strength, so he is made "equal" to all others by being forced to wear radio devices that pump noises into his ears to disrupt his thinking, thick glasses so he cannot unfairly read more than others, and weights to tie him down physically so he is weakened and made equal to others. The government uses a Handicapper-General to enforce the rule that all such gifted people never throw off their equalizing radios, glasses, and weights. Because nobody is allowed to be superior to another in any way, people are thoroughly equal, but society is characterized by mediocrity, conformity, and drabness. The zealous pursuit of equality has robbed society of genius, creativity, excellence, and noble accomplishments. Anyone with talent is penalized by handicapping devices, so talent is wasted.[19]

In Vonnegut's story, we can see various Nietzschean themes. First, equality becomes a basis for attacking those who would use their talents to become strong or intellectually dominant. The drive for equality means that the Handicapper-General enforces rules prohibiting anyone from rising above the "average" level. Second, equality is exposed as being a self-serving position; as a Nietzschean would say, equality is not a neutral concept but rather is a concept that harms some and favors others. In the short story, those who would not be able to successfully compete with the naturally gifted and strong Harrison are protected from having to do so by his radio, glasses, and weights. Harrison is harmed in the interest of their well-being.

We can look to Vonnegut's story as we think critically about several questions relating to the normative basis of equality:

- Is it possible to equalize all without harming some?
- Should individuals be equal in every way?
- Should laws pursue equality so diligently that laws provide for equality of capabilities rather than equality of opportunities?
- Can equality become a basis for oppression?

From Aristotle to Vonnegut, we see writers struggling with these questions. As you consider this ethical dimension of politics, think about which arguments you find most compelling. Is equality humane if it is viewed as equal consideration of all interests (Aristotle) but not if equality is imposed on people as a means of denying them the use of their individual talents (Vonnegut)? Is equality of results (Aristotle) more important than equality of processes (Mendes)? Is equality a linguistic and conceptual weapon whereby one group pursues advantages relative to another (Nietzsche), or is equality a fundamental natural attribute of human beings (Jefferson and Tecumseh)? In the next chapter, we take up the issue of equality again and explore how conservatism, liberalism, and other contemporary forms of applied theory try to sort out these questions and present their own views of equality through the medium of political platforms.

### Should States Be Organized to Maximize Their Own Power or Organized to Restrain This Power?

Are citizens better off living under a state that holds great power it can employ at home or abroad in a swift and decisive manner whenever a conflict may arise, or is it better to live under a state that is organized to prevent state leaders from having at their command such overwhelming amounts of power? This question has puzzled and divided political theorists for centuries.

Niccoló Machiavelli (1469–1527) presents an argument in favor of state organization for the purpose of maximizing state power in his classic work *The Prince*. Machiavelli wrote *The Prince* during the years 1512 and 1513, when he was exiled from politics and seeking to gain favor with the government of the city-state Florence. Indeed, he dedicated *The Prince* as a gift to Lorenzo de Medici, Florence's leader. Italy was divided into various warring and competing factions at this time, and Machiavelli hoped *The Prince* could offer the political wisdom needed to create order in the region. *The Prince* would tell Lorenzo how to be a powerful statesman, one who could best his enemies and maintain sovereignty over his lands. In the process of teaching these lessons, *The Prince* articulates for readers a complex and detailed blueprint for organizing states in a manner to seize and maintain power. As such, despite Machiavelli's other writings in favor of popular rule and limited government, *The Prince* has survived through the centuries to become a classic text on the mechanics of state power, and it has earned Machiavelli the reputation for justifying a "win at any cost" approach to governing.[20]

Read as a text for strong centralized leaders, *The Prince* recommends that states are most effective at maximizing their power if organized along the following lines. If possible, states should use cultural traditions and long-standing folkways to justify their use of power. If a state needs to attack an enemy, it is best to use religious or cultural symbols to legitimize the attack. Attack, but claim the attack is consistent with God's will, for example. This will win support for the state's actions. In addition, when a state seeks to expand its territory, it may be useful to colonize new territories in order to control them. In colonizing a territory, the state should move its own people into the land and confiscate land from the conquered population. Through these actions, the conquered population will be rendered too powerless to resist the state. Conquered peoples will suffer from such actions, but this is not necessarily bad. The suffering can be very useful, for it can serve as a visible warning of how the state can crush people at will.

Furthermore, a state must not allow its own populations to grow powerful enough to threaten the state itself. Thus, Machiavelli justifies state action to weaken economic classes to prevent them from becoming powerful rivals of state officials, and he also suggests that states keep their general population in fear. In a revealing discussion of whether it is better for states to be hated, feared, or loved by their own people, Machiavelli decides that fear is the optimum basis for ruling. The reason is as follows: A population that hates the state may rise up against it (and this would obviously impair the state's power if the revolt were successful), and a population that loves the state is uncontrollable (people give or withhold love of their own choosing, Machiavelli says, and thus it is impossible to *make* people love you), but a population that fears the state is controllable by the state (fear, unlike love, can be induced by the state and the levels of fear can be lowered or raised depending on the state's needs). For this reason, Machiavelli teaches, states maximize and secure their power if they rule through fear.

Indeed, rulers should use just the right amount of cruelty against their own citizens so that fear is created but popular vengefulness against the government is not. Use cruelty to make citizens fear politicians but not hate them, Machiavelli advised. A state so organized can maintain order and peace within its own borders. States that build up reserves of power and keep maximum power for ready use at any time are states that best provide protection and security to their own people. Thus, Machiavielli's work teaches, in being cruel the state is really being kind.[21]

Yet states that mobilize power so it can be used so extensively at home and abroad also possess the power to tyrannize over their own populations, according to some theorists. We may look to James Madison (1751–1836) to find a very different perspective on state organization. Madison was a member of the U.S. Continental Congress and the U.S. Congress, and he was elected the fourth president of the United States. He was one of the authors of the U.S. Constitution and, along with Alexander Hamilton and John Jay, an author of *The Federalist Papers* (1787–1788). As discussed in Chapter 3, *The Federalist Papers* was a series of articles that argued on behalf of the ratification of the U.S. Constitution. *The Federalist Papers,* like Machiavelli's *The Prince,* is a work that has endured beyond the original events inspiring its writing. *The Federalist Papers* presents what many readers have found a logically compelling argument for organizing states in such a manner as to restrict state power.

Madison argues that states should intentionally restrict their powers by a means of the institution of a *separation of powers* and a system of *checks and balances.* With respect to the former, Madison writes, legislative, executive, and judicial power must be divided among three different branches of government. If one branch is organized in such a manner as to hold all three powers, this branch becomes politically dangerous.[22] Such a branch is potentially tyrannical, Madison believes, because it possesses the power to make laws, enforce laws, and settle disputes on laws. Its power is final and absolute. Rather than concentrating all power in one branch, it is better to have one branch make laws (the legislature), one branch enforce laws (the executive), and still another branch settle disputes over the meaning of laws (the judiciary).

Separation of powers should be accompanied by a system of checks and balances, according to Madison. One branch should have the ability to obstruct the activities of a rival branch. This would have the effect of restricting state power even more than the separation of powers alone because it would allow the branches to *weaken* one another. The executive can weaken the legislature by means of a veto, whereas the legislature can weaken the executive by voting to override the veto. The judiciary can weaken either the legislature or executive by declaring legislative or executive actions unconstitutional by virtue of the power of judicial review, but the judiciary can also be weakened by the other two branches because the executive appoints and the legislature approves members to the highest court in the judiciary (that is, the U.S. Supreme Court).[23]

A Madisonian state is designed to shut down if its leaders ever consider imposing Machiavellian cruelties on the domestic population. An executive seeking to hold the citizenry in fear, for example, would be thwarted by one of the other two branches, if the system worked properly. A legislature bent on controlling the population through extensive regulations would similarly be "checked and balanced" and thus defeated in its endeavor. Notice how striking are the differences separating the logic of *The Prince* and that of *The Federalist Papers.* One was written in a period of chaos with the stated purpose of creating order through the actions of strong political leaders (*The Prince*), and the other was composed to justify a constitution creating a new government for a people who had recently revolted against a colonial power. Emphasizing different objectives, both *The Prince* and *The Federalist Papers* raise important questions about the ethics of political leadership. Which is more important, these works ask us to ponder, protecting citizens *from government* through an organizational mode that restricts power, or protecting citizens *by government* through an organizational mode that maximizes the power of the protector?

## Should States Try to Help Us Be Ethical?

When issues of ethics arise, is it best if the state leaves ethical decisions, as much as possible, to be decided by individuals; or should states take positions on ethical issues, decide what is ethical, and insist that citizens live consistent with the ethical positions taken by the state? Who is to decide what is ethical—individuals or states? Perhaps no normative question in political science is more difficult to resolve. On the one hand, states routinely enforce ethical positions. For instance, when states pass and enforce laws against murder, assault, theft, and other actions defined as crimes, states are imposing ethical codes on the population. On the other hand, we may look to the history of political theory to see that philosophers have disagreed on whether such enforcement should be as limited as possible or as extensive as possible. Some theorists have taken the position that states should seek to stay out of the moral decisions of individuals, whereas others have said that states should be intimately involved with this decision making.

John Stuart Mill (1806–1873) was an English philosopher whose works upheld the view that individuals should be allowed to judge ethical questions for themselves. According to Mill, governments should not interfere with individuals unless individuals posed a threat to others. Mill rejected the notion that government knows best. In short, Mill defended the widest possible range of individual freedom of thought and action.[24]

For example, if government and society suspected an individual's beliefs to be wrong, government and society still had an obligation to respect the individual's right to believe anything, as long as the individual did not harm others. Indeed, Mill wrote, people should have as much freedom to be wrong as to be right in their beliefs. In fact, he called on society to respect the individual's right to think any thought no matter how outrageous or unpopular.[25] The implications of Mill's argument are clear: Governments should not try to make individuals ethical, nor should governments become involved in individual lives to protect individuals from incorrect opinions.

Everyone benefits if government removes itself from questions of personal morality, according to Mill. Individuals benefit because they possess the liberty to live their lives as they please. Society also benefits because society gains whenever it encourages freethinkers to express themselves and explore new ideas. These far-sighted individuals can formulate bold and innovative approaches for moving societies forward. In fact, Mill was convinced that progress is made by people who refuse to accept conventional ways of thinking and acting. From Socrates on, Mill argued, iconoclastic thinkers have challenged traditional notions of ethics and have offered original insights on social and political problems.[26]

Yet what if an individual upholds an idea that appears destructive? What if a person upholds, for example, racism? What if the individual in question expresses his or her racism through public speeches and publications? Should society step in and try to stop the spread of this antihumanist idea? Mill considered the question of whether the consequences for society are harmful whenever individuals express erroneous opinions. After giving this question considerable thought, Mill concluded that the expression of incorrect ideas can also benefit society, in that the expression of error can give people a clearer view of what error looks like.[27] That is, one of the best ways of exposing error is to let proponents of error speak and show themselves to be charlatans. Thus, however tempting it may be, states should avoid the role of moral guardian.[28]

Mill's ideas are dangerous and are to be rejected, according to many religious fundamentalist political theorists. Fundamentalism—whether Christian, Islamic, or from a different faith tradition—upholds what it defines as religious truth: basic (fundamental) propositions that are validated by the religion itself. Fundamentalists are often described as ultraorthodox—that is, as advocates of what they regard as a strict, nonsyncretic approach to religious observance, an observance that claims not to dilute the purity and literalism of religious teachings by incorporating secular and competing religious practices into the original faith.

Fundamentalism includes a highly diversified and multidimensional range of political perspectives. In the United States, fundamentalism has often defined itself in opposition to science as well as to what it regards as secular forces seeking to alter traditional family structures, and in the Middle East and Central Asia fundamentalists have often been critics of international power structures seen as imperialistic.[29]

Despite variations in fundamentalist theory and practice, fundamentalists tend to assert that (1) religious truth is authoritative; (2) religious truth is compelling and not to be disregarded or reduced to being a mere option; and (3) if fundamentalism is to guide government policy, laws must codify the authoritative truths of the religion, not assume a posture of neutrality or silence on the issues of politics.

We can look to the teachings of the Afghan Taliban movement and the writings of Patrick J. Buchanan (born 1938) to see specific examples of fundamentalist critiques of Millian perspectives on state–ethics relations.

The Taliban emerged as the ruling power in Afghanistan in the mid-1990s, holding power in various regions of the country in 1994 and extending its range of control through the remainder of the decade. By November 2000, Taliban forces had 95% of the country under their control. Following 9/11, the Bush administration launched a military campaign that successfully dislodged the Taliban from power. In December 2001, Hamid Karzai assumed leadership of the interim post-Taliban government and later became leader of the Afghan Transitional Authority.[30]

The name Taliban means "students of Islam" and, while in power, the Taliban's governing policies reflected its particular fundamentalist view of Islam, as filtered through the perspectives afforded by Pashtun culture. The Pashtuns are the largest ethnic group in Afghanistan and the ethnic group from which the Taliban movement has drawn many of its supporters. Long-time student of Afghan politics Ahmed Rashid has noted that before the rise of the Taliban, Afghanistan was a religiously tolerant society in which the Sunni Muslim majority coexisted with Sufis,

Hindus, Buddhists, Sikhs, and Jews. Although divided by clan and ethnic divisions and complicated by the maneuverings of superpower and regional rivalries, Afghanistan's political process was not characterized by religious persecution.[31]

Taliban fundamentalism traced its intellectual origins to deobandism, a school within Sunni Hanafi Islam that many Taliban members learned from Pakistani religious leaders. This theology opposes the equality of women with men and also rejects tribal and clan authority in favor of religious authority. Both positions, according to Rashid, were implemented by the Taliban in extremist fashions that violated the integrity of the region's spiritual traditions. Not surprisingly, Muslims emerged as the harshest critics of the Taliban rulers. Many U.S. readers may be shocked to learn that whereas the Bush administration led the military effort that removed the Taliban from power, the Clinton administration had been among the Taliban's earliest supporters.[32]

What policies were introduced by Taliban leaders? Decrees requiring men to grow beards, forbidding girls and women from attending school and forbidding women to practice most professions, and restricting women from traveling in public without religious attire and without male escorts. Taliban decrees also banned most games, photography, American hairdos, and nonreligious holiday observances. All these provisions were presented by the Taliban as being required by religion, even though, for example, in cities such as Kabul, citizens had long been accustomed to a workforce and a civil society open to women as well as men. Indeed, before the Taliban took power, 40 percent of the physicians and 70 percent of the teachers in Kabul were women.[33]

Many of the country's women resisted Taliban restrictions. The most widely known resistance group is the Revolutionary Association of the Women of Afghanistan (RAWA). While the Taliban forces were in power, RAWA helped women learn skills such as weaving in order to empower them to work in their homes beyond the restrictive surveillance of Taliban officials. RAWA also defied the Taliban by running underground Afghan schools for girls and by teaching both girls and boys in refugee camps. Distancing themselves not only from Taliban actions but also from the fundamentalist foundations, RAWA has the following motto: "If you are freedom loving and antifundamentalist, you are with RAWA."[34] You can find this motto and information on its latest actions in post-Taliban Afghanistan by going to its Web site (http://www.rawa.org).

The anti–Millian perspectives of the Taliban are obvious. They are no less obvious in the fundamentalist politics of U.S. activist and 2000 Reform Party presidential candidate Patrick Buchanan. According to Buchanan, truly legitimate ethical positions are based on religion, and these positions should be expressed and enforced through a state's laws. In the United States, citizens have been turning away from religious-oriented ethics, Buchanan believes, and the result has been a crisis of morality. Following the teachings of the Christian Bible is the only way out of this crisis, Buchanan insists, for no source other than the Bible is legitimate as a foundation of law.[35]

Buchanan rejects the idea of tolerating all viewpoints. Government should not be neutral on issues but, rather, should uphold the moral position on policy questions. Thus, homosexuality should be identified for the sin it is, as should abortion and illegal drug use, Buchanan contends. Buchanan calls on citizens to exercise a profoundly important duty: Pressure politicians to rewrite the laws to encode fundamentalist teachings on all social, political, and economic matters.[36]

In the United States, questions regarding which normative approaches are to prevail—Millian ones or fundamentalist ones—arise with great frequency. Since 9/11, Millian critiques of the Bush administration's domestic security measures have been frequent. An examination of recent controversies in a number of U.S. states and cities indicates, however, that such issues divided U.S. citizens before the war on terrorism.

For example, in 1993, the state of Texas sought to confiscate documents from the Texas Knights of the Ku Klux Klan as a means of investigating Klan protesters who opposed an integration policy implemented in Vidor, Texas. The state of Texas claimed the Klan's actions were harmful, and government officials wanted to confiscate membership information in order to better monitor and restrict the organization. The state of Texas was opposed by the American Civil Liberties Union (ACLU), an organization long known for upholding a Millian position on matters of personal ethics. ACLU staff assisted the Klan in protecting its records, not because it believed in the Klan's racism but because it believed in keeping government out of questions of personal morality. People have the right to subscribe to any idea, the ACLU affirmed, and their right to be free in choosing their own ethical worldview must be respected. In the words of the ACLU attorney working on the case, one should not say that the constitutional protection of freedom of speech applies to some groups but not to others.[37]

Should all ideas be equally tolerated, as this attorney advises? Consider the following disputes subsequent to the preceding example from Texas. In spring 1994, Howard University was criticized by some for sponsoring a speech by Khalid Abdul Muhammad, who had earlier delivered an anti-Semitic speech at Kean College. Should Howard have sponsored a speaker who had expressed support for anti-Semitism? In 1995, a father took nude photographs of his daughter as part of a project for an art class but was jailed for endangering his child. Were his photographs pornographic, insofar as they were pictures of a nude child, and if so, should this activity be allowed or discouraged? Is one position on the question of photographs of nude children more ethical than another, and should the state (through the powers of arresting and prosecuting the man) uphold morality? In 1995, the Red Cross decided to be intentionally vague in its discussion of certain sexual practices in documents it distributed on AIDS education. Was this a responsible decision? Is a document containing candid discussions of sexuality destructive of divinely inspired morality? In 1996, Families against Internet Censorship organized to oppose efforts to restrict access to Internet materials deemed by some to be immoral. Is the organization to be applauded for standing up for a John Stuart Mill-like approach to freedom, or is the organization failing to serve its civic duty of promoting truth and morality? In January 2001, the mayor of Gary, Indiana, pushed for stiffer permit laws regulating groups wishing to protest within city limits as a means of trying to prevent the Ku Klux Klan from holding a rally in Gary. Was the mayor protecting democratic cultural values or subverting them?[38]

As these examples illustrate, questions concerning who is to decide what is ethical are unavoidable. Whether one finds Mill or Buchanan most helpful in resolving this issue, clearly these writers do us a great service in highlighting contrasting and provocative aspects of the debate. Whatever our personal understanding of ethics may be, we must all ask ourselves how best to deal with those who would disagree with our understandings of what is ethical. Is it best to uphold no single morality as the absolute truth? Should each person decide morality for him- or herself? If so, are all opinions to be tolerated? Or should we be seeking for an absolute truth in the religious traditions that have guided humanity for centuries and, on finding this truth, live in conformity with it? If we find such a truth, does our moral integrity not demand that we speak honestly—calling this truth what it is and struggling to uphold it against the errors of those who would deny it? If we live moral lives, does our morality not require that we speak up against immorality wherever we see it? Is ethical interaction a matter of recognizing that if each person's morality is to be respected, no absolute morality must be imposed on those who would reject it?

Each normative question explored in this chapter is addressed by the political ideologies of liberalism, conservatism, socialism, fascism, feminism, and environmentalism. Now that we have looked to the history of political theory to find some possible ways of thinking critically about these questions, we can turn to the political ideologies just listed. We will see that these ideologies draw on the historical debates we have examined, but they also base their platforms on an analysis of contemporary problems. These ideologies apply the historical, abstract normative questions we have discussed to an understanding of the present and, in so doing, develop proposals on how best to govern.

## SUMMING UP

- Political theory is a subfield of political science, which studies normative aspects of politics. In Plato's **allegory of the cave,** we see the process of political theorizing—the process of thinking critically and analytically about the ethical issues that constantly arise in our common, political lives. The Socratic method offers us a means of thinking beyond the boundaries of convention.

- Plato and Hobbes provide radically different perspectives on the role of the state. For Plato, the state must promote justice; for Hobbes, the state's justification is found in its ability to increase the chances of humanity's survival.

- Aristotle, Jefferson, Tecumseh, and Mendes are theorists of equality. Whether you think of equality in a manner reminiscent of Aristotle (equal consideration of interest), Jefferson and Tecumseh (equality of rights), or Mendes (equality of participation), you can find in the teachings of these diverse theorists creative ways to think about and argue in favor of equality. Nietzsche and Vonnegut, in contrast, challenge us to think about the intriguing possibility that government promotion of equality can bring harmful consequences.

- States can be organized to facilitate the use of maximum state power or to curb state power. If Machiavelli is correct, the first type of state—the one that maximizes power—is the more desirable state because such a state can better protect its citizens. Madison's theory would suggest otherwise, however. If Madison is correct, institutional protections against maximum state power (for example, separation of power) are necessary if citizens are not to be subject to the tyrannical power of Machiavellian states.

- From antipornography laws to antidrug laws, you can find evidence of state policies designed to shape people's choices. Sometimes it appears as though government were trying to make us more ethical. Should this be a goal of government? On this question John Stuart Mill parts company with fundamentalists such as Taliban members and Patrick J. Buchanan. For Mill, individuals judge best for themselves how to live. For fundamentalists such as Buchanan, governments have an obligation to pass laws that discourage what fundamentalism defines as immoral choices.

## STUDY QUESTIONS

1. What is an allegory?

2. Explain Plato's allegory of the cave: What is the setting, who are the characters, and what major events transpire? What does this allegory teach about the process of gaining enlightenment?

3. How does Plato describe justice? What are the three classes residing in the just society? How does Plato describe injustice?

4. What is the purpose of the state according to Hobbes? How does his answer to this question relate to his understanding of human nature?

5. Discuss Aristotle's concept of equality, and relate this concept to the six-part classification of governments outlined by Aristotle. Of the six types of government, which are proper (and why) and which are improper (and why)?

6. Jefferson, Tecumseh, and Mendes teach the benefits of equality; however, each writer may be viewed as anti-Aristotelian in conceptualizing equality. Explain this anti-Aristotelian element in Jefferson, Tecumseh, and Mendes by noting how Jefferson, Tecumseh, and Mendes separately define and explain equality.

7. How do the works of Nietzsche and Vonnegut offer a critique of equality? How does Nietzsche's discussion of equality relate to his analysis of slave morality?

8. How does Machiavelli describe effective states? How does Madison disagree with Machiavelli?

9. Compare and contrast answers given by Mill and the fundamentalists to the following question: Should governments pass laws to make citizens ethical?

10. Discuss three decrees introduced by the Taliban.

11. Did the U.S. government ever support the Taliban?

# FOLLOWING UP THROUGH
# INTERNET SOURCES

*Ethics and Politics*

- American Civil Liberties Union (http://www.aclu.org). An organization that follows an approach to ethics and politics similar to John Stuart Mill's theory, emphasizing individualism.

- American Center for Law and Justice (http://www.aclj.org). An organization that follows an approach to ethics and politics similar to fundamentalist theory, emphasizing traditional Christian morality.

- Revolutionary Association of the Women of Afghanistan (RAWA) (http://www.rawa.org). Updates, news, and background on RAWA's opposition to Taliban fundamentalist politics.

# 5

# Political Ideologies I

## Liberalism, Conservatism, and Socialism

Chapter 4 discussed some of the ethical questions central to the history of political theory. This subfield of political science, focusing on normative issues, is the study of how thinkers have sought to analyze difficult questions relating to such issues as equality, state power, and justice. This chapter continues the examination of political theory but shifts the focus to an analysis of political ideologies. Political ideologies are pragmatic applications of normative theories. Liberalism, conservatism, socialism, fascism, feminism, and environmentalism are examples of political ideologies. Each ideology draws on the history of political theory and seeks to apply the lessons of this history to the present. Thus, many conservatives look to the eighteenth-century writings of Edmund Burke to find solutions to the problems of immorality in politics, just as many socialists look to the nineteenth-century writings of Marx to find solutions to the problem of class conflict under capitalism.[1]

Ideological debates are fascinating testimony to the diversity of the human imagination. We will examine each ideology by looking at its origins and development.

### LIBERALISM

Liberalism is a term rooted in the Latin word *liber,* which means free. **Liberalism** advocates liberty, another word linguistically related to *liber.*[2] The theoretical roots of liberalism can be found in the seventeenth-century writings of John

Locke and the eighteenth-century works of Adam Smith. These early liberals are known as **classical liberals.** In the nineteenth century, liberalism was modified by theorists such as T. H. Green and Jane Addams. This later form of liberalism is termed **modern liberalism.**[3]

## Classical Liberalism

John Locke (1632–1704) was an English philosopher who is often credited with being the originator of liberalism. Locke lived during a period of political turmoil. In his lifetime, one king was executed and the institution of the monarchy was, in turn, abolished, reinstituted, and restricted in its powers. Despite the disorder surrounding him, Locke's personal life was one of accomplishment and success. He graduated from Oxford in 1656, taught philosophy, and published works on philosophy, politics, religion, and education.[4]

In his *Two Treatises of Government* (1690), Locke argues in favor of limited government and protection for individual rights. He builds a logical case for both propositions by extensively discussing human nature, the state of nature, laws of nature, and the origins of states. Locke's discussion of these topics culminates in his rejection of the political theory of English writer Robert Filmer (1588–1653), a very popular theorist who supported the doctrine of the divine right of kings. According to Filmer, God gives monarchs absolute authority over citizens. As Filmer saw it, citizens were born into subjection to the monarchy and had the duty to be faithful subjects. In contrast, Locke believed that people created governments by freely consenting to those governments and that governments should serve citizens, not hold them in subjection.[5]

Locke begins his liberal theory by examining human nature. He writes of human nature in reference to what he calls a *state of nature.* The state of nature was a period of time prior to the creation of governments. It was a time in human history when women and men lived in small groups and communities, and for Locke it was a very revealing period of human history. What was so important about the state of nature? Individuals living in this state of nature had not been influenced or shaped by laws or political decrees because governments did not yet exist. Consequently, Locke contends, we can look to individuals living in this natural state to see what humans are like at their most natural level. We can look into the state of nature to observe human nature itself.

If you find it unusual that Locke would refer to a long-ago state of nature in his discussion of contemporary politics, recall that Locke was writing before the development of modern geology and evolutionary biology. For Locke, therefore, history did not consist of a very long timeline. In fact, all human history was assumed to consist of a few thousand years. Thus, it made sense to Locke to assume that one could trace back the existing generation to a not-so-remote state of nature.[6]

According to Locke, what we learn from a study of the state of nature is that human nature is characterized by freedom, equality, and reason. Humans are naturally free, born with the duty to submit to no one. That is, in the state of nature there are no natural rulers to whom we owe obedience. On the contrary,

---

**BOX 5.1   Classical and Modern Liberalism**

*Classical Liberalism Teaches That*

- The individual is more important than the state and becomes a citizen of the state only through consent.
- The individual is rational and capable of making his or her own decisions; this makes the individual capable of autonomy and self-government.
- Progress is possible in political affairs, so change is not to be feared.
- State power should be limited.
- Economic inequality is not necessarily bad.
- Economic freedom (individual freedom to make economic choices) is more important than economic equality.

*Modern Liberalism Teaches That*

- Government intervention into individual and social life is sometimes necessary to prevent some individuals from denying freedom to others.
- Liberty should be understood in broad, expansive, positive terms: as the liberty to seek out ways to develop human potential and contribute in a meaningful way to society.
- Economic inequality is to be regarded with suspicion, as a condition likely to undermine the welfare of those who have lower incomes and thus to erode their chances of being free (freedom being defined as expansive liberty).

---

each person is naturally equal to all others, according to Locke. Each person is born equally free and equally in possession of certain natural rights (natural rights are rights we have just by virtue of being human). These rights are an element of our natural human nature. Locke believed that our natural rights include the right to life, liberty, and property.[7] Insofar as each of us is equally human, each of us has an equal claim to enjoy these rights freely.

As you can see, the concepts of natural equality, natural right, and natural freedom are logically connected in Locke's theory. These ideas are also closely related to Locke's concept of natural reason. Humans possess a natural capacity to reason and can use this reason to deduce a set of ethical codes by which to live. Locke calls these ethical principles the *laws of nature*. Notice the logic of his terminology. He has told us that reason is rooted in human nature; therefore, that which is deducible by reason is natural. It is a reflection of and product of nature. Laws of nature are commonsensical codes, ones that are obviously correct to reasoning men and women. Locke identified three specific laws of nature:

- *Preserve yourself.* Take care of yourself and your needs. Work to promote your own survival.

- *Do not harm others.* Do not seek out trouble by starting conflicts and wars. If you seek to harm others, this will put you at risk of being harmed and will thus violate the first law of nature.

- *Help others if possible.* Help others if you can help them without putting yourself at risk.[8]

According to Locke, each of these laws is self-evident to any thinking person. It makes sense to take care of yourself, to avoid creating dangerous situations in which you may die, and to help people who may later remember your good deeds and help you. Through his discussion of the laws of nature, Locke comes to a very important conclusion: People are capable of running their own lives because they have common sense. Government does not make people rational. Government does not make people fit for each other's company. People have within their own natural makeup the capacity for rational existence.

Governments are formed because rational people see that they are useful. In the state of nature, certain annoyances may arise. Individuals pursuing their own preservation and betterment (consistent with the first law of nature) may act in self-serving ways at times. In disputes, individuals may be biased in favor of their own positions. These biases may make it difficult to resolve disputes in an impartial manner that is fair to all parties. In addition, an individual may act contrary to reason. An individual may, on occasion, violate the laws of nature. Lockean theory, in positing that reason is a part of human nature itself, suggests that such acts of irrationality may not be so frequent as to become routine, but even if infrequent, such acts of irrationality create serious problems. If someone violates a law of nature—for example, if someone steals the property belonging to another—in the state of nature, individuals themselves must be the ones to enforce the laws of nature. In the case of the thief, individuals must find the thief, adjudicate any disputes over the thief's actions, and then execute the laws of nature to discourage future theft. These tasks are cumbersome and time-consuming. Would it not be nice to get rid of these annoyances? Would it not be nice to assign someone the task of enforcing the laws of nature so that those individuals who abide by the laws of nature need not do the enforcing? The desire for such a convenient arrangement is the motivation for creating government. Government can do the job of legislating, adjudicating, and enforcing rules in conformity with the laws of nature.[9]

Government is created when individuals come together and give clear, direct, explicit consent to the formation of the state. Only those who freely give their direct consent to the state are considered citizens of this state. That is, no one is forced to leave the state of nature, so no one's natural freedom is violated. In creating the state, Locke explains, citizens give it power, but only limited power. The state has the limited tasks of making civil laws (human-made laws), which uphold the laws of nature. In this way, natural rights are protected and made more secure by the existence of an institution (the state) with the specific responsibility of making and enforcing laws to protect life, liberty, and property. If the state ever exceeds its appropriate authority, it violates these rights. Locke calls such a state tyrannical, authoritarian, and illegitimate. After all, such a state is making war against reason and the laws of nature. Such a state has lost its integrity and is not worthy of obedience.[10]

In this discussion, Locke has made several points central to classical liberalism. First, he has established that *the individual is more important than the state*. The individual is the creator of the state and state authority. Without the explicit consent of individuals, states would not exist. Second, Locke has concluded that *the individual is capable of independence and self-determination.* Freedom is natural. Self-control and self-direction are natural to people because people can figure out the laws of nature. People are capable of making decisions for themselves and living their lives as they please and for the most part can do so without causing problems for others. Third, Locke has established an ideological basis for believing that *progress is possible in human affairs.* Because people are rational, they can take positive steps to improve and reform their societies. Change is not to be feared because rational humans can direct and steer change in ways that will promote well-being. Fourth, the logic of Locke's theory proposes that *state power should be limited.* States make our lives more convenient because they take on the burden of enforcing the laws of nature. This enforcement offers protection to us as we enjoy our natural rights. However, states are not in existence to make us moral, make us rational, or tell us how to live. Each individual, as long as he or she does not violate the laws of nature, should be left alone by the state so that the individual can decide how best to enjoy his or her natural freedom.[11] Thus, with reference to the debates discussed in Chapter 4, classical liberals such as Locke side with Madison over Machiavelli on questions of state power and with Mill over the fundamentalists on issues involving morality and politics.

Classical liberalism was elaborated on by Adam Smith (1723–1790). Smith was a Scottish moral philosopher whose economic writings offer an elaborate justification of both classical liberalism and capitalism. Indeed, in Smith's theory liberalism and capitalism are mutually reinforcing social arrangements. Liberalism and capitalism share a conceptual basis—both are founded on the premise of individual rationality. According to Smith, individuals pursue rational self-interest. In terms of economics, for example, individuals seek to satisfy their interests and needs by exchanging objects (money, goods, and services), and each party to the exchange seeks to better his or her position. If A desires object $X$ and can obtain $X$ on terms more favorable from B than from C, A's rational self-interest will incline A to exchange with B. B is rewarded and C is encouraged to improve his or her objects of exchange in order to benefit from future transactions. Capitalism—an economic arrangement in which individuals exchange their private properties according to their own self-interest with little or no state interference—is thus justified by Smith.[12]

Consider the parallels with Locke. Both writers argue that individuals are rational enough to decide what is best for themselves. Think back to the preceding example: A can figure out how best to meet his or her needs—trade with B, not C. Government is not needed to direct A's decision. Individuals deduce for themselves how to live well.[13] In short, both Smith and Locke agree that because individuals are so very rational, expansive regulatory governments are unnecessary. The departure from Filmer is a radical one; free individuals have no need of absolute monarchies. According to Smith, government's role should be restricted to providing security and public services such as public roads, bridges, and schools.

Under classical liberalism, natural equality does not lead to economic equality. Although Locke and Smith proclaim that individuals are naturally equal (that is, when individuals are born no one has any natural or preordained political authority over any other person), they conclude that individuals living in society will come to be divided into different economic groups. Locke asserts that economic classes of rich and poor will emerge as an economy develops. Locke attributes this class division to the use of money. He outlines his argument by explaining that in the early stages of economic development in any country, individuals tend to barter and exchange perishable objects. One person trades apples for beans, for instance. Because these objects of exchange are perishable, hoarding them for the purpose of stockpiling large quantities is very difficult. As a result, people's possessions remain relatively equal because no one can stockpile and acquire significantly more than anyone else. With economic development, however, societies begin to use money as a medium of exchange. Money does not spoil and can be hoarded. Some individuals can be expected to take advantage of the imperishable quality of money and start to store up increasingly large amounts. In this way, classes of rich and poor begin to appear.

According to Locke, this emergence of economic inequality does *not* create injustice or render the society illegitimate. Why? By using money, individuals imply that they are willingly consenting to the consequences of money. Economic inequality is consented to by rational individuals, whom Locke considers to be perfectly capable of deciding for themselves how to manage their own lives. Notice something very important in Locke's theory: The same logic that is used to justify limited government is used to justify economic inequality—namely, the notion that individuals know best, that individuals should be left alone to make their own choices.[14] If individuals consent to having economic inequality within their communities, then so be it.

Smith also argues that natural equality is not sufficient to produce economic equality. Smith's discussion is very candid.[15] He points out that, at birth, children are basically equal in terms of natural abilities. As children grow up, however, they enter different worlds. One pursues education, and the other does not. Consequently, as adults, they earn different returns on the labors they exchange. Physicians earn more than unskilled laborers. Like Locke, Smith accepts economic inequality. He sees society as making a rational trade-off when it embraces the capitalism in which the physician's and the unskilled laborer's lives are so very different. In return for economic inequality, society gains all the creative output from individuals producing goods and services as diverse as those created by physicians, unskilled laborers, and the other occupational groups comprising the economic sector.

Locke and Smith have arrived at some important conclusions, which go on to serve as basic precepts of classical liberalism's approach to economic policy. First, economic inequality is not necessarily unjust or unfair. Economic inequality is not a violation of natural equality. Instead, it arises from the free choices made by rational individuals sorting out the options available to them. Second, individual freedom is not to be sacrificed for the creation of economic equality. States are not to intrude into the economic interactions of individuals and mandate equal outcomes in terms of salaries, wages, prices, or property values. States are not to become "despotical" in order to give people equal incomes.

Over the years, classical liberalism has appealed to women and men who are drawn to its arguments in favor of keeping government small and limited. Classical liberalism has been praised by many for upholding individual liberty and freedom of choice in politics and economics.

Yet some writers have seen in classical liberalism something terribly flawed—even sinister. Is classical liberalism too comfortable with economic inequality, they ask? Does classical liberalism's concern with limiting state power turn it into an ideology that is insensitive to matters of social justice? Questions such as these led to critical disagreements among liberals. Out of the debate modern liberalism emerged.

## Modern Liberalism

English philosopher T. H. Green (1836–1882) was an advocate of modern liberalism. Modern liberals make the following revisions to liberal theory: They argue in favor of interventionist government and expansive liberty. **Interventionist government** is government that takes a role in regulating economic and social interactions. **Expansive liberty** is the objective sought by the interventionist government.

Green justifies his revised form of liberalism by pointing to what he considers to be the unacceptable implications of classical liberalism. Classical liberalism, he writes, views freedom in terms of freedom from state intervention. Someone is free, as the classical liberals see it, if he or she is not being regulated by or dictated to by government. For Green, this definition of freedom is too narrow. He prefers to define freedom as broader, more expansive, and more inclusive. Green's liberty is freedom to expand the boundaries of human potential and make a creative contribution to society.[16] Modern liberalism's expanded outlook conceptualizes liberty as maximizing individual potential and using that potential to be a contributing member of a society. It is a liberty involving living fully and actively, using one's talents and fulfilling one's potential.

Consider the ramifications of this revised definition of freedom. Think about hypothetical person Mary Smith. Let's say that she is unemployed and living in a homeless shelter. She is free to make personal choices in terms of where to look for a job, what kind of job to seek out, and how many hours to spend at the shelter or looking for employment. Of course, she is also free to make choices on private matters of conscience—whether to believe in God or not, whether to support capital punishment or not, and so on. Despite her freedom of thought and opinion, however, let's say she is demoralized by her poverty and feels defeated and hopeless.

Is person Mary Smith free? From a classical liberal standpoint, because she is not having choices dictated by an intrusive government and is not being interfered with, she is free. She is not happy, but she is free, and classical liberals would expect her to use her rationality to find a path out of this desperate, unhappy existence. From Green's perspective, however, Mary Smith is not free. Her potential to participate as a contributing member of society is being wasted. How very different her life appears, depending on how one defines liberty. If one moves from a classical liberal definition to a modern one, hypothetical person Mary Smith is transformed from a free person into an unfree (oppressed) one.

Green argues that an interventionist state is needed to promote the cause of this new expansive liberty, which is often called "positive liberty." States should not be limited to the protection of individualism (Locke and Smith are incorrect) but should intervene in society on behalf of those whose positive liberty is violated. Modern liberals such as Green supported government action to help those who lacked the resources needed to develop their own potential. Modern liberals have called for government assistance to working women and men who could not, in the absence of laws supporting them, demand that employers provide safe working conditions and increased wages. Modern liberals have also proposed that laws be enacted to regulate the amount of hours that employees could be required to work and that laws be passed to promote regulations to further public health. Did such laws interfere with negative liberty? Of course they did, Green argued. It was government's job to intervene in society and restrict the liberty of one person or group if that person or group happened to be carrying out actions that denied others the opportunities of pursuing the fullest realization of human potential (expansive liberty).[17]

Green's theory provides insights on the logic of modern liberal ideology. First, we can see from Green's writings that modern liberals believe that state intervention can promote and enhance individual freedom. Defining freedom as expansive liberty, modern liberals assert that state regulations protecting health, education, workplace conditions, and generally promoting the well-being of the less powerful sectors of society prevent exploitation and the denial of (positive) liberty. Increased state intervention in society can lead to increased levels of expansive liberty. Second, modern liberals are not as willing as are classical liberals to accept economic inequality. According to modern liberals, someone who is poor may have a difficult time realizing his or her potential; therefore, poverty is an impediment to expansive liberty and should be remedied by laws enacted by the interventionist state. In other words, modern liberals believe in both natural equality and economic equality. Third, modern liberalism promotes the social welfare of society. Indeed, we can see the parallels between Green's ideology and the logic of welfare policies designed to help the marginalized to achieve their potential.

Jane Addams (1860–1935) advanced the cause of modern liberalism in the United States. Addams was a founder of Hull House in Chicago. Hull House was a community center that offered assistance to immigrants, workers, young women, and others in need of social services. In addition, Addams campaigned for legislation to support social welfare programs, women's rights, consumer protection, and economic equality. Specifically, she worked on behalf of the 8-hour workday, the prohibition of child labor, and the right of workers to strike. Addams viewed these reforms in quintessentially modern liberal terms: If the state intervened to help those in need, this would take away the freedom of the powerful to exploit the weak and would therefore replace exploitation with expansive liberty. Thus, when Hull House and/or the state intervened to help the needy, this intervention advanced the welfare and freedom of the powerless.[18] If classical liberals were correct in saying that individual freedom is a wonderful thing, shouldn't the powerless enjoy it as well and thus become empowered? To Addams, the answer was obvious, and the state was needed to act as advocate and enforcer of expansive liberty.

Modern liberalism is reflected in many of the New Deal policies of the Roosevelt era. Franklin Roosevelt (1882–1945) was president from 1933 to 1945. During the years of the Great Depression, his administration established the following federal agencies and/or policies:

- *Federal Emergency Relief Administration.* Provided federal funds to state governments to finance relief programs to help the unemployed.

- *Works Progress Administration (WPA).* Created federally funded jobs for the unemployed.

- *Banking Act of 1935.* Established governmental controls over the banking industry.

- *National Labor Relations Act.* Provided federal government protection for workers who wished to unionize and prohibited employers from a number of antiunion activities.

- *Social Security Act.* Established a federal pension and unemployment insurance system.

Notice the logic of these New Deal programs. Through the New Deal, the state intervened in society to protect individuals from the loss of expansive liberty.

## Classical and Modern Liberalism Today

Think about how disturbing the ideas of Green, Addams, and Roosevelt must have seemed to the classical liberals of the period. Modern liberals were advocating the very outcome that classical liberals fought so fiercely against: big government. Addams's defense of state intervention sounded tyrannical to many classical liberals, just as Filmer's defense of monarchy had sounded authoritarian to Locke in the 1600s. Not surprisingly, classical liberals disassociated themselves from this new liberalism. Many classical liberals started calling themselves *conservatives* because they did not wish to be identified with what was passing for liberalism.

This trend continues. Thus, in the United States many of the Republican Party's positions resemble classical liberalism in criticizing what Republicans see as "big government," although the Republican Party calls itself **conservative.**[19] We can also see classical liberal ideas reflected in the British Conservative Party. For instance, in his 1996 New Year's message, Conservative John Major reminded British citizens that the Conservative Party viewed the individual as more important than the state and believed the state's powers should be limited.[20] The individual should live as free from state intervention as possible, Major asserted. Major himself was merely recapitulating the classical liberal ideology of his predecessor, Conservative and former Prime Minister Margaret Thatcher, who described herself as a Lockean-inspired conservative.[21] In contrast, in the United States the Democratic Party represents itself as the liberal alternative to the Republicans, but its liberalism is for the most part the later version of liberalism—modern liberalism.[22]

Some contemporary classical liberals call themselves **libertarians.** The Libertarian Party of Canada, for example, explicitly identifies itself with classical liberal ideology.[23] Like early classical liberals, libertarians favor strict limits on state action.[24] For example, the Libertarian Party of the United States supports the following policies:

- Legalization of drugs
- Legalization of prostitution
- Abolition of congressional subpoena powers
- Prohibition of censorship of books and movies
- Legalization of suicide
- Abolition of the Central Intelligence Agency (CIA)
- Support for abortion rights
- Support for gay rights[25]

Each of these policies, the Libertarian Party argues, would return power to individuals and take it away from government. Smoking marijuana, watching certain movies, engaging in sex for money—these and other actions should not be forced on anyone, but neither should they be denied as choices to naturally free, rational individuals.

In contrast to the libertarianism just noted, recent platforms of the Democratic Party reflect many ideas of modern liberal ideology. This party's platforms have argued for a government that intervenes in society to help the disadvantaged. It has often accused the Republicans of believing that the state has no responsibility for coming up with solutions to social problems such as poverty; in contrast, the Democratic Party has put forth a vision of using government policy to give citizens more power and equality in their lives. In 1992, for example, the party's platform supported laws to improve workplace safety, to provide universal public health care, to expand public transportation, to support Medicaid, to advance women's rights (including the right to obtain an abortion), and to protect civil rights. Although sharing classical liberalism's concern with freedom of conscience and personal choice (negative liberty) in many areas, the Democratic Party expresses modern liberalism's argument that people are not fully free unless positive liberty exists. Thus, one sees the influence of thinkers such as Green and Addams in the Democratic Party's positions.[26]

Summing up liberalism, we can see how the two forms of liberalism diverge in applying the lessons of political theory to the present. In terms of the debates over the ethical foundations of politics discussed in Chapter 4, classical liberals and modern liberals have very different views on how to leave the cave and achieve enlightenment. Although neither embraces Hobbes's call for authoritarianism, neither accepts Plato's concept of justice either. Classical liberals find justice and fairness in limited states, whereas modern liberals find it in interventionist states. Classical liberalism upholds natural equality but not economic equality, whereas modern liberalism advocates both kinds of equality. Neither form of liberalism is Machiavellian; however, clearly, on questions of state mobilization of power, modern liberals are more supportive of expanding state power than are classical liberals. Both classical and modern liberals advocate individual liberty, and as a result both tend to claim John Stuart Mill as an ally. Thus, we see, both types of liberalism draw on the history of political theory, but they disagree radically in terms of using that history to come up with pragmatic solutions for contemporary problems.

## CONSERVATISM

Conservatism is an ideology that is generally thought of as seeking to *conserve* or preserve some reality. Like liberalism, however, conservative ideology is complex and multidimensional.[27] There is no single form of conservatism. Indeed, we have already discussed one type of conservatism—classical liberal conservatism. Classical liberal conservatives argue for small government and thriving capitalism.

However, a second group of conservatives draw their ideas from the eighteenth-century teachings of Edmund Burke. These Burkean conservatives are called **traditional conservatives,** and their ideology differs dramatically from that of the classical liberal conservatives.

### Traditional Conservativism

British philosopher Edmund Burke (1729–1797) was both a scholar and a member of the British parliament. In both capacities, he opposed what he saw as the errors of liberalism. His most famous work is *Reflections on the Revolution in France* (1790), in which he uses the occasion of the French Revolution to comment on the importance of conserving tradition, authority, and moral values. Upholding traditional values is very important to Burkean conservatives. Indeed, as we will see, it is the driving force of their conservatism.

---

**BOX 5.2  Conservatism: Classical Liberal Conservatism and Burkean Traditional Conservatism**

*Classical Liberal Conservatism*

- Makes the arguments of classical liberalism (see Box 5.1)

*Burkean Traditional Conservatism*

- Asserts that because of the profound human tendency toward irrational behavior, humans need guidance and direction from traditional authorities for society to enjoy peace and stability

- Argues that traditional authorities should pass on long-standing moral teachings through the family, religious institutions, and governmental laws
- Insists that compliance with traditional morality is more important than individual liberty; in other words, people should not have the freedom to violate moral precepts

---

Burke begins his discussion of political ideology with a critical analysis of human nature. He emphasizes two points. First, Burke argues that human nature is not characterized by rational supremacy. Although individuals have the ability to reason, according to Burke, the ability is severely limited. Most people do not reason clearly. On observing history, Burke believes, one sees that people are often irrational, emotional, and unpredictable. Individuals most certainly do *not* possess the kind of reasoning capacity accorded to them by Locke and the classical liberals. In short, Burke explains, individuals are incapable of using their reason to run their own lives smoothly.[28]

Not only are people less rational than liberals believe them to be, but they are also naturally unequal, according to Burke. Burke asserts that differences in natural talents divide people into different levels of abilities. Recall that classical liberals, although never stating that people are equal in terms of all their abilities, argued in favor of the notion that people are naturally equal in terms of possessing natural rights to life, liberty, and property. Traditional conservatives such as Burke seek to emphasize a different point, namely that people naturally differ in political capacity. Some individuals are more capable of ruling than others; some individuals are better suited for political decision making than are others. Thus, society is best arranged when individuals who are natural rulers do the ruling. To call for equality in the laws and to demand that all people be placed on the same (equal) level of decision making would be erroneous, according to Burke.[29]

Moreover, Burke rejects classical liberalism's emphasis on natural rights. Classical liberals are wrong when they contend that the purpose of government is the protection of natural rights. This emphasis on rights confuses citizens, Burke asserts. People hear about having natural rights, and they begin to mistake rights for promises of power. As Burke explains it, if someone is told he or she has a right to something, he or she begins to expect it, begins to demand it. These demands place undue pressures on society, as people clamor for the power to enjoy all that they are told they have a natural right to possess. Thus, Burke concludes, although natural rights technically exist in an abstract, analytical sense, they should not be the basis of government decision making, nor should they be stressed in political speeches and platforms. If governments stress rights, they engender grandiose expectations among the populace.[30]

Government should take care of human needs rather than protect natural rights, according to Burke. Burke believes that humans have a fundamental need for order and control. Given the less than fully rational impulses of human nature, Burke writes, people have a fundamental need for stability, for a guiding direction in their lives to render social existence meaningful and harmonious.[31]

Burke gives long consideration to the implications of these insights. For example, he instructs his readers to ponder the ramifications of limits of reason. If reason is fragile, it is unreliable. Therefore, he concludes, classical liberalism must be wrong on two additional points. First, because reason is weak, it is impossible to deduce ethics (laws of nature) from reason. We need something other than reason to show us right from wrong. In looking to our reason to decide what to believe on euthanasia, for example, we can probably think of rational arguments in its favor. However, we can also probably imagine rational arguments against it.

Yet if reason can justify either position, what good is it for deciding moral questions? This is Burke's point. Reason cannot be considered a trustworthy guide to ethical decision making because reason alone is insufficient to generate ethical clarity. Second, if reason is so very weak, reason is inadequate as the primary or only basis for individual decision making and self-guidance. If an individual cannot depend on reason to deduce any laws of nature, to figure out the consequences of any potential decisions, or to logically select between any possible alternatives, then this individual's reason has left him or her completely helpless.

Something beyond reason is needed. Something solid and trustworthy is needed. Traditional values are needed. Instead of looking to reason for answers, look to the moral guidelines passed down by generations of women and men. These guidelines have comforted humanity, provided solace during periods of crisis, represented moral clarity during times of uncertainty, and offered encouragement and strength during times of ethical confusion. Which sounds more reliable, traditional conservatives ask, trying to rationally deduce your life from scratch as you go along or learning how to live well by following the ethical rules that have served humanity across the ages?

From the standpoint of political ideology, Burke has told us something very important. Traditional conservatives do not glorify traditional values just to be "old fashioned." They challenge us to conserve traditional morality because without traditional morality, we lose our connection with ethical certainty. Traditional values teach us right from wrong in a way that reason, as we saw earlier, cannot. Reason can only confuse us by suggesting that there are no moral absolutes (because any side of any ethical dilemma can be made to look rational).

We are wise, Burkeans believe, if we come to know the difference between trends and traditional moral values. A trend is something new and different, such as a fashion or a fad. Traditional moral values, in contrast, are based on what endures after fads are long forgotten. Morality should not be like fashion. It should not go out of style just because it is old. Indeed, the older the moral teachings, Burke argues, the more trustworthy those teachings tend to be. Hence, Burkeans are conservatives in a very literal sense, seeking to preserve older, tradition-oriented moralities, not replace them with something new in the name of progress.[32]

Civil institutions should teach traditional morality, according to Burke. Civil institutions are nongovernment organizations within society. Examples include families and religious institutions. By passing along long-standing moral values from one generation to the next, civil institutions prepare individuals to live peacefully and orderly. When civil institutions are operating in this manner, society functions smoothly, without the violence and disruption caused by upheavals such as the French Revolution. Governments are to support civil institutions by providing a secure setting in which they can operate. In protecting and nourishing these institutions, governments become part of a larger mission, participating in the grand process whereby each generation connects itself to those who came before, as the teachings of the past are conserved.[33]

Each of these points leads Burke to another conclusion. Morality is more important than unencumbered individual freedom. Individual freedom must be compromised so that individuals conform to the teachings of traditional values.

Freedom should not include the freedom to act in an immoral manner. People should not insist on the freedom to act out any impulse or desire. Thus, traditional conservatives believe in freedom, but freedom with boundaries.[34] It is not to someone's benefit, for example, to go out and do whatever is pleasing but destructive. It is not your true need to indulge your irrational and impulsive self. That would be comparable to living so boundlessly that you destroy yourself.

In the nineteenth century, English Cardinal John Henry Newman expressed this idea by contrasting good uses of liberty with bad ones. With regard to freedom of opinion, for example, Cardinal Newman explained that proper uses of liberty upheld morality, whereas improper exercises of liberty violated moral traditions.[35] Bad or improper liberty recognized no rules. For example, contemporary traditional conservatives might argue that pornography is a form of such liberty. Someone who publishes pornography and claims that doing so is a part of freedom of the press is taking freedom too far; he or she is exercising liberty of choice when he or she should be acknowledging traditional moral proscriptions against such behavior.

Thus, traditional conservatives favor freedom limited by an acknowledgment of the duty to live in compliance with goodness. Burke describes the society he favors in a revealing passage from *Reflections on the Revolution in France*. In the good society, we live according to the laws of God, as passed from one generation to the next by traditional authorities.[36]

## Traditional Conservatism Today

Contemporary traditional conservatives share Burke's goal of elevating the moral lives of their societies. For example, one can look to the Conservative party of Norway and find Burkean concerns expressed throughout the party's program. In 1992, the Conservative party program expressed support for Christian values and committed itself to the preservation of the moral values of the country. Like Burke, the party proclaimed that individuals require the guidance provided by the teachings of traditional institutions. Very significantly, the party rejected the classical liberal conservative call for limited government. The state's role should not be minimal, because the state's purpose is to support strong civil institutions that can provide the moral certainties needed by Norway's citizens.[37]

In contemporary U.S. politics, traditional conservative ideology has many proponents. Burkean ideology is reflected in conservative writer William Bennett's concern over the weakening of civil institutions, because such institutions are vital, Bennett believes, to the moral well-being of any society.[38] Burkean ideals are also articulated in many antiabortion arguments made in recent years by Republicans such as Robert K. Dornan of California.[39]

Alan L. Keyes organized his 2000 Republican presidential bid around antiabortion politics and traditional conservatism.[40] The Family Research Council (FRC) has also maintained a Burkean conservative posture in U.S. political debates in recent years. FRC members closely monitor candidates for office and assess their degree of compliance with what the group considers to be pro-family positions. The FRC defines "pro-family" in ways it defends as traditional; specifically, the FRC opposes gay civil rights, criticizes cohabitation by unmarried people, opposes no-fault divorce, and supports the view that children should be cared for by mothers, not commercial day care centers.[41]

Yet perhaps no group is more closely associated with traditional conservatism in U.S. politics than is the Christian Coalition. Formed in 1988, largely through the efforts of television minister Pat Robertson and Ralph Reed, the Christian Coalition has affiliates in all 50 states. The Christian Coalition has embraced the following positions:

- Antiabortion policy
- Opposition to legalization of gay rights, such as gay marriage
- Support for school prayer
- Opposition to sex education in the public schools
- Opposition to sidewalk sales of pornography

Notice the parallels with Burkean ideals. Individual freedom, it is believed, should be curtailed if that freedom veers into areas in which ethical taboos are violated.[42] Indeed, in a 1995 survey of the Christian Coalition, more than 60 percent of the Coalition's members stated that immorality was the most serious problem in the United States. To see the Christian Coalition's present strategies, consult http://www.cc.org.[43]

Ironically, if by immorality one means support for individual choice on matters of abortion and sexuality, one of the greatest contributors to immorality is arguably conservatism itself—classical liberal conservatism, to be more specific. Lockeans have been in the forefront of arguing that individuals are the best judges in matters pertaining to their own lives. Because many Lockeans have called themselves *conservatives* since the late 1800s, they and the Burkeans share an ideological label but not much else. As a result, conservative ideology is deeply divided, with classical liberal conservatives seeking to minimize state actions and traditional conservatives seeking to use the state's authority to make society more moral.[44] Classical liberals have been trying to convince individuals to be self-reliant, whereas Burkeans have been trying to convince people to submit to traditional authority. Not surprisingly, conservatives often come into conflict, as we see on examination of some recent controversies in conservative political ideology.

## Traditional Conservatism and Classical Liberal Conservatism in Conflict

Tensions between traditional conservatives and classical liberal conservatives have recently developed over issues relating to governmental regulation, the Contract with America, financial contributions to the 1996 Dole and 2000 George W. Bush presidential campaigns, Republican relations with conservative leader Barry Goldwater, and conservative responses to 9/11. With respect to the first controversy, conservatives split over the issue of governmental regulation of the pharmaceutical industry.

Conservatives like the ones shown here display Burkean concerns over what they see as the loss of traditional morality. How would classical liberal conservatives view their protests?

In 1995, the House Commerce Committee considered measures to ease such regulations. Doing so would be consistent with classical liberal conservative arguments in favor of limited government. Indeed, Republican Thomas Bliley, Jr., chair of the committee, and Republican Speaker of the House Newt Gingrich made stirring speeches in support of reducing regulations and fighting to end "big government." However, in 1995, other conservatives began pressuring the House Commerce Committee to *expand* federal regulation of drug companies in one particular area; these conservatives wanted massive regulations covering a drug called RU-486. This drug can be taken orally and can be used to induce abortions. Americans United for Life, a conservative pro-life group, lobbied vigorously for the committee to require extensive testing of the drug. They hoped that federal regulations in the form of innumerable testing and review procedures would effectively stall the pharmaceutical industry's plans to market RU-486. Here, classical liberal conservative goals of stripping government of excess power came into direct opposition to traditional conservative objectives of upholding traditional pro-life morality.[45]

Conservative ideology also became an arena of conflict and dissent during debates over the conservative-sponsored Contract with America. The Contract with America was put forward in Congress in 1995 as a means of reducing government spending and controlling taxes. Many conservatives believed that these two measures would spur economic growth and contribute to the country's financial strength. This made perfect sense from a Lockean/Smithian perspective. After all, who better than classical liberal conservatives can understand the need to work to create a society in which women and men pursue their rational self-interest without the meddlesome intrusions of an overspending government supported by excessive taxation?[46] However, as part of Contract with America's efforts to cut government spending, some conservatives proposed cutting the welfare benefits of children of single mothers as well as cutting payments to mothers who had additional children while on welfare. These provisions caused alarm among a number of traditional conservatives, who feared that such cuts would encourage women to have abortions. Indeed, some traditional-minded conservatives pronounced the Contract with America immoral.[47] Again, we see the complexity of conservative ideology: A conservative drawn to the ideology by Locke's arguments may have major conflicts with a conservative who identifies with Burke.

Bob Dole's 1996 presidential campaign was beset by conflicts involving contradictory pressures from classical liberal conservatives and traditional ones. In 1995, the Dole campaign received a contribution from a conservative group known as the Log Cabin Republicans (LCR). The Log Cabin Republicans support the Lockean/Smithian principles of capitalist economics and small government. They are also gay activists. To the LCR, government has no more business regulating sex lives than it does regulating business. Members of this organization liked Dole's commitment to rolling back taxes and government programs. Contributing to his campaign seemed rational and commonsensical. However, to some traditional conservatives, it seemed unacceptable for the Republican nominee for the presidency to be affiliated with a gay rights group. Dole's campaign returned the donation out of fear of antagonizing conservatives more Burkean than Lockean on the issue of gay rights; however, Dole later criticized his staff's decision to return the money. Dole attempted to strike a compromise between the Log Cabin conservatives and the traditional conservatives such as Gary Bauer, who attacked what he saw as Dole's indecisive wavering on an issue involving moral absolutes. In the 2000 presidential campaign of George W. Bush, during the Republican primaries the Log Cabin Republicans criticized Bush for being too much of a traditional conservative. The group accused him of being dominated by the Burkean wing of the Republican Party and insensitive to the Lockeans who were also depending on him for conservative representation. Responding to the criticism, Bush met with LCR members, and although the two sides continued to disagree on gay civil rights, LCR decided to endorse Bush. Indeed, LCR paid for $250,000 in pro-Bush radio ads to help him defeat Al Gore. In the Bush administration, the president has at times distanced himself from religious traditional conservatives, as was true when he rejected the claims made by Jerry Falwell and Pat Robertson that America's liberal sins (e.g., tolerating feminism, homosexuality, and abortion) had brought the

9/11 attacks on the country. Very quickly, President Bush made it clear that he regarded bin Laden and Al Qaeda—not liberalism—as the culpable parties.[48]

Conservative criticism of Dole and President Bush may be somewhat surprising, but recent conservative attacks on another Republican leader have been downright shocking to some observers. One might think that if anyone could earn immunity from conservative reproach, the late Barry Goldwater would have been that person. Goldwater was the Republican nominee for the presidency in 1964. He was considered so conservative that many mainstream commentators charged him with extremism. Goldwater took it as a compliment. Recently, however, Goldwater was called a traitor by a number of fellow Republicans. He provoked their ire by stating that the genuinely conservative position on abortion is the pro-choice one, and that the genuinely conservative position on gay issues is the pro-gay rights one. Goldwater's conservatism is clearly the conservatism of Locke and Smith. It is similar to the conservatism of Republican Christine Todd Whitman, who is pro-choice, pro-gay rights, and pro-affirmative action but at odds with the ideology of the Christian Coalition and the FRC.[49]

As these examples illustrate, traditional conservatives often disagree with their classical liberal counterparts as much as they disagree with modern liberals. Traditional conservatives challenge both classical liberals and modern liberals to learn from the allegory of the cave and avoid the misleading shadows represented by an erroneous faith in reason, equality, and unrestrained individualism. Traditional conservatives share with Plato a belief that the well-ordered society is one in which each group learns its place and fulfills its natural calling, even though this implies that groups do not exist on a level of natural equality. In fact, traditional conservatives reject the concept of natural equality for many of the reasons conveyed in Vonnegut's fictional account in "Harrison Bergeron." A society that tries to make people equal simply ends up pushing everybody down to the lowest level. Traditional conservatives are closer to fundamentalism than John Stuart Mill on the matter of government and morality. Mill's freewheeling tolerance would be disastrous for a society of irrational and impulsive individuals, traditionalists contend. Finally, although traditional conservatives abhor Machiavellian calls for abandoning morality in favor of expediency, they do believe in empowering states so that states are effective at safeguarding the well-being of civil institutions. They would view with alarm any measure to weaken state power through excessive Madisonian checks and balances, if such weakening left the state powerless to support their pro-family and pro-morality measures.

## SOCIALISM

The word **socialism,** coined in the early 1800s, referred to an ideology arguing that citizens are best served by policies focused on meeting the basic needs of the *entire* society rather than on serving the needs of individuals *as individuals*. From its inception, socialism has been critical of competing ideologies (such as classical liberalism) that rank individualism above the common good in terms of political priorities. Henri de Saint-Simon (1760–1825), Robert Owen (1771–1859), and Charles Fourier (1772–1837) were early socialists who taught that competitive individualist societies destroyed the possibility of collective harmony. Individuals are capable of living cooperatively, they insisted, and the socialist society would prove it.[50] Saint-Simon envisioned socialism as a large, complex social system in which scientific planners would coordinate economic activity to ensure that goods were produced in exactly the proper quantity and distributed evenly throughout society so that neither waste nor shortages occurred. Owen and Fourier believed in small self-sufficient cooperative societies in which socialism consisted of living in such a manner that all community members shared both the responsibility of laboring and the wealth produced by it.

Although the term *socialism* is of recent origin, the roots of socialist ideology are ancient and varied. You can find some of the oldest inspirations for socialist ideas in the Judeo-Christian tradition.[51] In the Book of Deuteronomy, for example, you can read in Chapter 15 about the year of release from debt. In this chapter, God commands that after every 7 years, debts be forgiven and property be given to any poor living within the community of God's people. If someone resists following these commandments, preferring to keep his or her individual property and/or insisting that any debts owed to him or her be paid, God's response is unambiguous. Resistance to this release of debt is considered an act of sin. Likewise, in the Book of Acts, in Chapters 4 and 5, you can read about early Christians selling their individual possessions and then contributing the proceeds to a common stock from which all lived. When one individual, Ananias, decided to hold back some of his property for himself rather than contributing to the common stock, he fell dead. Similarly, you can look into the First Book of Timothy and find the apostle counseling against the pursuit of self-gratification and worldly riches as meaningless but powerful distractions that tempt women and men from the more noble lives of righteousness, prayer, and good deeds.

Although biblical teachings are subject to as many interpretations as there are readers, you can see how socialist-oriented readers find insight in these passages. A recurring theme emerges in these passages: Individual needs may be called on to be sacrificed for the well-being of all. Consider, for example, how a Lockean might fare during the year of the release. A Lockean, seeing him- or herself as an autonomous individual, would likely argue that individuals have the natural right to be self-governing and decide for themselves how to dispose of their properties. A Lockean would not find economic inequality to be intrinsically problematic. Both a classical liberal conservative and a modern liberal would likely agree that Ananias has the right to make his own decisions about holding on to his personal possessions. Yet the biblical teachings in the passages just cited lead to outcomes different from those sanctioned by liberal and conservative ideas. In these passages, social obligations prevail over individual desires. The duties to God and God's people are more important than the preferences of any single individual.[52]

---

**BOX 5.3**   **Socialism: Marxism–Leninism and Social Democracy**

| *Marxism–Leninism Teaches That* | *Social Democracy Teaches That* |
|---|---|
| <ul><li>Society needs a centralized, vanguard party and does not need multiparty competition through peaceful, lawful political participation.</li><li>Imperialism has shaped the development of capitalism and altered the terms of revolutionary struggle from those outlined by Marx; namely, revolutions are more likely in less developed capitalist economies, contrary to Marx's theory.</li></ul> | <ul><li>Socialism and democracy are consistent with each other.</li><li>Economic oppression is no less harmful than political oppression, and therefore government should promote economic equality no less than political equality.</li><li>Socialism should be brought about through peaceful, lawful, democratic means.</li></ul> |

---

## Marxism

The contributions to socialist ideology made by German theorist Karl Marx (1818–1883) are so vast and complex that his theory of socialism has come to be known specifically as Marxism. Marx was well versed in political theory and completed a doctorate in classical Greek philosophy from the University of Berlin in 1841.[53] Marx was greatly influenced by German philosopher Georg W. F. Hegel (1770–1831), who believed that historical development takes place through a series of dramatic changes producing increasingly comprehensive systems of knowledge. With each epoch of historical development, new and old ideas clash and compete. New ways of thinking and conceptualizing reality emerge from the conflict, according to Hegel. One finds in Marx's work many parallels with Hegel, not the least of which is the notion that history moves forward from the push and pull of conflict and that each new period of history is a creative response to what has gone before. As abstract as this sounds, these ideas are important in providing glimpses of some of the most concrete dimensions of Marx's theory. For example, Hegelian influences are discernible in Marx's understanding of class conflict and social change.[54]

Although Marx is known as a socialist, the majority of his writings focus on analyzing capitalism. This is not surprising when one realizes that Marx lived under a capitalist system and, as a student of politics, wrote primarily about what he could observe. With his friend and collaborator Frederich Engels (1820–1895), Marx published *The Communist Manifesto* in 1848. In this and other works, Marx analyzed many facets of capitalist society. The better one understands capitalism, Marx contends, the more clearly one sees the rational basis for socialism.

How does Marx analyze capitalism? He begins by noting that capitalism is an economic system in which most people come to be members of one of two large classes. This division of people into two basic classes contrasts with the more complex class systems of antiquity and feudalism, in which numerous classes existed.[55]

The two prominent classes under capitalism are the proletariat and the bourgeoisie. The proletariat is the class that lives primarily by selling its labor power (laboring ability) for a wage. The bourgeoisie is the class that lives primarily by purchasing the labor power of others and using this labor to operate the factories and businesses owned by the bourgeoisie. Thus, generally, the proletariat consists of people who work for wages and the bourgeoisie consists of people who own businesses and hire employees. Very importantly, Marx was aware that many members of the bourgeoisie also work; indeed, business owners often have interminable workdays and remain at the office longer than any single employee. However, if an individual's economic position is premised on the ability to hire workers and run a business through the employees' labor, then this individual is a member of the bourgeoisie. At the same time, a member of the proletariat might supplement his or her income by taking in boarders, growing his or her own food, and so forth. If, however, an individual needs his or her wage in order to live, then the individual is a member of the proletariat.[56]

Notice what is absent from Marx's discussion of class. He has not defined class in terms of income levels. He has not come up with a formula for determining how much money one needs in order to qualify as rich or poor. Rather, he has defined class in terms of *functions*. If person A functions in society by selling her labor power in return for a wage, she is a member of the proletariat, regardless of how high or low her wage may be. In contrast, if she functions as someone who operates a factory by employing wage laborers, she is a member of the bourgeoisie, whatever her income level. This point is crucial to remember because when Marx later speaks of abolishing class, it is necessary to remember how he defines class. Because he does not define class in terms of income levels, he does not define the abolition of class in terms of eradicating income differentials.

According to Marx, under capitalism conflict between the bourgeoisie and the proletariat is inevitable. This is the case because both classes are rational. Both pursue what is in their respective interests. Consequently, the bourgeoisie and proletariat clash over the price of wage labor. It is in the interest of the bourgeoisie to lower the price of labor, whereas it is in the interest of the proletariat to raise it. Neither class can afford to abandon its interests, according to Marx. For example, if a capitalist pays a higher wage than that paid by rival capitalists, the generous capitalist will be unable to compete with his or her peers and will be ruined. Thus, the rational capitalist will pay subsistence wages to the employees. Subsistence wages are defined by Marx as the lowest possible wage for inducing sufficient numbers of capable workers to fill job openings. That is, the rational capitalist will pay only so much as he or she must in order to recruit qualified workers to come into the business and do the jobs. All capitalists will be motivated to compete successfully with their peers, so each will be inclined to pay subsistence-level wages. For the proletariat, of course, this means that every possible employer is operating according to an identical logic, one that is not exactly favorable to the proletariat.

Moreover, unless a capitalist holds back a part of the value created by employees through their labor, the capitalist will have nothing for him- or herself. Therefore, the capitalist keeps some of the value created by workers; this value is called *surplus value* (it exists as a surplus above and beyond what is returned to the workers in the form of wages) or profit. Yet the existence of profit is testimony to the fact that the workers have created a value in excess of that paid to them in wages. They are creating more worth than the amount reflected in their paychecks, and because their existence depends on their ability to earn these paychecks, their lives are insecure as long as wages are meager. As you can see from just this short discussion, both proletarians and capitalists live or die by the decisions surrounding the price of wages.

According to Marx, the state plays an important role in preventing the conflict between the classes from erupting into daily riots and rebellions. If workers rise up and attempt to take over a factory and demand higher wages, the state's law enforcement officers will suppress their rebellion. The state's judicial officers will prosecute, and the state's legislative officials may even respond by writing new laws to prevent future rebellions. In short, the state will work to prevent class conflict by enforcing law and order, which, under capitalism, indirectly supports the bourgeoisie's continued pursuit of profit through the payment of subsistence wages to workers. Logically, Marx points out, one can see that the class that benefits most from the status quo also gains most from the state's protection of the status quo.[57]

For Marx, however, capitalism is an entire social system. It involves more than states, wages, and profits. Capitalism also includes certain ways of thinking about the world and psychologically responding to it. For example, Marx believed that life under capitalism became an emotional ordeal for many proletarians/workers. *Alienation* is a term he used to describe the emotional, cognitive, and psychological damage done to the proletariat by capitalism. Alienation means loss. According to Marx, workers are vulnerable to different kinds of alienation. One type of alienation is alienation from the self. A worker alienated from his or her self has lost a sense of self-awareness and identity. Such a worker may go through the workday "on automatic pilot," barely aware of him- or herself as an individual with a mind, with thoughts, with a history, with feelings. Workers such as this live through the day, but they do not *experience* the day any more than the machines in the factories experience it. Proletarians are also likely to suffer alienation from the work process, from other workers, and from society, according to Marx. The creative, productive, and collaborative dimensions of working and living are lost to the proletarian, who has become almost as lifeless as the tools he or she uses. Not only has life become joyless, but the alienated worker does not even know any more that it is not supposed to be this way.[58]

Just as capitalism affects the psyche, it also influences the intellect. Marx asserted that intellectual systems (ideologies, for example) are shaped by the political and economic systems in which they arise. In other words, the existence of capitalism makes some ideas useful and, therefore, renders them means of obtaining and holding power.[59] As Marx put it, each political–economic system needs its own ideology to justify itself as moral and "natural." In a capitalist society, the prevailing ideology will be one that proclaims private property as natural (because the bourgeoisie can use this idea to help legitimize its class power). The prevailing ideology will also uphold individual freedom as a fundamental right. The idea of individual freedom is useful to the bourgeoisie because it allows the bourgeoisie to argue that making profit is simply an element of individual freedom. In addition, the bourgeoisie can always justify paying the proletarians less than the value created by the proletarians by proclaiming that if the proletarians do not like working for them, the proletarians have the individual freedom to quit and find other jobs. That is, the ideology of individual freedom is used to distract attention away from questions about fairness, social needs, and basic economic equality. Ideology is used to justify the economic dominance of the bourgeoisie.[60]

As a student of Hegel, Marx saw in all these dimensions of capitalism evidence of tension and strain, but also eventual progress. On the one hand, capitalism is inherently contradictory, according to Marx, and thus doomed to fall apart as a consequence of its own clashing pressures. For example, as capitalists pursue their self-interest and pay workers subsistence wages, they set in motion a logic whereby most people (wage earners) are paid so little that they cannot purchase the goods and services produced by capitalism itself. *Underconsumption* is a danger and forces capitalists to compete for foreign markets.[61] On the other hand, capitalism is much more than a system in which contradictory forces threaten disorder and chaos. Capitalism, according to Marx, is also progressive. It has given humanity many wonderful gifts and has inspired innumerable positive developments. Has Marx begun to contradict himself in praising capitalism like this? Absolutely not, he assures his readers; he is merely viewing capitalism in all its complexity.

What is positive and beneficial about capitalism? In promoting the pursuit of self-interest (for example, high profits for the bourgeoisie), capitalism pushes people to be extremely competitive. Out of this competition come technological advances, scientific discoveries, mechanical inventions, and productive innovations, all of which contribute to the creation of an abundance of goods and services. Every capitalist is driven to discover the most efficient way to produce the best-selling, most appealing product in order to become the next billionaire. This competitive drive for profits encourages the rise of expanding cities, huge corporations, and centralized banking, each of which facilitates producing and selling at unprecedented levels by bringing workers, know-how, technology, and money together in close proximity for maximum use. The drive for profits further stimulates international trade and cross-cultural contact, as the bourgeoisie traverse the globe in order to sell more goods. Society becomes more worldly and sophisticated, as urban centers and international communications expose people to ways of living and thinking beyond those taught by their own local traditions. Old-fashioned loyalties weaken; traditional notions of religion, family life, relations between men and women, and the like begin to die out because capitalism forces people to adjust to technological innovations and adapt to incredibly diverse ways of interacting with people and products. Marx applauds these developments as spectacular by-products of economic development.[62]

The challenge of socialism, according to Marx, is to find a way to build on the positive features of capitalism while eradicating the negative ones. Marx's solution is as follows: The socialist society will abolish class and thereby end the conflict between the bourgeoisie and proletariat, and it will distribute the abundant resources created by capitalism in a way that addresses social needs. Abolishing class entails ending the distinction between selling and purchasing labor power. That is, under socialism, all able-bodied adults will work and share ownership of the goods and services produced. These goods and services will be publicly managed, at first by state officials and later by local citizens. Public managers will centrally plan how goods and services will be produced and managed, Marx argues, so that they can examine the society as a whole and see what is needed, where it is needed, and how much is needed in order to most efficiently fulfill the needs of all. Credit, communications, manufacturing, transportation, agriculture, and other crucial industries will be operated and monitored by these state planners so that no individual can sabotage the collective good by demanding that his or her individual rights and needs take priority over the needs of society. Once class distinctions have been completely eradicated (and all people recognize that their interest is in working to ensure the welfare of the society as a whole), monitoring by state planners will be unnecessary and the state, no longer having any function to serve, will fall into disuse, according to Marx.[63]

Meanwhile, capitalism has created so much abundance that state planners have a wealth of goods and services to distribute to the population. Moreover, capitalism has done such a wonderful job of inspiring inventions and discoveries that the socialist society possesses the technological skill to continue producing goods and services for the fulfillment of future needs. In addition, by forcing people to give up old-fashioned and narrow-minded traditions, capitalism has prepared individuals to be forward-looking in their thinking and capable of adjusting to the new requirements of the socialist society.

Implicit in Marx's discussion is the notion that capitalism is an important precursor of socialism. Indeed, in Marx's discussion of the transition to socialism, he contends that capitalism is a significant contributing element to the formation of socialism. Although he explored the *possibility* of organizing socialism in societies that had not already developed capitalism, Marx emphasized throughout his writings the fact that socialism will construct itself in relation to a preexisting capitalism. For example, in explaining his theory of how socialism will be brought into being, Marx writes that violent revolution will be necessary for destroying capitalism and instituting socialism in most societies. He writes of the socialist revolution as a majoritarian movement, involving massive numbers of workers. Notice the assumption behind this statement: Capitalism is needed because it creates an economic structure in which the majority of people *are* wage laborers. In addition, Marx argues, in some societies—Great Britain and the United States—peaceful organizing for socialism may work to bring socialists to power. Here, the capitalist democratic structures of society are so well developed that socialists may be capable of campaigning openly for socialism without suffering violent repression and being forced to fight for socialism outside the legal structures. Note, again, however, how the presence of capitalism is presented as a variable conducive to the eventual movement toward socialism.[64]

Marx followed the political events of his time closely, and he found what he took to be many encouraging signs pointing to the soundness of socialist ideology. He welcomed the northern victory in the U.S. Civil War as a progressive historical development.[65] He participated in the International Workingmen's Association, in which French, Swiss, Polish, English, Italian, and German workers organized in opposition to the bourgeoisie.[66] Marx was ecstatic when, toward the end of his life, he saw his writings gaining influence in Russia.[67]

Marx's ideological legacy is a complex one. Since Marx's death in 1883, socialists have disagreed about the implications of Marx's theories. They have also disagreed about how best to advance socialism. Marxism–Leninism and social democracy are two forms of post-Marx socialism that have greatly influenced ideological debates.

## Marxism–Leninism

**Marxism–Leninism** is a form of socialism articulated by Russian theorist and revolutionary Vladimir Iylich Ulyanov, whose revolutionary name was Lenin (1870–1924). Lenin took certain ideas from Marx and added some of his own to create Marxism–Leninism, often referred to as communist ideology. Lenin's life was fascinating and dangerous. He was exiled in 1895 to Siberia for his opposition to the Russian czar, worked with socialists in western Europe prior to World War I, and returned to Russia during World War I to assume leadership of the Bolshevik revolution, which led to the establishment of the Soviet Union. As the Soviet Union's first leader, Lenin worked toward socialism (as he defined it) by enacting policies whereby the state assumed extensive control over industry and by creating a political framework of one-party government.

Marxist–Leninist ideology argues that socialists should organize their struggle against capitalism by creating a vanguard party to lead the revolution against capitalism. The Marxist–Leninist party is to serve as the vanguard, or leader, of the proletariat, according to Lenin. Lenin envisioned the vanguard party as highly structured and centralized, with each member scrupulously upholding the party's policies.[68] To make sense of Lenin's ideas on the party, it is necessary to realize that he formulated his theory with pragmatic considerations in mind. Like Marx, Lenin believed that working-class movements would be susceptible to repression by hostile governments. To survive this repression, Lenin asserted that socialists needed to be united among themselves and sufficiently organized to endure long periods of antisocialist activity. Not only was the tightly controlled vanguard party designed to survive governmental attacks, but it was also organized to instruct and teach. Party leaders were to educate workers in the intricacies of socialist ideology and guide them through a learning process whereby they would come to understand the necessity of overthrowing capitalism through violent revolution. The vanguard party was a necessary element in the process of socialist organizing, for it brought to the revolutionary movement the expertise, discipline, and leadership needed to create socialism, according to Lenin.[69]

Once the revolution was successful, according to Lenin, the vanguard party would manage society in the interest of the workers. The party would suppress any opposition forces, as well as manage the economy.[70] In these arguments, we find elements of the ideological basis for the repression of potential opposition forces carried out by the former Soviet Union.

Marxist–Leninist socialism is also associated with the theoretical concept of *imperialism*. Lenin's concept of imperialism is important in explaining two ways in which Lenin developed socialist theory beyond Marx's original contributions. First, Lenin used the concept of imperialism to explain why older capitalist societies had survived into the 1900s, despite Marx's arguments that they were beset by internal contradictions. Second, Lenin's theory of imperialism provided an explanation for why the prospects of socialist revolution in societies lacking capitalist traditions were so promising.

Lenin defined imperialism as a stage of capitalism. Specifically, it is a stage at which capitalists begin to export capital and use this capital to build industries abroad. In searching out a site for new industries, capitalists choose a location most conducive to their interests (making large profits). A location in a developing country in which cheap labor is abundant is especially attractive to capitalists. Capitalists go into this location, hire employees from the local pool of low-cost labor, and make enormous profits. Profits are brought back to the capitalists' home country, where the capitalists spend lavishly. Refunneling of this money into the home economy spurs economic growth and development, the benefits of which raise the standard of living of all groups. As living standards improve, even the proletariat of the home country notice a higher quality of life. This point is crucial, according to Lenin, because it means that the workers in the home country to some extent become middle class and status quo–oriented in their outlooks. Such workers lack revolutionary zeal and see themselves as beneficiaries of capitalism. Imperialism thus boosts the well-being of capitalist societies and enables them to fend off, at least temporarily, the destructive consequences of their own internal contradictions.

Workers in the foreign country, however, are suffering. Their low wages make the capitalists superrich, Lenin argues. Such workers have an interest in opposing capitalism. These workers, living in the country sought out by the imperialist-minded capitalists, possess a revolutionary potential. Logically, therefore, Lenin saw revolutionary possibilities in a developing society—a society into which capital had been invested but that had not yet developed long-standing capitalist processes in which the proletariat had become complacent as a result of comparatively high living standards.[71]

Lenin's theory was appealing to some socialists who hoped to organize socialist movements in developing countries. For example, Mao Zedong (1893–1976) could find in Lenin's work an ideological rationale for socialist revolution in China, despite the fact that China was not a capitalist society and lacked the sizable proletariat discussed by Marx in Marx's theory of revolution. Mao became communist leader of the People's Republic of China in 1949 and governed until his death in 1976.[72]

## Social Democracy

**Social democrats** (also known as *democratic socialists*) reject Marxism–Leninism. They see Marxism–Leninism's advocacy of a vanguard party as authoritarian. Social democrats believe in integrating socialism and democracy. Unlike

Marxist–Leninists, social democrats support peaceful, legal efforts to work toward socialism, and they believe in multiparty competition and civil liberties. They view socialism as a way of organizing society so that all groups are guaranteed some level of social well-being and economic security. They propose to distribute society's riches among all sectors of the population by enacting public policies very similar to those advocated by modern liberalism. Indeed, social democrats support extensive welfare programs. Such programs, they contend, can promote economic self-determination, just as democracy promotes political self-determination.[73] Historically a party of social democracy, the Labour Party of Great Britain has moved toward liberalism under the leadership of centrist Labour leaders such as Tony Blair. In fact, the party's 1997 general election program omitted the word *socialism* altogether.[74]

The Finnish Social Democratic Party embraces democracy as well as economic policies designed to improve the social and economic positions of workers. The party rejects communism (Marxism–Leninism) in favor of free elections. It calls for economic reforms such as shorter workdays, flexible working hours, low interest rates, and full employment.[75] In like fashion, the party of Catalonia's socialists specifically links socialism and democracy together and views the two as mutually reinforcing means of creating conditions of both fairness and liberty.[76]

Social democrats take from socialism a commitment to serving the needs of the entire society. They share Marx's dissatisfaction with the inequities in the bourgeoisie–proletariat relationship whereby the bourgeoisie ends up with profit while the proletariat suffers alienation and makes subsistence wages. These socialists have a vision that can be traced back to the story of the year of the release of debts in the Book of Deuteronomy. Property should be redistributed so that it is shared by all, they argue. As the Catalonian Social Democratic Party puts it, a socialist society is one in which nobody sees his or her basic needs overlooked.[77]

What would democratic socialism look like in the United States? The Socialist Party of America believes it would include support for racial equality, gender and sexual equality, the rights of citizens to participate in corporate decision making, public ownership of many businesses as a means of reducing economic inequality, and environmental protection. To see how the party spells out these positions, go to the document titled "Where We Stand" on its Web page (http://www.dsusa.org).

The debates between Marxist–Leninists and social democrats illustrate that socialist ideology is varied and diverse. In looking at Marxism–Leninism and social democracy in the context of historical questions in the field of political theory, one finds that both forms of socialism have a complex relationship to previous political philosophies. Both Marxist–Leninists and social democrats believe that society should aspire toward more than a Hobbesian blueprint for survival. They tend to share with Plato a commitment to organizing society so that a larger vision of justice is realized. The Marxist–Leninists also share with Plato a view supportive of elite (philosopher-kings or vanguard parties) decision making. Marxist–Leninists and social democrats decry the inequalities of capitalism and look to socialism as a more egalitarian system than capitalism. In addition, Marxist–Leninists reject Madison's argument for intentionally weakening state power through a system of checks and balances; however, social democrats often support such measures as consistent with democratic decision making. In terms of debates between fundamentalism and Millian individualism, Marxist–Leninists are opposed to both sides. They reject religious fundamentalism outright but also reject individualism if individualism is used to weaken the decision making of the vanguard party and, with it, progress toward socialism. Social democrats reject fundamentalism but, as noted earlier, try to reconcile individualism, democracy, and socialism.

## SUMMING UP

- **Liberal** ideology includes the **classical liberalism** of John Locke and Adam Smith and the **modern liberalism** of T. H. Green. Classical liberals stress the rationality of human beings and the desirability of limited government, whereas modern liberals believe that **interventionist government** can reform society and expand the very meaning of individual liberty (**expansive liberty**). In response to the emergence of modern liberalism, classical liberals came to describe themselves as classical liberal conservatives.

- **Conservative** ideology includes **classical liberalism** (the ideas of Locke and Smith) as well as Burkean **traditional conservatism.** Burke-inspired conservatism stresses the need to preserve and uphold traditional morality. Classical liberal conservatives and Burkean traditional conservatives disagree on many issues involving contemporary politics, as seen in the divergent paths conservatism has taken in leading the formation of the Christian Coalition and the Log Cabin Republicans.

- **Socialism,** like the preceding two ideologies, is not one-dimensional. Greatly influenced by Marx's theory of the inherently flawed but progressive nature of capitalism, socialists today include advocates of **Marxism–Leninism** and **social democracy.** The former rejects democracy, whereas the latter sees socialism and democracy as logically reinforcing.

## STUDY QUESTIONS

1. Compare and contrast classical and modern liberalism on matters of liberty and government.

2. What do classical liberals such as Locke and Smith teach about economic inequality?

3. What did classical liberals start calling themselves after modern liberalism came into being?

4. Compare and contrast classical liberal conservatives and Burkean traditional conservatives.

5. Identify a contemporary conservative group that embraces classical liberal conservative ideas. Identify a contemporary conservative group that calls for Burkean traditional conservatism.

6. When and how has President Bush been controversial to other conservatives? Give an example related to his presidential campaign and during his presidency.

7. What is a religious source of socialist ideology? Explain.

8. Why did Marx believe that capitalism necessarily generated class conflict?

What role did government play in this conflict?

9. Did Marx see anything positive in capitalism?

10. How do Marxist–Leninists and social democrats differ in their application of socialist ideology?

## FOLLOWING UP THROUGH INTERNET SOURCES

*Liberalism*

- Democratic National Committee (http://www.democrats.org)

- Democratic Leadership Council (http://www.ndol.org)

- Jane Addams Hull House Museum (http://www.uic.edu/jaddams/hull /hull_house.html); includes links to historical information on Addams and liberalism

- Libertarian Party (http://www.lp.org)

- Association of Libertarian Feminists (http://www.alf.org)

- Gays and Lesbians for Individual Liberty: Supporting Freedom for All (http://www.glil.org)

*Conservatism*

- Republican National Committee (http://www.rnc.org)

- Christian Coalition of America (http://www.cc.org)

- Focus on the Family (http://www.fotf.org)

- Eagle Forum (http://www. eagleforum.org)

*Socialism*

- Democratic Socialists of America (http://www.dsausa.org/dsa.html)

- Socialist International (http://www.dsausa.org/si/si.html)

- Marxists.org Internet Archive (http://csf.colorado.edu/mirrors/ marxists.org)

# 6

# Political Ideologies II

# Fascism

In 1938, Edith Hahn was a 24-year-old studying law in Austria. In the same year, Nazi Germany incorporated Austria into its political domain. This meant that Edith Hahn and other Jews lost control over their lives. Forced to leave school, Edith worked at home as a seamstress. In 1939, she, like other Jewish women, was assigned the middle name Sarah, was transferred into a Jewish ghetto, and was required to carry an identity card designating her as a Jew. In 1941, she was assigned to a Nazi labor camp. Just before she was to be sent to Auschwitz, she escaped to Vienna, and with the help of various people, she illegally obtained a food ration card, resumed her work as a seamstress, joined the German Red Cross, and eventually married a man who would be drafted into the Nazi military. She survived the Nazi regime and lives today in Israel.[1]

Edith Hahn's early life was one of resistance to fascism. As we will see in this chapter, **fascism** asserts that government is at its best when government is totalitarian.

## THE FASCISM OF MUSSOLINI AND HITLER

Benito Mussolini (1883–1945) and Adolf Hitler (1889–1945) advocated fascism as a response to what they identified as twentieth-century political problems. Fascism, they promised, would rescue countries from economic disorder, national weakness, and moral decline—societal maladies exacerbated, they contended, by the failures of liberalism, conservatism, socialism, and, more generally, by democracy itself. The philosophical ideas of socialism, liberalism, and democracy were attacked directly in fascist writings; conservative ideas were more implicitly critiqued. Fascism's appeal to antisocialist constituencies was evident in, for example, the Italian elections of 1921, when support for fascism was linked to opposition to socialist candidates. That is, studies of these elections reveal that a vote for fascism was perceived by many as a vote against socialism.[2] In Nazi Germany, socialist ideas and socialist and communist parties and individuals were especially targeted by the Nazis for repression and persecution; indeed, as we will see, some of the earliest concentration camps in Nazi Germany were used to imprison socialists and communists. Thus, in terms of both ideology and political practice, fascism, from its early twentieth-century beginnings, defined itself as a rejection of the ideologies discussed in Chapter 5. More particularly, fascism during these years put itself forward as a categorical and generally vituperative expression of antisocialism/anticommunism.

Many scholars describe fascism as having an antitheoretical tendency. That is, fascism is said to have consisted not so much of core political ideas accepted universally by fascists in varied settings as of improvised, culture-specific positions taken by self-avowed fascists. Thus, although Mussolini came to power in Italy in 1922 and ruled until 1943 and Hitler and the Nazis held power in Germany from 1933 until 1945, fascism in Italy differed greatly from fascism in Germany. Fascism beyond Italy and Germany differed still more. For example, Mussolini and Hitler supported Spain's Francisco Franco (1892–1975), and Franco also sought support from Spain's fascist Falange; however, on coming to power in 1939, Franco distanced himself from Mussolini and Hitler. Beyond Europe, one can look to Argentine leader Juan Peron's (1895–1974) politics as illustrative of fascist ideology. Recently, as we will see, U.S. skinheads and the Aryan Nations have espoused neofascist politics.[3]

Fascism's lack of theoretical unity and consistency can create interpretive and analytic difficulties for students seeking to delineate the ideology's central components. Indeed, as early as 1927 Italian historian Gaetano Salvemini pointed out that fascism's lack of theoretical clarity meant that fascists could often confuse both supporters and opponents. Neither necessarily knew what to expect from newly installed fascist regimes, Salvemini asserted. Exiled from Italy three years after Mussolini's assumption of power, Salvemini came to conclude that fascists could be understood by their

---

**BOX 6.1  Fascism**

- Argues in favor of a totalitarian state that regulates any and all parts of life deemed to be relevant to politics, as determined by state officials
- Asserts that the state is more important than the individual
- Rejects the idea that civil institutions should have an important role

- in limiting the power of states and in criticizing laws of the state
- Affirms that individuals are to gain a sense of purpose by psychologically identifying with a totalistic state and devoting themselves to service to that state
- Rejects the concept of equality
- Advocates nationalism and/or racism

actions, if not by their ideological propositions. Analyses such as those offered by Salvemini suggest that fascism, in practice, becomes a system of glorified violence directed at those too weak to resist successfully, a system concentrating power in an authoritarian leader, and a system stabilized by the lack of opposition to these state actions from established, influential sectors in society. Thus, Salvemini's picture of Italy during the early years of Mussolini was one depicting a government that ruled by means of force but also by means of popular support from people not themselves suffering from the state-directed terror. Salvemini's 1920s description of fascism as popularly grounded violence against marginalized individuals and groups, as we will see, could be used to describe many of the dynamics of Nazi Germany as well as of more recent neofascist politics. With respect to the former, for instance, members of the White Rose resistance to the Nazis understood that Nazism relied on more than concentration camps and execution squads in perpetuating Nazi rule—the Nazis relied also on maintaining the appearance (and the reality, as much as possible) of popular acquiescence to the state. Therefore, any measure that conveyed popular opposition to fascism could weaken fascism's support structure.[4]

In analyzing fascism, it is useful to examine the origins of the terminology. The word *fascism* is related to the term *fasces*. In ancient Rome, the *fasces* was an emblem symbolizing power through unity.[5] For fascists, this emblem was a compelling one because fascism called for the establishment of a unified society in

---

**BOX 6.2   The White Rose**

The White Rose was a resistance movement against the Nazis. It was organized in Munich by a small group consisting primarily of university students. The White Rose operated in 1942–1943. Its members wrote pamphlets calling on their fellow German citizens to carry out "passive resistance" to the fascist government. They copied their pamphlets on a duplicating machine that they carefully kept hidden; once copied, the pamphlets were left in public places in Munich and, as possible, transported to other cities—Karlsruhe, Frankfurt, Stuttgart, Freiburg, Saarbrücken, Mannheim, and Vienna—and distributed.

The White Rose pamphlets tried to dispel the notion that Nazism was a credible ideology. In fact, the second pamphlet written by the students denied that it was an ideology at all: Nazism was advocacy of murder and brutality, not a philosophy of life. One pamphlet quoted Aristotle on tyranny; others included prayers, poems, quota-

tions from Lao-Tzu, and clear, precise discussions of German history and politics. The pamphlets tried to remind Germans that there were alternatives to fascism; the pamphlets also offered assurance to any reader who might have felt her- or himself alone in wanting to resist the Nazis that there were like-minded antifascists close by. The pamphlets sometimes ended by encouraging readers to take the pamphlet, duplicate it, and then carefully leave copies in other public places. One pamphlet at a time, the White Rose conveyed the message that the so-called totalistic state was a failure: It had not silenced antifascist voices, it had not achieved totalitarian domination over all its citizens, and it had most certainly not achieved total deference among the citizenry.

The White Rose members knew they were in great danger. Hans Scholl, who was a founding member, heard a rumor of his impending arrest days before he was detained. Although he had opportunities to escape to Switzerland,

| BOX 6.2 *Continued* |
| --- |

he remained in Germany out of fear that his escape would put his family at greater risk. Hans, his sister Sophie, and friend and fellow White Rose member Christoph Probst were among the first of the group arrested. They were executed by the Nazis on February 22, 1943.

Today, the courage of the White Rose members and their astute deciphering of the ideological dynamics of Nazism are recognized by many students of fascism. A White Rose museum has been organized in Munich, where Hans and Christoph were medical students and where Sophie had just begun her studies in biology and philosophy. A Hans and Sophie Scholl Plaza was named in their honor in the western German city of Wuppertal, also the site where a group of German ministers in May 1934 issued the Barmen Declaration, a criticism of the Nazi posture of domination toward German churches.

SOURCE: Inge Scholl, *The White Rose: Munich 1942–1943*, trans. Arthur R. Schultz (Middletown, CT: Wesleyan University Press, 1983).

which each individual existed for the nation's purposes. When, in March 1919, Mussolini began formalizing his leadership over newly organized fascist groups in Italy, he chose the *fasces* as the official insignia.[6]

Fascists have sometimes embraced a strategy of explaining their ideology by describing what it is not. In Mussolini's *Fascism: Doctrine and Institutions*, this approach is followed. Specific arguments of fascism are delineated through a series of contrasts that highlight fascist alternatives to rival political perspectives. For example, fascism is presented as an ideology that opposes pacifism. Pacifism rests on the notion that countries can and should coexist peacefully and resolve disputes by nonviolent means. Pacifism is peace seeking and peace building. Mussolini's work explains why fascism rejects such thinking. Fascism regards peace seeking as consigning a country to weakness, as excusing cowardice, and as abandoning the very risk taking that might propel a country into a position of greater strength. Pacifists avoid conflict, Mussolini writes, yet conflict can become an occasion for winning against a competitor. Conflict can become an opportunity for territorial expansion. Conflict can become a means of taking power over government. Conflict can become a means of demonstrating superiority.[7]

Mussolini further describes fascism as an ideology promoting nationalism. Nationalism is defined as an alternative to both internationalism and individualism. With respect to the first concept, Mussolini rejects the argument that international alliances should be allowed to override national sovereignty. That is, he maintains, international structures should not be used to erode national authority; international alliances should not be used to try to undermine or constrain the decision-making powers of national leaders. Cosmopolitan, universal, international perspectives should not outweigh the concerns and needs of Italy, for example, on issues involving Italian national politics. National loyalties are potentially stronger sources of power than international alliances could ever be, according to Mussolini; in understanding this, fascists are able to draw out of a people its nationalist potentialities and direct those toward shared interests.

The concept of shared interests was especially important to Mussolini's point. Nationalist shared interests stood in contrast to particular interests exclusive to only certain individuals. *Every* member of the nation, Mussolini insisted, bene-fited when interests shared by the entire nation were mobilized. Thus, the two dimensions of nationalism (anti-internationalism and anti-individualism) proved to be reinforcing: Nationalism was a middle ground, of sorts, rejecting those claims that were above or larger than the nation (claims made by the interna-tional community) and those claims below or smaller than the nation (claims made by the individual). For example, internationalists might claim that peace would be good for the global community (even though Italy might view war as serving its territorial ambitions), and individualists might claim that freedom of speech would be good for those whose opinions were in the minority (even though Italians as a whole might find minority views treacherous). In these ex-amples, both peace and freedom of speech seem illegitimate, from a fascist per-spective, because both threaten to hijack the decision-making process that should reside in the nation acting for itself and place it in the hands of interlopers (in-ternationalists and individualists). Both peace and freedom of speech would con-stitute misspecifications of that which should be pursued through fascist politics.[8]

Had Mussolini completed his argument with this appeal to nationalism, he would have allowed a very big question to remain unanswered: What entity can represent and articulate the nationalist, shared interests? His answer was the state, if the state is properly constituted as a totalistic state. Thus, Mussolini's writings assert that fascism supports the creation of a totalistic state. Indeed, Italian fascists coined the word *totalitarian* to describe the proper boundaries of state authority. Any and all activities needed for the creation of a powerful nation should be directed by the state. Thus, one finds in the historical record of fascism ideological support for the regulation of economic, cultural, and political life. Italian fascist Giovanni Gentile (1875–1949) explained this view of the state in a 1925 lecture in which he pro-claimed that nothing was to be considered off limits for state regulation.[9]

Consistent with the principle of totalitarianism, the following decrees were articulated by fascists in Italy:

- A law of 1925 created a system of monitoring activities of individuals who participated in sports, drama societies, bands, orchestras, libraries, and theaters. For example, in 1939 the fascists decreed that Italian tennis players participat-ing in international competitions were required to wear fascist uniforms and to use fascist salutes instead of handshakes when greeting opponents.

- A law of 1926 outlawed strikes.

- A law of 1927 proclaimed that the nation was more important than the individual.

- A proclamation by Mussolini in 1928 announced that popular culture should reflect fascist ideals. As part of the fascist reforms, women would be forbid-den to wear pants.

- A pronouncement in 1929 stipulated that publishers were to submit political manuscripts to fascist representatives for approval.

- A 1934 law empowered corporations (groups of workers and employers under the dominant authority of state officials) to establish wages and prices.

- A regulation in 1935 stated that the Confederation of Fascist Corporations (a group dominated by the state) was the only authority that could negotiate on behalf of workers. Independent labor unions were prohibited.[10]

Under Hitler, German fascists also expanded the state's authority in ways reflecting the totalistic ideology.[11] The following laws, for example, illustrate efforts to implement extensive control by the state over economic matters:

- The Reich Entailed Farm Law of 1933 regulated farm holdings and declared it illegal for the owners of a farm to divide the land among different heirs.[12]

- The Law for the Regulation of Work Allocation of 1934 restricted freedom of movement within Germany by prohibiting migration to urban areas with high levels of unemployment.[13]

- The Law for Meeting Labor Requirements in Agriculture of 1935 legalized the procedure of requiring former agricultural workers to return to their jobs in agriculture.[14]

Notice how the state displaced the individual as the locus of economic decision making.

Mussolini, Gentile, and other fascist theorists made explicit their disagreements with older ideologies. Fascism's rejection of individualism in favor of nationalism placed it at odds with liberalism. In upholding the totalistic state, fascists denied that states should limit their own powers in order to maximize individual freedom and insisted, instead, that individuals acknowledge the superior authority of the state. Unlike traditional conservatism, fascism opposed civil institutions strong enough to exist independently of and in potential opposition to the government. Fascists asserted that the state should be the ultimate source of morality, and civil institutions should defer to state decisions. A former socialist himself, Mussolini was especially adamant in claiming that fascism differed radically from socialism. Whereas socialists viewed the state in terms of its economic utility (its usefulness in publicly managing the production and distribution of economic resources), fascists considered the state in more grandiose terms, according to Mussolini. The state, Mussolini contended, was not to be regarded merely as an economic manager. On the contrary, the state was to function as an emotional force in the lives of the people.[15]

Fascists argued that the state could fulfill psychological needs by representing a symbol of strength with which otherwise powerless individuals could identify. To serve such a state was to gain a sense of purpose, Mussolini argued. Indeed, being a part of the fascist state—through obedience to its decrees and participation in its activities—would lift people out of their isolated, petty, limited individual lives and attach them to something bigger, something heroic. Submission to the fascist state was thus presented as ennobling. Although any single individual would be but a small part of the fascist regime, because the regime itself would be powerful the individual would feel invincible.[16]

Mussolini asserted that the citizen should commit to being in a position of subordination to the fascist state but insisted that this subordination was a form of popular empowerment. Mussolini made a distinction between (1) subordinated citizens and (2) individualistic individuals. Subordinated citizens knew their own well-being was tied up with the ability of the nation and state to thrive; therefore, they did nothing to weaken either nation or state. They knew to obey the state, just as the hand knows to obey the brain in the interest of the survival of the entire body. In contrast, individuals and groups who lacked deference to the fascist state and who pursued their own personal objectives in opposition to the fascist state undermined unity; competition among individualistic people, each seeking his or her own agenda, tore apart societies and prevented the emergence of nationalist shared interests embodied in a totalistic state. Individualistic people might think themselves empowered, but they were not; as corrosive agents weakening nations and as opponents of totalitarian politics, such individuals undermined the one thing that could give them real power: membership in something much larger than themselves, namely membership in a nation governed by a unified totalistic government. Indeed, Mussolini was adamant in distinguishing his own fascist government from police states, absolutist monarchies, and other more conventional forms of authoritarian governments. These governments, Mussolini said, ruled over people and crushed them rather than empowering them; these states repressed people without giving them strength. Fascist states, in contrast, ruled over people but did so ethically, insofar as the states' repression kept the entire body of the nation unified and thus vigorous.[17]

These arguments are consistent with fascism's opposition to party and interest group competition. Historically, fascist governments have repressed dissent and banned or severely restricted any groups or institutions that could challenge the state's authority.[18] For example, by 1925 Mussolini had effectively destroyed parliamentary rivals to his authority in Italy. Specifically, he gave himself the power to issue decrees without consulting parliament, and he oversaw the enactment of a law prohibiting parliament from debating public issues. By 1926, Mussolini had destroyed the authority of local governmental authorities as well.[19] Similarly, in Germany, in 1933 Hitler declared his Nazi Party to be the only legal political party in the country and announced that anyone attempting to organize another party would be subject to a penalty of at least three years in prison.[20]

Fascism also opposed the concepts of natural and civil equality and supported, instead, the idea of elitism. According to fascism, individuals are not equal by birth (or nature) and should not be equal under the laws. To the contrary, individuals are divided by natural abilities and social worth, and society should be arranged hierarchically to reflect the differences between "naturally superior" and "naturally inferior" groups. Naturally superior individuals constitute the elite, who should be accorded the highest ranking within the social hierarchy. Different fascist leaders have offered varied opinions on who is to be designated the elite and who is not; scholars have noted that fascists have targeted different populations within their respective countries as non-elites. Thus, any group can become vulnerable to this labeling. Hitler added a psychosadistic element to fascist elitist ideology by proclaiming that the average person not only had an obligation to submit to the elites but actually *desired* to be dominated by them. Non-elites achieved gratification from being ruled by domineering masters, Hitler maintained.[21]

Fascism's support of elitism was conceptually related to its advocacy of nationalism and racism. Fascists tend to define what they regard as the "elite" groups in society in nationalist and racist terms. Recalling this chapter's previous discussion of fascism's lack of theoretical unity, it is important to take note of the fact that Mussolini and the Italian fascists were primarily nationalistic elitists, whereas Hitler and the Nazis were both nationalistic and racist in their elitism. With respect to Italy, fascists espoused nationalism from the earliest days of Mussolini's rule; however, not until the late 1930s did Mussolini add a racist and anti-Semitic dimension to this nationalism.[22] In contrast, from the very beginning of Hitler's regime, Nazism proclaimed a belief in Germany's superiority as a nation and the Aryans' superiority as a race.

Hitler's *Mein Kampf*, written during his imprisonment for treason in 1924, conveys the Nazi ideology of nationalistic and racist elitism. Hitler calls for racial purity, attacks Jews as "inferior," and asserts the racial and cultural "superiority" of whites or Aryans. He scapegoats Jews as the culprits for Germany's economic and political problems and accuses Jews of participating in an international conspiracy against "naturally superior" elites, such as Germans. Once in power, Hitler and the Nazis declared their position that Jews and Germans are different races and that Jews should be excluded from German citizenship.[23]

These ideas were translated into approximately 400 anti-Semitic decrees in Nazi Germany:

- The Law for the Restoration of the Professional Civil Service provided for the removal of Jews from civil service jobs.
- The Law against the Overcrowding of German Schools and Institutions of Higher Learning restricted Jews in terms of school enrollments.
- A law creating a Reich Chamber of Culture excluded Jews from cultural and entertainment professions.
- The National Press Law created state censorship of the press and excluded Jews from journalistic positions.
- The Hereditary Farm Law prohibited Jews from inheriting farm lands.
- The Law for the Reduction of Unemployment provided subsidies for couples wishing to marry, if both the man and woman were deemed racially superior.[24]

These decrees illustrate the vehement nationalistic and racist elitism that culminated in the Holocaust.

The elitist ideology of Nazism is also reflected in Nazi persecutions of other groups deemed to be natural and social "inferiors." In the concentration camps, "inferior" groups were identified by an emblem worn on their clothing for the purpose of signifying the nature of their "inferiority." Jews were assigned yellow stars; Jehovah's Witnesses, purple triangles; the Roma (gypsies), brown triangles; criminals, green triangles; political dissidents, red triangles; gay men, pink triangles; and lesbians and "antisocials," black triangles. Documents recovered from the Dachau camp offer a glimpse into the particular categorization of Jehovah's Witnesses, for example. Jehovah's Witnesses were required to denounce the "International Association of Jehovah's Witnesses" as an organization disseminating a "false doctrine"; had to pledge that they rejected this association and that they would turn in anyone they knew to be a member; had to agree that the association was

Remains of the Birkenau Concentration Camp

not really a religious organization but was actually a radical political group; and, finally, had to swear allegiance to the state.[25] The meticulous codification of "inferior" groups conveys the extent to which the Nazi ideology conceptualized individuals in hierarchical terms—not only were "elites" distinguished from "inferiors" by the terms of the ideology, but "inferiors" were further classified into their own subcategories of "inferiority."

The Nazi commitment to national and racial elitism inspired state-directed programs of eugenics (breeding), sterilization, medical experimentation, and euthanasia. Believing as they did that they were the "master race," Nazis sought to encourage reproduction and population growth among those they defined as "pure" Germans while simultaneously decimating other populations. Members of "inferior" groups could become forced participants in medical experiments involving tortuous levels of pain and probable death. Some "inferiors" were sterilized by exposure to intense radiation. In addition, in 1939, the Nazis began a state-directed euthanasia program. Under the terms of this program, people identified as disabled by physicians at state hospitals were shipped to special facilities and killed by tablets, injections, or gas. Mass executions of other groups soon followed. At Auschwitz-Birkenau alone, more than 1 million individuals were killed.[26] In these policies, the key ideals of fascism came together: The totalistic state was used to promote the power of the "natural elites" and was used to eliminate the "inferiors" as well as any potential source of opposition to the fascist system. Power through unity was furthered through the actions of an expansive state apparatus that used laws, decrees, propaganda, concentration camps, and violence to create the racially pure and nationally dominant German Reich (empire).

## BOX 6.3  Responses to the Nazi State: Gad Beck, the Chug Chaluzi, the Herbert Baum Group, the Eva Mamlok Group, and the Rosenstrasse Group

Gad Beck was living in Berlin in 1941 and recalls that, in this year, Nazi repression of Jews became more intense. Jewish families began receiving notices that they were to be sent to "work camps." Beck remembers that, prior to deportation, a family would receive a list of items they could take with them and instructions on when to report to a deportation center.

In the fall of 1942, the Lewin family received their notice. They were to report to the center on Grosse Hamburger Strasse for removal from Berlin to a camp somewhere in the east. According to Beck, the Lewins did not believe that they were going to be sent to a death camp, although BBC broadcasts had transmitted reports of atrocities, and friends had heard stories about Jews being killed in the camps. Even if the Lewins had known about the nature of the concentration camps, it was illegal for Jews to emigrate from Germany at this time. The Lewins reported for deportation as ordered.

Beck was himself at risk in Berlin; he was Jewish and gay, a member of two groups the Nazis deemed "inferior." He put himself at greater risk by taking on the task of trying to free Manfred Lewin, with whom he had fallen in love, from the deportation center. Beck went to Manfred's employer, whose son was in a Hitler Youth group, borrowed the Hitler Youth uniform, and wore it to disguise himself as a Nazi. Dressed in this way, Beck went to the deportation center to secure Manfred's release. The ruse worked. Within minutes of leaving the center, however, Manfred decided he had to return. He could not leave his parents and his siblings behind to endure alone whatever might lie ahead.

The Lewins and other Jewish families were deported. Beck survived the Nazis but never saw Manfred after that day.

It is unknown how many similar individual efforts at escape or rescue were tried. However, several group-level efforts at eluding, escaping, and resisting the Nazis were made inside Germany. The Herbert Baum group was organized in Berlin in the late 1930s; it consisted of Jewish and non-Jewish individuals who knew one another primarily through work. Estimates of its size range from 50 to 150 members. Most members were young, and most were socialists. The group staged an arson attack on a Nazi exhibit in 1942.

The Eva Mamlok group was a small resistance group consisting of Jewish women and centered in Berlin. The Chug Chaluzi was a Jewish resistance group that focused on observing the Sabbath, studying Jewish theology and history, and helping Jews with specific survival needs.

The Rosenstrasse group consisted of individuals who came together in 1943 to protest the recent arrests of some of their family members. Primarily consisting of non-Jewish women married to Jewish men, the Rosenstrasse group demanded that the Nazis release their husbands. After a week of protesting in downtown Berlin (in front of the deportation center on the street of Rosenstrasse), the protesters succeeded in gaining the freedom of more than 1,000 detainees. It is important to note that the Rosenstrasse group did not protest against Nazism itself, but rather, asked for the return of their family members. The fact that they did not challenge the political system's larger ideological purposes is probably what saved the protesters from being detained themselves.

SOURCES: Gad Beck, *An Underground Life: Memoirs of a Gay Jew in Nazi Berlin* (Madison: University of Wisconsin Press, 1999), pp. 56–70; Marian A. Kaplan, *Between Dignity and Despair: Jewish Life in Nazi Germany* (New York: Oxford University Press, 1998), pp. 193–216; Nathan Stoltzfus, *Resistance of the Heart: Intermarriage and the Rosenstrasse Protest in Nazi Germany* (New York: Norton, 1996), Chapters 14–15.

The Nazi state developed different mechanisms and institutions for implementing these ideological measures through the 1930s and 1940s. Scholars have noted that prior to 1941, the Nazi government relied heavily on three strategies of promoting its elitist objectives: (1) It encouraged individual citizens to participate in brutalizing Jews (such as insults, assaults, and boycotts against Jews and Jewish establishments, designed to communicate that Jews were regarded as "inferiors"); (2) it enacted laws such as the ones noted earlier in order to isolate Jews and take away any social, economic, or political power; and (3) it pushed Jews into ghettos, the two largest of which in 1940 were in Warsaw and Lodz. After 1941, the state shifted to the following strategies: (1) It increased its reliance on execution squads to murder Jews, and (2) it expanded its use of concentration camps to confine and exterminate Jews and also to enforce mandatory labor on Jews and non-Jews.

The concentration camp system itself evolved during the Nazi years. Early camps were used primarily for confining political opponents of the Nazis, especially opponents who were socialists, communists, or labor organizers. For example, records of the Columbiahaus camp from the mid-1930s show that officials of the Socialist Workers Youth, the German Communist party, and the Social Democratic party were detained at this camp. These early camps were publicized by the Nazis as visible messages of how the regime intended to deal with socialists, communists, and other anti-Nazi critics. Indeed, when the Dachau camp was opened in 1933, the Nazis held a press conference. By 1939, the Nazis were operating six concentration camps: The Dachau, Sachsenhausen, Buchenwald, Flossenbürg, Mauthausen, and Ravensbruck camps confined approximately 21,000 prisoners.

By 1944, 20 camps had been organized; in January 1945, these camps held 700,000 prisoners. In the 1940s, the camp system was used not only to try to silence the opposition but also to supply labor to industry and to kill Jews and other groups identified by the Nazis for murder. The use of the camp system for large-scale institutionalized killings began at Auschwitz-Birkenau, Treblinka, and other camps in 1942, the same year in which the Nazis held the Wannsee Conference in Berlin, at which Nazi officials formulated specific procedures for carrying out their stated objective of killing the entire European Jewish community.[27]

The Flossenbürg concentration camp, located in southeastern Germany close to the Czech border, exemplifies the three purposes the Nazis assigned to the camp system. First, the Flossenbürg camp was part of the Nazi apparatus of silencing political opposition. Protestant minister Dietrich Bonhoeffer, who participated in an attempt to assassinate Hitler, was executed at the Flossenbürg camp in 1945. Second, the camp system could be used by the Nazis to attack and eventually seek to annihilate those deemed "inferior." At Flossenbürg, medical tortures and experiments were carried out on and killed many Jewish and disabled prisoners. Third, the camp prison population provided labor for industry. Camp records document that thousands of Flossenbürg prisoners were sent on work details in the German defense industry. For example, the Messerschmitt Factory, which produced airplane components, had 5,000 Flossenbürg camp prison workers in 1944. During a visit to Flossenbürg in 1999, the author of this text was told by a local resident who grew up in Flossenbürg that he remembered as a little boy watching the camp inmates walking to the defense factories every morning.[28]

## BOX 6.4 U.S. Fascism: The Ku Klux Klan?

Some scholars regard the Ku Klux Klan (KKK) as an early expression of fascism. Formed as a white supremacist social group in Pulaski, Tennessee, in 1866, by 1867 the KKK had become a paramilitary organization. The KKK espoused a number of arguments that, taken together, resemble what will later be termed fascist: advocacy and use of violence in support of elitism/racism by a governing group seeking to place national supremacy above individualism. The KKK saw itself as the governing organization to enforce this supremacy and rejected the post-Civil War Reconstruction governments in the southern United States. The KKK declined in the 1870s.

A second Klan came into being in the United States during the 1920s. The message of the KKK of the 1920s was similar to arguments made by recent neofascists. The second Klan attacked immigration, immigrant rights, and those it perceived as immigrants and/or "foreign." Like Mussolini and Hitler, the second Klan was virulently antisocialist and anticommunist. It promoted "Americanism" as its nationalistic ideology. What "Americanism" meant in this context, according to the Klan, was patriotism and love of the nation of America, opposition to "foreigners" and "foreign ideas and ways," and working to defeat godless socialism. Calling on its members to be "good Americans" by doing these things, the KKK was often allowed by white Protestant churches to meet on their premises, was often urged on by white Protestant ministers, and even had help burning crosses from various white Protestant congregations.

Thus, although fascism's twentieth-century origins are generally thought to be European, an examination of the KKK might prompt a reconsideration. As one scholar has asked, could it be that fascism has U.S. roots?

SOURCES: On the question of whether the KKK is fascist, see Robert O. Paxton, "The Five Stages of Fascism," *The Journal of Modern History* (March 1998): 1–23; on the connection with Protestant churches, see Kathleen M. Blee, *Women of the Klan: Racism and Gender in the 1920s* (Berkeley: University of California Press, 1991), pp. 29, 138, 178; on KKK history, see Allen W. Trelease, "Ku Klux Klan" in *The Reader's Companion to American History*, edited by Eric Foner and John Garraty (Boston: Houghton Mifflin, 1991), pp. 625–626.

The ideology of fascism—mobilized in the service of the state-directed terror that almost killed Edith Hahn and that succeeded in killing many others—survived World War II. Neofascism is an ideology that has claimed adherents in both Europe and the United States in recent years.

## NEOFASCISM

Following World War II, fascist parties were banned in Italy and Germany,[29] but fascist ideology endured. A number of European political parties and movements have ideological ties to fascism. These new fascists (neofascists) include the National Alliance in Italy, the National Front in France, the Republikaner Party in Germany, the Freedom Party of Austria, and the National Party in Great Britain. These groups have either espoused fascist principles or explicitly appealed to constituencies supportive of those principles. None of these groups is strong enough to operate as a dominant power within its own country; however, each group has successfully placed candidates in office in recent years. For example, the National Alliance recently won more than 13 percent of the national vote in parliamentary elections and served as a member of the coalition government of Italy. In Germany, Republikaner leader Franz Schönhuber, a former member of Hitler's SS, has built up his party's base to the point of capturing 15 percent of the vote in some local races, and Schönhuber himself has served as a member of the European Parliament. In France, the National Front has received 10 percent or more of the popular vote in national elections for parliament and/or the presidency in recent years (for example, in elections in 1986, 1988, and 1993). In 1999, the Freedom Party of Austria (FPO) won 27% of the vote in national elections and went on to become a coalition partner in government, and the FPO's Jörg Haider is governor of the Austrian state of Carinthia.[30]

Neofascist ideology is evident also in the actions of a number of groups not formally affiliated with the parties just mentioned. These groups include skinheads, followers of neo-Nazi musical groups, and racist and anti-Semitic hate groups that explicitly link their politics with the legacies of Hitler and/or Mussolini. Such groups differ in terms of their level of organization, with some groups exhibiting a highly organized leadership structure, whereas others are very decentralized. What makes these groups significant in terms of modern ideologies is the fact that they illustrate the survival of fascism into the post-World War II period and are movements with sufficient power to affect government and society. In Germany in 1992, for example, authorities reported more than 2,000 acts of violence perpetuated by hate groups espousing, to varying degrees, neo-Nazi principles. Included among the 1992 totals were acts of violence carried out by approximately 600 skinheads and neo-Nazis against foreigners in the city of Rostock. The hate groups at Rostock shouted Nazi slogans as they attacked, leaving little doubt about the neofascist nature of the violence. After Rostock, skinhead violence spread to other German cities, including Mölln, where three people were murdered in December 1992. In 1992, the Emnid-Institut in Bielefeld, Germany, conducted a poll that asked German respondents how they would react to seeing a German attacking a foreigner. Very few Germans responded that they would view such attacks favorably. However, the most popular response was one indicating that the viewer would leave the scene and do nothing.[31] Neo-Nazis attacked individuals perceived to be "foreigners" in German cities such as Guben in 1999 and 2000.[32]

Neo-Nazi violence has been glorified in the lyrics of a number of recent European rock groups, including Störkraft (Destructive Force), Radikahl (Radical/Bald), Böhse Onkelz (Evil Uncles), and Cigany Pusztito Garda (Gypsy Destroyers Guard Regiment). For example, Radikahl released "Swastika" with lyrics stating that Hitler should be awarded a Nobel Prize. Störkraft's "Mercenary" details the action of a skinhead/fascist/racist/sadist, and Cigany Pusztito Garda performs "Gypsy-Free Zone," which calls for genocide against the Roma. The existence of these groups illustrates the penetration of neofascist ideology into European youth culture.[33]

In the United States, neofascist ideology is found in the teachings of groups such as the Aryan Nations and White Aryan Resistance (WAR). Aryan Nations, headquartered in Idaho, espouses white supremacy, anti-Semitism, racial purity, and racial nationalism. Aryan Nations maintains that Aryans should preserve their own race and culture, and the group calls for the establishment of Aryan sovereign political territory. Aryan Nations bases its arguments on a racist reading of the Judeo-Christian tradition known as Christian Identity. Christian Identity is a theology claiming that God created whites as a separate and superior race. WAR shares the racist and anti-Semitic stance of Aryan Nations. WAR has called for the establishment of a white-only state and for the deportation of Latino- and African-Americans. WAR's leaders have been linked to at least one racist-inspired murder in the United States. Like the European neofascist groups, U.S. groups such as Aryan Nations and WAR have a very limited following but have made themselves noticeable participants in ideological debates.

Relating fascist and neofascist ideology to the ethical debates analyzed in Chapter 4, both fascists and neofascists believe that if we learn from Plato's allegory and leave the cave of our ignorance, we will reject equality in favor of notions of national and/or racial superiority. The fascism of Mussolini and Hitler calls for a state with power beyond that imagined by Hobbes and Machiavelli. The fascist state would overpower individuals as well as civil institutions.[34]

## SUMMING UP

**Fascism** is an ideology that introduces totalitarianism as the objective of political decision making. Rejecting the ideologies of liberalism, conservatism, and socialism, fascism presents itself as an elitist response to modern social and political problems that the older ideologies leave unresolved. The fascism of Mussolini and Hitler has survived in modified form in the ideologies of neofascist organizations such as Aryan Nations and various skinhead groups.

## STUDY QUESTIONS

1. What is the connection between fascism and totalitarianism?

2. Compare and contrast the fascism of Mussolini and Hitler.

3. What was the White Rose?

4. Explain fascism's critique of (a) individualism, (b) civil institutions such as the family, and (c) pacifism.

5. In what respect is nationalism a middle ground for fascists?

6. In your estimation, is the KKK of the United States a fascist organization? Explain the basis of your answer. In addition, take the opposite position and explain the basis for that position.

7. How does Gaetano Salvemini explain fascism?

8. Under the Nazis, concentration camps served varying functions. What were these functions?

9. Identify one neofascist organization or individual in contemporary Europe. Identify one neofascist organization or individual presently operating in the United States.

10. Compare and contrast the resistance to the Nazis carried out by (a) Gad Beck, (b) the Eva Mamlok group, and (c) the Rosenstrasse group.

# FOLLOWING UP THROUGH
# INTERNET SOURCES

- U.S. Holocaust Memorial Museum (http://www.ushmm.org)

- Simon Wiesenthal Center (http://www.wiesenthal.com)

- Southern Poverty Law Center (http://www.splcenter.org)

# 7

## Political Ideologies III

## Feminism, Environmentalism, and Postmodernism

New questions. That's where feminism, environmentalism, and postmodernism can take us. For example, a feminist might ask, How democratic does the United States look if one takes gender equality seriously? Women comprise slightly more than 50% of the population, but in 2003 held only 13.6% of the seats in the U.S. Congress and 25.3% of the elected positions in the various states.[1] Does this seem just? And while we are considering the topic of justice, environmentalists might challenge us to veer into this area of inquiry: Why is justice typically understood as something that should be extended toward people but not toward ecosystems? What is the connection between oil and war, natural resources and political alliances, environmentalists might ask? Moreover, feminists and environmentalists might be puzzled about why the older ideologies discussed in the previous two chapters did not put these types of questions at the center of their analyses. What if the reason for the gaps in the older ideologies had something to do with the dynamics of power and language within those ideologies? A postmodern perspective might suggest that, in many cases, the older ideologies were put forward as metanarratives—that is, these older ideologies sometimes used language to describe themselves as disinterested, neutral descriptions innocently portraying a set of independently existing "truths," and therefore any perspective at odds with such descriptions was dismissible as biased, self-interested, subjective, and basically wrong-headed. Those social groups affirmed by the ideologies functioning as metanarratives were empowered and justified; those groups seeking to challenge them (feminists and environmentalists, for example) were disempowered and delegitimized. What if this postmodernist perspective is the answer to the puzzle?

As we will see in this chapter, feminism, environmentalism, and postmodernism can break open new areas of ideological exploration. Who knows where our thoughts might turn if we remove ourselves from the orbit of the older ideologies? Poet Audre Lorde once argued that this type of "breaking out" in one's thinking was necessary for those whose interests were marginalized; as she put it, if you are one of the oppressed you are likely to remain so until you stop thinking within the boundaries drawn for you by those with the power.[2]

# FEMINISM

**Feminism** opposes the political, economic, and cultural relegation of women to positions of inferiority.[3] That is, feminism critiques laws, customs, and beliefs positing that women are inferior to men, contribute to discrimination against women, privilege men over women, and value men's freedom and well-being over those of women. Feminism critiques historical, contemporary, national, and cross-cultural practices that deny women power over their own lives and thereby attempt to take away from women the possibility of living as free, self-governing individuals. Feminism is philosophically similar to liberalism in that both ideologies reject as illegitimate and unethical the notion that one person or group has a natural claim to dominate or to exercise arbitrary power over another.[4] Feminism shares with democratic theory a belief that all people should be empowered to participate in collective decision making, as well as the viewpoint that when people are denied this power, the agency doing the denying is oppressive.[5] As analyst Rosemarie Tong explains, although feminism is as diverse and divided an ideology as any discussed in this text, all feminists share the view that women should be as free as men.[6]

In upholding the fundamental equality of women and men, feminists have critiqued and argued against the institution of patriarchy. *Patriarchy* is a term used by many feminists to describe the rule of men as a social group over women as a social group.[7] A patriarchal system is a system based on a sexual hierarchy, whereby men exist in positions of superiority and women are accorded positions of subordination and dependency. According to many feminists, patriarchy has

---

**BOX 7.1　Feminism**

- Affirms that women should have equality with men and should possess as much autonomy as that enjoyed by men
- Rejects patriarchy whenever manifest in intellectual, cultural, religious, or political traditions and practices
- Includes liberal, radical, and diversity feminist perspectives

existed across various cultures and time periods. Although not every man has dominated women or even exercised power over women, men, *as a group,* have had the preponderance of power within society and have used this power to further their own interests at the expense of women, according to feminist perspectives. How do feminist thinkers support this view? Many feminists have pointed to the following evidence to demonstrate the existence of patriarchy:

- *Women have been denied equality of resources.* In 1980, the United Nations pointed to the following disparity: Although women represent 50 percent of the world's population, women owned only 1 percent of the earth's property and earned only 10 percent of the total income earned globally.[8] In 1994, *World Health* reported that women owned 20 percent of the earth's resources.[9] In 1995, the United Nations found that, worldwide, women tended to be paid 30–40 percent less than men performing the same work.[10] The pattern continued in 1996, when, according to UN representatives, women across the world earned only 50–80 percent of men's wages.[11] Not surprisingly, given these statistics, women are more likely than men to live in poverty. Indeed, a 1996 report indicated that women represent the great majority (perhaps in excess of 70 percent) of the world's poor.[12]

- *Women have been denied equality of political power.* According to a United Nations report in 1995, women, on average, held only 10.5 percent of the seats in the world's national legislatures. In only two countries—Norway and Finland—did the percentage of women in parliaments exceed 39 percent. Historically, only 23 women have been elected as head of state or executive leader of a country.[13] In 1995, only 6 women were heads of state: Prime Minister Benazir Bhutto of Pakistan, Prime Minister Gr Harlem Brundtland of Norway, President Violeta Barrios de Chamorro of Nicaragua, President Chandrika Bandaranaike Kumaratunga of Sri Lanka, Prime Minister Khaleda Zia of Bangladesh, and Prime Minister Tansu Ciller of Turkey.[14]

- *Women have been denied equality of educational opportunities.* Women comprise two-thirds of the earth's illiterate population.[15]

- *Women have been denied equality of basic health care.* In a number of countries, women and girls are given less food than their male counterparts. The World Health Organization has suggested that one-sixth of female infant deaths in India, Pakistan, and Bangladesh result from discriminatory attitudes toward females.[16]

- *Women have been denied equality of respect.* In some countries, girls are not respected and valued as highly as boys, and, as a result, females have been aborted or killed through infanticide. For example, in China in the early 1990s, 10,000 ultrasound machines were being manufactured every year; these machines are suspected to have been used to facilitate abortions of females by families who prefer sons. Sex selection for the purpose of ensuring sons rather than daughters has been practiced in South Korea as well.[17]

- *Women have been denied equal protection from violence.* Women worldwide are particularly vulnerable to violence, including violence perpetuated by family members. For example, a study of England and Wales found that 45 percent of female homicides were perpetrated by spouses/partners or former spouses/partners, whereas only 6 percent of male homicides were similarly committed by women who were present or former spouses/partners.[18] In the United States a women suffers a battering every 18 minutes, and in Latin America women's concerns over their vulnerability to violent attack by men has prompted the organization of more than 100 women's associations.[19]

■ *Women have been denied equal protection by the state.* Political institutions have established preferential systems whereby laws and policies discriminate against women and favor male interests. In Peru and Egypt, for example, husbands may legally beat wives suspected of adultery. In Brazil, the judicial system has recognized legal defense arguments in criminal cases suggesting that a man's violence against a woman is justifiable if the woman has wounded the man's honor.[20] In the United States, it was not until 1920 that women enjoyed federal protection of the right to vote (through the Nineteenth Amendment) and it was not until the 1970s that the U.S. Constitution's provision for political equality (in the form of the Fourteenth Amendment's equal protection clause) was interpreted by the Supreme Court to apply to women as well as men.[21]

According to feminism, empirical facts such as these clearly demonstrate the existence of a sexual hierarchy, and feminists further contend that this hierarchy/patriarchy has been held up as legitimate and justifiable by the teachings of numerous religions, intellectual traditions, and cultural authorities. For instance, feminists point out that the Judeo-Christian tradition has been invoked to convey messages of female subordination. In the 1200s, for example, St. Thomas Aquinas (1225–1274) pondered whether women's souls were different from men's, insofar as men were made in the image of God and women were crafted in the image of man (Adam).[22] Similarly, religious leaders have, at times, interpreted Islamic theology as condoning female subordination to men. One finds such interpretations of Islam in Iran, under the Ayotollah Ruhollah Khomeini (1900–1989), when women were denied the right to enter certain professions and were told by clerics that their basic duty was to be wives and mothers.[23] Palestinian women have also witnessed political and religious leaders in the liberation movement Hamas (an organization fighting for Palestinian autonomy relative to Israel) using religion to justify segregating women into confined, subordinate, and inferior social and political positions.[24] In some sects of Buddhism one also finds religion used as a justification for a sexual hierarchy: Women are denied the option of full ordination as monks and are restricted to lower positions (nuns) of leadership.[25]

In the intellectual traditions of Western philosophy, classical Greek theorist Aristotle (384–322 B.C.) was one of many philosophers who taught that women and men were fundamentally different and asserted that woman's highest function was having children, whereas man's highest purpose was intellectual creativity.[26] In the 1700s French philosopher Jean-Jacques Rousseau (1812–1867) continued the Aristotelian practice of using philosophy to legitimize patriarchy. Rousseau argued against tyranny and oppressive governments and in favor of individual liberty, as regarded men, but concomitantly taught that women should be subordinated to male authority within the family. A woman's duty was to please her husband, Rousseau asserted, and this was best accomplished by submitting to his will. Domination of men (by governments) was awful, according to Rousseau, but domination of women (by men) was natural and desirable.[27]

Outside the spheres of theology and philosophy, other cultural practices have often sanctioned and even glorified female submission to men. In the popular culture of the United States right after World War II, books and magazines told women to be happy wives and mothers and to avoid competing with men. A popular book from 1947 (titled *The Modern Woman: The Lost Sex*) proclaimed that ambitious, career-minded women were harmful to men. Women who sought educational and economic advancement were castigated as selfish, man hating, and family destroying. Indeed, in 1954 *Esquire* magazine labeled married working women a threat to society.[28]

Female subordination has been legitimized by cultural authorities outside the United States as well. In a number of African countries, female circumcision, also known as female genital mutilation (FGM), is a widely accepted cultural practice. FGM involves surgically changing a female's body in order to elicit male approval; in this procedure, a female (usually a young girl) has her clitoris (and, in some cases, surrounding tissue) removed, and her capacity for sexual pleasure is greatly diminished by this procedure. The resultant alteration and scarring of the genitals is also thought to increase male sexual pleasure during intercourse.[29] Whereas many U.S. feminists have supported efforts to end FGM, a number of African women have called on U.S. feminists to be reflective and cautious before rushing to condemn African culture. Indeed, U.S. readers of this book who may look on FGM as unthinkable might reflect on cultural practices in their own country involving altering the female body in order to stimulate male interest and desire (for example, plastic surgery, electrolysis, excessive dieting, liposuction, breast implants, and so on).[30]

Feminism includes more than a critique of patriarchy and its religious, philosophical, and cultural underpinnings. Feminism also involves policy advocacy, although feminists disagree as to which policies would best address the problems of patriarchy. Readers should not be surprised by this lack of consensus on the goals of feminism. Feminism, like the other ideologies discussed in this text, is a complex set of ideas and embraces a variety of outlooks. Liberal feminism, radical feminism, socialist feminism, and diversity feminism represent different feminist analytical and political perspectives.

## Liberal Feminism

Liberal feminists often trace their roots to the eighteenth-century writings of English philosopher Mary Wollstonecraft (1759–1797). Wollstonecraft wrote *A Vindication of the Rights of Woman* (1792). When Wollstonecraft was alive, English women were denied the right to hold office, to exercise custody over their children, to control property, and, in most cases, to divorce their husbands.[31] Wollstonecraft's

*Vindication* attacked the logic of this patriarchy by drawing on classical liberal ideology. As you recall from Chapter 5, classical liberals such as John Locke insisted that individuals had a natural right to be free and self-governing because individuals were naturally rational. The problem, Wollstonecraft pointed out, was that these Lockean liberal ideas were not made applicable to women. That which was construed as "human nature" (rationality) was really interpreted as *male* nature by writers (including Locke himself), who simultaneously proclaimed humans to be rational and women to be emotional, intellectually weak, and irrational. Wollstonecraft wanted women to be included within the concept of "human nature": She wanted women, no less than men, to be regarded as rational beings capable of self-determination and liberty.[32] Wollstonecraft argued that reason is a human trait, not just a male one.[33]

Wollstonecraft supplemented the preceding arguments with two other interesting observations. First, she contended that oppression creates vice. Specifically, when women are oppressed by patriarchy, women develop behavioral habits designed to appeal to male conceptions of proper femininity. Such traits include superficiality, obsequiousness, feigned weakness, supposed helplessness, and jealousy of other women. These behaviors are demeaning, irresponsible, and dishonest, Wollstonecraft argued. Men also develop vices under patriarchy. When society places men in a privileged position and tells them they are superior to women, men are in danger of becoming arrogant, full of themselves, and self-absorbed. Like children who have been spoiled by overly solicitous parents and who begin to feel that they always "deserve" the best presents, men can develop a sense of entitlement to the highest status in society. To end patriarchy would encourage both women and men to live more virtuously: If women were seen as men's equals, women would stop acting helpless and would begin to develop a sense of responsibility for their own lives, and men would stop relating to women from a position of condescension.[34]

Second, Wollstonecraft argued that love can be detrimental to women. Women have always been in a difficult position, according to Wollstonecraft, because the very group oppressing women is also a group whose members women love. Love and romance can impede women's ability to demand respect from men and equality with men. For these reasons, Wollstonecraft described romantic love as a potentially threatening and draining emotion.[35] Love could compel a women to continue submitting to men; after all, would it not be difficult for a women to be confrontational when dealing with a life partner and beloved husband? Could love not make a woman weak by diminishing her desire for autonomy? In making these observations, Wollstonecraft was not implying that women should sever their emotional ties to men. In fact, she believed that once women enjoyed equality with men, these emancipated women would make better wives and mothers. In her commentaries on love, Wollstonecraft was merely pointing out the provocative and intriguing thesis that women's struggle against male privilege would be complicated by the fact that, in a manner of speaking, women loved their oppressors.[36]

More recently, liberal feminism has been advocated by U.S. writer Betty Friedan (born 1921). Friedan was a founder of the National Organization for

Women (NOW) and is the author of various books and articles championing women's rights. Through her activism and her writings, Friedan has argued that women should enjoy the same freedoms accorded to men; that, for example, women should not be discriminated against in educational institutions, career growth, and economic advancement. As NOW's early organizing slogan proclaimed, women should be free to enter and succeed in the mainstream of society.[37] Liberal feminists have supported antidiscrimination measures, affirmative action, legalized abortion, funding for child care centers, flexible work hours, and other policies that would enhance women's ability to compete as the equals of men in existing economic, social, and political institutions.[38]

### Radical Challenges to Liberal Feminism

Many feminists reject liberal feminism. Socialist feminism contends that the mainstream of a society such as the United States should itself be radically changed. The goal should not be to bring women into the capitalist mainstream on an equal basis with men, but rather to organize for socialism. Socialist feminism conceptualizes capitalism and patriarchy as mutually reinforcing. For example, women's lack of equal access to economic resources—as seen in statistics indicating women's lower wages and lower levels of property ownership—promotes women's dependence on men (patriarchy). In turn, the social expectation that women will be "taken care of" by men (husbands making higher wages) justifies keeping women's wages low and thereby provides capitalism with a steady supply of cheap labor.

According to socialist feminists, capitalism and patriarchy also overlap through the **double day**—the workday during which women work for wages

---

**BOX 7.2  NOW and Feminism**

Established in 1966, the National Organization for Women (NOW) is a leading liberal feminist interest group in the United States. NOW has numerous state-level offices in the country, as well as chapters in Japan, Germany, and Great Britain. NOW has worked for abortion rights; nondiscrimination in terms of women's access to education, credit, insurance, pension coverage, and employment opportunities; antiviolence programs; lesbian rights; maternity leave for working mothers; and enforcement of child support laws. In support of these goals, NOW often works in alliance with a variety of other interest groups, including the League of Women Voters, Planned Parenthood, the National Black Women's Health Project, the Young Women's Christian Association, Delta Sigma Theta, the American Association of University Women, and the National Federation of Business and Professional Women's Clubs.

To see NOW's most recent press releases, newsletters, and activities, go to the group's Web site (http://www.now.org). As you can see, from the Web page you can join NOW, support its various activities, and get updates on the organization's goals from your own computer.

SOURCE: Sarah Slavin, ed., *U.S. Women's Interest Groups: Institutional Profiles* (Westport, CT: Greenwood, 1995), pp. 403–409.

(as employees at factories, offices, and so on) but also work for no wages (as wives and mothers in the family). The work at home, though unpaid, is crucial for the survival of capitalism because women rear new generations of future workers; provide a consumer market for goods and services the capitalists need to sell; and nourish, comfort, and care for other wage laborers (such as husbands) in the family so that these wage laborers remain healthy, reliable members of the workforce. Although men also perform unpaid labor in the family, they do so at rates considerably below those of women. For example, a recent study of U.S. families found that women engage in an average of 33 hours of unpaid family labor per week compared with 14 hours of comparable labor by men.[39] As a consequence, socialist feminists point out, the double day is primarily a female phenomenon. Socialist feminists also call attention to the fact that capitalist profits would be lowered if capitalists had to pay for these services. For socialist feminists, therefore, opposing patriarchy entails opposing capitalism.[40]

*Radical feminism* also rejects liberal feminism. Radical feminism shares with socialist feminism an opposition to mainstream institutions and politics. However, whereas socialist feminism emphasizes capitalism's complicity in the furtherance of patriarchy, radical feminism focuses on analyzing how men as a group have oppressed women and concentrates on offering alternatives to this oppression. In essence, radical feminists tend to view patriarchy as so thoroughly entrenched in the mainstream of most (if not all) societies that the only recourse to feminists is to advocate the fundamental (radical) alteration of the mainstream. For example, radical feminists have often critiqued the mainstream/traditional family as an arena of power in which women are oppressed by men, insofar as women have been expected to subordinate their interests, desires, and perspectives to those of fathers and husbands. Radical feminists have also maintained that everyday language tends to be patriarchal (for example, women are trivialized by male-oriented language such as "mankind," "salesman," "chairman," and so on), and that mainstream advertising and popular images of women are patriarchal (for example, images of women and notions of female beauty are narrowly constructed to cater to male desire rather than to affirm women's strength).

In addition, radical feminism has drawn on gay, lesbian, bisexual, and transgender activism to criticize mainstream attitudes toward sexuality. For instance, radical feminists have pointed out that a woman who lives as an independent individual (and who defines herself in a manner that does not include seeking out male approval) is vulnerable to charges of lesbianism. This charge is intended to censure and punish such a woman, insofar as the mainstream is characterized by *homophobia* (fear/hatred of gays and lesbians) and *heterosexism* (the view that heterosexuality is superior to homosexuality). Moreover, radical feminists have argued that the legal system of many societies is far from neutral on matters of gender. Many legal systems are patriarchal in that violence against and degradation of women are only partially criminalized. When depicted as art, such violence/degradation is protected as an acceptable form of entertainment, whether conveyed through "male" magazines, movies, or live performances. Degrading women is male sport, radical feminists assert, and a very popular sport, as indicated by the wealth generated by the pornography industry.[41]

As you can see from this brief overview of radical feminist perspectives, such feminists believe that moderate, liberal reforms designed to bring women into traditionally "male" careers and intended to boost the educational levels and earning power of women are pitifully inadequate in countering patriarchy. To launch a serious assault on patriarchy, one must commit to a process of rethinking our basic concepts of sexuality, language, law, and family.

*Diversity feminism* criticizes what it considers to be the narrow focus of liberal feminism. Diversity feminism draws on the experiences of women from multiple ethnic, racial, cultural, and international backgrounds.[42] It opposes the privileging of any single ethnic, racial, cultural, or national perspective on women's issues. Diversity feminism emerged, in part, because a number of feminists viewed other forms of feminism (especially liberal feminism) as concerned primarily with articulating the interests of a narrow cross-section (white middle class) of women. Diversity feminists contend that when one takes a cross-cultural/international approach to understanding women's issues, feminism comes to be understood in more inclusive, multicultural terms. For example, race may come to be seen as a feminist issue when one embraces a diversity feminism perspective. In this regard, many African-American and Latina feminists have argued that their oppression as women cannot be fully understood unless one takes into account how this oppression intersects with racial and ethnic oppression. Indeed, one of the interesting contributions made by a number of African-American and Latina feminists is the assertion that African-American and Latina women have been less likely than their Anglo counterparts to view the family as an institution of oppression. Whereas Anglo feminists have often seen women's traditional roles in the family as restricting women's choices, African-American and Latina women have been more inclined to see the family as an institution that helps hold their ethnic communities together and protects them from the debilitating effects of racism. Thus, Anglo feminists who offer generalized criticisms of the family as a patriarchal institution, without recognizing the family's importance in the lives of many African-American and Latina women, are myopic and exclusionary. In expanding feminist ideology to include an awareness of race, ethnicity, and culture, diversity feminism seeks to correct the myopia.[43]

Diversity feminism also maintains that "women's issues" vary cross-culturally and internationally. For example, in India, nineteenth-century women's rights advocates organized in opposition to youthful marriages, discrimination against widows, and unequal educational opportunities, and twentieth-century Indian women activists defined national independence from the colonial power Great Britain as a "woman's issue." Throughout the Indian independence movement, Mohandas K. (the Mahatma) Gandhi stressed the importance of national independence for Indian women and repeatedly drew on Hindu goddesses as symbols of strength and autonomy. By the time independence was achieved in 1947, many Indian women had contributed to the independence movement through their participation in women's organizations, their donations of money and jewelry to the independence cause, their picketing of British imports, their leadership in strikes and protest movements, and their clandestine actions against British rule.[44] Although not every feminist would see nationalism as a feminist issue, diversity feminists conclude that feminism should be inclusive enough to recognize those who do.

Diversity feminism argues that feminism should further acknowledge that in many developing countries illiteracy and poverty are major impediments to women's well-being and are therefore feminist issues.[45] In conclusion, diversity feminism challenges other forms of feminism to be careful to avoid misunderstanding women's lives by too narrowly defining women's experiences and concerns.[46]

As you can see, feminism addresses questions similar to those raised by Plato in the allegory of the cave. Enlightenment means embracing gender equality, feminism asserts, and, whether states are organized along Machiavellian or Madisonian principles, states should promote justice by passing laws that end sexual discrimination. In so doing, governments do, in fact, promote ethical outcomes (an abstract goal shared with fundamentalists), if, as Millians assert, living freely as self-regarding individuals is no less important for women as for men.

## ENVIRONMENTALISM

**Environmentalist** ideology asserts the importance of viewing natural resources from an ecological perspective. The term *ecology* was coined in the 1860s by German biologist Ernst Haeckel to refer to the disciplinary study of how organisms relate to their surrounding environments.[47] The study of ecology is the study of interdependence—of the connections between organisms and the life-sustaining materials (such as soil, water, and air) and processes (such as photosynthesis) that comprise ecosystems.[48] As advocates of an ecological perspective, environmentalists emphasize the importance of protecting the natural resources found within the earth's varied ecosystems. Environmentalists further point out that given the interconnections between elements of an ecosystem, the alteration or destruction of one element within that system is likely to have consequences for all the remaining elements.

Environmentalist ideology has been an important force in twentieth-century politics, but its roots are much older. As early as the 1600s, English observers were already documenting industrial pollution's harm to plant and human populations. At this time, advisers proposed the construction of higher chimneys to try to distribute toxins away from the immediate vicinity of people and plants. By the 1800s, English scientists were discovering acid rain. In the same century, French, Swedish, and U.S. scientists were putting together sufficient data to realize that increased levels of atmospheric carbon dioxide had the potential to alter climate patterns and eventually produce global warming.[49] During the same period, groups such as the French National Society for the Protection of Nature (established in 1854) and the British Society for the Preservation of Wild Fauna of the Empire (established in 1903) were working for the establishment of land reserves to be set aside and protected in near-pristine conditions so that hunters and adventurers could escape to unpolluted wilderness areas.[50]

Like many other ideologies, environmentalism has proven to be a complex set of arguments, and as the ideology has developed, tensions and disagreements among its advocates have contributed to the ideology's complexity. However, although individual environmentalists may offer divergent perspectives on an array of specific topics, environmentalism, like other ideologies, is held together by widespread agreement on key questions. What are the tenets of environmentalism?

## Basic Principles

Environmentalists argue that humans have a responsibility to use natural resources in a manner that is supportive of ecosystem integrity.[51] Ecosystem integrity (viability and health) may require that certain resources be protected from depletion; that land or water be conserved; and that development projects involving roads, dams, and buildings be curtailed. U.S. environmentalist Aldo Leopold (1886–1948) expressed this idea in advocating that humans recognize ethical obligations to nature. Being true to any ethical system that imposes obligations on us, Leopold maintained, entails limiting one's actions to those actions considered right by the terms of the ethical system itself. Although it is commonplace for individuals to subscribe to ethical frameworks (for example, religions) that dictate obligations to the human community, Leopold calls on us to desist from actions that harm natural ecosystems.[52]

Implicit in Leopold's writing—and in environmentalism generally—is the notion of *ecological stewardship*. Humans have a responsibility to act as ecological stewards, or caretakers, of the earth; an ecological steward is one who nourishes and protects what is left in his or her care. Such a steward may have the power to overfish a stream, pollute a river, litter a field, or overgraze a pasture, but would no sooner destroy these natural ecosystems than a devout religious person would defile a holy space.[53]

The concept of stewardship is linked to the idea of *sustainable development*. Sustainable development is development designed to use natural resources in a manner that neither depletes nor destroys elements of the ecosystem. It is oriented toward ensuring that a developed area within an ecosystem does not diminish the

---

**BOX 7.3   Environmentalism**

- Emphasizes preservation of ecosystem health and well-being
- Calls on women and men to assume obligations to nature
- Advocates environmental stewardship
- Proposes that any use of nature be done in a manner supportive of sustainable development
- Claims that owning natural resources does not imply complete

discretion over use of those resources

- Rejects the belief that humans are the center of the universe and masters of nature
- Suggests that economic value is not the only value to consider when calculating the worth of natural resources

ecosystem's viability. For example, sustainable development advocates have been critical of construction projects that threaten to reduce an ecosystem's biodiversity. As a result, environmentalists have opposed real estate, reservoir, and highway development in central coastal California that would threaten the California red-legged frog by draining the wetlands and enclosing the open spaces comprising its habitat.[54] Similarly, sustainable development advocates have been critical of land development in Utah that endangered local ambersnail populations and have organized in opposition to landfill projects in Massachusetts that posed threats to indigenous salamanders.[55] Other sustainable development advocates have argued against clear-cutting forests, insofar as such practices lead to the eventual exhaustion of timber resources, just as overfishing oceans and rivers threaten the depletion of fish. With respect to the latter, for example, overfishing in British waters has significantly reduced the cod population.[56] In each of these cases, environmentalists contend, development has destroyed ecosystem sustainability.

When you examine the stewardship concept closely, you can see that this concept challenges individuals to rethink the connections between ownership and use. The stewardship concept stands in opposition to the assumption that ownership is an entitlement to total discretion over use. Owning land gives the owner no greater claim to misusing land than is given to nonowners. For environmentalists, environmental obligations and the stewardship principle apply universally—to land that is owned by users as well as to land that is not owned by users.[57]

Indeed, the principle of ecological stewardship has prompted some environmentalists to call into question the concept of ownership in relation to natural resources generally. Although ownership is a useful notion in terms of demarcating territorial claims of humans, it may be illogical in terms of ecosystems. Specifically, although I may be able to survey my property and fence it off from your property, on "my property" other species have arguably as much claim, at any moment, to elements of the ecosystem as have I. As writer Sue Hubbell explains, after reflecting on whether she truly "owns" her farm in the Ozark mountains, the concept of ownership is something of an ecological fiction. Hubbell points out that her farm would not be worth owning were it not for the multiple life-forms and processes that contribute to its fertility and viability. Yet these life-forms and processes could not be more oblivious to her legal title of ownership. Hubbell realizes that, on her land, bugs, worms, bees, birds, and other animals interact with each other and the land and water to use, fertilize, replenish, and restore natural resources. These interactions involving the birth, death, decay, and reproduction of bodies sustain the ecosystem in countless ways—results that "owners" cannot accomplish for themselves but on which "owners" are dependent.[58]

Preserving ecosystem integrity, environmentalism teaches, requires abandoning a conquering or dominating approach to nature. To dominate something is to imply mastery over it. According to numerous environmentalists, humans lack any credible intellectual basis for thinking of themselves as masters of nature. Human knowledge of nature and natural processes is extremely limited, and one cannot exhibit mastery over something one cannot even know. For example, biologists have pointed out that much of the natural world remains uncharted. Biologists do not even know how many species of life exist on Earth.

There are at least 1.4 million species and, perhaps, as many 30 million different species,[59] but because our knowledge of ecosystems is fundamentally limited, we should be cautious and, perhaps, even humble—not domineering—in using natural resources.

Moreover, environmentalists maintain, it is clear that ecosystem viability is not based on human mastery over or centrality in relation to other species. Ecological perspectives point out that humans are not the center of the natural world nor the objective of species diversity and evolution. U.S. naturalist and environmentalist John Muir (1838–1914) expressed this point rather bluntly in a nineteenth-century essay on nature. Many individuals, assuming that the purpose of nature itself is to meet human needs, have perhaps not considered the implications of the fact that many animals can devour humans in minutes and that the natural elements can kill humans just as quickly. Indeed, does it not make as much sense to see humans as wild animal dinners than as masters of the universe? Would it not be just as logical to describe humans as naturally "decayable" as naturally supreme? Rather than positing that humans are the rightful masters of nature, Muir reasoned, it is more empirically and logically sound to view ecosystems as spheres within which multiple life-forms interact, alternate as predator and prey, and exist in relations of interconnectedness but not single-species (human) domination.[60]

Environmentalists argue that the effort to exert human mastery over nature has prompted many actions culminating in environmental degradation and human crisis. Examples abound, whether you look at affluent countries or at poorer ones. For instance, after World War II the U.S. government's decision to promote the Green Revolution in Central America (high-yield, technology-intensive farming) as preferable to lower-yield, labor-intensive farming encouraged agricultural dependency on highly toxic pesticides. This effort to master the land through pesticide-oriented agriculture provided enormous cash crops (cotton) but also produced pesticide-resistant insects, pesticide-related illnesses and deaths, and overfarmed land.[61] Problems no less serious confront citizens of Nepal, where deforestation has made fuel gathering so difficult for local families that up to one-fourth of the total amount of household labor is expended on this basic task.[62] In China, soil erosion has reduced the area of sustainable crop land and has contributed to population movements into already crowded urban centers.[63] In northern Canada, hydroelectric energy projects, logging, and pulp mill operations have threatened forests as well as the indigenous populations residing in the affected areas.[64] In central and eastern Europe, industrial pollution has damaged air, water, and soil in a number of countries. For example, in recent years, more than 50 percent of Czech drinking water has been reported as environmentally degraded and more than 40 percent of the forests in Poland, eastern Germany, and Bulgaria have been harmed by acid rain.[65]

In the United States, road construction, suburban growth, and agribusiness decisions to convert increasing acres of prairie into grain fields have destroyed ground covers, driven away naturally occurring predators such as wolves and bears, and consequently encouraged the overpopulation of raccoons, skunks, cowbirds, and other bird predators. As a result, grassland bird numbers are rapidly declining.[66] In U.S. forest reserves and public lands, decisions to impose human management over ecosystems by removing wolves and coyotes have contributed to deer overpopulation, which, in turn, has damaged indigenous plant life through overgrazing by deer.[67] At the same time, watershed and groundwater degradation caused by toxic runoff from industries, farms, logging operations, and urban sewage systems has compromised water quality. Indeed, according to the Environmental Protection Agency, between 1992 and 1994 almost one-sixth of the U.S. population was exposed to polluted drinking water.[68]

Perhaps no incidence of environmental degradation has received more attention from environmentalists than the case of the Amazon rain forest. The Amazon rain forest is the largest tropical forest on Earth and is also the site of one of the highest rates of deforestation.[69] Burning and clearing of forests for such purposes as cattle ranching have threatened indigenous peoples and plants. For example, curare extract, which pharmaceutical companies purchase from a number of indigenous peoples in the Colombian, Ecuadorian, and Peruvian sections of the Amazon, is increasingly scarce.[70] Deforestation has also threatened the extinction of knowledge regarding pharmacological benefits of native plants. Specifically, as local populations are pushed out of forests designated for burning and clearing, these people are forced to acclimate to new settings. Over time, their knowledge of how to use rain forest plants for food and medicine will likely die out, as well as any hope that this knowledge might hold for medicinal breakthroughs in preventing and treating disease.[71]

If environmental degradation is not checked, people are threatened with the eventual loss of wilderness itself, as well as the depletion of natural resources within wilderness areas. For example, when rivers and streams are polluted, the human population has not only lost a natural resource such as drinking water but also a contact point with nature itself. The two types of losses are very different but equally tragic, and environmentalists have been pointing to the dangers associated with both types of loss for two centuries. In 1854, Henry David Thoreau (1817–1862) published *Walden,* an account of his experiences living along Walden Pond in Concord, Massachusetts. Thoreau's essay suggested that something had been destroyed in the daily affairs of urban living. Most humans had begun to live artificially—measuring their worth and their accomplishments by means of arbitrary notions of "making it." How had this happened? Thoreau came to believe that the individuals had stopped living thoughtfully. They had lost their point of contact with nature—which, after all, is reality—and consequently they had forgotten how to live anything but artificial, unreal lives.

In his own sojourn in the natural world of Walden Pond, Thoreau found a means of distancing himself from the falsity and pretense of the humanly constructed world of materialism. By finding a contact point with nature, Thoreau learned to distinguish between what was real and what was phony, between what was truly necessary for living a good life and what was merely society's pretension.[72]

Yet what happens if Walden Pond disappears? What if the woods, ponds, and deserts are degraded to the extent that our contact points with nature are lost? U.S. writer Edward Abbey (1927–1989) has warned against such an eventuality.

We must preserve wilderness areas, Abbey argued, because we need places where we can experience ourselves and the world in biological, natural terms.[73] We need wilderness areas to remind us that we are biological creatures within larger ecosystems. Because so much of the humanly constructed world would make us forget that we are animals, we need to preserve ecosystems and wildlife areas in order to grasp our own biological nature.[74] We need to know what nature is so that we do not begin to mistake our materialistic culture as "natural." Otherwise we will become like the artificial individuals discussed by Thoreau. Thus, for Abbey, as for Thoreau, preserving nature implies something much more than conserving natural resources for human consumption.[75] Preserving nature implies holding tightly to that which tells us where we come from in a world of technological and material progress that would erode our animalistic and biological sensibilities. As fishing writer Le Ann Shreiber suggests, no state of consciousness seems more real and more complete than one experienced out-of-doors.[76]

Environmentalism concludes that nature is worthy of conservation even when there is no tangible economic benefit to humans. Songbirds, Leopold argued, lack any meaningful economic value, but they should be protected from destruction anyway.[77] Environmentalists have extended the same argument to wild trout, condors, swamps, and deserts. Indeed, considering that condors, wild trout, and the like cannot be recreated if they are lost, they are arguably more valuable—in terms of replacement value—than many items given enormous economic value by society.[78]

## Diversity within Environmentalist Ideology

Despite widespread agreement on the preceding principles, environmentalists differ on issues relating to land use and north–south questions. With respect to land use, two issues have recently divided environmentalists. The first concerns placing a price on wilderness. Some environmentalists have argued that environmental protection would be furthered by a policy of pricing access to wilderness. Perhaps hiking, swimming, fishing, and other encounters with wilderness should be subject to user fees (beyond those already in place in some public parks) as a means of encouraging the public to regard wilderness as a valuable commodity. So regarded, wilderness areas might be better cared for, some environmentalists contend. Such arguments strike other environmentalists as misguided. Critics of the fee-based conservation approach argue that the logic of environmentalism calls for an appreciation of nature on its own terms; to price nature would be to conceptualize nature in terms of human monetary values rather than the simple fact of its existence.[79]

A second disagreement among environmentalists concerns land use by indigenous peoples in areas susceptible to severe environmental degradation. Should areas of wilderness be protected from human encroachment altogether, or is human use of and settlement in such areas consistent with the ecological perspective? Environmentalism's emphasis appears to be shifting from a strictly protectionist perspective (focusing on preserving the wild lands from human use) to one supportive of limited human use. One sees this shift in environmentalists' support for the rights of indigenous populations in extracting forest resources in Guatemala, Venezuela, Brazil, and other countries. The Rainforest Action Network, for example, tries to promote sustainable development by supporting local Amazon communities that sell adobe bricks rather than wood. Rainforest Action Network provides funding for the brick production and contends that as long as bricks are profitable, local populations will have an incentive to avoid additional wood-cutting in the rain forest.[80]

North–south issues also raise fundamental questions for environmentalist ideology. The north–south division concerns the differences separating the more affluent and industrialized countries (which are predominantly north of the equator) from the less affluent and less industrialized countries to the south. Environmental issues become complicated when viewed from a north–south perspective, insofar as what is identified as the crucial set of problems and goals varies with one's perspective. Northern environmentalists have often called for controls on pollution-causing industry and have often blamed population growth (which tends to be higher in the South) for straining environmental resources. Leaders of the South have pointed to excessive consumption patterns in the North as a strain on the environment and have at times pointed out the possible hypocrisy of the North in calling for strict environmental controls on industry *after* the North has already industrialized. Indeed, an examination of population numbers and statistics on resource consumption reveals the dilemma. The South is home to three-fourths of the earth's population, but this population uses only one-sixth of the earth's resources. In the North, one-fourth of the earth's population consumes most of the planet's resources and also generates almost all the ozone layer-destroying gases in the atmosphere.[81] Which concerns are more pressing—population or consumption, clean industry or economic development?

Clearly, for environmentalists, to gain enlightenment in Plato's sense we must think about political obligations and choices more broadly than the other ideologies suggest. We must observe obligations to help sustain ecosystem integrity. We must evaluate ethical questions—whether the questions of Aristotle, Tecumseh, Madison, or Mill—in terms of their impact on nature.

## A NOTE ON POSTMODERNISM

The ideologies discussed up to this point make many ethical claims, but what if there are no ethical absolutes? What kinds of ethical claims could remain once absolutes disappear?

**Postmodern** perspectives contend that any ideology putting forward absolute statements as timeless truths should be viewed with profound skepticism. Indeed, postmodern theorist Jean-François Lyotard (born 1924) explains that postmodernism calls into question "metanarratives." A metanarrative is any system of thought that identifies its own explanation of reality as an undeniable truth having validation independently of the premises and structures that make up the system of thought itself. Metanarratives present themselves as descriptions of and prescriptions regarding an independently existing reality, when in fact they are not. Instead, metanarratives use language to create names for what the metanarrative labels as reality, as though reality were "just there" and as though the metanarrative were just a clear, neutral window allowing observation of the reality, without imposing any interpretation.[82]

Each of the ideologies previously discussed could be seen as examples of metanarratives, as understood by Lyotard. Liberalism and conservatism, for instance, are based on certain notions of human nature. But what if there is no such thing as human nature as liberals and conservatives describe it, except as it exists as a category within their own descriptions? Ideology as metanarrative imposes a meaning that would not exist in the way the ideology is presenting it, if not for the ideology. To return to our example of human nature, postmodernism posits that human nature is presented by liberalism and conservatism as a fact of life, whereas human nature is actually a phrase within an ideology's language and frame of reference that, through its usage by an ideology's followers, imposes a meaning on an array of human actions that in and of themselves are neither "natural" nor "unnatural." In and of themselves, such actions are just that—actions. It is the ideology's terminology that makes them seem like human "nature."[83] Many feminists have embraced postmodernism because its teachings offer a powerful critique of so-called ideological truths concerning male superiority; such "truths" are not true at all, but are instead claims that a man has a "nature" that is distinct from and superior to a woman's "nature."[84]

Not surprisingly, postmodernism is often associated with relativism. In denying any ideology's claim to absolute truth, postmodernism suggests that what we consider true is inevitably a product of our own individual frame of reference.[85] Socialist frames of reference produce truths distinct from the truths of religious fundamentalists, for example. To postmodernism's supporters, this relativism is seen as a liberating alternative to the rigidity of metanarratives.

Moreover, supporters of postmodernism have noted that postmodern perspectives highlight the importance of avoiding the temptation to see one's own frame of reference as somehow superior to all others because in doing so, one would be turning one's frame of reference into a metanarrative. As theorist Judith Butler explains, postmodern relativism challenges us to see ideological frameworks not as unquestionable truths but as various viewpoints about which we can debate. The inability to come up with ultimate truths, Butler writes, invites us to engage in critical thinking about political issues.[86] Indeed, a recurrent theme of postmodernism is the celebration of the diversity of thinking that logically follows from rejecting orthodox beliefs. If metanarratives are groundless, if truth is relative, then widely divergent notions of ethics, politics, and social relations—previously repressed by metanarratives that closed off all unorthodox explanations of reality—gain credibility as competing options.[87]

In contrast to postmodernism's sympathizers, critics have often found postmodernism's relativism disturbing and intellectually unconvincing. To assume a position that questions all claims of absolute truth has looked to some writers like a call for dismissing the existence of the world itself. After all, one might ask, if all knowledge/truth about the world depends on the frame of reference within which we operate, is this not an argument proposing that nothing other than our frame of reference is real?[88] In reply, a postmodernist might respond that the mere posing of the question (and the assumption that the question is important enough to pose) reflects the acceptance of numerous philosophical starting points (for example, that there is such a thing as reality that is knowable), and postmodernism can become an analytic way of seeing that these starting points are themselves created by people asking one sort of questions and excluding others. Starting points are never really starting points because they are not independently existing neutral or natural absolutes, according to postmodernism.

As to the question, What kind of ethical claims remain once absolutist thinking has been debunked?, postmodernism would suggest the following answer: Claims that present themselves as dependent on and rising out of the frames of reference that create them would remain, but not claims that present themselves as having an independence of their narrative, linguistic, ideological structures (as being meta or above any narrative or frame of reference).

## SUMMING UP

- **Feminism** advocates gender equality. Feminism has sought to point out deeply entrenched patriarchal assumptions in culture and intellectual traditions and to argue against systems of thought and political practices (e.g., the double day) that would elevate men's concerns and interests over those of women. Liberal feminism, radical feminism, and diversity feminism offer alternative feminist perspectives on gender issues.

- **Environmentalism** asserts that ecosystem integrity is a political issue. The destruction of natural resources threatens human communities no less than war, civil disorder, and other issues recognized as important by political ideologies. Humans should act as stewards of nature and expand the concept of political obligations to include obligations to preserve ecosystems.

- **Postmodernists** put forward the concept of metanarratives to describe ideologies (and outlooks generally) that posit objective truths (truths presented as intrinsically true rather than as mere propositions dependent on the metanarratives to make sense). Postmodernism rejects metanarratives as sources of intrinsic truth.

## STUDY QUESTIONS

1. How is feminism similar to liberalism?

2. What is patriarchy? Feminists point to many examples of patriarchy. Identify four of these points.

3. Compare and contrast liberal, radical, and diversity feminism.

4. Environmentalism asserts the importance of assuming an ecological perspective and of seeking to protect ecosystem integrity. What is an ecological perspective? What is ecosystem integrity?

5. Discuss the concepts of stewardship and ownership as they pertain to the environmentalist perspectives.

6. Should humans consider themselves masters of nature according to environmentalist John Muir? Explain.

7. Identify and discuss two debates causing disagreements among environmentalism in recent years.

8. What are metanarratives, viewed from a postmodernist perspective?

## FOLLOWING UP THROUGH INTERNET RESOURCES

*Feminism*

- Women Leaders Online (http://www.wlo.org)

- National Organization for Women (http://www.now.org)

- Center for American Women and Politics (http://www.rci.rutgers.edu/~cawp/index.html)

*Environmentalism*

- Rainforest Action Network (http://www.ran.org)

- Sierra Club (http://www.sierra-club.org)

- Green Parties of North America (http://www.greens.org)

# 8

❖

# Comparative Politics I

## Governmental Systems: Democracy and Nondemocracy

omparative politics is the study of how governments, political groups, political procedures, and citizenship vary across countries or time periods. Consider, for example, how different your life would likely be depending on whether you were a citizen of Nigeria or a citizen of Iceland. With a population in excess of 88 million, Nigeria is the most populous country in Africa. A former colony of Great Britain, Nigeria has been independent since 1960. Nigeria is home to a diverse population: Hundreds of dialects are spoken, and Muslim, Christian, and indigenous religions prevail. Although rich in resources, Nigeria is ranked by UN organizations as a low-income country. Nigerians have a life expectancy of less than 55 years, and fewer than 50 percent of the population has attended grade school. Politically, Nigeria has experienced civil war and authoritarian government since independence.

Iceland is one of Europe's smallest countries. It is the size of Virginia and has a population of less than 1 million. Ethnic and religious divisions are virtually nonexistent. Most citizens are of Norwegian or Celtic ancestry, and 95 percent of the population is Protestant. Iceland was an independent country from 930 to 1262. It was governed by Denmark from 1380 to 1918 and established complete independence in 1944. Iceland is a democracy with literacy rates (99 percent of the population) and life expectancies (76 years for men and 81 years for women) among the highest in the world.[1]

As this example illustrates, the range of potential differences separating one country from another is remarkable. This chapter explores some of the ways in which political scientists attempt to understand the logic of different political systems by means of comparative analyses. Specifically, in this chapter we compare the United States and other countries. This comparison can help us understand not only the United States and the other countries but also the role of U.S. politics as a component of the larger study of world politics. Such comparisons can help us avoid seeing U.S. politics in isolation, having no relationship to other systems or lacking any contextual grounding in larger comparative frameworks for analysis.

## DEMOCRACY AS A FLUID AND VARIED GOVERNING PROCESS

One of the most basic ways of comparing countries involves classifying governments as democratic or nondemocratic. **Democratic governments** are ones in which the people and the government are connected; in other words, the people are self-governed. The origins of the word *democracy* reveal this connection: *Democracy* is the combination of the ancient Greek words *demos* ("the people") and *kratein* ("to rule").[2] When the *demos* and the process of ruling are brought together through (1) elections in which the people are free to select and reject government officials, (2) ongoing access to the government by the people between elections, and (3) the enactment of laws and policies reflecting the interests of a self-governing people, then it is clear that the people and the government are connected in terms of inputs (the *demos* shapes and influences the government) and outputs (laws and policies coming out of government and affecting the lives of the *demos* reflect the interest of the *demos* as defined by the *demos*). It is clear in such cases that the government is democratic.

---

**BOX 8.1  Democracy: Definition and Presuppositions**

*Democracy defined:* Democratic government is government in which the people and the government are connected in terms of both the input and the output dimensions of government. That is, the people are self-governing in terms of input (people have freedom to put ideas into government and to shape government through elections, contacting officials, lobbying, and so on), and the output (laws and policies) of government indicates that government is in the hands of a self-governing people.

*Democracy Presupposes That*

- People are free to participate in the governing process (participatory democracy).

- *All* the people are free to participate in the governing process (pluralist democracy).
- People are aware of what they are doing when they participate in the governing process so that their participation is a process of achieving self-government (developmental democracy).
- Government is not tyrannical and oppressive toward the people (protective democracy).
- Governmental outputs in the form of laws and policies are a reflection of self-governing people's desire for well-being (performance democracy).

---

However, when studying and comparing actual governments, political scientists quickly discover that few clear-cut cases of perfect democracy exist. In such cases, political scientists often find it useful to speak of *degrees* of democracy.[3] From this perspective, you can think of democracy as a set of processes or arrangements to which actual countries may conform to varying degrees. Countries may, at various times, be in *transition*, moving toward or away from democracy. Moreover, a government that may look democratic from one standpoint may look undemocratic from another.[4] Given these complexities, it is helpful to think of democracy in disaggregated terms, that is, in terms that isolate the individual components of the *demos–kratien* connection. Specifically, democracy may be viewed as consisting of five components: participation, pluralism, developmentalism, protection, and performance.[5]

**Participation** in selecting government officials is one of the most obvious ways in which people can be connected to their government. Indeed, the existence of elections in which all eligible citizens are free to vote, campaign, debate, and otherwise participate is a basic element of democratic politics. From the standpoint of this component of democracy, a country would look highly democratic if, in elections, voters freely chose between alternative parties and candidates and voted in high numbers. In contrast, low voter turnout, corrupt elections in which some groups enjoy undue influence, bogus elections in which the outcome is rigged by a dominant party or clique, or the absence of elections altogether indicate low levels of democracy from the standpoint of participation.

The term **pluralism** refers to the multiplicity, diversity, or plurality of opinions and groups free to express themselves within a political system. Pluralism's relationship to democracy is crucial: Democracy requires that *all* the people— with all their differing ideologies, opinions, values, and so forth—be free to connect to government. Ideally, pluralism requires that no single group have a special claim to be heard before any others or to silence any others. In this sense, democracy affirms that all groups and opinions in a society must be free to compete for attention and for followers.[6] If some opinions and groups are suppressed, which would be indicated by lower levels of pluralism, then the level of democracy drops.

**Developmentalism** is a subtle component of democracy, difficult to define and measure with precision. The term refers to the extent to which the people develop their human potential sufficiently to possess an awareness of their actions as part of the democratic process, including an awareness of their civic actions such as voting. From a developmental democracy perspective we can ask, If the people in a country vote in high numbers and have exposure to a wide range of groups and opinions, but act without awareness of what they are doing, can we say that democracy exists in a meaningful way?[7] To be blunt: If self-awareness or consciousness of the need for self-governance is absent, how can self-governance (that is, democracy) be possible? Does democracy not imply some level of developed intellectual self-awareness? If not, then could we not say that interactive entities (such as computers) are capable of democracy? Would we not have to conclude that robots are capable of democracy, if we were to disregard the developmental dimension of democracy, because after all robots could be programmed to carry out the function of voting even if they lacked awareness of what they had been programmed to do?[8] These are the kinds of questions raised when we begin thinking of what it means for a people to govern itself, from a developmental democracy perspective.

The **protection** component of democracy is democracy's commitment to limiting governmental power so that governments do not become tyrannical. For democracy to be authentic, the demos must be protected from excessive governmental regulation and control inconsistent with the democratic principle of self-government. Democracies have many options for limiting governmental power. Governmental power may be restrained through constitutional protections of freedom of speech, press, association, and religion; through checks and balances that protect against the possibility of one branch of government becoming all-powerful; and through fixed terms of office for politicians, which protect against the rise of a governing elite who could proclaim themselves rulers for life. When comparing governments from the vantage point of protection, political scientists often evaluate systems as highly, moderately, or minimally democratic, depending on whether those systems have effective mechanisms such as constitutional bills of rights, fixed terms of office, or other provisions for protecting individual liberties. Governments lacking well-defined safeguards against the expansion of governmental authority into the lives of the demos receive low rankings on protective democracy.

Democracy also includes a **performance** component. If a government is democratic—if it is reflecting and serving the *demos*—then the *demos* should be living as well as possible given the resources available within the territory of the state. If not, one might ask whether the government is performing in a democratic (*demos*-oriented) manner. In the fifth century B.C., the Athenian leader Pericles (c. 495–429 B.C.) recognized the performance dimension of democracy. Athenian democracy, he explained, was characterized by many attributes, including rule by the people and equality under the law, but also by a standard of living that sustained the people's happiness.[9] Today, levels of democracy, in this sense, might be measured by examining the quality of life of the people, insofar as the quality of life is influenced by governmental laws and policies. Political scientists who study countries from the standpoint of performance democracy might examine such factors as income levels, literacy rates, life expectancy, access to medical care, vulnerability to crime, and other quality-of-life issues. High rates of poverty in a country rich in both natural resources and the technology needed to develop them, for example, might raise the question of whether government policies reflect and serve the interest of a self-governing people.[10]

What follows from an analysis of each of these components of democracy? Certain implications become clear. First, discussions of democracy seem inescapably subjective.[11] Even when democracy is defined in reference to specific components, it is a subjective matter to decide how to apply the components to actual countries. For example, U.S. history is replete with instances of governmental suppression of speech and thought, from the Sedition Acts that cracked down on antigovernment writings in the early 1800s to Richard Nixon's harassment of antiwar protesters during the Vietnam War.[12] Do these examples indicate the absence of protective democracy? Consider also that voter turnout in the 1996 U.S. presidential election was less than 50 percent of citizens of voting age and, in 2000, it was only 51.5 percent. In the midterm elections of 2002 and 1998, voter turnout was lower still—39.3% and 37.6%, respectively.[13] Does this render the United States undemocratic, minimally democratic, or moderately democratic from the standpoint of participation? As you can see, you, your friends, and your professor might have radically different answers to these questions, and all of you might be equally well prepared to logically and empirically defend your various positions. Indeed, it seems impossible to discuss democracy without encountering this subjective dimension. It is important to keep in mind that democratic politics is characterized by fluidity, as degrees of democracy increase or decrease within the same country over time and as linkages between people and government are made more meaningful or more problematic by changes in laws, voter turnout, and the like.

As you reflect on this subjective component of democracy, factor into your analysis the possibility that citizen rage may be informing much popular decision making in the United States. Public administration professor Susan Tolchin finds that U.S. citizens are often voting out of anger and ill will toward others.[14] Another scholar believes that U.S. citizens are lacking in the kinds of attitudinal traits that contribute to democracy, such as tolerance and respect for a wide plurality of viewpoints.[15] Do these observations indicate that the United States scores low on the pluralist democracy scale? Political science provides no uniformly accepted answers. However, similar factors have led analyst Wilson Carey McWilliams to comment that the United States just might fail a democracy quiz if such a test were available to administer.[16]

Second, democracy's various components may not necessarily coexist harmoniously. For example, protective democracy and performance democracy may come into conflict. A comparison of the United States and The Netherlands on energy policy provides illustration. Both countries have developed energy policies designed to reduce carbon emissions from automobiles. U.S. policy revolves around higher industry efficiency standards and voluntary participation in clean air projects. Policy in The Netherlands focuses on heavy taxation of automobiles and gasoline. In contrast, gasoline taxes in the United States continue to be among the lowest anywhere. Notice the differences in the policies. The U.S. policy is less intrusive than The Netherlands policy in both extracting resources from the citizenry and attempting to modify citizen choices by shifting choices away from gasoline consumption. Thus, when these policies are examined from the perspective of protective democracy, the U.S. policy appears more democratic.

However, policy analysts have predicted that future U.S. carbon emissions will likely be higher than those of 1990, whereas The Netherlands plan aims to reduce future emissions. If The Netherlands outpaces the United States in emissions reductions, you could argue that the quality of life for the *demos* in The Netherlands improved beyond that of the United States. Thus, you might argue further that The Netherlands would look more democratic than the United States from a performance perspective.[17]

Third, democracy involves more than government. Democracy's logic assumes the existence of certain societal requirements, such as the presence of diverse groups from which candidates for office, competing points of view, and organized political activity emerge.[18] That is, democracy presupposes a certain kind of *civil society*. Civil society is that part of a country's life that is neither the government nor the economy but, rather, the domain within which interest groups, political parties, and individuals interact in politically oriented ways. If civil society is alive with active groups offering multiple opportunities for political debate, association, and interaction, one may find, for example, developmental and pluralist democracy outside of the government.[19] Indeed, creating democracy outside of the government (within civil society) may be crucial to the formation of democracy within government. For example, numerous scholars studying eastern Europe's democratization following the demise of the USSR have observed that to the extent to which civil society was democratic, this democracy outside of government created pressures for increasing the level of democracy within the government. Specifically, the church and the union movement in Poland, the dissident group Civic Forum in Czechoslovakia, and the human rights group Charter 77 in Hungary were vehicles for challenging authoritarian political structures and demanding governmental reform.[20]

Fourth, democracy's forms are very diverse. Some democracies have written constitutions, whereas others do not; some democracies have two major parties, whereas others have several major parties. In some democracies, the judiciary has the power of overturning acts of the legislature, whereas in other democracies courts lack such authority. Some democracies create executive branches that are independent of legislatures (presidential systems), whereas others merge the executive and legislative branches (parliamentary systems), as we explore in Chapter 10.

The diversity of democratic arrangements is also evident when one compares democracies that appear to be stable with those so new that their stability remains uncertain.[21] Stable democracies are not necessarily very old democracies. Germany, for example, is presently a stable democracy but, as discussed in Chapter 6, was a fascist state as recently as the 1940s. In addition to Germany, the United States, Japan, Canada, Switzerland, Iceland, France, Britain, Australia, and New Zealand are examples of democracies generally considered by political scientists to be stable. Democratic processes are stable in these countries, insofar as elections are held regularly and are competitive, political parties and interest groups organize openly, and civil rights and civil liberties are protected by law. Stable democracies also tend to share certain economic characteristics. These countries tend to be among the most affluent in the world. Average income levels tend to be high by global standards. These societies are home to some of the most highly developed public education systems, the most advanced medical facilities, and the most sophisticated technological resources.

Other democracies include countries that have recently and/or partially democratized. South Africa, Chile, Argentina, Brazil, Venezuela, the Czech Republic, Poland, Hungary, Estonia, Lithuania, and Slovenia are often cited as examples of new or transitional or partial democracies.[22] The economies of these countries generally produce lower average incomes and lower levels of access to education and health resources than do the more developed economies of the stable democracies. As you can see, a comparison of democracies may yield as many dissimilarities as similarities.

# DEMOCRACIES COMPARED

## Participation: The United States and Switzerland

Voting for candidates in elections is one of the most fundamental ways of participating in politics. In fact, many U.S. citizens regard voting for candidates for office as the most obvious means of connecting citizens to government.[23] Taking the United States as a case study, voting may be analyzed from a variety of perspectives, some of which are discussed in Chapter 9. Consider for now, however, the concept of an **electorate**. An electorate consists of those people who are eligible voters. Obviously, the way in which a country defines its electorate has profound implications for participatory democracy. For example, during the early and mid-1700s the electorate in the United States was defined very narrowly. Voting rights were denied to such "ineligibles" as slaves, women, apprentices, minors, indentured servants, and males older than age 21 who were still living at home with their parents. What made these groups ineligible for inclusion in the electorate? In part, they were considered ineligible because they were deemed "dependents." Dependents were viewed as individuals who had no economic, social, or moral basis for governing themselves; as such, it was assumed that they were dependent on others to make decisions for them. Women, for instance, were seen as needing the guidance of fathers or husbands, just as men who were not independent of their parents by age 21 could be viewed as too weak or immature to be self-governing.[24]

After the American Revolution and the ratification of the U.S. Constitution (1787), the definition of the electorate became more democratic. By 1840, most adult white males were eligible to vote, regardless of the amount of property they owned outright or with whom they resided. South Carolina was the last state to dispense with property qualifications for voting; it did so only reluctantly, at the end of the Civil War. In 1870, after Congress proposed and the states ratified the Fifteenth Amendment to the Constitution, African-American males were included in the electorate. However, poll taxes and literacy tests were used to circumvent the Fifteenth Amendment and thereby prevent African-Americans—and, in some cases, impoverished whites—from voting. Indeed, as late as 1964 five states collected annual poll taxes as a condition of voting.[25] Poll taxes in federal elections were prohibited under the terms of the Twenty-Fourth Amendment in 1964, and with the passage of the Voting Rights Act of 1965, Congress outlawed literacy tests.

In 1920, the Nineteenth Amendment expanded the electorate to include women. Women had been fighting for voting rights for almost 100 years by the time this amendment was ratified. The women's suffrage movement began in 1848, and between 1848 and 1920 women formed numerous interest groups (the National Woman's Suffrage Association, the American Woman's Suffrage Association, the National American Woman's Suffrage Association, the National Association of Colored Women, the Women's Political Union, and the Congressional Union, among others), lobbied both major political parties, organized demonstrations and protests, and pressured politicians in state and federal governments on behalf of voting rights.[26]

In 1971, the Twenty-Sixth Amendment secured voting rights for 18-year-old citizens. To put this amendment in perspective, it is important to realize that before ratification of the Twenty-Sixth Amendment, 18-year-old men were considered old enough to serve in the military even though they were regarded as too young to vote. In fact, many of these men were actually serving in the Vietnam War when the amendment was ratified. Voting rights were further broadened in 1982, when Congress passed legislation providing for the use of bilingual ballots in elections.

Thus, depending on your race, your gender, your age, your economic class, and/or your language, the United States may start to look democratic from the standpoint of voting rights in, perhaps, 1840, 1870, 1920, 1964, 1965, 1971, or 1982. Even with the expanded electorate, however, U.S. voters still govern themselves only *indirectly*, insofar as their votes select the political leaders who actually write and implement the laws of the land.

Some democracies—most notably, Switzerland—provide for a more direct form of participation in the governing process. Specifically, Swiss democracy is one in which citizens vote in elections to choose officeholders and in national referenda to determine the details of public policy. A **referendum** is an actual proposal that citizens vote directly for or against. Whereas referendum voting takes place in state and local elections in the United States, in Switzerland referendum elections are held at the national level. To a greater extent than almost any other democracy, Switzerland uses the national referendum process to decide important political issues.[27] Thus, a comparison of Switzerland and the United States illustrates contrasting ways in which democracies approach the participation component of democratic politics.

Switzerland uses compulsory and optional referenda. A compulsory referendum is used to review all proposed constitutional amendments. That is, any amendment offered as a possible addition to the Swiss constitution *must* be submitted to Swiss voters for approval or rejection through a referendum. In addition, referenda are optional means of reviewing all laws passed by the legislature and all international treaties. For example, if Swiss citizens wish to exercise the option of reviewing a law or treaty by means of the referendum process, 50,000 citizen signatures (drawn from a population of 6.7 million)[28] in favor of the referendum must be collected. Once these signatures are obtained, the referendum is conducted. Moreover, citizens may use their voting rights to introduce their own constitutional amendments; the voting procedure of initiating amendments—referred to as *constitutional initiative*—stipulates that amendments can be proposed directly by voters on the collection of 100,000 citizen signatures in support of such initiatives. Once proposed, citizen initiatives must ultimately be reviewed by the same process governing all proposed amendments—that is, by referenda. If a referendum fails, it can be considered at a later time. In fact, a September 2000 referendum decision against imposing a quota on the number of foreigners allowed into the country was the sixth such vote taken on immigration quotas in a 30-year period.[29]

Under Swiss democracy, therefore, when the electorate was expanded through constitutional amendments, Swiss voters were directly involved in the process. In a 1971 referendum, Swiss voters included women in the national electorate; in 1991, a referendum vote expanded the electorate to include 18-year-olds (previously the voting age was 20 years old). Notice, however, that both groups—women and 18-year-olds—were granted voting rights *later* in Switzerland than in the United States.[30]

Which country looks more democratic from the standpoint of participation? The answer is not clear-cut. On the one hand, U.S. women and 18-year-olds were long accustomed to voting by the time their Swiss counterparts won similar rights. On the other hand, once groups are enfranchised in Switzerland, they have a more direct influence in policymaking than do citizens in the United States. Indeed, by means of recent referenda and initiatives, Swiss voters have directly participated in political decision making on policies as diverse as immigration levels, the rights of conscientious objectors, abortion, the legal age of sexual consent, nuclear power plant closures, prohibiting cars on Swiss roads on certain days, the number of paid vacation days offered by industry, the length of the work week, price controls, whether the Swiss army should be abolished, and whether Switzerland should join international associations such as the International Monetary Fund and the European Community.[31]

## Pluralism: The United States and Germany

Democracies can advance pluralism in a variety of ways. For example, the state may *actively* encourage the emergence and continuation of groups within civil society, or the state may avoid actively promoting such groups and choose, instead, to assume a position of neither encouraging nor discouraging their existence.[32] A comparison of U.S. and German church–state relations illustrates these distinct approaches to pluralism. The German government actively supports churches, whereas U.S. policy toward churches is guided by the U.S. Constitution's First Amendment principle of separation of church and state.

---

**BOX 8.2   How Are Amendments Added to the Constitution in the United States?**

The U.S. Constitution provides that amendments to the Constitution be proposed by U.S. congressional action and ratified by state action. The Constitution outlines two options for both proposal and ratification: Amendments may be proposed by a two-thirds vote in both houses of Congress or by a constitutional convention called by Congress on the request of two-thirds of the states. Amendments may be ratified by three-fourths of the states acting through their respective legislatures or in special ratifying conventions in three-fourths of the states. Most amendments have been proposed by Congress and ratified by state legislatures.

Notice the logic of these provisions. In neither the proposal nor the ratification stage are American voters *directly* involved in the amending process. American citizens vote neither to propose nor to ratify amendments. In this sense, the United States provides a striking contrast to Swiss democracy's use of the national referendum in approving amendments to the Swiss constitution.

U.S. readers of this text are probably very familiar with the idea of the separation of church and state. To appreciate the logic of separation of church and state, consider the case of Mary Dyer. Mary Dyer emigrated to North America in the 1630s, became a member of the Puritan community of Massachusetts, and converted to the Society of Friends (Quakers) in the early 1650s. Massachusetts, however, banned the Quaker religion. Refusing to renounce her religion, she was hanged on June 1, 1659. Massachusetts repealed this law in 1661. The execution of Dyer and others like her illustrates the potentially dangerous authority wielded by the state over matters of religion in the absence of an establishment clause.[33]

The establishment clause has been interpreted by the U.S. Supreme Court to mean that Congress—and by extension other administrative units of the U.S. government—cannot establish an official church and that government authority cannot be used to advance religion in the United States. For example, the establishment clause has been used by the Supreme Court to prohibit mandatory Bible readings and prayers in public schools. As the Court sees it, to permit public school officials (insofar as public schools are government supported) to conduct religious activities within the schools is inconsistent with the First Amendment's principle of separating official government functions from religious functions.

How does this relate to pluralism? The logic of church–state separation suggests that no single church should be promoted above any others and that churches should exist in accordance with popular wishes, not in conformity with government directives. Church–state separation purports to insulate churches from government and thereby to protect their status as independent (independent of government) institutions within civil society. Religious freedom and diversity are the intended outcomes of this church–state relationship.[34]

Germany's constitution, known as the Basic Law, states that citizens of its democracy are also guaranteed religious liberty. However, in contrast to the United States, Germany uses the resources of government to foster religious development. Specifically, the German government collects a "church tax" from citizens and returns the proceeds from this collection to the religious organizations participating in the church tax program. The German government gives official recognition to religious organizations such as the Roman Catholic Church, the Evangelical (Protestant) Church, the Greek and Russian Orthodox Church, and the Central Council of Jews in Germany (Orthodox and Conservative). The religious organizations given this official status by government can benefit from the collection of "church" taxes.

Viewed from the perspective of pluralist democracy, the logic of this arrangement suggests that insofar as religious institutions have an important contribution to make in a diverse, pluralistic civil society, the state has a legitimate role in actively supporting them through such mechanisms as the church tax. Most German churches receive their funds through this system, although a few churches (such as Baptists and Methodists) do not participate in the church tax process.

The German church tax works in the following manner. A citizen who is a registered member of a recognized church or synagogue has a portion of his or her income automatically withheld from his or her pay. The actual amount withheld is based on the size of the individual's income. Although collected by the government, the church tax is legally regarded as a charitable contribution; as a result, the church tax is deductible and can thus be used to lower the individual's payment of overall income taxes. The state transfers funds collected through the church tax to the participating religious organizations, based on the affiliations designated by the individual taxpayers. For example, church taxes paid by a member of the Evangelical Church are distributed by the government back to the Evangelical Church. The government has no authority to determine how religious organizations spend the funds collected through the tax. An individual who wishes to stop paying the tax must notify the government that he or she is leaving the church or synagogue. The government then informs the religious organization that the person in question is no longer a registered member.[35]

The German approach to church–state relations has been justified as a viable approach to achieving pluralism because it can be seen as creating a context within which religious organizations are assured of funding without having to rely on soliciting the support of the wealthy.[36] If supporters of the church tax are correct, a diversity of religious beliefs is promoted by a system that protects religious institutions from ideological domination by those who could make the heftiest financial contributions. In addition, religious organizations often provide social support services in their communities, and these services require extensive funds.

By looking at one type of group—e.g., churches—within civil society, it is evident that democracies have an array of options in seeking to realize pluralism. Which approach has been more successful? The U.S. doctrine of separation of church and state has been used to prevent the emergence of a state-ordained religion. However, fundamentalist Christians, among others, have often expressed dissatisfaction with the Supreme Court's interpretation of the establishment clause. To some Christians, Court decisions to prohibit mandatory school prayer and Bible programs constitute attacks on religion itself; if such assessments are accurate, the end of school prayer and Bible verse readings bode poorly for pluralism because they represent efforts to reduce the diversity of society by suppressing certain (Christian) groups. At the same time, other critics contend that separation of church and state is incompletely enforced in the United States. Noting the existence of religious references on currency, in oaths sworn on taking political office, and in federal government proceedings (such as prayers in the U.S. Congress), advocates of a stricter separation of church and state argue that pluralism suffers when such indirect support of religiosity persists.[37]

Although the German system offers an alternative to the U.S. approach, the German church tax has its own critics. Some Germans oppose the tax on economic and freedom of choice grounds; German tennis star Steffi Graf is perhaps the best known celebrity to have exited a church, reportedly as a means of avoiding the church tax. In addition, critics have pointed out that religious organizations not granted government recognition are discriminated against under the church tax system. Muslim organizations are not recognized in the church tax system. Another controversy has surrounded the Church of Scientology in Germany in recent years. Founded in 1954, the Church of Scientology has 30,000 members (out of a population of 82 million) in Germany. The Church of Scientology argues that the German government has discriminated against it.[38] Not only has the German government not recognized the Church of Scientology as a church (rendering it ineligible for participation in the church tax system), but also Germany's conservative political party—the Christian Democratic Union (CDU)—has a history of excluding Scientologists from party membership. In fact, the youth sector of the CDU called for a German boycott of the movie *Mission Impossible* because Tom Cruise is a Scientologist. The Hamburg offices of the opposition Social Democratic Party also denied party membership to Scientologists in recent years. Objections to Scientology have become so widespread and so intense that German government officials recently opposed a German performance by U.S. jazz musician Chick Corea, who is a Scientologist.[39] Although it might not have occurred to you that watching Tom Cruise and listening to Chick Corea could be politically dangerous acts, it is clear that neither the U.S. nor the German approach to pluralism has been entirely successful in accommodating the multiplicity of group interests within civil society.

## Developmentalism: The United States and Argentina

**Political socialization** is a process of political learning that shapes an individual's political attitudes, values, and behaviors. Political socialization is the process of learning what it means to be a part of the political life of a country. The political socialization process encompasses the barrage of messages, conscious and unconscious, that individuals receive about how to think and act politically.[40] In all countries, political socialization takes place through a variety of institutions: Within families, parents convey political information to children; schools instruct students in the politically useful values of patriotism and obedience to law; and leaders of parties, interest groups, and government make speeches intended to socialize whatever political beliefs are valued by the leaders. Indeed, were it not for people's ability to tune out much of the political instruction directed their way, citizens might experience sensory overload in response to the political socialization process.

Political socialization can either promote or obstruct developmental democracy. That is, a country's political socialization processes can encourage consciousness of one's role in a collective process of self-government or can neglect this dimension of democratic community formation.

In comparing countries on the question of developmental democracy, it is helpful to examine their political socialization processes. In the United States, one finds two school programs of political socialization deemed to be conducive to the development of democratic attitudes: the Character Counts program and student dress codes. Supporters assert that both programs teach lessons in citizenship (serving as part of the political socialization process) and encourage democratic attitudes and actions by increasing democratic awareness (promoting developmental democracy).[41]

---

**BOX 8.3  Should Public Schools Try to Mold Democratic Character?**

The Character Counts program and dress codes are not the only issues pertaining to developmental democracy and U.S. public schools. School officials often try to shape student attitudes and behaviors. Certain language may be disallowed, for example, if it is regarded as inconsistent with the value system the school is working to promote. Although supporters may see such efforts as conducive to the creation of democracy-supporting character formation, critics may regard these actions as political socialization processes in which school officials overstep their authority and violate student rights. Consider the following two cases involving the New Mexico public schools in 1997. In one school, a student wrote a story about a boy who was coming to terms with being gay. The editor of the school's literary magazine accepted the story for publication, but the story was dropped by another teacher. In the second case, a student was expelled for uttering the word *penis*. In these cases, are schools training students to grow into adults of upstanding character and, thereby, nourishing developmental democracy, or are schools imposing tyranny?

SOURCE: "ACLU-NM Docket," *Torch* 31 (July–August 1997): 4–5.

---

Character Counts attempts to teach elementary through high school students what the program identifies as basic values, such as getting along with others and interacting in positive ways. Insofar as each of these fundamental values is viewed by supporters as being crucial to democratic politics, students exposed to Character Counts instruction are, at least hypothetically, better trained in democratic citizenship, according to the program supporters.[42] After all, as discussed previously, appreciating diversity is appreciating pluralism, one of the components of democracy. If Character Counts socializes support for pluralism, it is socializing support for democracy.

School-imposed dress codes for elementary through high school students have been identified as measures to regulate student behavior and penalize students who would choose attire associated with antidemocratic values. Among the students targeted by such policies are those thought to be actual or aspiring gang members. Using dress code policies, school administrators who suspected, for example, hair nets, baggy pants, athletic shirts or shoes, and gold chains to be gang attire could block the wearing of such items by imposing a school uniform.[43] The logic was clear: If schools suppress "gang" clothing, they can better suppress "gang" attitudes and can better socialize antigang values. Supporters of dress codes have not always agreed on what constitutes "gang attitudes," but it is evident that dress code advocates view gangs—with their supposed automatic links to crime, violence, and drugs—as threats to democracy and democratic values.

Notice how neither Character Counts nor the school dress code had anything to do with school subjects such as math, science, history, and so on. Both programs were and continue to be attempts to induce a specific type of learned behavior and thought process: Good, democracy-supporting students believe in certain fundamental values and do not dress (or, by extension, think) like gang members. It is because these two programs attempt to develop democratic aware-ness within the student population that they are examples of efforts to promote developmental democracy.

Critics of Character Counts and dress codes point to what they view as the inconsistency associated with claiming to teach democratic values through a process that delimits student choices on what is deemed a fundamental value as well as an appropriate pant size. Even so, the U.S. government has used its influence to ensure that both programs become part of the long-term school political socialization and developmental democracy process. For example, in addition to former President Clinton's official endorsement of both programs, the U.S. Department of Educa-tion distributes a manual to help schools implement dress codes.[44] Here we see again the subjective aspect of democracy. Do you believe Character Counts and dress codes nourish the development of democratic awareness? Should President Bush push for their expansion?

As is true in the United States, Argentina's political socialization processes have important implications for developmental democracy. Argentina's transition toward democracy is of recent origin, stemming from the 1983 election of civil-ian president Raul Alfonsin. Under Alfonsin and his successors Carlos Menem, Fernando de la Rua, and Nestor Kirchner, Argentina has had regular elections but considerable social and economic conflict.[45] Having taken this step toward participatory democracy, Argentina has also instituted programs to facilitate the realization of developmental democracy. With respect to the latter, the Newspa-pers in the Schools Program was a project designed to foster democratic attitudes and behaviors.[46]

The Argentine Newspapers in the Schools Program was introduced originally in 1986 in Buenos Aires. In 1987, the program was broadened to include schools throughout the country. Through this project, newspapers were provided free of charge to schools for use in civics instruction in sixth- and seventh-grade classes. The details of the program were very simple: Students read and discussed articles they found in the newspapers. The logic of the program, however, was more complex. The program was intended to educate students about political matters, as well as to inculcate in them the view that debate, discussion, and disagreement over politics are positive and worthwhile activities. Indeed, a major goal of this program was to teach students to value the plurality of opinions that may emerge from rather lively and heartfelt political arguments. In fact, research suggests that students who participated in Newspapers in the Schools were more tolerant of diverse opinions than students who did not participate.[47]

Newspapers in the Schools has been viewed by supporters as especially important in Argentina given the "newness" of the country's democracy. After all, supporters ask, is it not reasonable to conclude that democratic values need to be given special emphasis in the political socialization processes of a country that until recently was accustomed to military rule? The profound commitment to this program felt by its supporters explains the decision to offer it to sixth- and seventh-graders instead of older students. Although supporters were aware that older students could possibly be more adept at processing abstract political issues, endorsers decided to launch the program in the earlier grades in order to reach more students. Especially in rural areas, large numbers of students leave school after the seventh or eighth grade.[48]

The U.S. and Argentine programs illustrate that what may look like purely personal decisions are, in reality, very politically relevant. Viewed in relation to developmental democracy, one's character, clothing, and willingness to engage in political debate are matters of public importance. As a result, democracies may take everything from clothes to reading habits very seriously and may attempt to socialize democratic choices; they may, in other words, make the political socialization process indistinguishable from the pursuit of developmental democracy.

## Protection: The United States and Great Britain

The **Bill of Rights** (the first 10 Amendments)[49] to the U.S. Constitution exemplifies one important way in which the United States seeks to realize protective democracy. The Bill of Rights proclaims that U.S. citizens are protected from a wide array of governmental intrusions into their lives, ranging from government control of the press to government confiscation of private property without fair compensation. The Constitution was ratified in 1787; the Bill of Rights was not added until 1791. The inclusion of the Bill of Rights was prompted, in great part, by ongoing criticism of the original Constitution; critics noted that the original Constitution gave scant attention to democratic freedoms but considerable support to the idea of a strong central government. Thus, while the Bill of Rights is a key element of U.S. protective democracy, the Constitution of which it is a part was originally written without explicit mention of the rights delineated in the First through the Tenth Amendments.[50]

Consider how different life in the United States could be if we lacked the following Bill of Rights protections:

- *First Amendment.* Provides for freedom of speech, press, religion, and association.
- *Second Amendment.* Protects rights to arms.
- *Third Amendment.* Protects citizens against arbitrary government requirements for the housing of troops.
- *Fourth, Fifth, and Sixth Amendments.* Provide for numerous rights of those accused of crime, including protections against unreasonable searches and seizures, double jeopardy, and self-incrimination. Further affirm that those accused of crime have the right to know the charges against them and to confront witnesses against them.
- *Seventh Amendment.* Provides for rights in common law cases.
- *Eighth Amendment.* Prohibits cruel and unusual punishment and excessive bail.
- *Ninth Amendment.* Protects against the denial of rights possessed by the people but not listed in the above amendments.
- *Tenth Amendment.* Provides for recognition of powers held by state governments.

In analyzing the significance of these amendments from the standpoint of protective democracy, it is instructive to keep in mind two points. First, the protective component of democracies calls for protection against *excessive* intrusion into people's lives by government, but not for the absence of any such intrusion. In fact, democracies sometimes justify the regulation of specific actions by individuals or groups in the interest of protecting public order in the absence of which popular government cannot thrive. Such was the argument of President Bush and Attorney General John Aschcroft in pushing for congressional passage of the USA Patriot Act after 9/11. The Patriot Act expands government's power to (1) monitor personal records (medical, reading, travel, and financial) of individuals, (2) prohibit third parties who are being required to release such information from informing the individuals in question; and (3) direct governmental authorities to enter and search private property. With respect to governmental surveillance of personal records, for example, Section 215 of the Patriot Act allows the FBI to obtain the library records of individuals, and library officials are required to keep such seizures secret.[51]

How is this possible under the conditions of protective democracy? If one looks to legal history, one finds that the Bill of Rights has never been interpreted by the U.S. courts as implying *absolute* freedoms. The First Amendment, for example, protects freedom of expression, but not absolute freedom of expression; expressions deemed libellous or obscene are subject to regulation, as are expressions of sexual harassment. In short, protective democracy restrains governmental power but does not leave government disempowered.[52]

Second, the *actual* protection afforded by the Bill of Rights depends on judicial interpretation and governmental enforcement. The mere presence of the Bill of Rights as a document means very little until the U.S. courts give meaning to the document through their interpretations and until these judicial rulings are enforced throughout the land. For instance, in 1965, when the Supreme Court rendered its decision in *Griswold* v. *Connecticut,* the Bill of Rights was interpreted as one part of the Constitution, implying that U.S. citizens had a *right to privacy,* which meant in this particular case the state of Connecticut could not forbid married couples from using contraceptives. In 1973, the Bill of Rights was one part of the Constitution used again by the Supreme Court to uphold an individual's right to privacy, which, in the case of *Roe* v. *Wade,* was said to include the right of a woman to decide to obtain an abortion.[53] As the U.S. government enforced these decisions, protective democracy was broadened to include these new privacy rights. These rights were "new" even though they were derived from amendments that were hundreds of years old. Ironically, the meaning of the Bill of Rights relative to reproductive rights was nonexistent for most of the amendment's life.

Great Britain's approach to protective democracy through constitutional government provides a contrast to that of the United States. In short, Great Britain has historically possessed no single written constitution nor any single, specific, written bill of rights. However, the traditions by which the constitution is constituted include both written documents, laws, and legal decisions as well as unwritten but long-standing practices. In other words, Britain has had an unwritten constitution consisting of principles and customs based on the country's legal traditions and its body of laws. Supporters of the British system assert that because it is *customary* in Great Britain to respect freedom of speech and press, these freedoms are assured of continued protection as new laws and policies are enacted by the country's legislature, known as the Parliament. Thus, whereas the U.S. government is limited in the kinds of policies it may enact by the written decrees of the U.S. Constitution, the British government is similarly limited by the expectation that it will be true to the traditions of the country.[54]

British constitutional traditions date back to the Magna Carta. The Magna Carta was signed in 1215 by King John. The document provided that England's king would acknowledge the rights of his subjects and would recognize the feudal rights of the nobility. Freedom of the church was also proclaimed. In the seventeenth century, England's kings were presented with a Petition of Right spelling out prohibitions against arbitrary taxation and arrest powers of the king and a Declaration of Rights affirming that monarchs were to acknowledge the liberties of subjects regarding such matters as protections against cruel and unusual punishment. Subsequent laws have built on and expanded the scope of rights suggested in the Magna Carta and the other historical documents. For instance, in October 2000 the Human Rights Act of 1998 took effect; this act upholds the standards set by the European Convention on Human Rights, which includes rights generally associated with a written bill of rights.[55]

This approach of protecting liberty through the process of passing laws consistent with customary principles—rather than listing specific liberties in a single written bill of rights—was defended recently by Britain's former Prime Minister John Major. Parliament is a legislative body elected by the country's citizens and therefore is the spokesperson of the citizens, Major pointed out. Consequently, when Parliament enacts laws, it is actually the citizens who are enacting the laws, albeit indirectly. What could be more democratic than this system whereby the Parliament/people define the boundaries of constitutional law, ask defenders of the British system?[56]

Constitutionalism and its relation to protective democracy are controversial topics within Britain. Charter 88 is a British interest group organizing in support of a written Bill of Rights. Charter 88 members point out that Britain is out of step with other democracies in having no written constitution. Charter 88 also believes that individual liberties would be more secure if certain rights were guaranteed *in writing*.[57] However Britain resolves the debate over its constitution, students of comparative politics know that the U.S. experience illustrates that a written bill of rights is not in itself a guarantee of any specific outcome. As the history of the U.S. Bill of Rights shows, a written right can exist in a constitution for years without providing citizens what later generations may say the written right signified all along. Also, in the aftermath of violent encroachment on its own sovereignty, a government with a Bill of Rights can become a government that magnifies its own domestic surveillance powers through the Patriot Act.

## Performance: The United States and India

According to advocates of performance democracy, a government of the people should be one performing in such a manner as to enhance the well-being of the people. Popular access to available economic resources constitutes one element of popular well-being. When comparing democracies on this element of performance, it is necessary, of course, to keep in mind differences in industrial and technological development, population size, natural resources, sensitivity to international economic fluctuations, and other variations that affect overall economic well-being. The United States is often referred to as a strong economic performer. In comparison, India is one of the world's poorest democracies. India is also the world's most populous democracy, encompassing a multiethnic population in excess of 900 million. The point of comparing performance democracy in the United States and India is not to try to hold India up to the economic performance levels of the United States; to do so would be illogical, given that the United States has had a very different political and economic history from India. Specifically, the United States has been politically independent since the 1700s, whereas India's independence was won only in the 1900s; in addition, the United States possesses an advanced industrial and technological economy. Less than 5 percent of the U.S. population is employed in agriculture. In contrast, 70 percent of India's labor force is employed in the agricultural sector.[58] A comparison of these countries on performance democracy is instead useful in illustrating how democracies possessing very different economic resources and challenges approach performance democracy.

With a population of more than 260 million, the United States is one of the most affluent democracies in the world. In recent decades, average annual income was in excess of $25,800. Only Norway, Denmark, Japan, Switzerland, and the United Arab Emirates reported higher average income levels.[59] Life expectancy for U.S. citizens averages 77 years. More than 90 percent of the population has access to primary and secondary public education. Infant mortality is very low, although not as low as infant mortality rates in most of western Europe, Australia, Canada, Hong Kong, and Singapore.[60]

However, the U.S. system has not been a "high performer" for every segment of the *demos*. In the most recent survey of such data, New York University Economics Professor Eric Wolff notes that the top 1% of U.S. households possess 38% of the country's total wealth, and the richest 20% of U.S. households own 83% of such wealth. This pattern of wealth and income inequality is further revealed by historical data collected by the World Bank. For example, in 1996, the World Bank examined the United States and other countries to determine patterns of income distribution. World Bank analysts looked at the percentage of income or consumption registered by different population groups within countries. With respect to the United States, for example, the World Bank found that the highest income group (the top 10 percent) accounted for 25 percent of the entire income or consumption spending in the entire country. In contrast, the poorest 20 percent accounted for only 4.7 percent of the income or consumption spending.[61] Not surprisingly, when public opinion survey organizations such as the Gallup Poll Organization periodically poll U.S. citizens about their attitudes regarding how well life is proceeding in the United States, a considerable number may express dissatisfaction. In fact, in November 2003 just over 50% (54% to be precise) expressed satisfaction with "the state of the country."[62]

Dissatisfaction with economic performance in the United States may be seen from another perspective when one shifts away from statistics and public opinion polls and starts to look at individual lives. Consider Roxana Machado, 10 years old, the daughter of migrant workers. Both her parents are U.S. citizens who travel from Florida to Maryland to work. Their work is vital to agricultural production, yet Roxana's parents and others like them tend to earn less than $5 per hour, work 10 to 12 hours per day, stooping over to pick crops or slaughter livestock, and live in cramped housing, and children such as Roxana have among the lowest school graduation rates in the country.[63] Granted, in no country are all citizens economically privileged; however, when 20 percent of a country's population possesses only 4.7 percent of the country's income or consumption spending, especially when the country is one of the richest and most technologically advanced in the world, one might ask how well the government is serving the entire *demos* in its economic decision making. Is the U.S. government democratic from a performance perspective?

In India, economic performance has improved considerably since the country became independent of Great Britain in 1947. Life expectancy has doubled, and education rates have quadrupled. The country's middle class has also grown. Economic exports have soared, as India has expanded agricultural as well as manufacturing production. Rice, wheat, maize, sugar cane, cotton, tea, and livestock are major industries. Steel, aluminum, motorcycle, commercial vehicle, engine, and iron production have also become key economic sectors. Licensed growers also produce opium and sell it to the Indian government. Opium is distributed for medical purposes and to addicts. International bans prohibit Indians from selling this product internationally.[64]

Despite economic gains since independence, more than a third of the population lives below the poverty level. With respect to income distribution, the most affluent 10 percent of the country accounted for 28.4 percent of income or consumption, whereas the poorest 10 percent accounted for only 3.7 percent. A 1996 Gallup Poll found that approximately 30 percent of Indian households owned a black-and-white television set, 12 percent owned a refrigerator, and 6 percent had a telephone.[65] Life expectancy in India is 62 years, and reports indicate that 48 percent of Indian adults are illiterate. Both figures are significantly lower than the life expectancy and adult literacy rates of the United States. Based on the recent data, 50 percent of the Indian population has access to health care, 55 percent has access to safe water, and 16 percent has access to sanitation.[66]

How has India's democracy responded to these economic challenges and sought to use available resources to achieve performance democracy? Since independence, India has generally adopted a more government-directed approach to economic policy than that found in the United States. For example, whereas most industries are privately owned and managed (though subject to governmental regulation) in the United States, Indian railroad, armament, atomic energy, and aviation have been government industries. In addition, the Indian government's management of iron, steel, oil, chemicals, banking, foreign trade, and shipbuilding has been very extensive. Indeed, for years following independence, India's approach to economic performance was characterized by government attempts to plan, direct, and shape the future growth of the Indian economy, moving it toward greater levels of industrialization and self-sufficiency.[67]

In recent years, however, leaders have experimented with reducing government controls and increasing private initiatives and foreign investments as a means of achieving economic development. For example, the National Development Council, which is the supreme economic policymaking body in the Indian government, implemented a 5-year plan (1992–1997) to reduce the number of government-owned industries and to curtail the government's involvement in investment decision making. India has also implemented family planning policies, including voluntary vasectomies, to control population growth.[68] Whether these policies will boost economic growth and stimulate higher levels of performance democracy remains to be seen.[69]

## NONDEMOCRACY: A FLUID AND VARIED GOVERNING PROCESS

The terrorist attack of 9/11 and the subsequent U.S. war on terrorism have prompted many U.S. citizens to learn more about the nondemocratic governments of Taliban-led Afghanistan and the Saddam Hussein regime in Iraq. When one analyzes nondemocratic governments, one finds that they can be as complex and varied as democratic ones. Nondemocractic governments may be in transition no less so than democracies. Nondemocratic governments are governments that have not linked the *demos* and *kratien*—the people and the process of ruling—by placing the former in charge of the latter. At its most basic level, **nondemocratic government** is government in which the people are not self-governing and are not, therefore, in a position to direct government policy toward the expression of the people's interests.[70] Nondemocratic governments are much more numerous than democratic ones. One political scientist recently estimated that, measured in terms of participatory democracy (free elections) alone, fewer than 30 percent of the world's governments that have enjoyed independence for at least 30 years have been continuously democratic.[71]

Nondemocratic governments are very diverse. Recalling that both democracy and nondemocracy are matters of degree, it is important to realize that nondemocratic governments may not be equally nondemocratic in all aspects. For instance, a government may be more nondemocratic in terms of participation than in terms of performance, or more nondemocratic in terms of pluralism than in terms of protection.

What does a nondemocratic government look like? Five points need to be emphasized. First, nondemocratic governments may be antiparticipatory, in that they do not provide freedom of participation to the people. Nondemocratic governments may actually mobilize the people by decreeing that the people act in certain ways (for example, attend political rallies) but may remove from the mobilized participation any opportunities for the expression of popular will. In short, if people are mobilized by government to participate in actions coerced by the government, the coercion precludes free participation. For instance, nondemocratic governments may deny genuine popular participation in elections and/or referenda altogether, may define the electorate narrowly to restrict participation to only certain segments of the people, may organize events in which populations are mobilized but are not allowed choices about what or whom to support, or may stage bogus elections in which meaningful choices among parties and candidates are absent. For example, when the Chilean military overthrew the democratically elected president Salvador Allende in 1973, the military immediately prohibited elections; General Augusto Pinochet assumed leadership of the government, used the government apparatus to smash opposition groups, and formalized his authority in a 1980 constitutional referendum. From 1948 to 1992, the South African government's official policy of apartheid—racial segregation premised on white supremacy—allowed for elections but during most years of its existence, it restricted voting and officeholding to the minority white population.[72]

Second, nondemocratic governments may maintain themselves, in part, by suppressing certain groups (such as students, journalists, opposition parties, and so on). This suppression not only precludes participation in politics to members of these groups but also violates the logic of protective democracy (by extending, rather than limiting, governmental authority over people through the imposition of rules regarding "acceptable" choices), pluralistic democracy (by quelling the open expression of some ideas and interests), and developmental democracy (by

---

**BOX 8.4    Nondemocracy: Definition and Characteristics**

*Nondemocracy defined:* Nondemocratic government is government in which the people are not self-governing in terms of inputs and outputs.

*Nondemocratic Governments*

- May be *antiparticipatory,* in that governments may deny freedom of participation by the people. Some nondemocratic governments may mobilize the people to act in certain ways (for example, to attend pro-government rallies) *decided on by the government;* insofar as this participation is not freely chosen by the people, this action represents mobilization but not democratic participation.
- May *suppress* various groups within society.
- May produce laws and policies that are not reflections of popularly defined and popularly articulated interests.
- Are diverse in terms of *leadership,* which may be drawn from a given family, party, or social (for example, military) sector, or may be concentrated in a single individual.
- May have unclear lines of *succession.*

socializing patterns of deference and submission rather than socializing the development of civic involvement and independent, critical decision making). Examples of such policies abound. When the military ousted Ecuadorian President Arosemena Monroy in 1963, for instance, military leaders proceeded to establish an authoritarian political system in which newspapers were censored, the Communist Party was banned, universities and labor unions were shut down, and opponents were jailed or exiled.[73]

In the African state of Malawi, former authoritarian leader President Hastings Kamuzu Banda (who ruled from 1964 to 1994) secured control by suppressing would-be political and economic rivals through a process that involved making himself head of state; head of his political party; minister of agriculture, foreign affairs, justice, and public works; rector of the university; leader of the Malawi Presbyterian Church; and owner of tobacco, oil, and banking monopolies. His regime attacked political dissidents and carried nondemocratic controls so far that those controls sometimes looked downright bizarre to outsiders. For example, he prohibited the playing of Simon and Garfunkel's song "Cecelia" (his "official hostess" was named Cecelia and the song had some sexually suggestive lyrics), he banned bell-bottom pants, and he proclaimed that men had to wear short (above-the-collar) hair.[74] Similarly, when the Iranian revolution overthrew the authoritarian government of Mohammad Reza Pahlavi in 1979, the new government under Islamic leader the Ayatollah Khomeini imposed its own form of nondemocracy, one that attacked pluralism just as Banda had done. [75]

Third, in nondemocratic governments, government outputs may delink the government and the people. To the extent that citizens have been closed off from democratic participation in the input aspects of politics, the citizens may be alienated from the product of government policy. Interestingly, however, nondemocratic leaders may conclude that their own self-interest is served by policies intended to increase living standards, literacy levels, health care, and other indicators typically associated with high levels of performance democracy. That is, autocrats may look as if they were trying to be performance democrats.

For example, from 1946 to 1981, Ferdinand Marcos ruled the Philippines through martial law. On instituting martial law, Marcos shut down the existing legislature and created a new one under his own command, closed newspapers, arrested writers, and took steps to weaken or ban opposition parties. Under Marcos, elections and referenda—in which Marcos rigged the results through miscounts, bogus ballots, and intimidation—were conducted.[76] One example of election rigging occurred just outside the capital city of Manila. The mayor of a small town was told that his town would be given special favors if it voted "correctly" in an upcoming election; when the election came, the mayor informed clerks at the town's voting booths that Marcos had to emerge victorious in the election.[77] Not surprisingly, a study by the University of the Philippines referred to such elections as government-controlled processes and certainly not examples of genuine participatory democracy.[78]

At the same time, however, Marcos used his power to enact land reforms. According to his Presidential Decree 27, such reform was geared toward improving the status of agricultural workers.[79] What was Marcos doing? According to one scholar, Marcos was trying to prevent pressures for democracy. He was trying to preclude the emergence of popular demands for multiple parties and interest groups. For example, Marcos knew that the Communist Party could gain credibility and support if the rural population saw its social position deteriorating. Thus, as one scholar explains, land reform was instituted to choke off support for Communists or any other party that could challenge the government.[80]

Not all nondemocratic governments seek to perpetuate their rule through the rhetoric and/or practice of improving the lives of the people. Burma (renamed Myanmar by its military rulers in 1990) is, according to recent statements from U.S. officials, one of the most authoritarian governments in the world.[81] Ruled by a military elite known as the State Peace and Development Council (SPDC), which came to power through a coup in 1988, Burma is one of Asia's (and the world's) largest producers of heroin. The SPDC actively promotes heroin production through policies that include forced labor and arrests of regime opponents. Farmers are encouraged to grow opium for both internal consumption and international markets, and workers in SPDC-owned and -managed jade mines are given the option of payment in drugs or money.[82] Although the SPDC is enriched by the booming narcotics trade, the opium growers themselves are living in poverty. For example, the Wa people, who produce perhaps 80 percent of the country's opium, lack access to hospitals, schools, and electricity and generally

---

**BOX 8.5   Democracy, Nondemocracy, and the Internet: The Case of (Burma)**

The Internet has become a battleground between the State Peace and Development Council (SPDC) military rulers of Burma and prodemocracy forces opposed to the government. The military regime sponsors a Myanmar home page. Readers can find information on the country's culture, religion, and industry. The home page is colorful, graphically interesting, and user-friendly in conveying an image that Myanmar is a nice place to travel, live, and do business.

However, if a citizen of Burma owns a computer with a modem capable of accessing this page or anything else on the Internet without SPDC approval, he or she is subject to arrest and imprisonment. The prison term for illegal modem usage is 15 years. It is also illegal to use fax machines without approval from the SPDC. Lee Nichols was one individual detained on charges of unauthorized faxing in 1996 and he died in prison.

Although such laws severely hamper prodemocracy forces within the country, prodemocracy supporters outside the country make extensive use of the Internet. The Free Burma home page, for example, carries news of prodemocracy activist Aung San Suu Kyi, human rights campaigns, and efforts to boycott businesses doing business in Burma. The home page also allows Internet users to link with groups supporting refugees from the SPDC-controlled state.

You can examine these very different uses of the Internet by going to the SPDC's Web site at http://www. myanmar.com/e-index.html. The Free Burma page (including information about the government restrictions on Internet, fax, and modem use) is found at http://sunsite.unc.edu/freeburma/noframeindex.html.

live in conditions of extreme poverty.[83] No doubt an extreme example, Burma's narcopolitics is, nonetheless, a clear-cut case of nondemocracy lacking even the *illusion* that government action is promoting the citizens' welfare.

Fourth, decision making within democratic governments may be shaped by military, party, family, or individual elites.[84] Greece, the USSR, Qatar, and Nazi Germany have, during different periods, represented examples of these four types of nondemocratic governments. Greece was governed by military forces from 1967, when a military junta came to power through a coup, until a provisional civilian president was elected in 1974. During these years, government was anything but stable. Plots and counterplots by different sectors within the military resulted in changes in military and political leadership, continued coup attempts, restrictions on civil liberties, and promises of elections followed by cancellations of elections.[85]

The USSR was a nondemocratic government under the direction of a dominant party: the Communist Party. Relations between the party and the state, as well as the party and society, were fluid in the USSR. For example, the party was less hierarchical under Lenin than under Stalin. Nonetheless, the party was the dominant ruling political organization, even during its least authoritarian years. Party membership was also the foundation for launching a career in government or for rising to positions of leadership in industrial management or academia. One scholar estimates that party members were elites, representing approximately 9 percent of the adult population in 1991.[86]

The oil-rich Middle Eastern state Qatar has been governed by the royal Al Thani family. A former colony of Britain, Qatar has been independent since

Aung San Suu Kyi is a leader in Burma's prodemocracy movement.

1971. In 1992, a small group of elite Qataris asked the Al Thani family to take steps to democratize the country by allowing for the creation of an independent legislature rather than the existing Consultative Council, whose members are appointed by the ruling members of the royal family. Although this request was denied, since coming to power in 1995 Hamad bin Khalifah Al Thani, the emir, has publicly supported the concept of moderate democratization.[87]

According to some comparativist scholars, Hitler's leadership of Nazi Germany provides an example of nondemocracy in the form of an individual ruler. It should be noted that individual rulers are usually attached to larger groups, such as political parties, political movements, military factions, or privileged families. One student of nondemocratic politics lists, in addition to Hitler, the following examples of individual rulers: the Ayatollah Khomeini (ruler of Iran 1979–1989), François Duvalier (ruler of Haiti 1957–1971), Jean-Claude Duvalier (ruler of Haiti 1971–1986), and General Alfredo Stroessner (ruler of Paraguay 1954–1989).[88]

Finally, rules governing political succession in nondemocratic regimes have often been unclear, especially to outsiders. In democratic systems, free elections can provide a means of transferring authority from one leader or party to the next. However, when elections are nonexistent or controlled, and when government operations are designed to close off public input and public scrutiny, procedures for succession may be unclear and unstable. For example, in the former Soviet Union, on the death of Communist head of state Lenin in 1924 a power struggle ensued, ultimately won by Josef Stalin.

## Questions About China

The difficulties that may accompany efforts at analyzing democratic/nondemocratic politics are illustrated in contemporary discussions of China. Is China most accurately regarded as a nondemocratic state, as a country in transition, or as something else (for example, as a country lacking clear political and economic definition at the moment)? No consensus on these matters has emerged. Scholars who stress China's nondemocratic components tend to concentrate on the fact that it has been and continues to be essentially a highly centralized one-party state. Yet other scholars note that since the late 1980s local village elections have been allowed, and in recent years have sometimes become highly competitive. In addition, China's economy has become increasingly open to international influences and nongovernment and non-Communist groups and individuals. Which, if any, of these tendencies will prove more influential in China's political future remains unknown.

To get a clearer sense of the fluidity of contemporary Chinese politics, it is instructive to take note of some of the most salient events of China's recent history. China has been governed by the Chinese Communist Party since 1949. Under Mao Zedung (1893–1973), China's first Communist leader, the state mobilized citizens in implementing key government policies designed to improve the living standards within the country and to secure the Communist Party's control. Two such policies were the Great Leap Forward (1958–1960) and the Cultural Revolution (1965–1976). The Great Leap Forward was geared toward boosting China's agricultural and industrial output. The policy defined China's people (not capital or technology) as the basic asset and the fundamental building block of economic development. Under Mao's direction, Chinese citizens were organized into labor-intensive communes and production units. As Mao saw it, China's future strength was dependent not on opening the country up to foreign investment but on maximizing the output of the nation's resources—primarily, its people. The Cultural Revolution mobilized citizens to attack those whom Mao regarded as ideological and political enemies. Among those targeted were writers, artists, and Communist Party members thought insufficiently supportive of Mao's leadership. Indeed, Deng Xiaoping—Mao's eventual successor—was ousted from the party in 1967 after he was labeled a "capitalist sympathizer."[89]

When Mao died in 1976, a succession struggle followed in which Mao's widow and other party leaders competed for dominance. Deng emerged as China's leader in 1978 and governed until his death in 1997. Like Mao before him, Deng sought to boost economic development and growth. However, Deng achieved a reputation as an economic pragmatist and was widely credited with shifting Chinese policy away from the Maoist stress on ideological purity. Whereas Mao used the state to direct economic affairs, Deng believed that economic growth would advance faster by curtailing state controls over economic activity. For instance, Deng promoted the Four Modernizations. This was a series of policies directed toward improving China's industry, agriculture, national defense, and technology through a reduction of state controls on economic activities, the granting of tax subsidies to attract investment, and the promotion of export industries.[90]

Deng was an economic reformer but not a democrat. This point was made tragically clear in 1989 when student demonstrators were killed in the Tiananmen Square prodemocracy protests, as well as in the subsequent imprisonment of prodemocracy activists. Deng once explained his opposition to democratic forms of governing to former President George Bush, Sr., by asserting that popular participation would lead to chaos in China. According to Deng, China's stability would be secured by economically opening the country to investment and trade while ensuring the country was not opened up to participatory democracy.

Jiang Zemin succeeded Deng in 1997. Jiang used the occasion of the Chinese Communist Party's fifteenth party congress in the same year to affirm his support for continued economic reform. Jiang has promoted such measures as increasing the range of private investment in industry, developing bankruptcy laws, and reducing government employment as means of sponsoring the growth of private enterprise. At the same time, his government has been criticized for human rights violations, in particular for repressive measures toward religious minorities and political opponents. On the matter of religion, in September 1999 Jiang stated that China should protect itself from religious cults. In October 2000, the Chinese Evangelical Fellowship reported that 53 of its members had been arrested in a government campaign to eradicate what the government viewed as cults; these arrests followed earlier detentions of Muslims, Tibetan Buddhists, members of the Fangcheng Church, and supporters of Falun Gong. In 1999, China's Supreme Spirit Sect saw its leader not only detained but also executed.

Hu Jintao assumed the presidency and the leadership of the Chinese Communist Party in 2003. Hu has a record of using strong government measures against separatists in Tibet, a stance that some scholars regard as evidence of his antidemocracy leanings. At the same time, Hu has shown support for economic openness and reform.[91]

Weighing these many events, analysts who make the case that China appears to be in a transition toward democratization often suggest that recent economic reforms are likely to create a growing number of economically influential leaders who will represent a set of checks and balances, of a sort, against the Communist Party's influence; this will nurture pluralist, performance, protective, and participatory democracy, such scholars believe. Similarly, such analysts continue, economic reforms will likely increase the exposure of citizens to a broader range of ideas, and this exposure to diversity is likely to push the country toward greater degrees of pluralism and perhaps developmental democracy. In addition, the fact that in 1987 China introduced elections for seats on village committees is beginning to show democratic results, some political scientists point out. A recent study of 56 Chinese villages found that elections to the village committee—a governing body consisting of three to seven seats on which members have terms running in three-year increments—can be very competitive. In the village of Anhui, for example, 83 candidates vied for committee positions. Participating democracy may be directly promoted by such competition, and the remaining components of democracy may be indirectly nourished. If so, Deng's comments on the prerequisites of China's stability (promoting economic reform but opposing democratization) may be disproved in the future.[92]

## SUMMING UP

- **Comparative politics** is the study of how governments, political groups, political procedures, and citizenship vary across countries and/or time. By examining U.S. politics in reference to comparative politics, you can analyze how the United States is similar and dissimilar to other countries, and you can also see U.S. politics as part of the larger process of world politics.

- **Democracy** links people and government in terms of inputs and outputs of the governing process. In thinking about this linkage, you can see that democracy presupposes certain participatory, pluralist, developmental, protection, and performance elements. If all the diverse segments of society (**pluralism**) are free to get involved (**participatory**) in the process of governing and are aware of their actions as part of a self-governing process (**developmental**), if government laws are not tyrannical (**protective**), and if government is characterized by laws and policies (**performance**) that reflect the direction of a self-governing people seeking their own well-being, then government is linked to the people in terms of inputs (involvement in government by all segments of a society of people aware of their acts of self-governance) and outputs (laws and policies that are not tyrannical and are indicative that government is in the hands of—and thus serving the interests of—the self-governing *demos*).

- Analyses of democracy are often subjective. Indeed, readers of this book may disagree on whether the United States is democratic. Some readers may conclude that the United States is highly democratic, whereas others may argue that the United States is not very democratic at all. Moreover, when compared to other countries, the United States may look more democratic on some points and less democratic on others. In addition, some components of democracy may exist in conflict with other components of democracy, as illustrated in the comparison of the United States and The Netherlands on the issue of energy policy.

- A comparison of Switzerland and the United States on participation reveals the diversity of democratic processes. In both countries, the expansion of the **electorate** also expanded the meaning of participatory democracy, as voting rights were extended to additional groups. In Switzerland this has meant expanded participation possibilities not only in voting for candidates for office but also in voting on national **referenda**.

- A comparison of Germany and the United States reveals that democracies can promote pluralism in highly divergent ways. The church tax in Germany is a means used by government to encourage a vibrant and pluralistically diverse civil society by offering assistance to institutions (churches) within civil society. In the United States, the separation of church and state outlined in the U.S. Constitution is intended to promote pluralism and diversity by preventing the government from promoting any certain viewpoint on or approach regarding religion.

- **Political socialization** takes place in all political societies. Political socialization can either promote or discourage the realization of democracy, in that political socialization can either promote or discourage people from viewing self-government in positive, intellectually aware ways. Thus, when studying democracies from the standpoint of developmentalism, it makes sense to analyze a country's political socialization processes to see whether citizens are being socialized to become consciously aware, self-governing individuals. In Argentina, the Newspapers in the Schools program seeks to include prodemocracy messages in the political socialization process. In the United States, advocates of Character Counts and mandatory dress codes also assert that such programs inculcate democracy-supporting values as part of the political socialization process.

- Democratic governments are governments in which the people are protected from oppressive government authority; this describes the protective component of democracy. Great Britain's protective democratic approach differs from that found in the United States because the United States has a written Constitution with a **Bill of Rights**, unlike Great Britain.

- If the people are self-governing, then governmental outputs in the form of laws and policies should, logically, reflect the people's desires for well-being. Thus, if we wish to examine democracy from as many vantage points as possible, we need to look at the performance of government to see if governmental performance reflects the people's interest. Analyzing this performance component of democracy—whether looking at a high-income country such as the United States or a lower income country such as India—can entail assessing quality-of-life measurements, such as income levels, access to basic goods, and patterns of income distribution within countries.

- **Nondemocratic governments** are ones that do not link the people and government in a manner culminating in the self-governance of the people. There are many ways to be nondemocratic: Nondemocratic governments may be antiparticipatory, may practice suppression of various groups, may perform (produce laws and policies) in a manner that is not a reflection of popularly defined desires for well-being, may be ruled by groups (such as the military, a party, or a family) or individuals, and may have unclear succession processes.

## STUDY QUESTIONS

1. Describe comparative politics as a subfield of political science.

2. What is the definition of *democracy*? What is implied by this definition? That is, what does democracy presuppose? What is implied by the concept of *transition* when used in discussing democracy/nondemocracy?

3. Would you rank the United States as high, low, or medium on a democracy scale? Explain your answer by discussing the United States in relation to each of the five components—participatory, pluralist, protective, performance, and developmental—of democracy. Why might others find it so easy to disagree with your interpretation; that is, why are discussions of democracy often subjective?

4. Compare and contrast Switzerland and the United States on the question of participatory democracy. What is a referendum?

5. Compare and contrast Germany and the United States on the question

of pluralist democracy. What is a church tax?

6. Compare and contrast Argentina and the United States on the question of developmental democracy. Include in your answer a discussion of political socialization, Character Counts, dress codes, and Newspapers in the Schools.

7. Compare and contrast Great Britain and the United States on the question of protective democracy. Which of the two countries has a written constitution? Identify the following: Magna Carta, Declaration of Rights, and Charter 88.

8. Discuss India and the United States on the question of performance democracy.

9. What is the definition of a nondemocratic government? The chapter discusses five components of nondemocracy. Identify and discuss these five components. Give an example of a country illustrating each component.

# FOLLOWING UP THROUGH
# INTERNET SOURCES

- University of Michigan, *Government Resources on the Web* (http://www.lib.umich.edu/libhome/Documents.center/govweb.html). Information on various governments and regions.

- *The World Factbook 2000* (http://www.odci.gov/cia/publications/factbook/index.html). General reference work on governments worldwide.

- Georgetown University, Organization of American States, Canadian Foundation for the Americas, *Political Database of the Americas* (http://www.georgetown.edu/pdba). News, government information, constitutions, elections, and economic data on Latin America.

- National Archives and Records Administration. Office of the Federal Register (http://www.nara.gov/fedreg). Information on the U.S. government, including presidential documents and information on the U.S. Constitution and legal/governmental issues.

# 9

※

# Comparative Politics II

## Interest Groups, Political Parties, and Elections

Political controversies can involve almost anything, and they can appear very odd to those not in the middle of the conflict. Consider, for instance, one of the knock-down–drag-out political fights of the nineteenth century. In the late 1880s, interest groups and politicians became embroiled in bitter contests over standardized vs. local time zones, a matter of great interest to railroad companies standing to make enormous profits if they could figure out how to coordinate reliable train schedules from city to city. Standardized time made such coordination possible. Today's controversies over matters such as spam may seem similarly strange or quaint to U.S. citizens 100 years from now.

Just as the subject matter of political controversies is virtually limitless, so is the variety of ways in which citizens may participate in political activity. One can look to the example of gay rights to find wide-ranging diversity of participatory strategies. In recent years, school officials in Topeka, Kansas, offered students extra credit to picket the funerals of individuals who died from AIDS while carrying signs declaring that God does not love gays.[1] In Iowa during the 1996 Republican primary, Republican organizers called on voters to condemn gay rights as Satanic.[2] A year earlier, in Albuquerque, New Mexico, the National Federation of Republican Women tried to send a similar message by selling bumper stickers commenting, in a light-hearted, joking manner, about AIDS wiping out the gay community.[3]

Exhibiting a similar combination of the creative and the shocking, animal rights activists have pursued their interests through a wide rage of participatory actions in recent years. For instance, a Philadelphia school teacher recently gave sixth graders a homework assignment of writing protest letters to companies using animals in product testing.[4] Animal rights groups such as the Animal Liberation Front and People for the Ethical Treatment of Animals stage protests over the wearing of fur, demonstrate against the inclusion of animal acts in rodeos and circuses, and conduct educational campaigns against the use of animals in medical experiments.[5] As these examples illustrate, whatever the issue, political participation strategies are virtually limitless in their diversity. Interest groups, political parties, elections, and media outlets provide innumerable opportunities for participation.

# INTEREST GROUPS

**Interest groups** are defined as groups of individuals and/or institutions united by shared opinions or interests and organized together in an effort to influence political outcomes.[6] Interest groups sometimes try to pressure government directly and, at other times, prefer to keep their distance from government even while they seek to shape public attitudes and beliefs. In comparing how interest groups operate across countries, we will see that interest groups can be either partners or competitors with government.

## Interest Groups in the United States

U.S. interest groups use a number of strategies in their efforts to influence politics. **Direct lobbying** is a strategy whereby interest groups make personal contact with political officials and try to persuade them to support the aims of the interest group.

The number of interest groups lobbying government at any single time can be mind-boggling to outsiders. At the end of the U.S. congressional session in 2003, Senate Majority Leader Republican Bill Frist of Tennessee pointed out that 358 different interest groups had mobilized to support President Bush's Medicare bill. When health care reform was being debated during the first Clinton administration, members of Congress reported scheduling nightmares as they tried to accommodate lobbyists representing chiropractors, dance therapists, social workers, masseurs, and other care providers, all competing to convince Congress to include their respective treatments in any health care reform bill.[7] When Congress was considering tobacco legislation, the National Association of Convenience Stores, Armstrong World Industries, Consolidated Rail Corporation, and W. R. Grace & Company were among the interests that converged on Congress. Why were these different groups so interested in tobacco? The National Association of Convenience Stores lobbied to prevent stringent congressional regulations on how convenience stores could display tobacco products, not an inconsequential matter considering that tobacco items represent almost 30 percent of all convenience store sales.[8] The remaining groups were asbestos corporations lobbying Congress to require tobacco companies to help pay for lawsuits won by individuals suing asbestos manufacturers because, the asbestos lobby asserted, smokers were at greater risk for asbestos-related lung cancer than were nonsmokers.[9]

Direct lobbyists target public officials carefully. Rather than maximizing the number of officials with whom they meet, lobbyists tend to concentrate on contacting a small group of officials whom the lobbyists identify as key decision makers. For example, when sugar producers fought to maintain tight restrictions on sugar imports as a means of keeping the price of domestically produced sugar high (approximately twice as high as international prices), lobbyists focused their efforts on members of the House and Senate Agricultural Committees, both of which had jurisdiction over the writing of such laws.[10] Similarly, when Southwest Airlines sought to influence congressional decision making on airline taxation levels in 1997, its spokespeople gave special attention to lobbying Senator Trent Lott, who, not coincidentally, was the Senate majority leader at the time. During the lobbying effort, Southwest Airlines announced it was preparing to begin service to Jackson, Mississippi. What was this about? Perhaps it had something to do with the fact that Senator Lott was from Mississippi and had complained loudly about the lack of airline service to his state.[11]

The success of lobbying efforts is often linked to two factors: the expertise of the lobbyist and the ability of the lobbyist to establish close connections with influential decision makers. Lobbyists who are professional experts on an issue tend to have a tremendous advantage over their more amateurish and less knowledgeable counterparts. Indeed, lawmakers have often remarked that they depend on lobbyists to provide them with technical information. A lobbyist who can do so makes officeholders look good and sometimes saves them from making embarrassing mistakes. Imagine, for example, how you might have felt had you been a member of the Senate Finance Committee in 1992. Committee members received a letter informing them that a proposed tax law had placed certain tax deduction provisions in the wrong section of the tax code; these provisions, having to do with deductions for club dues, had been written into Section 172 but technically belonged, the lobbyist explained, in Section 264. A congressional staff member later admitted that this writer probably understood these tax provisions better than anyone in Congress or in the U.S. Treasury Department. When the tax code was later revised, the writer's proposed revisions were included.[12]

In such cases, the line between lobbying for a law or policy and actually writing the law or policy is blurred. It is not, in fact, unusual for lobbyists to participate actively in drafting legislation for introduction in Congress. In addition to the case just noted, members of Congress have been known to consult with lobbyists working for electric utility companies when drafting laws to regulate utilities[13] and to look to the cigarette industry lobby when passing laws to regulate cigarettes. With respect to the latter, for example, when Congress passed legislation in 1965 requiring labels on cigarette packages, the legislation enacted included provisions proposed by the cigarette industry.[14] A 1995 bill to roll back protections for endangered species introduced by Washington Senator Slade Gorton was written by lobbyists hired by Idaho Power Company, Chevron, and Kaiser Aluminum, all companies interested in reducing species protection and opening up lands for mining, logging, or commercial development.[15]

Knowing the importance of expertise, interest groups often look to professional consulting firms when hiring direct lobbyists. In fact, it is not uncommon for interest groups on different sides of an issue to employ lobbyists from the *same* professional firm. Hospitals favoring higher taxes on cigarettes and the U.S. Tobacco Company opposed to such taxes hired professional lobbyists from the same firm when both groups were lobbying Congress on health care reform. The Association of Trial Lawyers of America and the National Association of Life Underwriters did likewise when they needed lobbyists to work on behalf of a cause of special importance to both groups. Even though the two groups were on opposite sides of the issue of whether the government should impose caps on medical malpractice fees, both hired lobbyists from the prestigious firm of Patton, Boggs & Blow to try to convince Congress of the merits of their respective positions. Not surprisingly, in February 2000, the *National Journal* reported on how one experienced Washington lobbyist approached a newly elected member of Congress. The lobbyist asked the member of Congress how he felt about sugar price supports and, before he could answer, the lobbyist added that if the member opposed the supports he could get the member some money from candy makers, whereas if he favored the price supports the lobbyist could get the member some financial contributions from his sugar-producing clients. The member of Congress decided to let the lobbyist choose which group of clients should have the honor of making cash donations to the member.[16]

Lobbyists not only need expertise but also need access to powerful officials. As a result, former politicians and former employees of politicians often turn out to be highly sought-after lobbyists. Ex-politicians and ex-staffers benefit from having well-placed friends.[17] The Washington firm of Verner Liipfert, Bernhard, McPherson and Hand considered former Senate majority leader and unsuccessful presidential candidate Bob Dole so valuable as a lobbyist that it employed Dole for $800,000 per year.[18] Moreover, when the American Dietetic Association wanted to lobby the Clinton administration, it looked for someone well connected to the Clintons. It found Betsey Wright, former Clinton gubernatorial campaign manager, gubernatorial chief of staff, and presidential campaign aide.[19]

Often an interest group concludes that its goals will be better met by using a strategy other than direct lobbying, or it will decide that direct lobbying efforts must be used in conjunction with other strategies. **Grassroots lobbying** is the strategy of trying to convince voters and members of the public to support the interest group's positions. The interest group may try reaching voters and the public through mass mailings, television or newspaper ads, telephone calls, Internet postings, e-mail, or door-to-door campaigns.

When the National Restaurant Association wanted to kill tax reform aimed at undercutting tax deductions for business meals in the early 1990s, it decided to conduct a grassroots campaign. The association put together a commercial in which a waitress expressed her fear of losing her job if the tax reform passed. She was not just any waitress—the commercial made it clear that she was mother to three children and needed her job to support her family. The commercial also claimed that the proposed reform would likely throw more than 100,000 workers out of their jobs. At the end of this sad and scary tale, a toll-free telephone number was presented, and viewers were asked to call their senators and persuade them to save jobs and help out workers by voting against the tax reform. The National Restaurant Association ran this commercial in four states: North Dakota, Arkansas, Louisiana, and Maine. Why these states? These were the home states of senators on the powerful Senate Finance Committee, a committee having jurisdiction over the proposed reforms. Consider the logic behind the selection of the interest group strategy: If the association had simply hired a direct lobbyist to pressure Congress, the association might appear greedy in its efforts to keep its own profits high at the expense of tax reform; however, by trying to scare voters about potential job losses, the association made tax reform seem cold-hearted and hurtful toward average, hard-working Americans.[20]

As with direct lobbying, interest groups often hire professionals to conduct their grassroots lobbying. In 1992, the Wexler Group advised the Coalition to End Abusive Securities Suits—which included Sears, Roebuck & Company; Prudential Securities; RJR Nabisco; and other companies—to persuade their employees to write letters to Congress on behalf of legislation favored by the coalition. However, as professionals in the grassroots lobbying trade, the Wexler Group knew that some potential letter writers might not know the names of their senators and representatives, might not fully understand securities law, or might simply be uninterested in going to the trouble of writing at all. So Wexler set up a toll-free number for these "writers" to call. Callers simply gave an operator their names and addresses. Using this information, the firm looked up the senators and representatives of the callers and then actually did the writing and mailing of the letters "from" the callers.[21]

As you can see, grassroots lobbying sometimes creates confusion about what is reality and what is illusion. In fact, this may be one reason for choosing it as a strategy. If interest groups do not want to be identified as the backers of a cause, they can hire a professional firm to "create" a grassroots movement on behalf of that cause. The interest group can then simply step back and let the grassroots momentum take over. That is exactly what the Washington firm of Apco Associates made happen on behalf of unnamed clients in 1993. Apco's clients wanted various legal reforms in Mississippi. Apco advertised on behalf of the reforms by renting billboard space for signs attacking "greedy" lawyers, and passers-by who agreed with the slogans could call a telephone number to join the campaign. Apco then presented itself as simply speaking on behalf of these "members" in its advocacy campaign. Meanwhile, the real client, which originated the demands for reform, remained invisible throughout the entire effort.[22]

Not surprisingly, interests linked to foreign countries have been especially interested in pursuing legal but cloaked ties to professional lobbying firms. During the Gulf War, for example, the Kuwaiti royal family formed the interest group Citizens for a Free Kuwait. Citizens for a Free Kuwait wanted to boost U.S. public support for American military intervention to drive Iraq out of Kuwait. Citizens for a Free Kuwait hired the U.S. public relations firm of Hill & Knowlton to advise them. Earning a fee in excess of $10 million, Hill & Knowlton conducted an intensive effort on behalf of Kuwaiti interests. Hill and Knowlton drummed up American support for war against Iraq—just like the Kuwaiti royal family wanted—by providing local television stations free film footage of testimony about Iraqi human rights abuses and by showing video clips supportive of the Kuwaiti royal family (indeed, clips provided by the royal family) during NFL games on Thanksgiving Day. Suddenly, the Gulf War had grassroots support. Similarly, in 2000 the government of Turkey found professional lobbying assistance from former House of Representatives members Bob Livingston, a Republican from Louisiana, and Stephen Solarz, a Democrat from New York. Livingston and Solarz contracted to lobby on behalf of Turkey in the country's bid to obtain U.S. attack helicopters and financial support for a pipeline construction project.[23]

Interest groups may also pursue strategies of **campaign involvement**. Interest group activity in campaigns may take the form of registering voters working on behalf of certain candidates, convincing candidates to support certain positions, joining political parties and shaping party decisions from the inside, or making campaign contributions. The National Association for the Advancement of Colored People (NAACP), for instance, set out to register 1 million African-American voters in an effort to shape the outcome of the 1996 elections.[24] Other groups have pressured political party members to support certain nominees over others. In 1980, the National Education Association lobbied Democratic Party delegates to support Jimmy Carter's presidential nomination.[25] In the 1996 Republican presidential primaries, conservative religious interest groups tried to pressure Texas Senator Phil Gramm to agree with their stands on abortion. A frustrated Gramm was reported to have snapped that his interest was politics, not religion. However, later, apparently fearful of losing their support, Gramm tried to appease religious conservatives by sending out mass mailings in which he expressed his Christian beliefs, in particular his faith in the impending second coming of Christ.[26]

Interest groups wishing to support specific candidates have several options for doing so in campaigns. A straightforward way is offering him or her an official endorsement. Although simple, this tactic appears to be giving way to two more indirect ways of supporting candidates: "grading" candidates and working inside parties to promote certain candidates over others. Technically, rankings are presented as mere information, not as endorsements. By grading candidates rather than officially endorsing them, interest groups such as the Christian Coalition have been able to maintain their tax-exempt status as educational and informational organizations. Grading a candidate (rather than coming forward with an official endorsement) also helps prevent possible backlash. In the presidential election of 2000, for instance, the National Rifle Association (NRA) chose not to endorse George W. Bush for fear of generating anti-NRA momentum for Al Gore.[27]

Interest groups can encourage their members to join a political party, run for leadership positions within that party, and thus gain great influence in deciding who will be nominated for office by that party. Indeed, the interest group may build such a strong base within a political party that it can sometimes nominate its own members to run for office using the party's label. That is, the interest group can essentially use a political party for its own purposes. The Christian

Coalition was very successful in using this strategy in local races in California in the early 1990s.[28]

Perhaps no dimension of campaign involvement has received closer scrutiny of late than campaign contributions. Interest groups and individuals can contribute money to campaigns through **direct contributions** or through **independent expenditures**. Direct contributions are contributions made to candidates themselves, whereas an independent expenditure is money spent on behalf of candidates but not directly given to them. Moreover, individuals may make contributions to political parties, in addition to direct contributions to candidates. When individuals make contributions to political parties in their states (often called soft money contributions) they may, of course, be helping specific candidates win elections. Interest groups often use **political action committees (PACs)** to make direct contributions to candidates. For example, in the 1996 elections the Sierra Club channeled $700,000 in campaign contributions through its PAC.[29] Both corporations and labor unions are prohibited by federal law from making direct contributions to candidates—neither can go up to a candidate and actually hand over money to him or her—so PACs are especially important. Members of both groups can give money they have raised voluntarily to PACs, which in turn give it to the candidates.

PACs are sophisticated and strategic in making their donations to candidates. For example, fully aware that incumbents are more likely to be reelected than challengers in congressional races, PACs have tended to give more money to incumbents and have thereby positioned themselves to be on friendly terms with probable winners.[30] PACs have further exhibited a tendency to give to both candidates in an election; this ensures that no matter who wins, the PACs have someone in office with whom they have established a record of support.[31]

Interest group-affiliated PACs have worked with PACs linked to specific politicians. Politician-affiliated PACs are typically organized by politicians for the purpose of raising money to help with their own campaigns or the campaigns of fellow political party members. For example, Ronald Reagan formed the Citizens for the Republic PAC to assist his 1980 presidential campaign.[32] More recently, Trent Lott established the New Republican Majority Fund PAC, a PAC so successful that it distributed $1.3 million in contributions to House and Senate Republican candidates in the 1996 elections.[33]

Rather than giving money through PACs, interest groups may decide to use **bundling** as a means of making direct contributions to candidates. Bundling is the process of combining numerous individual contributions together to make a single large contribution. When Democrat Jim Cooper decided to run for a Senate seat in Tennessee in 1994, he announced that he was going to refuse all offers of PAC money. PACs, he told voters during his campaign, represented special interests (interest groups) but not the public's interest nor Tennessee's interest. However, at a single breakfast meeting with individuals associated with pharmaceutical interests, he accepted more than $14,000 in bundled contributions. He ended up raising more than $2 million in his campaign in overall contributions, even though he accepted no PAC money. As you can see, bundling is a way of taking money from interests while allowing yourself to go on the record as taking an ethical stand against PACs.[34]

Direct donations have been regulated by federal law since the 1970s. Even so, a chorus of voices has alleged an excessive influence of big money in U.S. politics. According to former Democratic Senator Bill Bradley, those who can make large donations have been able to dominate political outcomes.[35] Former Democratic Representative James McClure from North Carolina once admitted that tobacco industry contributions shaped his votes on tobacco legislation.[36]

The reality described by Bradley and McClure was made possible, in part, by the decision of Congress to regulate some types of campaign giving but not others. Specifically, when Congress passed laws in the 1970s to regulate direct contributions, Congress purposefully excluded independent expenditures from the mandated regulations.[37] Thus, in 1996 Democrats threw a birthday party for Bill Clinton and charged $10,000 for tickets; the funds were spent on behalf of Democratic candidates and in support of Democratic issues. No laws were broken because these contributions were not given *directly* to any candidate. Nor were any laws violated when tobacco company Philip Morris spent $1.6 million to help the Republican Party, when Joseph E. Seagram & Sons Inc./MCA Inc. spent $620,000 to help the Democratic Party, or when AT&T split $743,000 in (indirect) contributions between the two parties.[38]

Soft money is used for party-building programs and activities. Get-out-the-vote drives, voter registration, and political ads designed to boost the party's support are examples of the type of party-building events soft money can finance.[39] Of course, these events can be scheduled strategically so that they just happen to help individual candidates. For example, in 1996 Republican soft money was spent on party activities that happened to coincide with key races by Republican candidates in Rhode Island, New Jersey, Wyoming, Colorado, and Kansas.[40] Gearing up for a single congressional race in New York, Republicans spent close to $800,000 on pro-Republican commercials in 1997 as part of a strategy of schooling voters to think Republican; it so happened that these commercials were aired in a district in which Republicans hoped to hold onto a seat they had controlled for 17 years.[41]

Soft money, bundling, and PAC contributions make for extremely expensive campaigns. In August 1997, *Congressional Quarterly* reported that Senate candidates had already raised $23.9 million and House candidates had already raised $56.2 million for the 1998 congressional elections. A Federal Election Commission press release of January 9, 2001, stated that congressional campaigns cost $858 million in 1999–2000, a 39 percent increase from the amounts registered in 1997–1998.[42] Not surprisingly, one campaign manager has confessed that raising money was so much a part of his job that he did it in his dreams at night as well as during his waking hours.[43]

In response to public criticisms of the role of big money in politics, in March 2002 President Bush signed the Bipartisan Campaign Reform Act (BCRA). Whether BCRA will significantly reduce the role of money in elections is unclear because the law is so new and the issues involving money and elections are so complicated. Among BCRA's provisions are stipulations limiting individual direct donations to candidates to $2,000 per candidate per election and individual direct donations to national party committees to $25,000 per year. The new law prohibits soft money contributions to national political parties but not to state offices of the political parties. Soft money contributions cannot be used to buy ads for candidates running in a federal election.[44]

Interest groups may also pursue their goals by following a strategy of **judicial involvement**. Interest groups may try to shape judicial decisions by filing **amicus curiae briefs**. These are "friend of the court" briefs, briefs filed by an entity (such as an interest group) that is not an actual party in the case. A "friend of the court" brief may be used when an interest group considers a case's outcome relevant to its goals. Thus, civil rights groups and women's rights groups often file such briefs in cases involving issues concerning racial and sexual discrimination.[45]

Judicial involvement can also include interest group decisions to file civil (noncriminal) suits, to offer legal assistance to individuals in court cases, to try to shape judicial appointments, and to try to influence judicial opinions by publicizing the interest group's viewpoints.[46] As an example of how judicial involvement can become an important interest group strategy, one can look to the NAACP of the post-World War II period. Since its founding in 1909, the NAACP has worked for civil rights. In the 1940s and 1950s, the NAACP decided to focus its efforts on using judicial strategies to fight racial segregation in public schools. It found the case of Homan Sweatt a perfect opportunity to pursue this goal. Sweatt, an African-American, was denied admission to the University of Texas, which did not have a single African-American student. The NAACP provided legal assistance to Sweatt, who proceeded to sue the university. The NAACP and Sweatt won. The use of the judicial involvement strategy did not stop with the Sweatt case, but was continued by the NAACP, which soon thereafter won perhaps its most famous decision—*Brown* v. *Board of Education*—in 1954. In the *Brown* decision, the U.S. Supreme Court declared segregation in public schools unconstitutional.[47] As you can see, judicial involvement proved an excellent choice of strategies.

The American Center for Law and Justice (ACLJ) is an interest group that has learned from the NAACP's example. Like the NAACP, it concentrates on judicial strategies. In contrast to the NAACP, it is a conservative group. Founded by Pat Robertson (who also founded the Christian Coalition) in 1990, the ACLJ has a staff of attorneys who offer legal assistance to groups pursuing conservative religious objectives. The ACLJ has helped students in public schools fight for Bible clubs, prayer groups, and Christmas celebrations.[48] The examples of the NAACP and the ACLJ are significant in illustrating that interest group strategies are not in themselves liberal or conservative; indeed, once a group demonstrates the value of a strategy, other groups of various ideologies tend to mimic it.

**Protest** is another interest group strategy. Pickets, demonstrations, sit-ins, and marches may be used to publicize an interest group's viewpoints and sway public opinion. For example, in 1997 the human rights interest group Global Exchange organized a protest rally in San Francisco against Nike. Global Exchange wanted to educate the public about Nike's plants in Vietnam and Indonesia.

These plants operate by paying low wages and working employees long hours. At the protest, Global Exchange tried to convince U.S. consumers not to buy Nike products. Trying to drive home the point by going after the company's most famous spokesperson, protesters chanted slogans suggesting Michael Jordan was selling himself like a prostitute.[49] Such actions can be dramatic and startling and, with media coverage of the protest action, can draw excited attention to an interest group's cause, as was the case with many of the antiwar protests against the Bush administration's campaigns in Afghanistan and Iraq after 9/11.

## Interest Groups Compared: Democracies

Whether you focus on the example of Global Exchange, the Sierra Club, the Christian Coalition, or any of the other U.S. interest groups discussed already, you find that interest groups in the United States relate to the government in certain patterned ways. Specifically, whatever strategy they choose, U.S. interest groups operate as entities outside of the government, pursue their choices of strategies independently of government directions or coordination, and compete with a variety of other interest groups to influence politics. This pattern is called **interest group pluralism**. Similar to the concept of pluralism discussed in Chapter 8, interest group pluralism calls attention to the presence of interest group diversity in a society and the fact that interest group activities are chosen by the groups themselves, not mandated by government. Interest group pluralism functions in Canada and New Zealand as well as the United States.[50]

Advocates of interest group pluralism point out that these patterns (interest groups operating outside of and independently of government in a competitive interest group environment) create positive outcomes. Advocates assert that the presence of multiple interest groups competing for influence provides numerous outlets for citizens to get involved in politics. Citizens can join groups as different as the Sierra Club and the Christian Coalition. Supporters also point out that the existence of multiple interest groups ensures that many points of view get expressed in society and in political laws and decrees. Critics, however, state that interest group pluralism can have negative outcomes as well. First, interest group pluralism can result in so many demands being placed on government that government can fail to operate smoothly. Government can become overburdened by interest group pressures. Second, under the conditions of interest group pluralism, interest group demands may be narrow and one-sided so that when government focuses on trying to satisfy interest groups, broader issues of public interest may be ignored. That is, government may become so concerned with looking at what interest groups want that it fails to consider what is good for society as a whole. Third, critics note that not all groups are equally equipped with money, time, and other resources to compete for influence and, consequently, interest group pluralism is no guarantee that all segments of society will actually be represented by effective interest groups. Poorer citizens, for example, may be unable to compete for influence with affluent citizens.

**Democratic corporatism** is an alternative to interest group pluralism. Democratic corporatism describes patterns of government coordination of interest groups, government incorporation of interest groups into the actual governing process, and the presence of peak interest group associations. That is, democratic corporatist societies are ones in which interest groups are not outsiders relative to government but rather are partners with government. Under the terms of democratic corporatism, democratic governments designate interest groups as formal participants in the decision-making process and coordinate the activities of the groups. Given the official role created for interest groups within government itself, those groups within these formal positions tend to emerge as the official spokespeople for their members. As such, these groups tend to become large "peak" associations.

Democracies that organize interest group involvement in a democratic corporatist manner include Austria, the Netherlands, Norway, Sweden, and Denmark. In Sweden, for example, the governmental office of the Labor Market Board is composed of business and labor interest group members who use their government positions to implement economic policy. In addition, business groups and labor unions have had their bargaining sessions orchestrated by the Swedish government, which has coordinated the actions of both interests in order to control wage increases.[51] Thus, summing up the Swedish corporatist system, W. Lance Bennett and Erik Asard explain that Swedish interest groups do not have to fight as outsiders for influence in government but rather are actively sought out by government to join in the political decision-making process.[52] In general, Scandinavian corporatist practices have brought governments and interest groups into formal unions whereby interest groups are represented on government boards and have enforced government policies.[53]

Democracies having elements of both interest group pluralism and democratic corporatism include Germany, Britain, Japan, France, and Switzerland. In France, for example, some scholars have suggested that agricultural interest groups have exhibited democratic corporatist patterns, whereas labor-oriented interest groups have not. As such examples illustrate, interest group pluralism and democratic corporatism should be viewed as matters of degree, not as absolutes, in comparative analyses of interest groups. In addition, it should be noted that interest group patterns can become more or less pluralist or corporatist over time. Some scholars have pointed to declining levels of corporatism and increasing levels of pluralism in both Scandinavia and Great Britain since the 1980s.[54]

In some democracies, governments enact legislation in a manner that is somewhat insulated from both interest group pluralism and democratic corporatist patterns. In such cases, governments originate policy on their own, rather than responding to interest group pressures. This pattern of interest group–government relations is known as **state autonomy**. In this pattern, state officials implement policies consistent with their own viewpoints and, in so doing, act independently of even the most powerful of interest groups. Some studies of British economic policies suggest that key economic decisions have sometimes been made by the government under conditions of state autonomy.[55]

How does state autonomy emerge? How can governments act so independently of interest group pressures? Some scholars believe that state autonomy is more likely to characterize interest group–government relations when state officials are confident of the soundness and expertise of their own positions; in contrast, if state officials are uncertain about how to proceed on a needed policy, interest groups—patterned along either pluralist or corporatist dimensions—may become more influential as advisers and lobbyists.[56]

A comparison of interest groups across democracies also reveals that interest groups differ in terms of membership characteristics. Whether they are operating under conditions of pluralism, corporatism, or state autonomy, interest groups can be membership organizations or nonmembership organizations. **Membership organizations**, as the name suggests, are interest groups that have official members. In the United States, the NRA, the National Organization for Women, the Christian Coalition, and the NAACP are membership organizations, insofar as they have actual members who have formally joined. **Nonmembership organizations** include groups such as universities, corporations, and hospitals. Nonmembership organizations possess a formal organizational structure (for example, a university has its own bureaucracy as a university) but do not have members who have officially "joined"; yet, insofar as the staff, stockholders, and clients have shared interests and act to shape political events in a manner consistent with those interests, the nonmembership organization acts as an interest group.[57] In a recent study of interest group participation in state politics in the United States, for example, scholars found that most interest groups were nonmembership organizations. Specifically, fewer than one-fourth of registered interest groups were organized as membership organizations.[58]

Interest groups may also be compared and classified according to their levels of organization. **Anomic interest groups** exhibit the lowest level of organizational identity, spontaneously arising in response to a very specific event. Suddenly appearing, they are likewise sudden in their demise. Prompted into action by a specific occurrence, they quickly dissipate, perhaps in a matter of hours or days. Of course, the group could endure and transform itself into a more permanent group, but in this case it would no longer be anomic. An example of an anomic group is a crowd that forms spontaneously as people hear about a suddenly announced government decision and takes action to try to influence the aftermath of the political decision, but then breaks up after the intensity of spontaneous feelings about the decision falters.[59]

**Nonassociational groups** are also groups exhibiting low levels of organization; however, they have a more enduring organization than do anomic groups. A nonassociational group is an interest group to the extent that it meets the definition just noted—a group with shared beliefs or interests acting to shape political events—but with such a low level of organizational structure that it may not even look like a group. It is a group without an actual leadership structure and without official designated procedures of operation. In fact, its participants may be strangers to each other. Lacking official structures, nonassociational groups generally have no formal name.[60]

For example, in Montgomery, Alabama, in 1955, African-Americans and white women formed a nonassociational group. This group emerged within the context of a boycott of the city's bus system. The boycott itself had been launched by civil rights activists in opposition to the segregation policies of

Montgomery's buses. Because African-American boycott supporters were not riding the city buses, they often walked, drove, or sought out rides to work. White women employing African-American maids began helping African-American boycott supporters by giving maids and other workers rides to and from work. Overlapping interests brought the white women and the African-American boycott supporters together: The white women wanted their employees to show up for work, and the boycott supporters wanted to keep the boycott alive by finding alternative transportation. Thus, the group came into being. Quintessentially nonassociational, the group members remained strangers to one another. One woman recalls that African-Americans taking rides from the white women often refused to give their names or even admit that they were supporting the boycott because they did not fully trust the white women. The group had no formal members, leaders, or name. However, unlike an anomic group, it endured. It lasted for months as the civil rights movement kept the boycott alive and the white women kept their maids coming to their homes to work.[61]

In contrast to both anomic and nonassociational groups, **associational groups** are highly organized interest groups. Such groups possess formal rules of operation, designated leaders, official structures, and an official name known to both those inside and outside the group.[62] Associational groups may be membership organizations or nonmembership organizations, depending on whether these highly organized groups have formal members (such as the American Association of Retired Persons in the United States) or merely staffs assembled into a highly organized bureaucratic structure (such as a corporation).

## Interest Groups Compared: Nondemocracies

Whether interest groups are capable of organizing in nondemocracies depends on the degree to which the government is committed to repressing groups within civil society and the extent to which the groups possess opportunities to communicate their goals and develop support for their positions. Moreover, interest groups in nondemocracies, like those in democracies, can assume a variety of organizational and membership types. For instance, studies of recent Chinese student protests suggest that nondemocratic regimes may become less repressive toward interest groups during periods in which the government leadership is in crisis or, at least, divided against itself.[63] In other cases, leaders within nondemocratic regimes show virtually no inclination to repress interest groups generally. Indeed, such leaders have been known to encourage the development of interest groups as a means of promoting their own agendas. In the former USSR, for example, Soviet leader Gorbachev encouraged groups to organize and participate in his effort to reform the Soviet system; from 1986 to 1988, some 30,000 such groups emerged. Gorbachev's plan for these groups to confine their demands to issues that would not challenge his leadership, of course, failed, as the eventual demise of the USSR made clear.[64] Nonetheless, the Gorbachev example testifies to the complexity of interest group politics in nondemocracies and, like the Chinese example, demonstrates that interest groups may and often do emerge in nondemocratic and transitional systems.

In other nondemocratic regimes, government officials may try to maintain their rule by attempting to control or prevent interest group activities. For example, the Polish government used arrests and harassment against Poland's Solidarity movement. Solidarity was a union movement that formed in 1980 to challenge the denial of human and economic rights under Poland's communist state. By 1981, Solidarity had more than 7 million members. Concerned by Solidarity's growth, Polish leaders used the country's military to arrest the movement's leaders and drive it underground.[65]

Interest group relations in a nondemocratic or transitional country may also take the form of **state corporatism**. Like democratic corporatism, state corporatism refers to government *coordination* of interest groups and governmental inclusion of interest groups into the formal governing process. Under state corporatism, the purpose of interest group activity is to promote the government's agenda through a process in which interest group leaders convince their constituents to defer to decisions negotiated by the interest group leaders and government officials. In this process, the interest group members may or may not even be consulted. Thus, under state corporatism, interest groups are not self-regulating entities pressuring, pushing, and demanding that government respond to citizen claims that the government might wish to ignore; rather, interest groups, under state corporatism, are intended to serve as subordinates to the government and are expected to *prevent* citizen demands from becoming boisterous and unruly.[66]

Many political scientists have described Mexico as a government that has historically exhibited characteristics of state corporatism.[67] To see why, consider the case of Armando Hernandez. A citizen of Mexico, Hernandez is a welder employed in a Korean-owned *maquiladora,* a foreign-owned company in the border region of Mexico that hires Mexican workers to assemble its products; the company receives tax benefits when shipping these products out of Mexico. Hernandez earns 85 cents per hour. A member of a union he regards as having long-standing ties with dominant state interests, Hernandez and a number of his coworkers have accused union representatives of serving state interests over those of rank-and-file members.[68] For example, work stoppages that might serve workers' demands by weakening the hand of management could be viewed as disruptive from the standpoint of government officials seeking stable economic conditions. Sorting out the role of the interest group in such situations becomes very complex, as analysts try to sift through data suggestive of democratic participation and that pointing to the restriction thereof.[69]

## POLITICAL PARTIES

**Political parties** are organizations that put forward proposed leaders whom they support for official positions in government. In democracies, for example, parties generally nominate candidates to compete in elections for office. In nondemocracies, governed by ruling parties interested in preventing rivals to their power, parties may become the major obstacles to electoral competition and may place their leaders in power by proclamation. In both democracies and nondemocracies, some parties may be subversive and seek to gain power by putting their proposed leaders in office by force. That is, parties may operate by competing for office, by curtailing competition for office, or by attempting to impose their leaders through revolutionary channels.[70]

## Political Parties in the United States

Bill Clinton and Newt Gingrich provide good starting points for understanding U.S. political parties. Both men learned that when it comes to dealing with members of your own party, you have to watch your back. Consider Clinton's difficulties during his first term as president. He desperately wanted congressional passage of the North American Free Trade Agreement (NAFTA) as a measure to expand international trade. Clinton pushed hard for NAFTA and made it clear this was a policy he believed in. Yet despite the fact that he occupied the most powerful position in the Democratic Party, who stood up against him on NAFTA? Congressional Democratic leaders such as Richard Gephardt of Missouri and David Bonior of Michigan.[71] In Clinton's second term, after working for passage of a balanced budget bill, whom did then President Clinton find to be among his most strident critics? Again, congressional Democrats. Indeed, Gephardt not only worked against Clinton's budget proposal but also blasted Clinton's policy as unfair.[72] With comments like these coming from Democrats, one wonders whether the former president had any time to worry about the Republicans.

Newt Gingrich had a lot in common with Clinton. As Speaker of the House of Representatives, you might think he could have banked on a fairly steady stream of respect from members of his own party. Instead, Republican House members tried to undermine his efforts to negotiate budget provisions with Clinton in 1995.[73] In 1997, a group of Republican House members tried to remove him as Speaker of the House.[74] While all this was going on inside Congress, Republicans on the outside were also on the attack: Moderate Republicans criticized Gingrich for being brash and uncompromising; economy-minded conservative Republicans accused him of being too tentative in fighting for tax cuts; and conservative Christian Republicans seethed at him for being a friend and supporter of fellow Republican Steve Gunderson, the only openly gay Republican member of Congress at the time.[75]

Neither Clinton nor Gingrich should have taken these matters personally because, despite their sometimes combative personality traits, their experiences are fairly typical of what can be expected, given the nature of U.S. political parties. First, U.S. parties are *broad-based organizations* in the sense that they are inclusive of anyone and everyone who wishes to identify with them.[76] U.S. parties are open to any citizen who happens to register as a party member. There are no tests, qualifications, or dues for members. As a result, both Democrats and Republicans tend to have diverse and, sometimes, contentious members. When parties are so broadly inclusive, no leader—not a Bill Clinton nor a Newt Gingrich—will speak for all party members on all party issues.

Second, U.S. parties are highly *decentralized*. Although both Democrats and Republicans have national committees and national chairpeople serving as official leaders, both parties allow individual members considerable autonomy on party decision making. Throughout the 50 states, local party members have considerable discretion over how parties will be formally organized in their states, over how party leaders at the state level will be selected, and over what parties at the state and local level will actually do. In fact, if you were to call your local Democratic or Republican Party headquarters right now, you might find that the individuals staffing the local office are altogether unaware of the names of the members of their party's national leadership committee. That local party members can be so oblivious to the formal leadership of the party is evidence of the relative decentralization of both Republicans and Democrats.[77] Thinking back to the travails of Clinton and Gingrich, it becomes clear that their experiences are unexceptional: Decentralized parties are parties with no one in absolute command at the top.

Third, U.S. parties are more focused on election needs than platforms.[78] Although both parties have official platforms—statements of what the party stands for—neither party requires its members to support the platform. In fact, both parties often nominate candidates who are opposed to some official position taken by the party in its platform. This is the case because both parties are more interested in finding candidates who can win elections than candidates who swear allegiance to the platform.[79] As a result, although Republicans are the more conservative of the two major parties and Democrats are the more liberal, any individual Republican or Democrat may take conservative, liberal, moderate, or idiosyncratic stands on particular issues and still retain credibility. For example, in past elections Republicans nominated senatorial candidates Nancy Kassebaum (Kansas), Olympia Snowe (Washington), and Kay Bailey Hutchinson (Texas), as well as gubernatorial candidate Christine Todd Whitman (New Jersey), even though each of these candidates opposed the Republican Party platform's antiabortion provision.[80] Once in office, a politician who proves to be popular with voters is likely to continue to receive party support, despite positions taken in opposition to the party.[81] Once again, we find that Clinton and Gingrich had to reap what their parties sowed: Both Clinton and Gingrich found themselves trying to lead disunited parties.

Politicians such as Hutchinson and Whitman are not the only party members divided on the issues. Rank-and-file members of the parties also reflect deep divisions on many key questions. Within the Republican Party, for example, polling expert Tony Fabrizio has found evidence of five separate groups. Surveys of Republicans reveal that some Republicans are interested mostly in a balanced budget; some are interested mostly in cutting taxes; some are interested mostly in stopping abortion and gay rights; some are interested mostly in changing welfare and affirmative action policies and attacking crime and drugs; and some are Republicans who are liberal and who have more in common with the Democratic Party than with other Republicans. Thus, Fabrizio's findings disclose a Republican Party whose members are so far apart in terms of priorities as to preclude any but the most watered-down consensus.[82] The Republican Party can be viewed as the quintessential election-focused, rather than platform-focused, party. After all, if there are no core principles unifying the party's members, the party cannot exactly put forward a platform of principles and expect it to be followed.

Finding electable candidates is a central concern of both parties, especially given the fact that U.S. parties must try to appeal to sizable numbers of Independent voters. The number of U.S. citizens who identify themselves as Independents (not identified with either Republicans or Democrats) or as members of a third party has increased in the past three decades. When polled in 1960, Independents and minor party members constituted 23 percent of the population; in the 1990s, that number averaged 33 percent of the population. In fact, in the 1990s, the number of Independents (33 percent) exceeded the number of people identifying with the Republican Party (29 percent) and equaled the number of people calling themselves Democrats (33 percent).[83] Reading these numbers, one can quickly see how Ross Perot could conclude that an Independent could make a competitive run for the White House in 1992 (when he won 19 percent of the votes cast) and 1996 (when he won 9 percent). However, as bleak as these national figures are for the major parties, the degree of declining party identification in some states is more somber. In Alaska, for example, more than half of all registered voters are Independents or members of minor parties; not even one-fourth of registered voters are Republicans and not even one-fifth are Democrats.[84]

Studies of these Independent voters have suggested that most Independents actually prefer one of the major parties over the other and generally tend to vote for the preferred party. Independents leaning toward the Republican Party tend to vote Republican, and Independents leaning toward the Democratic Party tend to vote Democratic.[85] This is very significant because it indicates that so far, both Republicans and Democrats have been able to capture enough votes from the Independents to prevent the emergence of a strong third party that might challenge the dominance of the two major parties. Whether the major parties will continue to win the support of Independents or whether the rise in numbers of Independents signals an impending collapse of the Republican and Democratic parties as organizations capable of representing U.S. voters is unclear.[86] What is clear, Newt Gingrich reportedly told a meeting of Republicans in 1997, is that if the major parties wish to woo supporters in the era of the Independent voter, they will have to sell themselves to voters the same way companies market soft drinks to consumers: They will have to figure out how to create loyalty to their product brand rather than their competitor's brand.[87]

To see how well the Republicans and Democrats are doing in their efforts to appeal to U.S. voters, consider the data (on the following page) from the past two presidential elections.[88]

The success of Clinton and Gore in appealing to lower-income groups, union households, Catholics, Jews, African-Americans, and Hispanics in the election is consistent with an overall pattern that political scientists described some time ago as the **New Deal Coalition**. The coalition, which emerged in the 1930s, consisted of lower-income, minority, and Southern voters in support of President Franklin Roosevelt's New Deal.[89] The South appears to be breaking out of the New Deal coalition, as increasing numbers of Republicans are elected to Congress from the South.

| Group | Percent Supporting Clinton | Percent Supporting Dole | Percent Supporting Perot | Percent Supporting Gore | Percent Supporting Bush | Percent Supporting Nader |
|---|---|---|---|---|---|---|
| All voters | 49 | 41 | 9 | 48 | 48 | 2 |
| Men | 43 | 44 | 10 | 42 | 53 | 3 |
| Women | 54 | 38 | 7 | 54 | 43 | 2 |
| Whites | 43 | 46 | 9 | 42 | 54 | 3 |
| African-Americans | 84 | 12 | 4 | 90 | 8 | 1 |
| Hispanics | 72 | 21 | 6 | 67 | 31 | 2 |
| Asian-Americans | 43 | 48 | 8 | 54 | 41 | 4 |
| Family income under $15,000 | 59 | 28 | 11 | 57 | 37 | 4 |
| Family income $30–50,000 | 48 | 40 | 10 | 49 | 48 | 2 |
| Family income $75–100,000 | 44 | 48 | 7 | 44 | 53 | 2 |
| Family income over $100,000 | 38 | 54 | 6 | 43 | 54 | 2 |
| Catholics | 53 | 37 | 9 | 49 | 47 | 2 |
| Jews | 78 | 16 | 3 | 79 | 19 | 1 |
| Household with union member | 59 | 30 | 9 | 59 | 37 | 3 |

Both Republicans and Democrats count on their parties to provide certain benefits to members. Parties not only recruit and sponsor candidates designed to appeal to members' values and preferences but also

- Provide opportunities to participate in politics, in that parties offer members channels for attending party meetings, for volunteering in campaigns, for getting involved in voter registration drives, and so forth
- Provide educational information to voters, giving their members a perspective by taking certain stands on issues such as abortion, crime, and drugs
- Provide a specific link between citizens and their government, in that parties serve as vehicles through which citizens themselves can seek government office or participate in deciding who does seek it

These processes include both interest articulation and interest aggregation.[90] Interest articulation concerns the communication of political ideas, as when the Republican Party articulates an antiabortion stance and, in so doing, tries to educate its members on the importance of abortion policy.[91] Interest aggregation refers to mobilizing members to vote for a winnable candidate or policy issue. For example, when the Republican Party has mobilized all five of the factions identified by Fabrizio to form a united front around a single candidate or in support of a single issue, it has "aggregated" or combined its various forces into a sizable, winnable constituency.

Yet some parties are appealing to their members because they are *not* primarily interest aggregation organizations. Indeed, these parties would likely alienate a sizable number of their members were they to emphasize the formation of winnable blocs as a top priority. These parties are known as **third parties**—parties other than the two major (Republican and Democrat) parties. Many third parties emphasize ideas, doctrines, and causes. These causes are very diverse, as indicated by the presence of fascist parties (the American Nazi Party), single-issue parties (Prohibition Party), environmentalist parties (Green Party), communist parties (Revolutionary Communist Party), civil rights parties (La Raza Unida), and feminist parties (National Woman's Party).[92]

Although third parties have failed to topple the national dominance of the two major parties, some third parties have been effective organizations. Third parties have sometimes influenced major parties to modify their party platforms. This is far from surprising, given the desire of both major parties to expand their membership bases by "stealing" members from other political groups. In the 1996 presidential elections, for example, more than 9 million votes were cast for third-party candidates, and in the 2000 presidential election, Green candidate Ralph Nader won 2.7 percent of the popular vote.[93] Republicans and Democrats viewing these numbers can readily see that a sizable group of potential major party supporters is there for the stealing if either party can figure out how to do it. Indeed, estimates have suggested that if Al Gore could have won 1,000 of the 96,837 Florida votes given to Nader, he would have been the president of the United States. In addition, some third parties have been successful because they have concentrated their efforts at the state or local level rather than trying to compete with Republicans and Democrats at the national level. The Minnesota Farmer-Labor Party, for example, has been effective in Minnesota, although it has lacked a nationwide following. Examples of third-party success at the state and local levels abound: The Reform Party's Jesse Ventura was elected governor of Minnesota, and although in 2000 Nader lost, 20 Green candidates were elected to state office.[94]

## Political Parties Compared: Democracies

In examining political parties in democracies, one finds numerous variations. First, parties differ in terms of organizational centralization or decentralization. For example, most European parties are more centralized than are U.S. parties. Specifically, European parties tend to require that potential members submit formal applications for membership; these applications are reviewed by the party, which may turn down applicants.[95] Although U.S. citizens (who become party members simply by registering as such) may consider this system unusual, European parties, by requiring that potential party members undergo review, offer a greater degree of organizational direction and leadership than that possessed by the highly decentralized U.S. parties. In addition, the presence of parliamentary forms of governing (discussed in the next chapter) reinforces the centralizing tendency within many European parties, in that the parliamentary systems are ones in which parties are more successful in holding elected officials accountable to the parties' platforms.

Second, parties in democracies differ greatly in terms of numbers. If you look at the number of electable parties (that is, parties that have won and/or are strong enough to be capable of winning seats in the national legislature) in various democracies, you find that a system of four or more electable parties is not uncommon in the world's democracies. Consider the examples of parties that have won legislative office in the sample of democracies in the following list:

- *Norway:* the Norwegian Labor Party, the Christian People's Party, the Conservative Party, the Center Party, the Socialist Left Party, the Liberal Party, and the Progress Party

- *Iceland:* the Independence Party, the Social Democratic Party, the Women's Party, the Progressive Party, and the People's Alliance

- *Germany:* the Christian Democratic Union, the Free Democratic Party, the Social Democratic Party, the Green Party, and the Party of Democratic Socialism

- *France:* the Communist Party, the Socialist Party, the Rally for the Republic, the Union for French Democracy, and Generation Ecology

- *Japan:* the Liberal Democratic Party, the Social Democratic Party of Japan, the Clean Government Party, the Democratic Socialist Party, the New Party Harbinger, and the Japan Communist Party

- *South Africa:* the African National Congress, the National Party, the Inkatha Freedom Party, the Freedom Front, and the Democratic Party

- *Switzerland:* the Radical Democratic Party, the Social Democratic Party, the Christian Democratic People's Party, the Swiss People's Party, the Independents' Alliance, the Swiss Party of Labor, the Evangelical People's Party, the Swiss Democrats, the Liberal Party, the Progressive Organizations of Switzerland, the Green Party of Switzerland, the Vigilance Party, the Swiss Car Party, the Ticino League, and the Union of Federal Democrats

Viewed from a U.S. perspective, democracies with four or more electable parties might give the impression that politics in those countries is characterized by instability. U.S. voters might wonder how so many parties could cooperate enough to govern effectively, or how voters could ever begin to choose among so many political party alternatives. In reality, however, the existence of numerous electable parties does *not* necessarily lead to instability or confusion. Democratic countries with several parties can be stable or unstable, just as democracies with two parties can be.

In comparing democracies by examining parties, some political scientists make a distinction between countries with party systems leading to majoritarian outcomes and those with party arrangements that tend to produce multiparty outcomes. In addition, one can examine whether democracies have party configurations that are generally consensual, conflictual, or consociational.[96]

Democracies with **majoritarian outcomes** are ones in which only two major parties are organized or with minor as well as major parties, although the minor parties are unable (usually because of elections laws, as discussed in the next section) to prevent the major parties from capturing majorities within the national legislature over time.[97] The United States and Great Britain are

---

**BOX 9.1    Political Parties in Great Britain**

Political parties in the lower house of the British legislature—known as the House of Commons (discussed in Chapter 10)—are centrally organized parties that stand in sharp contrast to decentralized U.S. parties. In the House of Commons, every Friday, members of Commons are presented a *whip*. The whip announces the next week's bills to be voted on and also tells members how important each bill is as far as the party leadership is concerned. If a bill is unimportant, it is underlined once; if it is somewhat important, it is underlined twice, and if it is very important, it is underlined three times. Bills underlined three times are ones the party leadership fully expects all its party's members to vote on *as deemed by the party leaders*. That is, on these issues, members are to uphold their party's official position regardless of their own viewpoints or opinions. Of course, a party

leadership sensing serious division in the party on a certain issue may be influenced to modify the party's official stance, and individual members of Commons sometimes go against party leadership and vote against party positions. Nonetheless, despite the give-and-take between leaders and nonleaders within parties, a party member who refuses to uphold the party's official position on key bills can be penalized, removed from his or her party, and ultimately removed from the House of Commons.

SOURCES: Jorgen S. Rasmussen, *The British Political Process: Concentrated Power versus Accountability.* (Belmont, CA: Wadsworth, 1993), pp. 115–116; Jurg Steiner, *European Democracies*, 4th ed. (New York: Longman, 1998), pp. 65–66; Richard Rose, "British MPs: More Bark Than Bite?" in *Parliaments and Parliamentarians in Democratic Politics*, ed. Ezra N. Suleiman (New York: Holmes & Meier, 1986), pp. 10–39; Phillip Norton, *The British Polity*, 2nd ed. (New York: Longman, 1991), p. 308.

---

generally considered examples of majoritarian systems. In contrast, in **multiparty outcomes** systems the existence of numerous parties and the absence of election laws that work against minor party competition combine to create a situation in which no single party gains control of the legislature; as a result, parties must form coalitions in order to govern.[98] In Germany, for example, the Free Democratic Party has, at varying times, formed a governing coalition with either the major party Christian Democratic Union or the major party Social Democratic Party. In Iceland, the Progressive Party has been a coalition partner with the Social Democratic Party as well as the country's Independence Party.

When a democracy's various parties are fairly united on fundamental issues involving politics and economics, the democracy tends to be characterized by what some political scientists have termed **consensual party relations**, rather than conflictual or consociational party relations. The United States and Great Britain exemplify consensual party systems: In both countries a major liberal party (Democrats and Labour, respectively) competes with a major conservative party (Republicans and Conservatives, respectively), but in both cases the two competing parties share basic beliefs in democracy itself, a commitment to the peaceful resolution of conflict, and the continuation of the constitutional order. Disagreements between such parties are typically limited to matters of how best to achieve the realization of commonly agreed-on values, such as how best to secure democratic outcomes or strengthen capitalism.

In democracies in which parties are divided by sharp ideological disagreements, party politics is characterized by **conflictual party relations**, and party coalitions tend to be less stable than those of consensual party systems. Italy is an example of a democracy with conflictual party relations. During the past 20 years, for example, Italy's government has been beset at various times by conflict among parties such as the Christian Democrats, the Communists, the Socialists, the Republicans, the Democratic Socialists, the Liberals, the Democratic Party of the Left, the Northern League, and neofascist alliances. Here, disagreements among parties concern basic, core values: capitalism versus communism, fascism versus democracy, and so on.[99]

**Consociational party relations** are ones in which parties differ radically on fundamental issues (as in conflictual systems) but possess established routines of bargaining and compromise conducive to stable government (as in consensual systems). The Netherlands, Belgium, and Switzerland are often described as consociational systems. In these democracies, power sharing across parties creates incentives for otherwise contentious parties to cooperate. Power-sharing coalitions into which diverse parties have entered can be sustained because each member of the coalition may determine that its own interest is promoted by the continuation of the coalition itself. Very significantly, a comparative analysis of these examples makes evident that neither the actual number of parties nor the presence of extreme ideological divergence among parties necessarily renders democracy unstable.[100]

## Political Parties Compared: Nondemocratic and Transitional Systems

A country in transition toward democracy may further the transitional process by reducing constraints on the development of rival parties, as has happened in recent years in Mexico. The Institutional Revolutionary Party (PRI) of Mexico came to power in 1929. For decades, the PRI maintained its position not by disallowing opposition parties (which is an alternative used by some nondemocracies) but by attempting to render these other parties so ineffectual that they have been unable to compete as strong competitors of the PRI.[101]

Historically, the PRI used several measures to obstruct the development of strong opposition parties. First, the PRI, as governing party, benefited from special access to media outlets. Using the media, the PRI tended to characterize the opposition parties as dangerous and generally incapable of offering competent leadership. Second, the PRI used its position as governing party to access government funds to conduct its campaigns. Third, the PRI used its position in government to distribute government benefits to citizens just before upcoming elections, as when, in 1994, to the chagrin of opposition candidates, the PRI handed out direct payments to farmers under a government agricultural program. The PRI has often been charged with attacks on opposition supporters. Fourth, better funded than opposition parties, the PRI has been Mexico's only party with organizers and staff throughout the country mobilizing support among the citizenry. Fifth, the PRI employed fraud and deception to "count" votes in its favor in those cases in which opposition parties posed challenges to its dominance. Why did the use of fraud not backfire against the PRI? Electoral fraud was officially investigated under provisions established by the govern-ment—controlled by the PRI—and was routinely found to be nonexistent by "official" investigators.[102]

Since 1929, these measures have generally served the PRI well, until very re-cently. The PRI never lost a presidential election until 2000, and it never lost a senatorial election until 1988 nor a gubernatorial election prior to 1989.[103] Until the opening of the 1997 Mexican legislature, the PRI was the overwhelmingly dominant party in the country's congress. Indeed, the 1997 legislative session was the first one in which seats controlled by opposition parties outnumbered those filled by the PRI.[104]

What contributed to this transition toward party competition? Scholars have pointed to democratization within the PRI itself on the matter of select-ing presidential candidates, increased media access for opposition parties, the recent distribution of funds for use by opposition parties, and the formation of an independent elections board during the 2000 elections. In the election of 2000, three presidential candidates emerged as serious contenders: the PRI candidate, the opposition party PAN (National Action Party) candidate, and the opposition party PRD (Party of the Democratic Revolution) candidate. In the election, the voter turnout was 64%, and the winning presidential candi-date—the PAN's Vicente Fox—won 42.5% of the vote, edging out the PRI candidate, Francisco Labastida, who received 36% of the vote, and the PRD's Cuauhtemoc Cardenas, who won 16.6% of the vote. Fox ran especially well among younger, urban, and male voters, whereas the PRI found its support confined primarily to rural, older voters and women.[105] The election of 2000 suggests that Mexico has made a transition from a single PRI-dominated sys-tem to one in which multiple opposition parties operate and sometimes win. Nondemocracy and democracy are fluid concepts, and transitions toward de-mocracy—in this case, participatory democracy—can emerge from single-party dominant systems.[106]

## ELECTIONS

Electoral politics—like interest group politics and party politics—are often infused with high drama, tedium, scandal, and enough surprises to keep even the most obsessive student of election history off balance. Elections can be so very competitive that it takes weeks or months of recounting votes to de-termine winners and losers. Moreover, elections can be such complicated af-fairs that they engender ongoing debates among political scientists and politicians over what motivated voters to vote as they did, what prompted nonvoters to abstain from participating, and how the choice of alternative campaign strategies by parties and candidates might have produced different electoral outcomes.

Long lines of voters form outside the voting station as women and men wait to
participate in South Africa's first all-race elections, April 27, 1994.

## Elections in the United States

U.S. elections have changed radically over the years. Consider, for example, elections during the colonial period. The electorate was generally confined to white male property owners over the age of 21, most people paid little or no attention to elections, and entire campaigns lasted only a few days or possibly only the morning of the election. As future president John Adams noted, candidates generally needed to go only to local bars to find supporters.[107]

In contrast, today's elections are often characterized by campaigns so long that some analysts have termed them "endless" and by the incessant search for strategies to capture votes from groups far more diverse than the tavern crowd mentioned by Adams. An examination of (1) Bill Clinton's 1992 and 1996 presidential campaigns and (2) the 2000 Bush–Gore presidential campaign outcome provides insight on the nature of contemporary elections. In running for the presidency in 1992, Clinton's campaign strategies included the following:

- On October 3, 1991, Clinton officially declared himself a presidential candidate. He had already forged strong links to the Democratic Leadership Council, a group advocating centrism rather than liberalism as the best strategy for Democrats. Presenting himself as a moderate, Clinton began a long campaign of directing his appeals to broad groups of voters and reminding them that during George Bush's presidency, the economy had declined on many fronts—in lost jobs, bank crises, increases in unemployment, and declining corporate profits. Indeed, Bush's approval rating with American voters fell from over 90 percent just after the Persian Gulf War in 1991 to less than 50 percent in 1992.

- On January 16, 1992, as Clinton was campaigning for the upcoming New Hampshire presidential primary, Clinton deputy campaign manager George Stephanopoulos was tipped that *The Star* tabloid would soon be publishing a story on an alleged affair between Clinton and Gennifer Flowers. To try to save his reputation with as many voters as possible, Bill and Hillary Clinton gave an interview on *60 Minutes*. A large audience was guaranteed, given the fact that the show immediately followed the Super Bowl. Meanwhile, campaign manager James Carville started attacking the press for its sensationalism.

- On February 12, 1992, Clinton called a press conference to explain his alleged draft evasion during the Vietnam War. His managers scheduled *focus groups* in which group participants were presented possible explanations for the draft evasion and asked to respond as to whether they found these explanations convincing. This helped the Clinton campaign develop an official answer to the charges of draft dodging. Their answer was to try to shift voters' attention away from Clinton's character to what they termed President Bush's poor economic performance. Clinton's campaign would later begin using dial groups as well as focus groups. Used masterfully by Ronald Reagan in his presidential campaigns in the 1980s, dial groups are groups assembled to watch a video of a candidate and turn a dial to a position between 0 and 100 to indicate opposition or approval to the candidate as the candidate speaks. These data can then be analyzed to reveal what typical Americans like or dislike about a candidate's presentation. Using focus and dial groups, the Clinton campaign carefully modified the content and style of Clinton's speeches to appeal to the tastes of the public. For example, focus and dial group data indicated that voters responded favorably to Clinton when he emphasized the importance of the work ethic; consequently, Clinton was coached by campaign manager James Carville to talk about work in every speech.

- By June 1992, Clinton's level of support among voters dropped significantly as Ross Perot gained momentum as an Independent candidate. Clinton responded with a frenzy of fundraising activity; with attacks on rap artist Sister Souljah, whom he called a racist (an attack some civil rights leaders considered a cheap appeal to white voters); with increased emphasis in his speeches on the need to strengthen the economy; and with an appearance on the *Arsenio Hall Show.*

- In July 1992, Perot withdrew from the election just before Clinton formally accepted the Democratic Party's nomination at the party convention. During the convention, the party ran a prime-time documentary on Clinton's impoverished boyhood and his victimization by an alcoholic stepfather. The content of the documentary was based on additional focus group research, which indicated that large segments of the public viewed Clinton as rich and pampered. Throughout the remainder of the month, Clinton continued to have trouble with some voters over his handling of allegations of marijuana use; his response continued to be that although he experimented with the drug, he "didn't inhale."

- In late summer through early fall of 1992, Clinton overtook Bush in public opinion polls, in presidential debates (during one debate, for example, Bush was caught on camera looking at his watch as though he were bored), and in the sheer number of campaign appearances.

- On November 3, Clinton beat Bush by winning 43 percent of the popular vote (and 370 electoral college votes) to Bush's 38 percent of the popular vote (and 168 electoral college votes) and Perot's 19 percent of the popular vote (and no electoral college votes). Exit polls of voters revealed that the major issue for voters in the election was the poor state of the economy.[108]

One might argue that Clinton's reelection campaign began the day after he was inaugurated as president. Campaign manager Carville remained with Clinton to develop a strategy for broadening Clinton's appeal among Democrats during his first days in office. Stanley Greenberg, Clinton's polling expert during his campaign, stayed on to advise Clinton on how to win over the 19 percent of the electorate who had voted for Perot.[109] In fact, Clinton advisers were worried about the 1996 election as early as May 1993, when, despite help from Greenberg, polls showed that as many as one-fifth of voters expressed support for a Perot candidacy in 1996.[110] A year and 2 months later, Bob Dole also started campaigning for the presidency, even though the election was still more than 2 years away.[111]

The 1996 presidential election was one in which Clinton reused the 1992 strategy of trying to appeal to a broad group of middle-of-the-road voters. According to Stephanopoulous, on potentially divisive issues Clinton would choose a strategy of taking no clear-cut position in order to avoid upsetting anybody.[112] Clinton campaign staffers also noted that Clinton's image as a leader was strengthened after the bombing of the Oklahoma City federal building; although Clinton was able to carry the image of himself as a strong president who helped the country endure the tragedy of Oklahoma City into his 1996 campaign, he portrayed Dole as an "extremist" who would hurt Americans by cutting programs such as Medicare if elected.[113] Like Bush in 1992, Dole attacked Clinton's character and, also like Bush, failed to marshal these attacks into a strategy capable of overcoming the political consequences of the country's economic indicators. Specifically, although economic problems helped Clinton win in 1992, economic growth and stability during his own administration helped him win reelection in 1996.[114] Still, Clinton failed to win over the 1992 Perot voters; half of those who voted for Perot in 1992 chose Dole in 1996, whereas the remainder of the 1992 Perot voters split their support between Perot and Clinton in 1996.[115] Although Clinton won the election, he captured less than 50 percent of the vote—49 percent voted for Clinton, 41 percent voted for Dole, and 9 percent voted for Perot. These figures translated into 379 electoral college votes for Clinton and 159 electoral college votes for Dole. Moreover, voter turnout (only 49 percent of the voting age population) was the lowest for a presidential election since 1924.[116] Perhaps equally disturbing if you are Bill Clinton, more than half of those voting said they doubted Clinton's integrity and truthfulness. It appears that a large segment of the electorate agreed with Bush's and Dole's charges against Clinton's character but just as firmly believed Clinton's economic performance was more important than his ethical missteps.

When the 2000 presidential campaign began, few, if any, could have imagined that the campaign between George W. Bush and Al Gore would have intensified *after* election day. An examination of postelection actions reveals both candidates struggling to control media and public images, fighting over which candidate was the genuine choice of voters, and scrambling to find a way to win that did not elicit accusations of crass self-promotion. Gore scored higher in public opinion polls than did Bush after the party conventions, but Bush did better than Gore in the presidential debates. When election day finally came, in the course of 36 hours from the time that voting ended, Bush appeared to be the winner, Gore offered a concession, and then Gore retracted the concession. In the contested state of Florida, Bush's lead over Gore jumped and fell depending on which ballots were recounted on which day: On November 9, Bush led by 1,784 votes, on November 10 by 327, on November 14 by 300, and on November 18 by 930. In New Mexico, the vote was even closer (in comparison with the November 18 Florida recount number): Gore won by only 486 votes. Gore won by 4,130 votes in Iowa, by 5,698 votes in Wisconsin, and by 6,595 votes in Oregon.

Having 25 electoral college votes, Florida became the battleground of the close states. In Florida, counting itself became controversial as incompletely scored chad ballots raised conflicting opinions over how they should be reviewed. At least 445 felons were found to have voted illegally in Florida. In Miami-Dade County, 5 percent of ballots were unreadable by the voting machines. In Palm Beach County, more than 19,000 ballots were disqualified for having more than one selection marked among the presidential candidates. In Duval County, 22,000 ballots were similarly disqualified. Fifteen hundred overseas ballots were disqualified for lacking postmarks, registration information, or verifiable signatures. Some African-American voters reported that they were illegally prevented from voting at all. The election held on November 7 was not over until December 13, following the U.S. Supreme Court's 5–4 ruling to end recounts in Florida, after which Gore conceded defeat.

In the end, as you can see, the number of contested votes in Florida far exceeded the margin by which George W. Bush won Florida and the state's 25 electoral college votes that pushed him to victory in the electoral college. Nationwide, Gore won the popular vote by a margin of 539,897 votes or 0.5 percent of all votes. Bush won 271 electoral votes and Gore won 266 electoral college votes.[117]

By looking at Clinton's two campaigns and the Bush–Gore election outcomes, you can discern various important features of U.S. elections. First, election strategies are influenced heavily by election rules concerning the counting of votes. Presidential candidates had to develop a strategy based on whether votes were counted according to plurality or majority rules, popular or electoral college vote rules, or alternative rules. Lest you think simple mathematical reasoning is enough

Bronx church fans remind worshipers to vote in the U.S. presidential election of 2000 (right), while voting links the people and the government in Scotland on election day (below).

© James Estrin/NYT Pictures

© Reuters/Jeff Mitchell/Archive Photos/CORBIS

to count votes and determine election winners, examine the following U.S. election rules stipulating the means by which votes are tallied:

- Presidential elections are decided by **electoral college** votes, not popular votes. The electoral college consists of a group of people who vote officially for president and vice president. To win the presidency, a candidate must receive a majority (270) of electoral college votes. The number of a state's electoral college votes equals the number of senators plus representatives in that state. The presidential candidate who wins the popular vote of a state receives all the state's electoral college votes, with the exception of Maine and Nebraska, which split electoral college votes among candidates based on each candidate's popular vote.[118] If no presidential candidate wins a majority of electoral college votes, the House of Representatives selects the president from the top three contenders and the Senate chooses the vice president. As you can observe, candidates have the incentive of paying especially close attention to voters living in large states (such as California) possessing large numbers of electoral college votes. As you can also imagine, it is possible to win the popular vote and lose the electoral college vote. On four occasions, we have had presidents who lost the popular vote: In 1824, John Quincy Adams was named president by the House (when no candidate received a majority of electoral college votes), although Andrew Jackson had more popular votes than Adams; in what historians have described as a highly corrupt presidential election of 1876, Samuel Tilden had more popular votes but fewer electoral college votes than Rutherford B. Hayes; in 1888, Grover Cleveland had more popular votes but fewer electoral votes than Benjamin Harrison; and in 2000, Al Gore won more popular votes than George W. Bush but lost the electoral college vote.[119]

- Congressional elections and most other U.S. elections are decided by **single-member plurality (SMP)** rules. Under SMP rules, the winner of an election is the candidate who receives more votes than anyone else. The key to understanding SMP is to realize that winners can win *without* getting a majority of votes, and runner-up candidates get nothing at all, even if they win almost as many votes as the candidate coming in first. A candidate winning only 40 percent of the vote, for example, can win the election as long as he or she has more votes than any other candidate. SMP rules are also known as "winner take all" systems: No matter how close rival candidates may make a race for office, as long as a candidate gets just one more vote than anyone else, he or she wins.

- In some states, one finds examples of alternative voting rules. For example, **cumulative voting** has been used in elections for offices such as county commissions and school boards in some localities in New Mexico and Alabama and has been recommended for county judicial elections in Hamilton County, Tennessee. Under cumulative voting rules, voters cast as many votes as there are offices to be filled; voters can combine their votes for a single candidate or split their votes among two or more candidates. Among the candidates, the top vote recipients are the winners. For example, if there are five offices on a school board to be filled, the top five vote recipients are the winners. Cumulative voting provides an opportunity for minorities (who can combine their votes around a single candidate) to succeed in getting candidates they favor elected to office.[120] A **single transferable vote (STV)** rule is used in city council elections in Cambridge, Massachusetts, and in some community school board elections in New York City. Under this rule, voters can rank candidates on the ballot as first, second, third, and so on choices; when all votes are counted, second, third, and so on choices are taken into account to reward candidates other than first-place winners.[121] The significance of cumulative voting and single transferable voting is related to the fact that both systems offer an alternative to the "winner take all" dimension of SMP rules and allow smaller segments of voting populations to compete more successfully with majorities.

Second, election strategies are based on candidate perceptions of voter decision making. Trying to figure out how voters make their choices in elections is a major concern of candidates and political scientists. Although voter decisions are probably too complex to allow for broad generalizations, studies have suggested the usefulness of the following perspectives on voter choice: sociological cleavages, retrospective voting, and prospective voting. The **sociological cleavages** perspective emphasizes that voting decisions are sometimes affected by one's membership in certain groups; because all members of such groups are likely to be concerned with issues relevant to the group, members of the group are likely to exhibit similar voting choices. For example, members of the same economic class, ethnic group, religious group, and so forth may vote similarly because of their shared interests and similar group affiliations. This perspective helps explain, for example, the broad voting patterns known as the New Deal Coalition.[122]

Yet the fact that no group votes unanimously for one party or candidate in any election raises the possibility that other factors often influence voter choice. The **retrospective voting** perspective on voter decision making suggests that voters sometimes make up their minds by looking at the present and/or past performance of candidates or parties and then either reward or penalize those candidates or parties on the basis of this performance. For example, if a voter makes a decision on the basis of retrospective voting he or she might ask, "Have I been better off economically since Clinton has been in office?" If so, according to the retrospective voting model, that person will likely vote for Clinton; if not, he or she will likely vote against Clinton. As you can see, the retrospective voting perspective emphasizes the individual's rational perceptions of candidate and party records in contrast to the sociological cleavage perspective's emphasis on membership in social groups. As you will recall from the discussion of the Clinton presidential campaigns of 1992 and 1996, Clinton's strategy consisted of reminding voters of the economic hard times under Bush and, later, economic recovery during his own first term. These campaign tactics are consistent with the retrospective voter model's proposition that voters make individual calculations of rational self-interest and either reward or penalize candidates based on how well voters feel themselves to be doing.[123]

In some elections, some groups of voters seem to be influenced by **prospective voting** considerations. A voter who makes his or her decision on a rational assessment of probable future benefits is a prospective voter. For example, a voter who voted for Dole over Clinton in 1996 because he or she believed Dole would likely do a better job of managing the economy and creating job opportunities would be characterized as having made a voting choice on the basis of prospective voting decision theory. The salient point here is the following: Unlike both sociological cleavage models (emphasizing the impact of group membership on voting decisions) and retrospective voting (emphasizing voter attitudes about past or current performance) perspectives, the prospective voting model suggests that voters look ahead and rationally analyze parties and candidates and then vote on the basis of their individual predictions as to which parties and candidates will bring better benefits to voters.[124] As you can see, voter decision making is so complex and varied that no single perspective can fully describe how all voters vote. Which model (if any) best describes your decision-making process in the election in which you last voted?

Third, election strategies are based on candidates' knowledge that not everyone who is eligible to vote will vote. In the United States, on average, only approximately 50–55 percent of eligible voters have voted in presidential elections in the 1980s and 1990s; the voter turnout in local elections has been even lower (approximately 25 percent). Nonvoting occurs more frequently among the members of the population who are economically disadvantaged and who have low levels of education.[125] Consider how different elections might be if candidates knew that, for example, 80–90 percent of the voting age population planned to vote. Imagine the range of issues that might be debated in elections if candidates knew that they had to compete for the support of the poorest and the most marginalized members of the populace—those very members who can presently be ignored by the Clintons, Doles, Bushes, and Gores.

## Elections Compared: Democracies

Democracies differ dramatically in terms of electoral rules governing the counting of votes. One finds examples of various uses of **single-member plurality (SMP), proportional representation (PR), and single transferable votes (STV)** rules. As discussed earlier, the United States uses, with few exceptions, SMP rules for measuring the vote. Great Britain also uses SMP rules. Under SMP provisions, the candidate who receives more votes than any of his or her competitors in an election wins the election.

**Proportional representation** provides an alternative to SMP. Under PR rules, parties (and their candidates) receive a percentage of offices based on the percentage of votes received in an election. For example, in legislative elections, if a party wins 40 percent of the popular vote, its candidates will fill 40 percent of the seats in the legislature. Democracies can use a straightforward, pure PR system, or they can, like Germany, use a variant of PR; Germany elects a part, rather than all, of its legislature according to PR rules. PR systems often operate with a *threshold* provision; that is, a party must receive a certain percentage of the popular vote to qualify for legislative seats. In Germany, for example, the threshold is 5 percent; in Israel, it is 1 percent; in Denmark, it is 2 percent; in Norway and Sweden, it is 4 percent.[126]

Very significantly, the PR system is more conducive to the emergence of multiple parties than is the SMP system. Runner-up parties, third-place parties, fourth-place parties, and often even smaller parties are rewarded with officeholding in PR systems, whereas in SMP systems they could turn out to be perpetual losers to the first-place parties. Knowing that votes are counted in such a manner as to reward smaller parties as well as large ones, voters in PR systems may find it rational to vote for parties that are not in first place, whereas these same voters might conclude that a vote for a small party is a "wasted" vote in a system based on SMP. Thus, democracies that want to encourage the development of multiple parties (as opposed to just two major parties) find PR preferable to SMP.[127]

As mentioned earlier, in reference to the United States, STV systems are similar to PR measurements, insofar as they distribute votes in such a manner as to reward parties not in first place. In STV systems, as used in Ireland, voters mark on their ballots their ranking of candidates in order of preference. Winning candidates must win a certain quota of votes, with the quota based on the number of votes cast and the number of offices to be filled in the election. Once a candidate achieves the quota, any extra votes cast for that candidate are then distributed to the voters' subsequent choices for office, as indicated on their ballots. Similarly, candidates who are losers in the election (who have failed to attain the quota through either first-choice votes or transferred votes) have their votes transferred to the alternative choices, as indicated on the ballots. This system rewards parties that are popular enough to be second choices but not first choices; thus, like PR measurements, STV systems tend to be more supportive of smaller parties than are SMP systems.[128]

Democracies are also notable for the variations in voter turnout in elections and for the attendant rules governing timing, scheduling, registration, proportional representation, and compulsory voting in elections. Students of comparative politics have long known that voter turnout in the United States is significantly lower than voter turnout in most European democracies. Political scientists have found that voter turnout in elections is often related to the following factors:

- *Timing.* Europeans may have the occasion to vote two or three times in a 4-year period, whereas U.S. citizens may have 10 or more elections in which to vote during the same period. Less frequent elections seem to result in higher levels of voting.[129]

- *Scheduling.* European democracies generally do not schedule elections for workdays (for example, elections may be held on weekends), whereas U.S. elections tend to be scheduled on workdays. Voter turnout may increase when elections do not occur on workdays.[130]

- *Registration.* European voters generally are registered to vote by the state, whereas U.S. voters have historically had to register themselves to vote. The ease of registration for European voters compared to U.S. voters has long been thought by political scientists to be a factor explaining higher turnout in European elections.[131]

- *Proportional representation measurements of the vote.* Most European democracies use some form of PR measure for counting votes; PR appears to increase voter turnout because the pool of people finding it rational to vote is larger than the corresponding pool in SMP systems. This is the case because insofar as PR systems reward small parties as well as large ones, voters supportive of small as well as large parties have the incentive to vote. In contrast, in SMP systems, voters who are supportive of the Green Party, the Libertarian Party, the Prohibition Party, or similar small parties may feel that voting is a waste of time because the first-place large party is the only party rewarded.[132]

- *Compulsory voting.* A number of European countries have used compulsory voting—that is, have required by law that voters go to the polls and vote. The Netherlands had compulsory voting until 1970. When compulsory voting was abolished, voter turnout fell by approximately 10 percent. Studies of Belgium have indicated that if this country terminated compulsory voting, voter turnout would drop as it did in The Netherlands.[133]

### Elections Compared: Nondemocracies

Elections can play important roles in nondemocracies, as countries become transitional societies opening up avenues for democratization. In other nondemocratic situations, elections can be used by dominant parties to make themselves appear more legitimate and to squelch dissent. For example, the ruling party of Singapore, the People's Action Party (PAP), has used elections in this manner. Since Singapore's independence in the late 1950s, the PAP has attempted to hold onto its virtual monopoly of power by using elections rather than doing away with them. Opposition parties are simply weakened by harassment campaigns and unequal access to resources so that, although they officially exist, they are unable to topple the PAP. In 2001, for example, PAP won 27 seats in government and opposition parties won only 2 seats. In Burma, the military regime has also experimented with the use of noncompetitive elections as a means of bolstering its own dominance. In 1989, for example, the military officially recognized more than 200 parties as legal entities permitted to run candidates in an election. The government apparently thought this maneuver would effectively splinter any opposition so badly that no opposition party would be able to build a sizable base because when opponents to the government rallied behind a single opposition movement, the government nullified the results of the elections.[134]

### SUMMING UP

- **Interest groups** are groups that try to shape political outcomes. Interest groups can be organized in many ways. **Membership organizations** have official members, whereas **nonmembership organizations** do not. **Anomic groups** represent the lowest level of organization, and **associational groups** represent the highest; **nonassociational groups** lie in between the two others in terms of organizational level.

- U.S. interest group strategies include direct lobbying, grassroots lobbying, campaign involvement, judicial involvement, and protest.

- **Direct lobbying** is defined as contacting government officials as a means of influencing political outcomes. Direct lobbying can be a very effective interest group strategy if direct lobbyists can offer government officials expert information. This information can be crucial to government leaders, as they proceed to make political decisions. Former politicians often go on to become direct lobbyists; such individuals have a wealth of experience and contacts that may be invaluable assets to interest groups.

- **Grassroots lobbying** is the process of contacting the public in an effort to influence politics. Contacts can include person-to-person meetings but are increasingly likely to be telephone- and computer-based grassroots contacts.

- Interest groups use numerous tactics to get involved in campaigns and elections. Making financial donations, ranking candidates, registering voters, joining political parties, supporting some candidates rather than others, and pressuring candidates to support interest group positions are possible avenues of **campaign involvement**.

- **Judicial involvement** is an interest group strategy that can include the filing of **amicus curiae** briefs and offering professional legal services to individuals involved in judicial controversies of importance to an interest group.

- **Protest** is still another interest group strategy. Protest can be a dramatic, engaging, and thought-provoking way of publicizing an issue, as when Global Exchange publicized Nike's low wages to international workers by questioning Michael Jordan's ethics in being a Nike spokesperson.

- **Interest group pluralism** encompasses interest group–government relations in which interest groups are outsiders competing for influence over government. In contrast, **democratic corporatist** societies are ones in which interest groups are insiders or partners with government. **State autonomy** describes a relationship between interest groups and government in which the government is fairly insulated from and autonomous of interest group pressures.

- Interest group politics in nondemocratic societies is anything but simple. Interest groups may be repressed, tolerated, encouraged, and/or controlled. One pattern of interest group–government interaction is **state corporatism**, a pattern said to exist when states control interest groups by incorporating groups into government in ways that make the groups subordinate and submissive to government itself. Such groups are not partners with government but rather are servants of government.

- **Political parties** put forward proposed leaders of government.

- U.S. political parties have a *broad-based* diverse membership, are decentralized, and are more intent on winning elections than on insisting that their members and candidates agree with party platforms.

- In U.S. elections, both Democrats and Republicans try to appeal to Independent voters as well as their own members.

- Studies that examine political parties in democracies suggest that parties differ in terms of degree of *centralization*, *number*, and whether **majoritarian**, **multiparty**, **consensual**, **conflictual**, or **consociational** party relations exist.

- Parties and elections often play important roles in nondemocratic countries. Indeed, elections can be used by dominant parties to strengthen their own rule. Dominant parties can maintain themselves by repressing rival parties or by allowing their existence but checking their ability to gain influence.

- Elections can operate under a variety of rules. In the United States, the **electoral college** uses unique rules for selecting presidents. Created by the writers of the Constitution, the electoral college bases the number of electoral college votes per state on state population and accords victory to the presidential candidate winning a majority of electoral college votes. **Cumulative voting** is another unique set of election rules used in some U.S. localities.

- Most U.S. elections operate under **single-member plurality** (**SMP**) rules. SMP rules define an election's winner as the candidate receiving more votes than any other candidate. Some democracies use **proportional representation** (**PR**). Elections under PR rules are ones in which parties receive a percentage of government offices in accordance with the percentage of popular votes won. Democracies using **single transferable vote** (**STV**) rule allow voters to rank candidates on election ballots and have those ranking preferences considered in determining election winners. Democracies may combine or revise these systems so that, as in Germany, a variant of PR is used.

- Voter turnout in the United States is lower than in most other democracies. Why? Factors such as election *timing*, *scheduling*, *voter registration*, *PR*, and *compulsory voting* have been suggested as possible influences on levels of voting. Citizens who do vote may make decisions based on **sociological cleavages** or **retrospective** or **prospective voting** perspectives.

## STUDY QUESTIONS

1. Compare and contrast interest groups and political parties. How is each type of party defined?

2. Identify and give examples of interest group strategies used by U.S. interest groups.

3. Identify and define PACs, independent expenditures, and bundling. Explain the legal limitations on the amount of money that can be spent on campaigns.

4. Compare and contrast interest group pluralism, democratic corporatism, and state autonomy.

5. What is the difference between a membership organization and a nonmembership organization?

6. Discuss the differences separating anomic, nonassociational, and associational interest groups.

7. How does state corporatism differ from democratic corporatism?

8. Describe the characteristics of political parties in the United States.

9. Why do Independents represent a significant force in U.S. elections?

10. Are third parties in the United States always ineffective? Explain.

11. Identify three ways in which parties can differ across democracies.

12. Do parties exist in nondemocratic countries? Do elections? Explain.

13. Discuss three characteristics of U.S. elections.

14. Compare and contrast SMP, PR, and STV election systems.

15. How do voters make decisions about which candidates they prefer? Explain how retrospective, prospective, and sociological cleavages models answer this question.

## FOLLOWING UP THROUGH INTERNET SOURCES

- Lijphart Elections Archive (http://dodgson.ucsd.edu/lij). Election schedules and results from numerous countries.

- University of British Columbia Library, *Political Parties and Electoral Behaviour* (http://www.library.ubc.ca/poli/electoral.html#Parties). Links to parties, election results, party platforms, etc., from various countries.

- Federal Election Commission (http://www.fec.gov). Provides historical overview of the development of U.S. laws on campaign contributions, explains legal limitations on campaign contributions, and provides specific election data.

- Republican Party (http://www.rnc.org). Link to U.S. Republican Party.

- Democratic Party (http://www.democrats.org). Link to U.S. Democratic Party.

# 10

❖

# Comparative Politics III

## Governing Democracies: Executives, Legislatures, and Judiciaries

Democratic governments have a wide range of options for specifying the relations among different institutions of government. Executives may be linked to legislatures in a manner that emphasizes executive independence or in one that pushes executives and legislatures into close partnership. Courts may or may not have the authority to override the decisions of legislatures. As you survey governing processes within various democracies, you can easily see why democracy is often thought of as a very flexible form of political decision making. In analyzing this flexibility, this chapter focuses on a comparison of U.S. and British executive, legislative, and judicial processes.

### EXECUTIVE-LEGISLATIVE RELATIONS: PRESIDENTIAL AND PARLIAMENTARY SYSTEMS

Democracies have tended to adopt, to varying degrees, one of two types of executive-legislative arrangements. **Presidential systems** are ones in which executive-legislative relations operate as follows: (1) Executives and legislatures are elected in distinct, separate elections for fixed terms of office; (2) executives cannot be removed by votes of no confidence; and (3) executive power is separated from legislative power. In a presidential system, as in the United States, both presidents and members of Congress are elected in distinct, separate elections, and the powers of both institutions remain separate. If the president is opposed by Congress, Congress cannot force the president out of office (except through the very difficult and cumbersome process of impeachment), nor can congressional disapproval of a president force a calling of early elections. Indeed, insofar as the branches are separate and independent, the president and Congress may become antagonists rather than partners in governing.

In contrast, **parliamentary systems** are ones in which (1) legislatures select executive leadership; (2) executives can be removed by votes of no confidence, and new elections may be necessitated; and (3) executive and legislative powers are combined—not separated—in order to forge a working partnership between the two branches of government. Citizens in parliamentary systems elect members of the parliament, but the parliament itself names the country's executive leader. After parliamentary elections put in place a legislature, the major party within the legislature names the leader of that major party as chief executive. If no single party has a majority of seats in the parliament, a coalition of parties names the executive leader. In this way, the power of the executive and that of the legislature are combined. The executive is further connected to the legislative branch in that executives who lose the confidence of a majority of the parliament can be removed from office. A loss of confidence can be expressed through parliamentary refusal to pass legislation deemed important by the executive or through actual votes to rebuke the executive. The possibility of such actions is intended to motivate executives to work productively with parliaments. Although parliamentary systems vary in their procedures for no-confidence measures, often such measures are followed by elections for a new parliament, which in turn will name a new executive leader. For this reason, and also because in most parliamentary systems executives generally can call for early parliamentary elections even in the absence of votes of no confidence, neither executive nor legislative terms are fixed. Specifically, parliamentary systems stipulate a certain period within which parliamentary elections must be held (for example, within 5 years in Great Britain), but elections are often called earlier than the stipulated due date.[1]

## The U.S. Presidential System: The Executive

In the United States, executive authority—the authority of executing the laws of the country—resides primarily with the president and to a lesser extent with the vice president and cabinet. The nature of the president's authority is outlined in

| BOX 10.1 **Presidential and Parliamentary Systems** | |
|---|---|
| *Presidential Systems* | *Parliamentary Systems* |
| ▪ Separation of power | ▪ Connected powers |
| ▪ Separate elections | ▪ Legislature names executive leader |
| ▪ Absence of votes of no confidence | ▪ Votes of no confidence |
| ▪ Fixed terms of office | ▪ Terms of office are not fixed |

the U.S. Constitution, which states that the president's powers and responsibilities include

- Serving as commander of the country's military forces and state militias

- Granting pardons, except in disputes involving impeachment

- Negotiating treaties, in consultation with the Senate

- Appointing, in consultation with the Senate, ambassadors, Supreme Court justices, and other officials

- Making a State of the Union address to Congress

- Proposing laws to Congress for consideration

- Convening and adjourning Congress

- Approving or disapproving laws passed by Congress

- Receiving foreign officials and ambassadors

- Ensuring that the country's laws are implemented[2]

Presidential authority is enhanced by two factors: the ability to persuade and the ability to draw on precedents establishing expanded presidential powers. First, to be most successful, presidents need to be able to use persuasion in their dealings with Congress.[3] Whether a president wants Congress to pass a certain bill, not to pass a certain bill, or to support a certain presidential nominee for public office, a president is in no position to *demand* that such objectives be carried out; instead, presidents must bargain, coax, and persuade Congress if presidents are to be successful in developing productive working relationships with the legislative branch.

President Bush was called upon to be both tireless and unrelenting in his persuasive campaign to establish the Department of Homeland Security (DHS) after 9/11. The formation of the DHS was a major reorganization of the U.S. federal government, one that DHS itself proclaims to be the most all-encompassing consolidation of centralized state power since the 1947 reorganization of the Armed Forces under the Department of Defense. For fiscal year 2004, DHS had a budget in excess of $37 billion to enhance port, aviation, border, coastal, and emergency security forces. Even with the country's insecurities after 9/11, President Bush had to bargain with Congress in order to see the DHS through to completion. As a *Wall Street Journal* headline put it at one point in the debate over homeland security, "Bush Security Plan Faces Obstacles." Representative Don Young was skeptical of transferring Coast Guard authority to a new agency, Senator Evan Bayh worried about the growth in governmental centralization and the possible loss of efficiency, Senator Bob Graham voiced doubts about whether the Bush plan could not be replaced by something more logical, and Senator Richard Shelby criticized what he saw as inattention to intelligence-gathering needs.

President Bush's months-long campaign to build congressional–as well as public and international–support for the attack on Iraq in 2003 also demonstrates the strategy of persuading, not demanding, in presidential policymaking. In his State of the Union address in 2002, President Bush referred to Iraq as part of an "axis of evil." He described Iraq as a regime supporting terror and as a state intent on nuclear, biological, and chemical weapons development. A month later, President Bush stated that it would be disastrous for a hostile state such as Iraq to successfully forge an alliance with an international terrorist organization such as Al Qaeda. In March 2002, he declined to rule out unilateral action to constrain Iraqi threats to international security, and in April 2002, President Bush and British Prime Minister Tony Blair asserted that peace-loving people would be "better off" if Saddam Hussein were removed from power. While he denied that he had actual plans for an attack in place in June 2002, President Bush, in August 2002, speculated about how fitting it would be to give future generations the gift of a planet without dictators in possession of weapons of mass destruction. However, it was not until September 2002 that President Bush explicitly linked Saddam Hussein and Al Qaeda, and it was not until October that he suggested the imminence of a preemptive strike against Iraq. By January–February of 2003, President Bush was highlighting the importance of regime change in Iraq—for the betterment of Iraqis, for the safety of the world, and for the security of the United States. In short, a lengthy, detailed persuasion campaign served as a prelude to the attack itself.[4]

Former President Clinton's relationship with Congress further illustrates the importance of persuasion to presidential success, in this case, in terms of domestic policy. During his first term, Clinton failed to convince Congress to enact widescale health reform. Rather than abandoning his ideas, Clinton simply altered his persuasive strategies during his second term. He arrived at the following conclusions: (1) Congress can be more readily swayed to approve an idea if the idea does not look totally new and radical, and (2) Congress is more easily persuaded to enact small-scale ideas than large-scale ones. Thus, as his second-term strategy Clinton began trying to persuade Congress to pass health reform laws that were repackaged measures already enacted in various states, and he began presenting his ideas on health care little by little to Congress so that no single proposal looked too sweeping. These persuasive tactics proved remarkably successful: Clinton saw Congress enact health insurance regulations protecting workers in August 1996, pass further insurance regulations covering obstetrics in September 1996, and pass measures to expand health care for children in 1997. Moreover, Clinton learned that his persuasive tactics were less likely to be met with overwhelming interest group opposition if his focus remained on details so small in scale that they attracted only limited interest group attention.[5]

The importance of persuasion to presidential success may seem surprising, given the fact that presidents possess the power to **veto**, or negate, bills passed by Congress. A presidential veto prevents a bill passed by Congress from becoming law; however, Congress can override a presidential veto if it votes by a two-thirds majority in both chambers to do so. From the president's perspective, a veto can be *formally* enacted by a president; or, if a bill is sent by Congress for the president to sign into law, and if the president simply does nothing with the bill—provided that Congress is adjourned within 10 days—the bill is killed *informally* through a **pocket veto**. Although vetoes give presidents leverage with Congress, they are no substitute for persuasion. Not only can Congress override vetoes, but Congress can also

---

**BOX 10.2   Presidential Veto Power**

The actual or threatened use of a veto affords presidents leverage in the law-making process. Below is a list of recent presidents and the number of vetoes they used, as well as the number of vetoes overridden by Congress. How extensively President George W. Bush will use or threaten vetoes is yet to be determined.

| Congressional Sessions | President | Number of Vetoes | Number of Vetoes That Congress Overrode |
|---|---|---|---|
| 73—79 | Roosevelt | 635 | 9 |
| 79—82 | Truman | 250 | 12 |
| 83—86 | Eisenhower | 181 | 2 |
| 87—88 | Kennedy | 21 | 0 |
| 88—90 | Johnson | 30 | 0 |
| 91—93 | Nixon | 43 | 7 |
| 93—94 | Ford | 66 | 12 |
| 95—96 | Carter | 31 | 2 |
| 97—100 | Reagan | 78 | 9 |
| 101—102 | Bush | 44 | 1 |
| 103—106 | Clinton | 37 | 2 |

SOURCE: U.S. House of Representatives, Office of the Clerk, Presidential Vetoes, http://clerk.house.gov/histHigh/Congressional_History/vetoes.

---

remember vetoes a long time, so long that veto memories may be very fresh the next time the president has an idea he or she wants Congress to enact.

Presidential success also depends on the ability of presidents to put the expanded powers attached to the office through custom to effective use. Certain powers have come to be associated with the office of the presidency either because they are viewed as logical extensions of constitutional provisions or because presidents simply undertook certain actions that came to be viewed as legitimately "presidential." With regard to the former, for example, President Lincoln drew on his constitutional role as commander in chief to claim the right to force individual states to remain in the United States during the Civil War. With regard to the latter, President Washington created the practice of having regular meetings with his cabinet, a practice that grew into a custom available for later presidents. President Franklin Roosevelt began the practice of using the media—specifically, the radio—to communicate with the public; today, no president can afford *not* to use this custom of trying to build popular support through media appeals. As these examples illustrate, through the development of customs, presidential powers and actions have grown and diversified beyond those originally spelled out in the U.S. Constitution.[6]

The expansion of presidential power has prompted some political scientists to refer to the U.S. president as a *presidential lawmaker.* That is, presidents are in a privileged position relative to the other branches of government, so much so that presidents (if they are skillful in using the powers available to them) can shape the laws passed by Congress and can take the lead—relative to Congress and the judicial branch—in shaping the country's political agenda.[7] Several factors beyond the ability to persuade and to take advantage of customary practices also contribute to the ability of presidents to act as presidential lawmakers. First, Congress has passed laws enlarging the president's authority, according presidents key roles in setting budgets, negotiating international trades, and committing U.S. troops abroad in the absence of actual declarations of war. With the passage of every such law, the power resources available to presidents increase. Second, presidents since Harry Truman have had official staff members whose priority it is to pressure Congress to support presidential objectives. For instance, President Reagan had a Legislative Strategy Group, whose full-time job was to lobby Congress to support Reagan's proposals and to put together coalitions of congressional supporters large enough to vote these proposals into law. With a coterie of staff assigned the task of pushing presidential proposals through Congress, presidents can greatly increase their legislative influence. Third, presidents can reward members of Congress with favors, such as visits to the White House, complimentary speeches, and budgetary allocations for federal programs in their states. The ability to grant or withhold such favors can certainly make the president's job as persuader of Congress easier. Fourth, presidents can present themselves as leaders of the entire country–whereas Representatives and Senators are likely to be viewed as leaders only of their districts or states–and this can be used to convince Congress to defer to presidential objectives.[8] This deference may be especially pronounced on issues involving foreign policy, especially during periods of international tension or conflict.[9]

Although very important, these reservoirs of power provide no guarantee that all presidents will succeed in becoming chief legislators. Indeed, presidents who lack popular appeal may lack clout with Congress and may fail to become effective leaders. In addition, even popular presidents are limited in what they can expect in the way of support from Congress. As discussed in Chapter 9, U.S. parties are decentralized and members of Congress will likely look to voters in their home states and districts and, on issues important to those voters, side with the voters even if that means opposing a president's plan. Finally, insofar as presidents are seen by voters as leaders of the entire country, presidents have very high expectations placed on them to solve national problems. More than members of Congress, presidents may be blamed when their plans fail. If the blame sets in and a president's public approval rating drops, Congress may see no reason to accept a president as a legislative leader.

Whether or not presidents succeed as presidential lawmakers, they enjoy an independence from Congress not known in parliamentary systems. Even ineffective presidents are independent of Congress. To understand this, it is necessary to examine *presidential tenure*. Presidents are elected for fixed 4-year terms, which, since ratification of the Twenty-Second Amendment in 1951, cannot exceed a total of 10 years. A president's 4-year term of office cannot be cut short by Congress, unless Congress uses its **impeachment** powers. As spelled out in the Constitution, the House of Representatives has the power to impeach (charge) presidents on matters of "Treason, Bribery, or other high Crimes and Misdemeanors" and the Senate has the authority to try and convict on the charges. If impeached, tried, and convicted, a president is removed from office. Impeachment powers are very difficult to use against presidents, as indicated by the fact that only three presidents faced serious threats to their tenure because of impeachment: Andrew Johnson was impeached but not convicted during the 1800s, and Richard Nixon resigned prior to impeachment in the 1900s. Bill Clinton was impeached in December 1998; in February 1999, the Senate acquitted him. In contrast to no-confidence votes, which can cut short an executive's tenure in a parliamentary system, impeachment proceedings cannot be used simply to express displeasure with a president's leadership; impeachment can be used *only* if presidents are thought to have committed impeachable acts.[10]

## The British Parliamentary System: The Executive

Executive authority in Great Britain is vested in the prime minister and cabinet. The prime minister is selected by the House of Commons, which is the elected chamber of the British parliament. The prime minister is leader of the majority party in Commons and is also a member of the chamber. At present, Tony Blair is the prime minister. Blair's Labour Party won 413 seats in the 2001 general election. The Conservative Party won 166 seats, and the remaining seats in the 659-seat House of Commons were divided among smaller parties, including the Liberal Democrats, the third largest party at 52 seats in Commons.[11] The prime minister names and presides over a cabinet, which customarily consists of members of the majority party in Parliament. Custom dictates that the cabinet consist of approximately 18-25 members.

Typically, the cabinet meets weekly, conducts much of its work—for example, preparing bills favored by the prime minister to be presented to Parliament—in committee, and operates according to the tradition of collective responsibility. The term **collective responsibility** refers to the cabinet's custom of publicly supporting positions taken by the executive. That is, whatever their personal opinions on measures desired by the prime minister, cabinet members are expected to stand together in support of executive decisions. For instance, when Prime Minister Tony Blair was criticized by fellow Labour members of Parliament in 1997 because of announced welfare reforms, collective responsibility necessitated defense of the prime minister's program by cabinet members. Accordingly, in immediate response to the criticisms, the chancellor of the exchequer publicly expressed full support for Blair's proposed reforms.[12] Despite its customary importance, collective responsibility has faltered in some well-publicized cases in the 1970s when Labour ministers criticized the prime minister and in the 1980s when cabinet minister Michael Heseltine, serving as defense secretary, publicly criticized Conservative Prime Minister Margaret Thatcher.[13]

The British prime minister is generally considered to be in a potentially dominant position relative to the British Parliament. This position of dominance is not due to formal, delineated powers outlined in a constitution. Indeed, the range of powers held by prime ministers is not codified because Britain has no single written constitutional document. Rather, the prime minister's authority is based on custom and authority granted by Parliament. What are these sources of the prime minister's powers? First, the prime minister is head of his or her party, which is the major party in Parliament. As discussed in Chapter 9, British parties, unlike parties in the United States, are centralized ones in which leaders have extensive authority.[14] Second, prime ministers have wide-ranging appointment powers. Prime ministers have the power to appoint (and remove) cabinet members and key administrative personnel. These powers enable prime ministers to shape the British civil service, which is responsible for implementing laws.

Although presidents in presidential systems have no guarantee that the majority party in Congress will be their own party, British prime ministers do generally have this guarantee, insofar as elections in Britain typically result in a majority for either the Conservative or Labour Party; after all, if their party is not the majority party, either singly or in coalition, they will not become prime ministers. This connection between the executive and legislature joined by control of the same party gives prime ministers an advantage lacking for presidents under presidential systems. Because prime ministers are usually guaranteed a parliamentary majority consisting of their own party members and the parties tend to be centrally organized and platform oriented, prime ministers are generally well positioned to see their proposals passed by Parliament.[15] Thus, the British parliamentary system can reach a degree of executive effectiveness the U.S. presidential system generally does not attain.[16] Indeed, a recent study comparing U.S. President Ronald Reagan and British Prime Minister Margaret Thatcher during the 1980s found that Thatcher was much more effective in carrying out conservative policies than was Reagan, not because of any fault of Reagan but because Thatcher had those benefits of the parliamentary system just discussed.[17]

Yet this effectiveness is not synonymous with independence. If a British prime minister loses the confidence of a majority of the House of Commons, the prime minister and cabinet are forced to resign and new elections for the House of Commons as a whole may follow. Moreover, British prime ministers may call early elections for Parliament. This signifies an absence of fixed terms of office for prime ministers and Parliament. Insofar as the British parliamentary system has built-in procedures promoting effectiveness, the system produces prime ministers who look strong in comparison with parliaments; however, to the extent that prime ministers are forced to be attentive to party members' wishes in order to preclude declines in party unity and possible votes of no confidence, the British parliamentary system creates prime ministers whose actual power may turn out to be rather limited relative to Parliament. Not surprisingly, as political scientist R. A. W. Rhodes notes, scholars who study the British executive often disagree among themselves over how much emphasis should be placed on the characteristic of effectiveness and how much should be accorded to the attribute of dependence. As a result, these same scholars disagree on the question of how strong individual prime ministers have actually been in their dealings with Parliament.[18]

## Other Examples of Executive—Legislative Relations

Democracies differ greatly in the types of president-oriented or parliament-oriented executive-legislative relations they choose. For example, France has what scholars often refer to as a mixed system, combining elements of presidential and parliamentary relations. France has a president elected by the citizens, as well as a prime minister named by the president. In France, the president has been the dominant of the two executives.

Germany also has a president as well as a chancellor (the equivalent of a prime minister). Unlike France, Germany is considered an example of a parliamentary system, insofar as the chancellor—selected by a majority of the legislature—is the powerful executive. Germany's parliamentary system is unique in two ways. First, the chancellor cannot dissolve the legislature and call for early elections, as prime ministers can generally do under the terms of a parliamentary system. Second, the German legislature cannot cast a no-confidence vote unless it also agrees on whom to name as a new chancellor. This is known as a **constructive vote of no confidence**. As you can see, the constructive vote of no confidence is more difficult for legislatures to use than is a simple vote of no confidence, and as a result it is viewed by supporters of the German system as a stability-producing mechanism that discourages potentially ill-advised and frequent use of votes of no confidence.

Japan has a parliamentary system, but one that has created a uniquely weak prime minister. The Japanese prime minister's relative weakness is related to the fact that until recently, the majority party in the Japanese legislature was splintered into various factions. This party—the Liberal Democratic Party (LDP)—was the dominant party in Japanese politics from 1955 to 1993. The LDP recaptured control of the legislature in 1996. As the major party in the legislature during most of the period since World War II, the LDP has been positioned to name prime ministers from its own ranks, and the party has chosen to do so by selecting executives who could appeal to broad factions within the LDP. This has meant, however, that Japanese prime ministers have been vulnerable to these diverse factions and, operating in a culture that expects leaders to build consensus with competing groups and to accommodate the expertise of a powerful Japanese civil service, have occupied an unenviable position, in comparison with British prime ministers, who can draw on more cohesive party support.[19]

## The U.S. Presidential System: The Legislature

Although presidents may become legislative leaders in actual practice, the U.S. Constitution gives the legislative, or lawmaking, authority to the U.S. Congress. Congress consists of two chambers: (1) the House of Representatives has 435 members, who serve 2-year terms, with each state receiving an allotted number of members based on the state's population, and (2) the Senate has 100 members, who serve 6-year terms, with each state accorded two senators. Originally, members of the Senate were selected by the legislatures of the states; since the ratification of the Seventeenth Amendment in 1913, however, senators have been elected by citizens.

Congress passes laws in accord with the Constitution, as follows: Tax bills must originate in the House and, by custom, appropriations bills are introduced in the House; bills concerning any other issues may start out in either the House or the Senate but must pass both chambers and receive presidential approval in order to become law. When a bill is introduced in the House or Senate, it is assigned to a committee, which, in turn, may send it to a subcommittee. Committees and subcommittees are assigned the task of doing the initial screening of bills (by holding hearings on the merits of the bills, for example) to determine whether the bills put forward, in the judgment of Congress, are workable ideas. For example, in 1997, the House Judiciary Committee screened out (killed) a bill to prohibit the use of race and gender considerations in hiring for federal jobs. Although leading Republicans had been critical of affirmative action in their campaigns, the committee's Republicans voted with committee Democrats to kill the proposed bill because they considered it highly controversial.[20]

Because committees have the ability to kill bills, chairing committees is an important source of power in Congress. Committee membership and committee chairs are assigned on the basis of majority party status and *seniority* in Congress and on committees. That is, the party having the most seats in Congress is given the most seats and the chairs of the committees. The term *seniority* refers to the number of years of uninterrupted service a member of Congress has given in the same party in Congress and/or on particular committees, and although its influence has declined in recent years, seniority is still an important factor in gaining committee membership and chairs of committees.

---

### BOX 10.3 Leaders of Congress

In both the House of Representatives and the Senate, Republicans and Democrats designate leaders from their own ranks to coordinate the congressional actions of their party members in Congress. For example, the majority party names majority leaders and assistants (such as whips). The majority party in the House of Representatives also names the Speaker of the House, who is powerful in shaping a range of decisions, including committee assignments, schedules for debate and consideration of bills, and the distribution of campaign resources and office space. The coordinating activities of the party leadership in the House and Senate help shape votes on bills in Congress along party lines, not to the extent that more centralized European parties do, but to a greater degree than one might otherwise expect in such umbrella-like (see Chapter 8) parties as the Republican and Democratic parties.

Who are the Republican and Democratic leaders in Congress? The following Internet pages list the leadership of both the House and Senate. To visit the House page, go to http://www.house.gov/leadership_officers.html. The Senate page is found at http://www.senate.gov/senator/leadership.html.

SOURCES: Gary Cox and Mathew D. McCubbins, *Legislative Leviathan: Party Government in the House* (Berkeley: University of California Press, 1993), p. 277; Joseph Cooper and Gary Young "Partisanship, Bipartisanship, and Crosspartisanship in Congress since the New Deal" and Lawrence C. Dodd and Bruce I. Oppenheimer, "Congress and the Emerging Order: Conditional Party Government or Constructive Partisanship," both in *Congress Reconsidered*, 6th ed., edited by Dodd and Oppenheimer (Washington, DC: Congressional Quarterly Press, 1997).

Bills are sent to specific committees or subcommittees on the basis of the language used in the bill. For example, a bill dealing with agriculture will be assigned to a committee or subcommittee with jurisdiction over agriculture. It is important to realize that writers of bills know this and deliberately word the provisions of a bill so that the language corresponds to the jurisdiction of friendly committees whenever possible. For example, New Mexico Republican Pete Dominici once strategically wrote a bill on freight regulations in such a manner as to avoid using the word *tax* in the bill, to prevent the bill from being assigned to a hostile tax committee in the Senate.

It is also significant that bills may be assigned to more than one committee or subcommittee. Since 1975, the House of Representatives has allowed for bills to be referred to multiple committees. The shift toward multiple committee referrals was justified on the grounds that many bills contain provisions covered by the jurisdiction of several committees (and their attendant subcommittees). In 1995, 40 percent of House bills were sent to more than one committee for consideration. Since 1977, multiple referrals in the Senate have been permitted, as long as leaders of both majority and minority parties favor such action; however, multiple referrals in the Senate are rarer than in the House.

If committees and subcommittees approve a bill, the bill is generally revised during committee and subcommittee consideration and reported to the entire chamber in which it originated for a vote. The process whereby committees or subcommittees edit and revise the bill is known as "marking up" the bill. **Markups** can involve lengthy processes in which committee members, interest group lobbyists, and presidential staff jostle to determine the bill's actual terminology and provisions.

Most bills are killed by committees and subcommittees. Committees and subcommittees can kill bills simply by refusing to approve them and thus refusing to refer them "out of committee" and onto the House or Senate floor for a vote. In some circumstances, a committee's power to kill a bill can be taken away. In the House of Representatives, for example, a procedure known as a **discharge petition** can be used to bring a bill out of committee and to the House for a vote. Discharge petitions can be used only with the support of 218 members of the House. In the Senate, a senator can challenge a bill's assignment to a particular committee, and if he or she obtains majority party leadership support, a Senator can act to maneuver a bill successfully out of a hostile committee.

If a bill survives committee and subcommittee scrutiny and is voted on favorably by one chamber (such as the House), then, in order to become law, it must be voted on favorably in the other chamber (such as the Senate). A special committee called a **conference committee** can be convened to settle differences in the wording of a bill if the two chambers are in disagreement on specific provisions in the bill. The conference committee consists of members from both the House and the Senate. The conference committee can be vital to the lawmaking process because any bill that is to become law must be passed in both chambers with no differences in wording from one chamber to the next. If both chambers vote in favor of the bill, the bill is sent to the president

---

**BOX 10.4    Committees in Congress**

The following are standing (permanent) committees in the House of Representatives and the Senate:

*Standing Committees in the House of Representatives*

Agriculture
Appropriations
Banking and Financial Services
Budget
Commerce
Economic and Educational Opportunities
Government Reform and Oversight
House Oversight
International Relations
Judiciary
National Security
National Resources
Rules
Science
Select Intelligence
Small Business
Standards of Official Conduct
Transportation and Infrastructure
Veterans' Affairs
Ways and Means

*Standing Committees in the Senate*

Agriculture, Nutrition, and Forestry
Appropriations
Armed Services
Banking, Housing, and Urban Affairs
Budget
Commerce, Science, and Transportation
Energy and Natural Resource
Environment and Public Works
Finance
Foreign Relations
Governmental Affairs
Indian Affairs
Judiciary
Labor and Human Resources
Rules and Administration
Small Business
Veterans' Affairs
Select Committee on Ethics
Select Committee on Intelligence

SOURCE: Steven S. Smith and Eric D. Lawrence, "Party Control of Committees in the Republican Congress," in *Congress Reconsidered,* 6th ed., edited by Lawrence C. Dodd and Bruce I. Oppenheimer (Washington, DC: Congressional Quarterly Press, 1997), pp. 170—171.

---

for his or her signature or veto. If approved by the president, the bill becomes a law. As discussed earlier, Congress can override a presidential veto by means of a two-thirds majority vote in both chambers.

Major differences separate the House and Senate in the process of lawmaking. Because the House is much larger than the Senate, the House has stricter, more centralized rules governing committee assignments of bills and debate on bills. In the House, the Rules Committee determines the guidelines the House will follow in debating any bill recommended to it by its own committees. For example, the Rules Committees can limit the time for debating bills and can prohibit amendments to bills. As you can see, decisions by the Rules Committee can greatly affect the nature of debate on bills considered in the House. Members to the Rules Committee are nominated by the speaker of the House, the presiding leader of the House of Representatives, who is drawn from the major party in the House.

Lawmaking in the Senate is less formal than in the House. The Senate has no rules committee, and leaders from the majority and minority parties generally work in concert to schedule bills for debate. In debating bills, the Senate allows its members to use customs such as the **hold**, a practice whereby a senator can request of his or her party leaders in the Senate that a bill not be scheduled for consideration. Although not all requests for holds are honored by party leaders, the custom continues to be viewed as a legitimate part of the chamber's process. **Filibusters** are another resource available to senators. A filibuster is a process of "talking a bill to death"—that is, talking and debating on a bill for an indefinite period in order to delay any vote on the bill. Through a vote of **cloture**, requiring a three-fifths majority vote, the Senate can terminate debate and thus kill filibustering efforts.[21]

In 1957, South Carolina Republican Strom Thurmond talked for more than 24 hours in a filibuster. In case you are wondering how anyone could think of enough things to say to keep talking for so long, it is instructive to note that a filibuster does not have to stay on the topic at hand. Thurmond took up time by reading aloud the Declaration of Independence, the Bill of Rights, George Washington's Farewell Address, and other items. As for other matters that could also make talking for more than 24 hours difficult, Thurmond was well prepared on that score as well. Before starting the filibuster, he had a steam bath to dramatically reduce his body fluid levels. Why such effort? Thurmond was trying to prevent passage of a civil rights bill by trying to make sure that no one could ever vote on it.[22]

It may seem to you that the process of lawmaking just described is cumbersome and generally unfavorable to bills themselves. If you have inferred this, you are correct. Indeed, the structure of lawmaking guarantees that most bills introduced in Congress fail to become laws: Committees can kill them, subcommittees can kill them, Rules Committee members can stipulate provisions that hinder them, filibusters can subvert them, the House can vote them down, the Senate can vote them down, presidents can veto them, and either chamber can vote to kill a veto override. Indeed, from 1995 to 1997, more than 6,800 measures were introduced in Congress. Fewer than 400 passed.[23]

Despite the importance of lawmaking, passing laws is not necessarily the primary objective of all members of Congress. Many members of Congress spend more time on **constituency relations** than on lawmaking. The term *constituency relations* refers to contact with and services performed for the voters back home. As discussed in Chapter 9, campaigns for office are expensive and complex contests involving media coverage, interest group pressures, and PAC contributions. Members of Congress often try to gain an edge on their competitors in upcoming elections by spending a lot of time interacting with constituents through town hall meetings, newsletters, and—increasingly—Internet pages and e-mail. These interactions provide members of Congress ample opportunities to present themselves to voters as concerned leaders, as problem solvers. For example, when New Mexico Senator Pete Domenici learned that one of his constituents was having problems with state officials, he put his staff to work on solving this one constituent's difficulty. What was the problem? A disabled resident of the small New Mexico town of Mora had had his wheelchair taken away by the government; this man lived alone, had no legs, had no indoor plumbing, and was dependent on an outhouse more than 100 feet from his house. When Domenici heard about this, getting this constituent's wheelchair returned became the Senator's objective.[24]

This example is fairly typical, in the sense that members of both chambers of Congress report tremendous expenditures of time and staff resources on constituency relations. Indeed, in 1993, 68 percent of members of Congress stated that they spent considerable time in contact with voters from their home districts or states, but only 25 percent reported spending comparable amounts of time on researching and passing laws.[25] You may spend more time studying for your exams than members of Congress spend on studying some laws.

Constituency relations not only competes with lawmaking in terms of congressional energy and time but also affects the kinds of laws passed. One way to please constituents is to pass **pork barrel legislation**. Pork barrel laws are narrow in terms of benefits and are passed to help a congressperson's district or state; these laws create programs or services that receive federal funding. In other words, if your senator passes a pork barrel law, he or she is "bringing home the bacon to you"—your state gets programs or services courtesy of the federal taxpayers. In the early 1990s, for example, Pennsylvania Democrat Paul E. Kanjorski used pork barrel politics to secure $30 million from different federal budgets to fund an organization called Earth Conservancy, located in his state and run by his brother.[26] Airports, military contracts, highways, municipal centers, and sewer systems are other examples of pork barrel projects passed by members of Congress to boost services, employment, and benefits enjoyed by the voters back home. For example, former Senator Fred Harris notes that in 1987 more than 80 percent of military contracts were awarded to businesses in the home states of the senators sitting on the Senate Armed Services Committee and the Senate Subcommittee on Defense Appropriations.[27]

## The British Parliamentary System: The Legislature

The British legislative body, or Parliament, consists of two chambers. The House of Lords is the upper house of Parliament. Members of the House of Lords are not elected. Historically, the House of Lords was made up of members who had hereditary title to a seat in Lords, those who were appointed to the Lords for life, those who were named archbishops and bishops of the Church of England, and those named lords of appeal who serve as judges. In 1997, the youngest "member" of the House of Lords was an 8-year-old earl holding hereditary claim to a seat in the chamber; however, members cannot actually assume their positions in the House of Lords until age 21. The House of Lords Act recently altered procedures by which the chamber is constituted. No longer are hereditary peers automatically granted seats in the House of Lords; rather, peers who once would have inherited their seats must now be appointed to the House of Lords. As of November 2003, only 92 members of the House of Lords held their seats by virtue of hereditary claims. The House of Lords Act, in its very first section, calls for the end of hereditary assumptions of seats in the upper chamber.[28]

Members of the lower chamber, the House of Commons, are elected. With more than 600 members, the House of Commons is the more powerful chamber in the British Parliament. As discussed previously, the majority in Commons names the prime minister. Unlike the U.S. speaker of the House of Representatives, the presiding officer of the House of Commons acts as a nonpartisan in managing the business of the chamber. With few exceptions, the introduction of bills and the scheduling of debate on bills is determined by the prime minister.

In the British Parliament, the opposition party (the losing party of the two major parties) is given formal recognition. For example, since 1985, the House of Commons has set aside 17 days per session as Opposition Days. On Opposition Days, the opposition party (at present, the Conservative Party) can schedule debate on issues. In addition, the House of Commons has institutionalized Question Time, during which the prime minister fields questions from members. During Question Time, the leader of the opposition is guaranteed the right to ask specific questions of the prime minister. The opposition party also provides a shadow government. The shadow government consists of the leaders of the opposition party—that is, those individuals who would be serving as the country's prime minister and cabinet were their party the majority party of Commons—who publicize their differences with and their policy alternatives to the actual government. These opposition leaders also work in concert to coordinate the opposition's parliamentary strategy when bills are debated and brought up for votes in Commons.[29]

Lawmaking in the British Parliament is somewhat similar to lawmaking in the U.S. Congress. As in Congress, laws may originate in either chamber, and they are submitted to both chambers of Parliament for review and approval. Like the Senate, the House of Lords is a chamber in which debate is less structured and less controlled than is debate in the corresponding lower chamber (for example, the Commons and the House of Representatives). In addition, the British Parliament uses committees in the process of lawmaking. Finally, in the House of Commons, as in the U.S. Congress, legislators spend great amounts of time on constituency relations.

However, major differences characterize the U.S. and British legislative systems beyond these points. First, members of the British executive hold seats in Parliament as well as in the executive office; as just discussed, cabinet members and prime ministers are drawn from the legislature. For example, British cabinet ministers sitting in Parliament are expected to work at pushing through executive-supported bills and to argue in support of the executive's position on bills whenever debate comes up.[30] This practice of having executive ministers hold seats in the legislature, of course, provides a striking contrast with the U.S. system of separating executive and congressional powers and offices.

Second, the House of Lords has a role in lawmaking unlike that of either chamber of the U.S. Congress.[31] If a bill is approved by Commons, it is sent to Lords for approval. If the House of Lords approves, the bill is passed. However, if the House of Lords disapproves, the House of Lords can suggest revisions, unless the bill is a money bill, in which case the Lords has no power over its content. No conference committee is convened, as would occur in the United States. In the 1994–1995 session of Parliament, the House of Lords proposed more than 1,200 revisions to bills brought to it from the House of Commons; of these, 9 revisions failed to be reconciled between the two chambers. During the same session the House of Commons made more than 1,000 revisions to bills from the House of Lords, and all revisions were reconciled between the two chambers.[32] Yet if the House of Commons does not wish to incorporate changes in a bill recommended by the House of Lords, the bill can be reintroduced in the House of Commons and passed by Commons alone. In this instance, the power of the House of Lords is the weaker of the two chambers, having only the power of delaying the passage of laws. Money-related bills are passed by Commons alone.

Third, committees have very different functions in the British Parliament and in the U.S. Congress. As analyzed previously, committees in the U.S. Congress serve the function of killing most bills introduced in Congress. In the British Parliament, committees *expedite* the passage of bills, most of which, as previously explained, are the favored projects of the prime minister and his or her cabinet. Specifically, in the House of Commons, bills are assigned to committees only *after* they have received an initial screening and general approval in Commons. After the bill is pushed through Parliament, the committee—unlike the standing committees in the U.S. Congress—is disbanded.[33]

## JUDICIAL REVIEW VERSUS PARLIAMENTARY SOVEREIGNTY

The U.S. Constitution divides authority at the national level of government among the executive, legislative, and judicial branches. As discussed earlier, U.S. executive and legislative authority are separated rather than connected. Judicial authority is also separate from the authority of the other two branches. This separate judicial authority is no less important in shaping the contours of U.S. politics than that authority held by presidents and legislators.

In 1803, the U.S. Supreme Court issued a decision in the case of *Marbury* v. *Madison,* and the decision's significance has only grown with time. *Marbury* is important because it firmly established the Supreme Court's power of **judicial review**, the power to overturn laws and actions of government officials on the grounds that such laws and actions violate the U.S. Constitution. This power of judicial review establishes the judicial branch—and, within it, the U.S. Supreme Court—as the ultimate authority for determining the soundness of governmental actions. In *Marbury*, the Court overturned a section of a law passed by Congress. In later years, the Court used judicial review to overturn laws and actions by state governments as well as directives issued by the executive branch. Thus, judicial review can be used to strike down actions by state or federal and legislative or executive officials.[34]

The Supreme Court has not used judicial review indiscriminately. Political scientist Henry J. Abraham has noted that the Supreme Court has overturned approximately 140 federal legislative acts. More than 95,000 such acts have been passed over the years, so 140 constitutes a very small percentage. Judicial review has been used more aggressively against state acts, with more than 1,200 such acts reviewed and struck down.[35]

It is also important to realize that judicial review is not an unlimited power. Although the Supreme Court can strike down laws and actions, the Court depends on other offices of government to apply Court decisions. In short, the Court lacks the power to enforce its own decisions and needs federal and state politicians to interpret the Court's ruling and to carry out the enforcement. Like anything else in life, interpretation and enforcement of Court decision can be conscientious or lax, good-faith or bad-faith efforts. In addition, amendments can be added to the U.S. Constitution through a process involving proposal by Congress and ratification by the states. This means that if the Court strikes down a measure passed in the form of a law, the very same measure can be rewritten as an amendment to the Constitution and, if proposed and ratified, it stands as a part of the Constitution and is outside the realm of judicial review. In addition, Congress and state legislatures can reintroduce into law any measures previously struck down by judicial review (perhaps revised in response to the judicial review itself), and unless the Court uses judicial review again, the measure stands. As you can see, judicial review is not a dictatorial power but instead is a power to which other offices of government can respond and adapt.[36]

What is the logic of judicial review? Judicial review is premised on the notion that as an appointed body rather than an elected one, the Supreme Court can draw on its legal training and professionalism to assess and review actions by the more politically oriented (elected) branches and offices of government. Advocates of judicial review contend that although state politicians, presidents, and members of Congress may be tempted to surrender to political whims and fads, the Supreme Court Justices—appointed for life (unless they are removed for having committed impeachable offenses), with no worries about making popular decisions to get reelected—can examine laws and policies in an independent, fair, scholarly manner and thus render better decisions than those made by politicians. Who better, then, to have the ultimate authority to decide the soundness of laws and governmental actions?

However, critics of judicial review often note that it would be more democratic for a popularly elected branch of government to have such supreme authority. These critics point out that Supreme Court Justices, having been appointed by presidents and approved by the Senate, lack a connection to the people themselves, which presidents and members of Congress possess. No matter that elections can be confusing because of the increased role of interest groups, dial groups, focus groups, and other campaign groups (as discussed in Chapter 8), elections still put *citizens* in charge of choosing officeholders in the executive and legislative branches. Moreover, critics add, Supreme Court Justices are politically minded and no more neutral on controversial issues than anyone else. Justices inevitably take political positions; therefore, the fact that they are not voted into office is irrelevant. Would not executive review or legislative review be better than judicial review, the critics ask?[37]

Whatever the merits of the supporters and opponents of judicial review, comparisons of countries show that approximately 70 countries use judicial review. Judicial review is more likely to be found in countries that have a federal rather than a unitary structure.[38] As explained in Chapter 3, federal structures divide government authority between central and state levels, whereas unitary government structures concentrate authority in a central structure. Australia, Canada, Germany, and India are examples of countries other than the United States that practice judicial review.[39]

Great Britain represents a vivid contrast to the United States and the other governments just listed. Rejecting judicial review, Great Britain practices **parliamentary sovereignty**. Parliamentary sovereignty exists when Parliament—not a separate judicial branch—exercises ultimate authority to determine the soundness of laws and governmental actions. No judicial branch can overturn an act of Parliament. Parliamentary laws are supreme. If a law is in need of change, the change occurs when Parliament passes another law to revise or replace the original one. Parliamentary sovereignty has a straightforward logic: Parliament is elected by the people, laws are to serve the good of the people, and therefore Parliament is best positioned to exercise ultimate judgment on the soundness of the laws. If in the opinion of the people the currently constituted Parliament fails to correct a bad law, a new set of members of Parliament can be voted into office.[40] What could be more democratic, supporters of parliamentary sovereignty ask, than having the legislative branch—elected as it is by the people themselves—have the ultimate authority to decide matters of law?

## SUMMING UP

- Democratic governments may organize executive-legislative relations as presidential or parliamentary systems or as modified (as in Germany and France) forms of presidentialism and parliamentarism.

- **Presidential systems** separate executive and legislative branches. Elections for the two branches are separate, and members of the two branches have fixed terms. Votes of no confidence are not used.

- **Parliamentary systems** combine and link executive and legislative authority. Legislatures name the executive leader. No-confidence votes are used. Terms of office are not fixed.

- In the United States, presidential authority is based on constitutional provisions, persuasion, and presidential usage of customary powers. Presidents have sometimes drawn on these three sources of authority so effectively that they have acted as virtual presidential lawmakers, despite the fact that the U.S. Constitution technically accords lawmaking authority to Congress, not to presidents.

- In Britain, the prime minister, assisted by his or her cabinet and its tradition of collective responsibility, is leader of Parliament and the major party of Parliament. As leader of both, he or she is well positioned to guide and direct Parliament, to an extent that U.S. presidents are not positioned to lead Congress. Yet leadership is not synonymous with independence; no-confidence votes can topple executives.

- U.S. Congress members have both lawmaking and **constituency relations** responsibilities. Constituency relations can involve getting **pork barrel**

**legislation** passed as well as troubleshooting problems of individual voters in one's district or state. In terms of lawmaking, members of Congress see most proposed bills defeated rather than successfully passed into law. The defeat of proposed bills can come in committees or subcommittees, through **holds** or **filibusters**, because **conference committees** fail to resolve the wording of bills favored by the two chambers, or because presidential support is lacking.

- The British Parliament consists of two chambers: the less powerful House of Lords and the more powerful House of Commons. Although the House of Lords has a delaying power, the House of Commons is the core lawmaking chamber, one in which executive leadership and committee structures expedite the passage of laws.

- The U.S. system of **judicial review** and the British system of **parliamentary sovereignty** represent two alternatives for democracies on the matter of judicial relations. Under judicial review, judicial decision makers have ultimate authority on the constitutionality of laws. Parliamentary sovereignty accords this authority to Parliament.

## STUDY QUESTIONS

1. What defines and differentiates presidential and parliamentary systems?

2. Which system—presidential or parliamentary—employs fixed terms of office? In which system are votes of no confidence used?

3. What is a veto? What is a pocket veto?

4. How can U.S. presidents make themselves into presidential lawmakers?

5. What is collective responsibility?

6. What makes British prime ministers potentially dominant in their relations with Parliament? What renders them ultimately dependent on Parliament?

7. What is a constructive vote of no confidence? Which country uses this?

8. Identify three aspects of lawmaking in the United States, and explain three ways in which lawmaking in Britain differs from that of the United States.

9. How do judicial relations differ in the United States and Britain?

## FOLLOWING UP THROUGH INTERNET SOURCES

- Web Sites of National Parliaments (http://www.ipu.org/english/parlweb.htm). Links to various parliaments arranged by country.

- House of Commons (http://www.parliament.uk/commons/hsecom.htm)

- House of Lords (http://www.parliament.the-stationery-office.co.uk/pa/ld/ldhome.htm)

- Parliamentary Channel (http://www.westminster-digital.co.UK/parliament). Coverage of Parliament.

- The Times (London) Internet Edition (http://www.the-times.co.uk). Coverage of Parliament and politics.

- The White House (http://www.whitehouse.gov)

- U.S. House of Representatives (http://www.house.gov)

- U.S. Senate (http://www.senate.gov)

- Capweb, *The Internet Guide to the United States Congress* (http://www.capweb.net)

- Library of Congress. Newspaper & Current Periodical Reading Room, Official federal government Web sites (http://lcweb.loc.gov/global/executive/fed.html)

- THOMAS Legislative Information on the Internet (http://thomas.loc.gov)

# International Relations I

## Introduction

On October 4, 1957, the Soviet Union launched the satellite *Sputnik*. Capable of orbiting the earth in 90 minutes, *Sputnik* represented enormous possibilities as well as complicated problems for governments. Exploration of outer space could advance scientific knowledge but could also become a means of militarizing the cosmos. After all, if governments could launch satellites into outer space, what would stop them from launching rockets over vast distances to attack enemies? Moreover, what would stop governments from developing satellites capable of spying on enemies?

In the aftermath of *Sputnik*, the United States had reason to be especially concerned with the first possibility—the development of long-range rockets. Although the United States had access to bases in Japan, Turkey, and western Europe from which to launch conventional arms against its Cold War rival, the Soviet Union, the USSR lacked access to favorably located bases close to the United States. Therefore, the development of Soviet long-range rockets had the potential for eroding the U.S. advantage.

At the same time, the Soviets had great concerns about the second possibility— the development of satellite-based spying. Prior to *Sputnik*, the Soviets had greater access to information about the United States than the United States had about the USSR. However, as the Soviets realized, if satellite technology advanced to the point of providing minutely detailed data from outer space, the information edge held by the Soviets could be compromised.

Clearly, both superpowers had an interest in shaping the terms under which governments would use outer space in the post-*Sputnik* era. Should outer space be regarded as free and open territory for exploration by any government that could launch a probe, or should the outer space directly above a government's territory be regarded as an extension of that territory and thus under the authority of that government? In assessing these questions, the United States and the USSR eventually came to the following agreement: Both outer space and the celestial bodies within outer space (such as the moon) would be considered open territory. That is, space would be available for the common exploration of governments. Governments could not "govern" the outer space directly above their earthly domains for the purpose, for example, of controlling the entry and exit of probes into outer space.

One could interpret this agreement as evidence of the ability of rival governments to cooperate for the sake of common interests. Perhaps both the United States and the USSR concluded that by keeping space open to exploration by any government rather than tightly controlled by competing governments, scientific exploration could proceed without encumbrance by politically inspired regulations. Perhaps both superpowers were demonstrating the ability to cooperate for the mutual benefits to be derived from the peaceful uses of outer space.

Yet one could also see this agreement as a manifestation of power politics. Perhaps both the United States and USSR were simply trying to protect their own positions of power. For example, maybe both governments decided to keep the moon as an open celestial body because both the Americans and the Soviets calculated that diverting vast resources to moon militarization would weaken earthly military preparedness. Or perhaps both governments decided that, given the earth's rotation and the consequent difficulty of tracking which part of outer space was above which government at any moment, it would be irrational to divert resources to controlling outer space and away from more traditional defense allotments. Or maybe the Soviets favored regarding space as open territory because by 1962 they had developed their own reconnaissance satellites and wanted no government to interfere with their usage, just as the United States wanted the same for its own spy satellites.[1]

The *Sputnik* example illustrates that outcomes in international relations are rarely subject to only one interpretation, either by governments or by the political scientists studying them. The processes by which governments make international decisions—and the means by which those decisions are analyzed by political scientists and citizens—are influenced by different **models of analysis**. A model of analysis is a set of fundamental operating assumptions. It is a theoretical perspective defining the logical parameters for assessing why things happen as they do. This chapter begins with a discussion of two models of analysis—idealism and realism—that have been very influential in the political science subfield of international relations. After reviewing idealism and realism, think about which of the two models, if either, seems more helpful in making sense of the post-*Sputnik* decisions of the United States and the USSR. Consider also the philosophical issues raised by idealism and realism as they pertain to the post–World War II period and to international politics after 9/11. With respect to the latter, in the final chapter, we will examine why some political scientists believe one must look beyond both idealism and realism if one wishes to grasp international relations in its full complexity.

# MODELS OF ANALYSIS

## Idealism

Idealism is sometimes referred to as liberal idealism because idealism draws on liberal theoretical debates and principles such as those discussed in Chapter 5.[2] **Idealism** is a perspective that makes both normative (value) and empirical (factual) claims. In terms of its normative arguments, idealism proposes that governments should pursue *ethical principles* when making foreign policy decisions. For example, idealists over the years have championed efforts to promote peace, justice, and respect for human rights, whether through international organizations such as the League of Nations and the United Nations (UN) or through nongovernmental organizations such as Amnesty International. In terms of its factual dimension, idealism posits that human nature (or human psychology) is capable of reason and peaceful, harmonious interaction. Humans, idealists contend, are not intrinsically prone to violence and destructive behavior, so political decision making need not assume the worst of humans.

Drawing together the normative and empirical claims, idealist models of analysis tend to assert that in many cases governments can gain mutual benefits from participation in projects involving the sharing of recourses, the provision of humanitarian assistance, the promotion of human rights, the pursuit of ethical standards in foreign policy making, and the curtailment of military power. Indeed, according to idealism, if governments seek to maximize their power—especially military power—relative to other governments, this may trigger war, which brings certain costs and only possible benefits to participating states. Power seeking is risky. Thus, rather than interacting with each other in ways designed to amass and exert superior power, governments should seek cooperative agreements.[3]

Idealists often stress the concept of interdependence. For example, many economic exchanges link societies together, idealists contend, and thus the overall economic fates of countries are similarly linked. An economic crisis in Asia can affect economies in Europe, Africa, Latin America, and North America. Likewise, an environmental disaster in Europe can cause problems in the Americas, Africa, and Asia. Civil wars in one country can generate human migration patterns and refugee populations affecting countless other countries; health epidemics in one region can soon become international in scope. Indeed, you need think only of Chernobyl, AIDS, acid rain, or the breakup of Yugoslavia to realize that politically relevant issues—be they environmental, economic, or military—rarely remain local. It is only rational, therefore, according to idealism, for governments to relate to one another in a cooperative manner rather than a domineering one. It takes little imagination to see that in an interdependent world a dominated, crushed country can potentially pull down the seemingly dominant country with which it is linked.[4]

Idealists also tend to stress the importance of "human security" as an element of government security.[5] If governments pursue the ethical principle of peaceful cooperation in the international arena, idealism argues, this better allows those same governments to invest more fully in human security programs (rather than military programs) within their own territories. In short, pursuing and maintaining peace allows governments to spend less on the military and more on programs to improve the quality of life. Human security programs could include programs to expand educational opportunities, policies designed to improve access to health care, or government-sponsored efforts to broaden job training programs. As you can see, idealism proposes that security issues involve not just security against attacks from a foreign country (military security) but also security against illiteracy, premature death, or perpetual impoverishment (quality-of-life security).[6]

Idealists emphasize the potential utility of international organizations in facilitating peaceful cooperation among governments. By participating in international organizations such as the UN or the European Union, governments can formulate rules for mutually beneficial peaceful interaction. Although organizations such as the UN cannot guarantee peace, they can improve the odds of obtaining it, idealists believe. Such organizations can promote increased communication between governments, international peacekeeping deployments, and international aid programs—all of which have the potential to reduce the chances of international conflict. Those idealists who focus on the concepts of economic interdependence of states and the importance of international organizations are often referred to as a particular type of idealist: **liberal institutionalists**.[7]

One can look to the historical example of the Iroquois League to find specific illustrations of idealist principles. The Iroquois League was a federation created by the Cayuga, Mohawk, Oneida, Onondaga, Seneca, and Tuscarora nations in the northeastern United States. The league was formed sometime around 1450 and lasted until 1777. It had the purpose of maintaining peace among the nations, which, before the formation of the league, had fought one another in numerous wars. The league worked according to the following principles:

- Each member nation retained its own customs and traditions but agreed not to attack any other member nation of the league.
- Each member nation pledged to defend all other nations within the league.
- League membership was up for renewal every 5 years, at which time member nations could declare their intent to renew their membership or to leave the league.
- Each member nation participated in league decision making by naming members to the Great Council, which was the governing body of the league.
- The Great Council met at least once per year to discuss any issues of importance to league members.

By organizing an international body (the league itself) to promote observance of these rules, the various nations were successful in reducing (and according to some accounts, virtually eliminating) war among themselves.[8]

## Realism

**Realism** is an alternative perspective on international politics, but like idealism it includes a normative and empirical dimension. Some realists draw on the lessons of Machiavelli and Hobbes (discussed in Chapter 4), concluding that human nature is naturally prone toward violence and destruction. Other realists

---

*Idealism Asserts That*

- Human nature is rational and capable of peace.
- States should follow moral principles in foreign policy.
- States should seek cooperation.
- States should promote human security.
- International organizations can enhance state efforts to exist peacefully.
- States tend to exist in a world that looks increasingly interdependent to many idealists such as liberal institutionalists.

*Realism Asserts That*

- Governments cannot count on the existence of a peaceful and cooperative

human nature to produce harmonious interactions.
- States must be cognizant of the fact that anarchic relations in world politics place each state in position of needing to advance its own power.
- Foreign policy must be based on a state's need to protect and advance its own power, not on morality (if power and morality come into conflict).
- International political relations are prone to conflict.
- When governments act rationally in advancing their own power, their decisions are often similar, regardless of the different ideologies subscribed to by the governments in question.

---

choose not to base their assumptions on concepts of human nature but nonetheless concur with their Machiavellian and Hobbesian peers that political behavior (perhaps not because of human nature itself but because of structural arrangements) is conflict oriented. Given this fact, realists contend, from a normative perspective it is best if government decision making is guided by the requirements of amassing power, not pursuing morality at the expense of power.

Thus, realism suggests that the interests of governments are best promoted when governments gain and hold power relative to other states. Power includes military and economic power. States that neglect the task of acquiring and maintaining power are vulnerable to attack by other states. Thus, from a realist standpoint government security is understood primarily as military security, not quality-of-life security. Although it is clearly not in the national interest of states to maximize their power to the point of actually provoking attacks by other governments, it is in the interest of states to have military power sufficient to ensure their own protection and to advance their own welfare. Indeed, it is a primary task of statesmanship to calculate losses and gains associated with various foreign policy alternatives for the purpose of determining which alternative provides the optimal level of military security.[9]

Realists point out, for example, that if one examines the history of U.S. interventions in Third World conflicts between 1945 and 1989, one finds that the United States was inclined to intervene when governments it viewed as hostile were also intervening; U.S. intervention was therefore strategic and geared toward protecting U.S. military power relative to its enemies. Ethical, humanitarian, and cooperative motives did not influence decisions on whether to intervene or not. Nor was intervention an automatic response. In fact, in most conflicts during the period the United States abstained from both direct military intervention and intervening indirectly through provisions of military assistance. In short, U.S. intervention was prompted by strategic military security motives.[10]

To realists, basing foreign policy on strategic military objectives is thoroughly rational, in part because governments exist in relations of international anarchy and anarchic conditions are prone to conflict. **Anarchy** is the absence of any overarching world government that enforces rules of peace on existing governments. According to realists, because international organizations such as the UN lack the capacity to actually implement rules independently of the wishes of powerful governments, such organizations cannot be counted on to play decisive roles in international politics. For example, although international organizations such as the UN may articulate international rules of peace, these international organizations cannot independently enforce these rules; if such rules are enforced at all, it is because of the decisions of governments—exercising dominant influence both within and outside organizations such as the UN—powerful enough to enforce them. As you can see, realism sees outcomes in international politics as being shaped primarily by the actions of governments, not by independent actions of nonstate organizations such as the UN. Thus, according to realism, in an anarchic world states that wish to survive must be powerful or allied to the powerful.

© Chang W. Lee/The New York Times

A child ventures outside in the village of Charykari, Afghanistan after the village was bombed by the U.S. in the aftermath of 9/11. After the raid on the village, nearby unexploded bombs posed safety problems for residents. In this photo, a basin is used to cover a cluster bomb canister, not itself explodable, but indicative of the literal spillover of the war into the backyards of villagers.

One major implication of realism is the notion that moral principles cannot outweigh military security in international decision making. Given the conditions of anarchy, governments cannot afford to emphasize ethics at the expense of their own security needs. For example, realists can point to pre-9/11 U.S. policy in Afghanistan as an example of realism in practice. In September 1996, the Taliban seized control of Afghanistan's capital, Kabul, and used its base in Kabul to extend control through various sectors of the country. Outside Afghanistan, Muslim leaders, human rights groups such as Amnesty International, and peace advocates quickly came forward to criticize the repressive policies of the Taliban.

What was the response of the U.S. government? Did the United States, in ide-alist fashion, work through international organizations to convince the Taliban to respect human rights in Afghanistan? Officially, the United States took no steps to either help or hinder the Taliban. However, the United States made clear that it was interested in discussing with the Taliban the possibility of opening an embassy in the new Afghanistan. Although the United States later backed away from this position, its lack of opposition to the Taliban was seen by a number of other coun-tries as a form of quiet assent to the Taliban's rule. Why would the United States take such a position? Realists point out the importance of the following factors in influencing U.S. policy. First, the Taliban movement was a religious and political rival to nearby Iran; a strong Taliban could mean a weaker Iran. Second, U.S. and Saudi Arabian oil corporations had investments in the area, and Saudi Arabia and Pakistan had successfully negotiated secure trade routes through the areas under Taliban control. In other words, the Taliban's presence helped contain Iran's influ-ence and appeared to stabilize trade routes important to U.S. interests.[11]

This example brings up a further point in the fundamental logic of realism: Governments tend to behave similarly whatever their political ideologies.[12] Under conditions of international anarchy, democratic governments are under the same pressures to survive as are nondemocratic governments. Hence, both types of governments will be likely to respond in similar fashion to similar inter-national pressures. Democratic governments cannot be counted on to stand up consistently for human rights in Afghanistan or anywhere else, just as nondemo-cratic governments cannot be assumed to be automatic allies of repressive regimes. Indeed, political scientists point out that the acceptance of realist princi-ples by U.S. leaders over the years helps explain why the United States has a record of supporting nondemocratic leaders such as former President Marcos in the Philippines, even though the United States likes to think of itself as a voice for democratic values.

As you can see, idealist and realist models are useful in prompting us to con-sider varied issues confronting political leaders, governments, and international organizations. Although neither model is entirely comprehensive in spelling out the logic and details entering into every international interaction, idealism and realism highlight alternative ways of exploring key questions in world politics: What is security, and how does our understanding of security change in response to world events and technological development (see Box 11.3 on p. 251)? What is the role of ethics in foreign affairs? Are international organizations effective channels of peaceful cooperation, or are they primarily institutions dominated by powerful governments pursuing their own national objectives? Should foreign policy decisions always promote human rights?

Whether one is looking back to *Sputnik* or ahead to international politics in the twenty-first century, the philosophical issues raised by idealist and realist perspectives challenge us to think critically about contemporary and future international relations. As the following discussion illustrates, although the middle of the twentieth century witnessed bipolar international politics, the outlines of twenty-first century international relations are difficult to decipher, whether examined from the standpoint of idealism, realism, both, or neither.

# INTERNATIONAL RELATIONS: OUT OF BIPOLARISM AND INTO THE TWENTY-FIRST CENTURY

## Bipolar Politics

Soon after the end of World War II in 1945, international politics could be seen as a **bipolar system**, a system in which two superpower governments—the United States and the USSR—emerged. A *cold war* (ongoing tensions and rivalries but not actual military attacks on each other) ensued between the superpowers. For example, one can see both cold war suspicions and superpower maneuvering in the following policies pursued by the United States: containment, the Truman Doctrine, the Marshall Plan, and the formation of the North Atlantic Treaty Organization (NATO).

**Containment** was the name given to U.S. foreign policy objectives in the years immediately after World War II. George F. Kennan spelled out the logic of containment policy in 1946–1947. Kennan argued that U.S. foreign policy should contain and limit Soviet expansionism. Containment policy was premised on a view of the USSR as a hostile rival to the United States, a rival that could be expected to try to expand its influence over territory beyond even eastern Europe and into, perhaps, the Middle East, the Mediterranean, and other regions. By containing any potential Soviet expansionist push, Kennan reasoned, the United States would not only curb the Soviet Union's sphere of influence but also impose strain and pressure on the Soviet system by perpetually thwarting its goals. Thus, in the long term, a containment policy could possibly compel a reconfiguration of the USSR into a less expansionist form of government.[13]

Containment ideas were reflected in the **Truman Doctrine**. Announced by President Truman in 1947, the Truman Doctrine stated that the United States would aid countries in resisting what Truman called the "totalitarian" threat posed by the USSR. The Truman Doctrine claimed that the interest of the United States was served by providing economic assistance to countries that might otherwise come under Soviet influence. Greece and Turkey were foremost in Truman's mind in 1947, but his doctrine opened up possibilities for aid to numerous countries.

Indeed, beginning in 1948 the **Marshall Plan** provided U.S. economic aid to Europe, consistent with the containment philosophy. Fearing that the economic damage to Europe during World War II would render it vulnerable to Soviet influence, the United States asked European governments to submit plans for economic rebuilding; in return for U.S. aid in this rebuilding process, the United States asked each recipient country to share its budgetary data with the United States and required that U.S. exports play a key role in the rebuilding effort. Although the Soviet Union rejected both requirements, a number of European countries accepted the terms of the Marshall Plan and used U.S. aid to restore their economies. Food, coal, electricity, oil, steel, and transportation sectors were targeted for immediate rebuilding.[14]

The **North Atlantic Treaty Organization (NATO)** was formed in 1949. NATO provided for a common defense of member countries. The original members were the United States, Canada, Denmark, Iceland, Italy, Norway, Portugal, Britain, France, Belgium, The Netherlands, and Luxembourg. Members pledged to defend any other member attacked. Under these terms, NATO was intended to provide a deterrence against Soviet military expansion, a threat that became even more complex when the Soviets exploded their own atomic bomb in 1949 and when the Soviets formed the Soviet–Eastern European military alliance known as the Warsaw Treaty Organization (Warsaw Pact) in 1955.[15] Indeed, from the articulation of U.S. containment policy in 1946–1947 until the withdrawal of U.S. troops from Vietnam in 1973, bipolar superpower tensions surfaced in a variety of locations:

- Germany was divided into West and East Germany in 1949, with West Germany allied with the United States and western Europe and East Germany allied with the Soviets.

- The Korean War (1950–1953) began with what the United States considered to be a Soviet-inspired decision by North Korea to attack South Korea. The United States supported South Korea.

- The United States used covert operations in Iran in 1953 and in Guatemala in 1954 to undermine governments the United States considered unfriendly to U.S. interests.

- The United States sent CIA and military personnel to assist South Vietnam in 1954 in an effort to oppose communist forces.

- The Soviet Union sent troops into Hungary in 1956 to maintain Soviet interests.

- The United States launched the Bay of Pigs invasion of Cuba in 1961 in an effort to inspire uprisings against Fidel Castro, who, during the previous year, had entered into alliances with the USSR.

- The Soviets put in place the Berlin Wall in 1961, a few months after the Bay of Pigs invasion; the wall separated Berlin into Eastern and Western spheres of influence and prevented freedom of movement.

- The Cuban missile crisis developed in 1962, when the United States discovered Soviet missile sites in Cuba and demanded that the Soviets remove their missiles from Cuba.

---

**BOX 11.2  The European Union**

The European Union (EU) was formed by the Treaty of European Union in 1991. Formerly known as the European Community, the EU promotes cooperation on economic, foreign, and social policy among its members. In January 1991, the EU established the euro as currency for EU members, with January 2002 designated as the date for the origination of notes and coins. Other recent decisions include the following:

- Proposed improved safety standards for water transportation vehicles serving EU member countries
- Studying ways to improve environmental conditions around offshore oil platforms
- Assisting European airlines to compete more favorably with U.S. carriers in Japan
- Increasing access to Ukrainian automobile markets for European auto companies
- Ensuring open competition for Europe-based companies within EU countries

The members of the EU are Austria, Belgium, Denmark, Finland, France, Germany, Greece, Ireland, Italy, Luxembourg, The Netherlands, Portugal, Spain, Sweden, and the United Kingdom. The presidency of the EU rotates among the member governments every 6 months.

A vital question confronting the EU is organizational expansion. Cyprus, the Czech Republic, Estonia, Hungary, Latvia, Lithuania, Malta, Poland, the Slovak Republic, and Slovenia are scheduled to become EU members in May 2004. To join the EU, countries must demonstrate that they possess

- A stable democratic form of government
- A strong market economy
- A capacity to meet fully the requirements of EU membership concerning all economic, foreign, and social policies in force within the EU

SOURCES: EU at http://europa.edu.int/index_en; Arthur S. Banks, ed., *Political Handbook of the World: 1994–1995* (Binghamton: State University of New York/CSA Publications, 1995), pp. 1057–1065; European Union, "What Is the European Union? 15 Member States and Maps" (http://wuropa.eu.int/index.htm); BBC News, "Special Report: European Union a Growing Union?" (http://www.news.bbc.co.uk/hi/english/spec...997/euoropean_union/newsid_3800/38407.stm, accessed 12 December 1997); European Union "European Commission to Investigate State Aid to Spanish Ferry Company Transmediterranea (Transmed)"; "Commission May Start Dispute Settlement Procedure against Ukraine over Daewoo and Second Hand Car Discrimination"; "European Commission Proposes New Safety Measures for Roll-On/Roll-Off Ferries and High Speed Passenger Craft Operating in the European Union"; "European Commission Urges Japan to Treat European Air Carriers Fairly by Allocating Airport Slots According to International Rules"; "Commission Recommends to End Dumping of Disused Offshore Platforms in the Sea"—all available through the EU's RAPID database Web service available at http://europa. eu.int/rapid/start/cgi/guesten.ksh?qry; "Going Too Fast," *Wall Street Journal* (8 November 2000): A22.

---

- The Soviet Union sent troops into Czechoslovakia in 1968 to maintain Soviet influence.

- The United States had more than 540,000 troops in Vietnam by the end of 1969 and justified the deployment on the grounds of preventing communist expansion in South Vietnam.

Cold War tensions between the United States and USSR did not end at any specific moment. Conflict abated under Nixon's presidency of the early 1970s. Meanwhile, China, India, Japan, and Europe emerged as potential superpower entities—of either a military or economic type—under the bipolar system and prompted some observers to ponder whether bipolarism truly existed. The 1980s turned out to be the decisive decade for the end of the postwar bipolar system. Coming to leadership in the USSR in 1985, Mikhael Gorbachev instituted a number of policies that transformed the USSR, eased tensions with the United States, and served as a prelude to the demise of the USSR in 1991.[16]

## After Bipolarism

Long before 9/11, political scientists cautioned that the post-Soviet, postbipolar international system looked neither simple nor peaceful. Political scientists and international observers debated whether the international system had become unipolar (with the United States as the sole superpower) or multipolar (with competing economic and military powers represented by the United States, China, Europe, and perhaps other countries and regions, depending on the political scientist consulted) in the aftermath of bipolarism. In terms of peace and security questions, the former Yugoslavia emerged as an immediate and obvious refutation of any thesis of post-Soviet international harmony. Tensions in the former Yugoslavia erupted in 1991, when the Yugoslav states of Slovenia and Croatia proclaimed themselves independent and were opposed in their independence efforts by Yugoslav authorities. The Yugoslav army, with a Serbian majority, resisted Slovenia's, Croatia's, and, later, Bosnia-Herzegovina's independence moves and fought to hold Yugoslavia together. Although Serbian, Bosnian, and Croat leaders signed a December 1995 treaty to end the fighting, the region remained unstable.[17] The conflict produced thousands of fatalities and a refugee community in excess of 3 million.[18]

Elsewhere, controlling nuclear materials and technologies raised additional security challenges. With the dissolution of the USSR, the newly independent former Soviet states of Russia, the Ukraine, Kazakhstan, and Belarus possessed nuclear weapons. In addition, Russia and the Ukraine controlled nuclear power plants. The presence of nuclear materials created possible environmental, health, and military threats. International smuggling became a major worry, insofar as the new governments of the former Soviet region were not always equipped to safeguard nuclear materials against theft. In addition, fears that the Ukraine and Russia would be unable to operate their nuclear power plants safely prompted the U.S. government, through the U.S. Nuclear Regulatory Commission and the Department of Energy, to offer assistance for the development of effective regulations, safety upgrades, personnel training, and risk reduction programs.[19]

Civil war and U.S./UN military intervention in Somalia in 1992, as well as U.S./UN military intervention in Haiti in 1995 and 1996, provided further evidence that the post–Cold War order was subject to insecurities emanating from a variety of sectors. In Somalia, intervention was initially justified as a means of supplying food to communities ravaged by war, but it later became a battle against one of Somalia's most powerful warlords, General Mohammed Farah Aidid. Intervention in Somalia was ended in 1995. In Haiti, military intervention restored the presidency of Reverend Jean-Bertrand Aristide, whom Haitian military leaders had ousted soon after his election to the presidency in 1990. Placing the cases of Somalia and Haiti in a larger context, one finds that between 1990 and 2001, more than

**BOX 11.3    Technology, Military Operations, and Changing Concepts of Security: Clocks to Computers**

Technology can change the way wars are fought, the meaning of military preparedness, and the definition of national security, as the following examples illustrate.

- *Clocks and synchronization.* The invention of pocket watches in the 1500s made it possible for small, portable timepieces to be carried into battle and used to synchronize troop movements. By World War I, the role of clocks in conducting military operations was monumental: Timed maneuvers allowed arms and troops to be placed so that weapons could be stationed far removed from the troops they were protecting.
- *Muskets and weaponry advance.* Muskets were important weapons during the American Revolution. Muskets had begun to replace bows during the 1500s and represented technological progress in terms of weaponry, in part because soldiers required less training in the use of muskets than in bows. However, muskets could be somewhat tedious to load. Soldiers needed to be able to bite off cartridge sections and pour powder into their muskets. As a result, during the American Revolution, the American Army insisted that soldiers have at least two front teeth.
- *Telegraphs and rapid communications.* Telegraph communication during the U.S. Civil War facilitated troop and supply assignments. Of course, destroying telegraph lines became a key element of warfare.
- *Railroads and enhanced transportation.* The U.S. Civil War demonstrated the effectiveness of railroad

transportation. Because railroad lines, like telegraph lines, were easily sabotaged, however, the advent of this technology prompted large commitments of troops to stationary guard posts around railroad lines. Military strategy had to adapt to the new machines of war.
- *Computers and "soft power."* Computer technology promises to make the twenty-first century information-rich in ways unimaginable to previous generations. Information collection, storage, analysis, and retrieval may become at least partly the basis for new approaches to national security because national security may come to be linked to what some political scientists call "soft power." Soft power is the power to achieve objectives through peaceful persuasion and by example. If the United States can be an appealing example to other states, and can serve as a model state sharing its computer-oriented information technologies, then the United States can possibly promote its security through nonmilitary ways. In this scenario, the United States can influence other states not through military force but through its own example of peace and affluence.

SOURCES: Kenneth Macksey, *The Penguin Encyclopedia of Weapons and Military Technology: Prehistory to the Present Day* (New York: Viking, 1993); Andre Corvisier, ed., *A Dictionary of Military History and the Art of War* (Cambridge, MA: Blackwell, 1994); Norman Desmarais, *Research Publications' American Journey: History in Your Hands* (Woodbridge, CT: Primary Source Media, 1995); Joseph S. Nye, Jr., and William A. Owens, "America's Information Edge," *Foreign Affairs* 75 (March–April 1996): 20–36.

---

What did it mean to endure the Cold War at home? For U.S. citizens, it sometimes meant risks of exposure to nuclear fallout and biological agents—from actions not by the USSR but by the United States.

First, between 1951 and 1959 the U.S. government carried out 100 aboveground nuclear tests at Yucca Flat and Frenchman Flat, Arizona. Troops were routinely sent on maneuvers into the test areas following the explosions. Former Marines recall seeing blinding lights, burned test dummies, and incinerated remains of test animals.

Second, in the 1950s and 1960s, the U.S. Army released non-health-threatening biological agents in some U.S. cities to study the spread patterns of such agents. In one test, the Army introduced the bacteria *Bacillus subtilis* and charcoal into the New York subway system. When these biological exposures became public in the 1970s, the programs were ended. The Army maintained that no one was sickened by the exposures; however, the Army acknowledged that it did not do follow-up monitoring on the health of the exposed populations.

SOURCES: Phil Garlington, "Government May Open Nevada Atomic Test Site to Tourists," *Albuquerque Journal* (11 January 1998): C1, C4; Leonard A. Cole, "It Can Happen Here—And Did," *New York Times* (23 March 1995): A15.

---

50 major violent conflicts ensued. Five conflicts were in the Americas, 19 were in Africa, 16 were in Asia, 9 were in the Middle East, and 8 were in Europe.[20]

## International Security Questions

Would peace be better served by operating from the standpoint of idealism, realism, a combination of the two, or some entirely different perspective? In analyzing these matters, we can look specifically at two questions confronting governments and decision makers.

First, what is the role of the UN? The UN is an intergovernmental organization (IGO). IGOs have states as members. IGOs, states, and nongovernmental organizations (NGOs) such as the International Red Cross are all potentially key actors in international relations.

To understand the contemporary challenges facing the UN, it is useful to examine the organization's background and structure. The charter establishing the UN was created by representatives from 50 governments in 1945. Chapter One of the UN Charter suggests that the purposes of the UN include efforts

- To promote peace and security
- To support principles of equality and self-governance of all people
- To support human rights, freedom, and justice
- To help governments in pursuit of mutually supportive objectives[21]

The charter further calls on member governments to abstain from threats and violence against any other governments, to assist the UN in carrying out its purposes, and to abstain from aiding any government against which the UN is

## BOX 11.5  The Gulf War

Interpretations of the Gulf War shift, as one examines the war from different models of analysis, and debates about the war have intensified since 9/11 and the ousting of Saddam Hussein.

What was the Gulf War about? In August 1990, Iraq invaded Kuwait. In response to the invasion, under the leadership of the United States, the UN imposed economic sanctions against Iraq and issued a January 15, 1991, deadline for Iraq's withdrawal. When the deadline passed with no Iraqi pull-out, UN forces attacked Iraq. After more than 100,000 Iraqi casualties, Iraq withdrew from Kuwait.

This war and its aftermath highlight many issues of continuing importance in international relations. First, the outbreak of the war served as a reminder of the fragile nature of peace. Whether initiated by states acting from aggression, miscalculation, or rational self-interest, war is an ever-present possibility in international affairs. Knowing this, the United States had actually identified Iraq as a hostile state prior to Iraq's invasion of Kuwait and, according to a Pentagon report, had outlined a plan of action (air strikes followed by ground troops launched from Saudi Arabia) in the event of war with Iraq.

Second, the Gulf War illustrated the extent to which arms proliferation enhanced the war-making capacity of states. Having ended a war with Iran in 1988, Iraq was well armed by the time of the Gulf War, in part because of arms supplied from Europe, Brazil, the USSR, and the United States. From 1986 to 1990, Iraq purchased more than $10 billion in weapons, making it the fourth largest arms buyer in the world.

Third, the Gulf War called attention to the deadliness of present-day weapons. For instance, international scholars worried about Iraq's capacity for deploying biological weapons. Yet the problem of destructive weapons transcends any single country. Indeed, the presence of weapons—nuclear, chemical, or biological—in any country places untold numbers of people at potential risk. After the war, for example, the Pentagon reported that some U.S. troops had been exposed to radioactivity from the U.S. Army's use of depleted uranium ammunition during the war. Depleted uranium ammunition is made from radioactive waste materials.

Fourth, questions of economics were never far from the center of debates on appropriate action toward Iraq after the invasion of Kuwait. Specifically, as long as Iraq was in power in Kuwait as well as its own territory, Iraq held control over massive oil reserves. Leaders from Japan to Europe to the United States were alarmed by the economic power such control represented. Indeed, the standard of living of some of the richest countries of the world was threatened by events in Kuwait.

Fifth, the conduct of the war highlighted the environmental costs of war as well as the importance of environmental issues in contemporary calculations of national security. Iraq's destruction of oil wells and the U.S. military's systematic pesticide sprays over areas in which U.S. troops were stationed caused alarm in many quarters, especially after the war when some veterans developed illnesses possibly related to pollution caused from oil field fires or toxic water used for bathing.

Sixth, in justifying the UN response against Iraq, the United States and other participants tried to call the world's attention to Iraqi violations of human rights in both Iraq and Kuwait. As is often true in international conflicts, language and concepts associated with idealism (human rights and ethics) merged with those of realism (power) as states hastened to explain their decision to retaliate against Iraq.

**BOX 11.5** *Continued*

SOURCES: Information on the war and its aftermath is found in Michael Brzoska and Frederic S. Pearson, *Arms and Warfare: Escalation, De-escalation, and Negotiation* (Columbia: University of South Carolina Press, 1994), pp. 222–224; John Spanier and Steven W. Hook, *American Foreign Policy since World War II*, 14th ed. (Washington, DC: Congressional Quarterly, 1998), pp. 275–279; Michael T. Klare,

"Making Enemies for the '90s: The New 'Rogue State' Doctrine," *The Nation* (8 May 1995): 625–626; Bill Mesler, "The Pentagon's Radioactive Bullet," *The Nation* (21 October 1996): 11; Laura Flanders, "Mal de Guerre," *The Nation* (7 March 1994): 292–293; Christopher S. Wren, "Weapons Inspection Chief Tells of Iraqi Tricks," *New York Times* (27 January 1998): A6.

taking actions.[22] The enforcement of the UN Charter depends on the resources and support that member governments give to the UN.

The UN consists of five major divisions: the General Assembly, the Security Council, the Economic and Social Council, the International Court of Justice, and the Secretariat.[23] The General Assembly is a large body whose members include representatives from all states belonging to the UN. In December 2003, the UN listed 191 member states. Each state has one vote in the General Assembly. The General Assembly has the authority to debate and render advisory recommendations on any matter involving international politics relating to UN purposes. In essence, this means that the General Assembly debates issues of broad scope— ranging from promoting peace to ending violations of human rights. Very importantly, however, the General Assembly cannot enact its own recommendations.

The Security Council is smaller but much more powerful than the General Assembly. The Security Council has five permanent members: the United States, Russia, China, France, and Great Britain. Each permanent member has a veto power that can be used to prevent a council decision. In addition to the permanent members, 10 other members are elected by the General Assembly to 2-year terms on the Security Council. The Security Council has the authority to enact sanctions against hostile states, to call for cease-fire plans in the event of conflict, to send peacekeeping forces to a conflict, and to authorize military actions by member states. In peacekeeping operations called into being by the Security Council, UN member governments provide troops on a voluntary basis, and the governments—not the Security Council—exercise final authority over their own troops. This means, for example, that a country that commits military personnel to a peacekeeping endeavor can withdraw its personnel at its own discretion.[24]

The Economic and Social Council, made up of 54 members, oversees UN projects on economic development, human rights, and environmental issues. This council reports to the General Assembly. The range of international political issues within the jurisdiction of the Economic and Social Council is indicated by the variety of commissions under its authority. These include

- Commission on Population and Development
- Commission for Social Development
- Commission on Human Rights and Subcommission on Prevention of Discrimination and Protection of Minorities

---

**BOX 11.6 Biological Warfare**

The use of biological warfare is very old. Consider the following examples:

- Evidence from the 1300s suggests that one tactic employed by warring forces was the strategic placement of plague-infected corpses in towns for the purpose of infecting enemy populations.
- In the 1400s, combatants deposited corpses and excrement in enemy territories for the purpose of inducing sickness.

- In the 1700s, British colonial administrators in North America corresponded about, planned, and, apparently, carried out actions to deliberately expose Native Americans to smallpox.

SOURCE: Stockholm International Peace Research Institute, *The Problem of Chemical and Biological Warfare: A Study of the Historical, Technical, Military, Legal and Political Aspects of CBW, and Possible Disarmament Measures.* Vol. 1, *The Rise of CB Weapons* (New York: Humanities Press, 1971).

---

- Commission on the Status of Women
- Commission on Narcotic Drugs and Subcommission on Illicit Drug Traffic and Related Matters in the Near and Middle East
- Commission on Science and Technology for Development
- Commission on Crime Prevention and Criminal Justice
- Commission on Sustainable Development[25]

The International Court of Justice (World Court) issues advisory opinions and hears cases involving states. The court consists of 15 members who serve for 9-year terms. Members are elected by the General Assembly and Security Council. The members of the World Court are not to be spokespeople for their individual countries but, rather, are to decide cases and issue opinions in an impartial manner. Only cases involving states (not individuals) are decided by the Court. The World Court cannot require states to participate in its proceedings. In the late 1990s, World Court cases included fishing controversies between Spain and Canada, disputes over crimes of genocide involving Bosnia and Yugoslavia, conflicts surrounding the destruction of oil platforms involving Iraq and the United States, and disputes between Libya and the United States over terrorism.[26]

The Secretariat—directed by the secretary-general—does the job of administering the work of the previous four organs. The present and seventh secretary-general is Ghanaian Kofi Annan, whose second term will end in December 2006.

In addition to these five divisions, the UN also includes a number of departments, such as the World Health Organization (WHO), the Office of the UN High Commissioner for Refugees (UNHCR), the UN Children's Fund (UNICEF), and the UN Development Program (UNDP). These departments support a variety of international programs. For example, the WHO carries out programs that provide assistance relating to HIV/AIDS, children's health, tropical diseases, drug management, food safety, tuberculosis, leprosy, mental health, blindness, chemical safety, noncommunicable diseases, reproductive health, and environmental health.[27]

How effective can the UN be in working for peace and justice? Three factors suggest that the UN does have the potential to be effective. First, it provides a forum for international debate among diverse governments and this debate can foster greater understanding among countries. In turn, greater understanding can promote diplomatic and nonviolent relations among states, UN proponents assert.

Second, the record has shown that the UN can be effective in increasing levels of military security (as emphasized by realism) and human security (as emphasized by idealism), as indicated by the following examples: The UN has helped negotiate more than 170 peaceful settlements of conflict since 1945; it has funded immunization, nutrition, health, and education programs in more than 100 countries; it has overseen nuclear reactor inspections and thus reduced the possibility of nuclear proliferation; and UN efforts have been central to campaigns to eradicate smallpox and polio.[28] Success stories such as these indicate that the UN is not simply a "hollow" organization powerless to shape international military, economic, and social decision making, according to UN advocates.

Third, insofar as the UN routinely works in cooperation with NGOs, the UN provides citizens and social movements an arena for participating in politics beyond the borders of their own countries. For example, the Subcommittee on Racism, Racial Discrimination, Apartheid and Colonialism is one human rights NGO whose members have worked closely with the UN to develop policies on nondiscrimination issues. By linking people and movements to UN programs, NGOs can provide alternative models of analysis (perhaps beyond both idealism and realism) that take into account perspectives other than those of superpowers and politicians. Citizen involvement through NGOs can facilitate international cooperation and ease tensions that might otherwise lead to societal disorder, UN proponents assert.[29]

Yet two important factors point to the limitations of the UN. First, as noted previously, the UN depends on its member states. Member states provide funding and, in the event of peacekeeping and military operations, troops. For example, in 1994 the secretary-general requested 35,000 peacekeeping troops for Bosnia-Herzegovina, but member states contributed only 7,600. In the same year, the Security Council unanimously called for the immediate creation of a peacekeeping force of 5,500 for assignment in Rwanda; however, almost 6 months elapsed before the troops were amassed. In December 2003, the UN reported that only 5,900 military personnel out of an authorized 15,000 had been provided by member states for assignment to a peacekeeping mission in Liberia. Indeed, while the UN organizational structure names all member states as responsible for contributing to the UN's programs, in October 2003 only 91 states were sustaining the personnel and military needs of the organization's peacekeeping forces. For example, in October 2003, Pakistan, Bangladesh, India, Ghana, and Uruguay were the top five states in terms of contributing military personnel to UN peacekeeping missions. Whereas Pakistan contributed 5,252 troops to UN peacekeeping efforts, the U.S. provided only 430 security personnel.[30] As these examples illustrate, the UN, as an organization, is actually in a subordinate relationship relative to states.

No less an authority than World Court Judge Mohammed Bedjaoui has made the same point. Speaking of the role of the World Court, Judge Bedjaoui has noted that the Court's effectiveness is dependent on government decisions both to articulate international rules of peace and justice and to supply the material and personnel resources needed to implement those rules. The Court can only resolve disputes about the rules of peace and justice; it cannot make governments abide by its decisions.[31]

Second, just as the UN reflects a hierarchy—with the Security Council possessing considerably more power than the General Assembly—the governments on which the UN depends exist in a hierarchy. Thus, some critics contend, the UN is actually dominated by superpower states, such as the United States. As such, rather than providing a forum for peacefully mediating disputes to the mutual benefit of member states, the UN serves the interests of the powerful, these analysts maintain, and cannot effectively provide an independent and/or egalitarian perspective on world issues.

In weighing the merits of such an argument, it is imperative to consider that if dominance is exercised, it is not one-dimensional and universal, especially in cases in which powerful member states are at odds over proposed policies. One can look to the example of the events leading up to the U.S. and British-led war on Iraq in 2003 to find evidence of the UN and a powerful member state—the United States—in opposition. In statements released on January 27, February 19, March 10, and March 19, Secretary-General Annan was urging a peaceful resolution of U.S.–Iraq tensions. When, on March 20, 2003, Annan was called upon to comment on the commencement of war, he expressed regret that negotiations had not been given more time to work by the Bush and Blair administrations. That is, the UN was critical of, not the mouthpiece of, the U.S. position on Iraq.[32]

Whether the UN can be effective, as you can see, is unclear, as is the fate of state sovereignty in the case of UN interventions. Specifically, UN intervention calls into question the reality of state sovereignty for the state that is the site of the intervention. As discussed in Chapter 3, sovereignty (the actual capacity to make and carry out ultimate rules within the territory of a state) is claimed by states. UN intervention against a state's wishes not only violates the state's claim of sovereignty but also may undermine the self-governance and self-determination of the people of the state, if the state is perceived by the citizens as a legitimate organ reflecting the popular will. Indeed, routine UN intervention into the affairs of states may hasten the decline of state sovereignty, a process already well under way according to some scholars, as noted also in Chapter 3.

In addition to discussing the role of the UN in contemporary international relations, it is also important for students of world politics to consider a second security question: What role should NATO play? As discussed earlier, NATO was formed to provide for the common defense of its members in 1949, and throughout the Cold War NATO viewed the USSR as the major threat to European security. In addition to the original NATO members noted previously, NATO expanded to include Greece (1952), Turkey (1952), Germany (1955), Spain (1982), the Czech Republic (1999), Hungary (1999), and Poland (1999). Bulgaria, Estonia, Latvia, Lithuania, Romania, Slovakia, and Slovenia are candidates for NATO membership in 2004. Like the UN, NATO's operation as an organization depends on its member states.[33]

Given its origins, however, some might have expected NATO to dissolve rather than expand. NATO's restructuring through expansion was made possible by negotiations undertaken in the early 1990s. NATO leaders met in July 1990 in London and put forward a new organizational plan. NATO's new strategic plan asserted that NATO's presence could stabilize Europe in a post–Cold War era likely to be threatened by new sources, such as

- Nationalist and ethnic tensions in Europe
- Economic conflicts in Europe
- Instability in transitional countries such as Russia
- Tensions in southern and eastern Europe in proximity to volatile regions such as the Middle East
- Arms control and nuclear materials control in Europe[34]

Given the seriousness of such threats, NATO leaders asserted that a common defense alliance was still needed. Indeed, NATO participants argued that a strong NATO could facilitate arms control, deter aggression, and promote the sharing of information on military technologies among its members. In other words, if NATO supporters were correct, both realists and idealists should have been happy to see NATO endure and expand: NATO was conceptualized as a bulwark of military security (consistent with realism) and as a catalyst for resource sharing by states in an interdependent world (consistent with idealism).

NATO proceeded to establish official links with a number of central and eastern European states formerly in the Soviet sphere of influence or formerly part of the Soviet Union. For example, the North Atlantic Cooperation Council (NACC) was formed in 1991 to promote information exchanges between NATO members and central and eastern European states on defense and disarmament issues.[35] NATO also established formal relations with the Ukraine in 1991. NATO leaders were especially concerned with pushing the Ukraine to dismantle its nuclear weapons.[36]

NATO announced the Partnership for Peace (PFP) program in 1994. Through PFP, NATO created links with non-NATO states, including central and eastern European states, for the sharing of defense and arms information, for the promotion of openness in terms of military budgets and preparation, for the promotion of civilian control of military affairs, and for the development of international coordination of military and peacekeeping exercises.[37] Perhaps most controversial of all the immediate post-USSR moves by NATO was the decision to expand to include three central and eastern European states as full members in 1999. At the time, critics of the expansion worried that NATO's enlargement might intensify Russian instability by fueling forces within Russia that wanted Russia to militarize and establish itself as a superpower state. Cognizant of such threats, NATO established direct ties to Russia by including Russia as a member of the PPF in 1994, by including Russia in peace and security plans embodied in what came to be known as the Founding Act of 1997, and by forging the NATO–Russia Council in 2002. The NATO–Russia Council links NATO members with Russia for the purpose of common security planning. Between 1996 and 2002, Russia collaborated with NATO countries in peacekeeping efforts in both Bosnia-Herzegovina and

Kosovo. In fact, Russia proved to be the most generous non–NATO member contributing to NATO operations in the former Yugoslavia.[38]

Whereas questions about the future of NATO in a world without a cold war absorbed scholars and political leaders for much of the 1990s, the question of NATO's role in an international arena dominated by questions of international terrorism is currently drawing the attention of political scientists and governments. Did NATO have a response to 9/11, the war against Afghanistan, and/or the war on Iraq? NATO's reaction was swift and varied. Within 24 hours of the 9/11 attack, NATO defined the attack as a strike against all 19 member states. NATO increased intelligence communications among members, initiated naval patrols in the Mediterranean for surveillance purposes, committed NATO Airborne Warning and Control Systems (AWACS) to support U.S. security by providing early warning of any additional threats, and accelerated efforts by NATO-led forces in the Balkans to identify any Al Qaeda supporters. The NATO–Russia Council affirmed common interests in antiterrorism efforts as well. Although the war against Afghanistan was not a NATO operation, NATO publicized that its member states contributed troops, and, in 2002, NATO provided command support for security operations. It assumed leadership of command functions for the International Security Assistance Force in Afghanistan in the summer of 2003. The war on Iraq was not a NATO campaign, but, as with the war in Afghanistan, NATO countries contributed troops. In addition, NATO provided security assistance to member states—e.g., Turkey and Poland—involved in the campaign. For example, NATO committed missile defenses and surveillance forces for Turkey.[39]

How will NATO and the UN respond to future international crises? How will new tensions and new possibilities shape these IGOs? These questions are no less difficult than the question that opened this chapter—what *really* explains the decisions of the United States and USSR during the post-*Sputnik* years? Whether looking to the past or the future, international political issues have been debated by idealists, realists, and those taking modified or alternative perspectives. As we see in the next chapter, when one's focus in international relations turns from models of analysis to questions of globalization, the questions do not get any easier and the controversies analyzed remain subject to a myriad of interpretations.

## SUMMING UP

- Idealism and realism offer alternative **models of analysis** for interpreting international relations. Idealism and realism make descriptive and prescriptive claims.

- **Idealism** asserts that governments should pursue moral principles in making policy and that this is a feasible approach because humans are rational and capable of peaceful interaction; international organizations have the capacity to promote peace, human rights, and human security, in a world that to many idealists seems interdependent.

- **Realism**, in contrast, emphasizes that power considerations, not morality, must guide government policy. According to realists, states exist in a condition of **anarchy**, in which there is no ultimate enforcer of rules and therefore states must guard their own power in order to defend their interests in a world characterized by conflict and the threat of conflict.

- The Iroquois League can be seen as an example of idealism, and U.S. intervention in Third World conflicts during the 1940s–1980s can be viewed as an application of realism.

- International politics is no longer characterized by the **bipolar** relations that shaped the post-World War II period. The end of bipolarism raises fundamental questions about the role of the UN and **NATO**. The UN's' effectiveness and the role of an expanding NATO are two questions dividing international observers in the postbipolar world.

## STUDY QUESTIONS

1. What is a model of analysis?

2. What defines idealism as a model of analysis?

3. What defines realism as a model of analysis?

4. Should human rights dictate foreign policy decisions? Compare and contrast how idealists and realists might answer this question.

5. What is bipolarism?

6. Identify three examples of foreign policymaking after World War II that were influenced by bipolar considerations.

7. Identify three divisions of the UN.

8. What are the arguments in favor of viewing the UN as an effective organization? What are the arguments against this position?

9. What is NATO? How might idealists and realists differ in their views of NATO's role in the postbipolar period?

10. Did NATO respond to the 9/11 attack?

## FOLLOWING UP THROUGH INTERNET SOURCES

- United Nations (http://www.un.org)

- European Union (http://www.europa.eu.int)

- NATO (http://www.nato.int)

# 12

# International Relations II

## Contemporary Issues

The acts of terrorism on September 11, 2001 killed more than 3,000 people in New York, Washington, and Pennsylvania. The 9/11 attack was preceded by Al Qaeda strikes against U.S. targets in Saudi Arabia in 1995 and 1996, Kenya in 1998, Tanzania in 1998, and Yemen in 2000. President Bush quickly stated that Al Qaeda leader Osama bin Laden was behind the attacks and later announced that bin Laden was wanted "dead or alive." Using Pakistan as an intermediary, the United States demanded that Afghanistan's Taliban government surrender bin Laden to the United States and destroy all terrorist capabilities within the country. The Taliban's representatives responded by demanding proof of bin Laden's involvement and by requesting a motion from the Organization of the Islamic Conference, an organization consisting of more than 50 Muslim countries. Taliban spokespersons also insisted that if bin Laden were to be released to another state, it would have to be to a third party, not to the United States.

On September 20, President Bush declared that in terms of retaliation, he would make no distinction between the 9/11 terrorists and those who gave them protection. Indeed, he announced a campaign against global terrorism and suggested that as many as 60 states had terrorist cells or individuals within their borders. By this time, Taliban leaders had announced that they had instructed bin Laden to leave Afghanistan. President Bush rejected the move as inconsequential. As late as September 27, the Taliban government requested continued negotiations with the United States as well as proof of bin Laden's culpability. On October 7,

U.S. and British forces bombed Afghanistan. By November 13, Taliban forces were surrendering Kabul. On November 27, talks that would lead to the formation of a post–Taliban interim governing authority were beginning. Although the war removed the Taliban leadership from power, it did not lead to the capture of bin Laden. In fact, Al Qaeda proved to be resilient, as indicated by the fact that Al Qaeda carried out seven terrorist strikes against Western targets between April and December 2002 and, in so doing, killed more people than had been killed by Al Qaeda terrorism during the three years immediately prior to 9/11.[1]

When one examines 9/11 and its aftermath in reference to the concepts discussed in this text, one finds political science offering a number of analytical insights on 9/11. First, if one conducts a comparative analysis of the suicide terrorists—with terrorism understood as the use of violence by nonstate actors for political objectives—who carried out the 9/11 strikes in reference to other suicide terrorists, one discovers that the 9/11 attackers are not fully representative of suicide terrorists. The 9/11 attackers expressed religious motives and identified themselves with a particular reading of the Islamic faith. Comparative analysis demonstrates that, worldwide, suicide terrorists are not necessarily likely to be Muslim or religious. Specifically, studies of suicide terrorist acts between 1980 and 2001 indicate that despite media tendencies to focus on Islamic examples, the Liberation Tigers of Tamil Eelam (LTTE) carried out more acts of suicide terrorism than did any other single group; LTTE recruits primarily in the Hindu region of Sri Lanka and espouses a Marxist–Leninist politics. Among suicide terrorist groups having a cultural connection to Islam, secular grievances constitute 30 percent of the documented motives for suicide terrorism.[2]

Second, some political scientists believe that 9/11 provides evidence for a claim that antedates 9/11: that the realism and idealism models of analysis discussed in Chapter 11 have severe conceptual limitations insofar they devote too little attention to the potentially decisive role of nonstate entities in shaping international relations. Both realism and idealism are state-centric models of analysis. That is, both models seek to understand international politics by directing scrutiny to the actions of states. However, as Al Qaeda's terrorism on 9/11 shows, nonstate actors can radically alter international politics. Do we not need a model of analysis that gives greater attention to such possibilities?[3]

With respect to such questions, political scientist Joseph Nye has suggested for some time that international politics is best understood as being constituted by three spheres: (1) the sphere of military power (which is primarily unipolar with the United States as the dominant state), (2) the sphere of economic power (which is multipolar with many economic rivals, such as the United States, Europe, China, and Japan); and (3) the sphere occupied by "transnational" organizations that move across state boundaries and challenge state sovereignty. Transnational organizations can be international terrorist groups such as Al Qaeda, international drug cartels, or international businesses legally moving currencies across states. In other words, 9/11 is a tragic and vivid example of something much deeper in international affairs, according to a number of political scientists. These scholars believe that the events of 9/11 clearly demonstrate what 100 smaller events each day might disclose less clearly: the vulnerability of governments to nonstate transnational entities in a way that neither realism nor idealism can explain. Ironically, states may respond to exposures of their own vulnerabilities with a hyperstatist agenda; that is, states may further centralize and extend their power in sphere 1 (to use Nye's terminology) in response to the absence of sovereignty in sphere 3. Indeed, President Bush's decisions to heighten domestic security and to attack Iraq as well as Afghanistan on grounds invoking 9/11 could be argued to be possible examples of this hyperstatist response.[4]

Third, political scientists often view 9/11 and its aftermath in the context of globalization. Globalization is a slippery term lacking a settled, uniform definition. It can be used as a popular catch-all expression, as indicated by the fact that more than 700 articles using the term *globalization* appeared in the *Washington Post* and *New York Times* in the late 1990s, whereas fewer than 100 appeared in the mid-1980s. Used here, globalization refers to internationalization—that is, a loosening of ties that might have held people, things, and symbols to a single place and thus bracketed in their mobility, influence, and exposure to people, things, and symbols in other places. With globalization, more permeable boundaries replace more closed boundaries. For example, a product becomes global or globalized when its influence becomes international in reach because it has found borders to be penetrable, not rigid and closed. Globalization (of some things) has been going on for centuries. Examples include international voyages of exploration, international population migrations, international religious crusades and missionary programs, international trade, and international communication networks.[5]

Much of what happened on and after 9/11 was possible only within a context of globalization. A terrorist organization used porous borders to move money and people across the globe, struck targets a world away from the land wherein most of the terrorists' grievances were said to have been experienced, used global telecommunications to plan and coordinate its attack, chose vehicles epitomizing global travel to carry out the attack, and utilized global satellite media to tell its story and that of the daring escape of its leader to a worldwide audience.

In this chapter, we will explore two issues that promise to be of continuing importance in global relations. Both issues have a relationship to 9/11 as well as a central place in world politics on their own merits: (1) questions relating to the media and politics and (2) questions relating to international economics and politics.

## MEDIA AND POLITICS

Political scientists have studied the relationship between media and politics from a variety of perspectives. Here, we will focus on four aspects of media—politics interactions. First, media relations illustrate both the sweep and the unevenness of globalization. That is, media coverage of political events is broader in its reach than ever before—consistent with the notion of porous boundaries in a globalized arena—even though its coverage is unevenly dispersed. With respect to the latter, for example, Susan Carruthers has pointed out that while U.S. and European residents are increasingly likely to rely on satellite technology and Internet news sources, more than half of the world's population has yet to make a telephone call.

The number of televisions in Britain exceeds that in the entirety of Africa. The 29 richest countries are home to more than 90 percent of all the world's computers. Thus, the *global media* does not actually reach all parts of the globe.[6]

Still, the media's range is far-reaching to an extent that is surprising by the standards of the recent past. Consider the point made by political scientist Brigitte L. Nacos in her comparison of media coverage of the attacks on Pearl Harbor and that of 9/11. It was not until 3 hours after the bombing of Pearl Harbor that radio audiences in the U.S. heard of the event. It was a week later before photographs appeared in the newspapers. In contrast, on 9/11, coverage of the attacks was immediate and international in scope. For example, surveys noted that almost 100 percent of citizens in Hungary knew of and followed the events of 9/11 from the beginning of news reportage. CNN alone dispatched 400 media personnel to the World Trade Center site to maximize coverage.[7]

Second, a number of political scientists have asserted that although government boundaries may have become more porous in a period of globalization, media relations continue to be shaped by government structures. That is, whether a government's structure is democratic or nondemocratic impacts media's coverage and creation of news content. Media scholar Holli A. Semetko provides a very useful model for comparing the media's role in different countries. According to Semetko, the media–politics relationship has the following important dimensions, which vary considerably from one country to the next. In some countries, various media outlets are government funded, whereas in others, including the United States, media organizations are mostly privately owned. In addition, countries differ in terms of the degree to which the media's content and reporting are free of control by the government; in nondemocratic systems, government leaders may see media outlets as primary avenues for perpetuating the political status quo. Finally, countries differ in the degree to which parties, interest groups, and political participants have access to the media. Clearly, if only dominant parties or groups have the opportunity to convey messages through the media, this severely restricts the range of democracy within civil society.[8]

Employing Semetko's classification scheme, among democracies, a number of countries have operated media outlets that are either partially or entirely government funded and have been major competitors with privately owned media entities. In Great Britain, the British Broadcasting Corporation (BBC), formed in 1927, is government funded through license fees collected from households possessing color televisions or VCRs. Although it is so funded, the BBC's official operating charter provides for its independence from government control as well as control by any party or interest group; that is, neither government officials nor partisan activists dictate the content of news broadcast on the BBC's television and radio stations. The BBC provides a useful example of a media organization that is connected to government but not a tool of government. The example of the BBC thus illustrates that government funding of media need not violate the democratic (especially protective democracy as noted in Chapter 7) principle of freedom of the press. Indeed, the BBC's credibility as a source of independent news is recognized beyond Britain. It has been widely noted that former Soviet leader Mikhail

Gorbachev depended on BBC broadcasts over the BBC Russian Service to monitor events affecting his political and personal fate during his confinement by coup leaders during the disintegration of the USSR.[9]

In contrast, Nazi Germany represents a case of nondemocracy in which media–politics relationships were characterized by extreme government domination. When Hitler came to power in Germany in 1933, the Nazis created a government agency known as the Ministry for Public Information and Propaganda. Keenly aware of the popularity of radios among Germans at the time, the Nazis took steps to use radio broadcasts as a means of extending their reach over the country's population. Specifically, the ministry took control over radio programming to ensure that only pro-Nazi "news" and entertainment were broadcast. Music by Jewish composers was forbidden; jazz and popular music were removed from radio schedules. The ministry also prohibited Germans from listening to foreign broadcasts.[10] Viewing these measures in reference to Semetko's categories, one finds in the case of Nazi Germany a prime example of a government-controlled media lacking any foundation for independent reporting and thoroughly closed off to any non-Nazi group that might seek to present anti-Nazi views through media outlets.

In China, the government exercises a high degree of control over the publication, broadcast, and content of popular print and electronic media. Government-directed news is broadcast on all three of China's national television channels during the early evening, just as government-sponsored news and entertainment are carried on the country's five national radio channels. Educational programs have become an important part of China's media offerings. For example, China created a Television University in 1960; viewers can watch programs teaching a variety of classes, one of the most popular of which is English. Interestingly, the government permits advertising by Chinese and foreign companies. Japanese and U.S. products are heavily advertised. With respect to the latter, for instance, Chinese viewers see the U.S. Marlboro Man riding his horse, looking cool, and smoking cigarette after cigarette on their television sets. China's decision to exercise political control over the media while simultaneously allowing international advertising access to the media has raised interesting questions.[11] It is too early to tell whether the Chinese Communist Party will see its authority eroded as diverse ideas are marketed with the products advertisers can try to link them with, or whether the Marlboro Man will turn out to be apolitical and innocuous.

Third, political scientists have pointed out that media's relation to political events can be multidimensional, with media coverage appearing sometimes to shape and other times to be shaped by events. That is, media sometimes appears to "make" the news and other times to simply report the news made by others (e.g., terrorists, political leaders, governments, and nations).

We can return to the work of Nasco to see this multidimensionality. Taking 9/11 as a case study, one can argue that media organizations simply responded to an event, that they merely covered it; that is, they did not carry out the terrorism but, rather, conveyed images and data relating thereto. On the other hand, one could also make the argument that in the editorial choices made following

9/11, media representatives generated, molded, and gave form to a certain frame of reference for making sense of 9/11. If such is true, media organizations, at least in part, could be said to have "made" what we came to think of as "the news." For example, Nasco has documented that after 9/11, U.S. television stations gave more attention to Osama bin Laden than to President Bush. She also found that news coverage of Islam and Muslims skyrocketed after 9/11 as media representatives undertook to answer "why do they hate us?" One might step back and ask, Why this frame of reference rather than another? How might an alternative frame of reference invite a different understanding of what constitutes news? For example, what if news coverage had drawn the U.S. public's attention to a comparative analysis of suicide terrorism like that noted earlier in this chapter so that U.S. citizens had learned that suicide terrorists were more typically recruited in Hindu regions by the LTTE than by Islamic religious fundamentalists? Or, what if the focus of post-9/11 media coverage had directed attention to early efforts by many members of the international Muslim community to warn against the Taliban, even while the U.S. government was courting Taliban support as a means of neutralizing Iran, as noted in Chapter 11? One cannot answer such questions, but one can note that the media representatives who gave coverage to topics other than these shaped what counted as news and what did not.[12]

Fourth, political scientists have pointed out that reliance on different media outlets—electronic vs. print, hourly vs. daily coverage, for example—can influence the presentation and processing of news. For example, when television began covering political party conventions in the United States in 1940, a changed political environment was in the making. Forty years later, presidential candidates were claiming that no policy proposal taking longer than 10 seconds to explain would ever be heard by voters because television coverage demanded succinct quotes.[13]

U.S. citizens tend to rely on electronic media such as TV rather than print media. This was no less true of 9/11 than it has been with political campaigns and other political events. TV news tends to provide numerous visuals and abbreviated textual information. Although TV news stories pitch "live shots," "on-the-scene reporting," and other eye-catching images to viewers, the actual stories are generally so brief that were the reports transcribed into newspaper copy, no single story would have enough text to cover a third of a page. It is remarkable to consider how little information is conveyed between all the exciting visuals. It is also remarkable to stop and think about how inadequately informed citizens may be if their primary source of political knowledge is the picture-rich and data-poor TV evening news.[14]

Moreover, because U.S. media companies are primarily privately owned, media professionals are under pressure to present news in an entertaining way in order to expand their audiences and corresponding advertising revenues. Large audiences create higher profits from advertising sales. With the exception of the Public Broadcasting Service and National Public Radio, both of which are supported by public monies, U.S. TV and radio stations are like other businesses: They need to generate money to cover operating costs and make profits. If media professionals are convinced that viewers want entertaining news rather than in-depth details, this

assumption affects the kind of news they produce. Not surprisingly, political scientists have found that news coverage of campaigns tends to focus on the personal
lives of candidates rather than on issues, and when issues are reported the emphasis
is often on the immediate and most dramatic implications of the issues, not on the
historical, long-term, or global dimensions of those issues.[15]

At the same time, insofar as television and Internet-based news must be generated quickly, time pressures impede extensive independent investigations. U.S.
citizens think of news as something that happens many times per day. Imagine,
for instance, the shock of turning on your TV or consulting your Internet source
and finding that there was no news to report. Of course there is news, you might
think; it is 9 AM (or 12 PM, 5 PM, etc.) so, by definition, there is news. Because
U.S. citizens conceptualize news as something occurring by the hour or minute,
U.S. media professionals are often putting together news stories under severe
time restraints. Some analysts believe that this increases the tendency of reporters
to get information from official sources rather than from the reporters' own independent investigations of newsworthy events. Think about this issue from the
standpoint of reporters and editors. If you are a reporter assigned the task of doing
a story on a state's new prison system, for example, you will find it is quicker and
easier to get a governor's press release on the new prison than it is to go to libraries,
data banks, and university research centers to investigate the topic on your own. If
you have to do a story on homeland security, you will see the obvious time-saving
benefits of attending a politician's press conference on the subject and simply taking notes on the presentation compared with spending days searching for facts at
the Library of Congress and various federal and state government departments.
These hypothetical examples are not intended to suggest that investigative journalism never occurs; rather, the examples are meant to illustrate that time pressures tend to encourage the use of information provided by official sources (for
example, political leaders and their press secretaries) rather than the collection of
facts through ongoing independent research. Knowing this tendency, political
leaders and political interest groups place great emphasis on "handling" the media
through carefully prepared official statements and official press releases. Government officials do the same.[16]

## ECONOMICS AND POLITICS

Economic issues are no less salient in discussions of international relations than
are questions of media relations. Although the range of topics in international political economy is enormously varied and complex, some of the most prominent
debates in recent years have centered around three intergovernmental organizations (IGOs): the World Bank, the International Monetary Fund (IMF), and the
World Trade Organization (WTO).

The World Bank and the IMF were created in 1944 at a meeting in Bretton
Woods, New Hampshire, by a delegation of representatives from 44 states. Sometimes referred to as the "Bretton Woods Institutions," the World Bank and IMF
were designed to facilitate order, openness, and predictability in international

---

**BOX 12.1    Media Sources during the War against Iraq**

Surveys of U.S. citizens reveal interesting patterns of how people made choices among competing media outlets during the war with Iraq. Did the Internet prove to be more popular than TV news for Americans following the war? The results show the continued dominance of TV news as a source of information. The following data were published as part of a study of U.S. media coverage of the Iraq war in *Colombia Journalism Review*:

- Top sources of news about the war: TV (87%), newspapers (21%), Internet (17%)

- Top Internet sources of news about the war: U.S. television news pages (32%), U.S. newspaper pages (29%), U.S. government pages (15%), foreign news pages (10%)

- Top Internet sources located outside the U.S. as sources of news about the war (in order of popularity): BBC, Al-Jazeera, and The Guardian.

SOURCE: "By the Numbers." *Columbia Journalism Review* May/June 2003, p. 27.

---

economic relations. The founders of these IGOs described their efforts as representing key steps toward precluding the reemergence of the kind of economic instability that preceded the outbreak of World War II.[17]

At Bretton Woods, the World Bank was assigned the task of extending long-term loans to countries for the purpose of funding economic development projects. Once in operation, the World Bank's initial loans were extended to European governments needing developmental assistance to recover from World War II, but since the early 1950s World Bank lending has been concentrated in developing countries. Bank-funded projects have included the construction of electric power plants, roads, dams, natural resource development facilities, water treatment plants, and public health programs. In 2000, the World Bank reported $15.3 billion in loans, with the largest loans going to fund transportation projects in India and China. Although sizable, the bank's 2000 lending level was down from the $29 billion it loaned in 1999.[18]

The IMF was founded to facilitate orderly currency exchanges between states and to provide short-term loans to member states experiencing temporary balance

---

**BOX 12.2    Unequal Access to the World's Resources**

- More than 1 billion people try to survive on less than $1 per day.
- 125 of 1,000 children born in the world's poorest countries do not survive to age 5; their deaths would be highly preventable in richer countries.
- More than 50% of all the people alive live in poverty and the number

is predicted to be reduced by only 10% by 2015.

SOURCES: IMF Fact Sheet (September 2003), http://www.imf.org; Prakash Loungani, "The Global War on Poverty: Who's Winning?" *Finance & Development* December 2003: 38–39.

of payments problems. With respect to the latter, a state that found itself unable to make a loan payment to a foreign lender could seek a short-term loan from the IMF to cover its foreign debt payment. The presence of the IMF as a "backup" source of funds was expected to be a stabilizing influence in international affairs. Temporary balance-of-payments problems could be smoothed over rather than allowed to set in motion an economic crisis, and IMF member states could be assured of a "a little extra help" to recover from the effects of natural disasters, economic downturns, or other hardships that might complicate their debt repayment schedules. Working in conjunction with the World Bank, the IMF was counted on to harmonize economic interactions between governments and to increase the confidence level of states whether they were lenders or debtors in the post–World War II new economic order.[19]

In 2003, IMF activities included approving more than $11 million in loan programs for Dominica, disbursing $502 million in a lending package approved for Turkey, and working with the World Bank to implement $334 million in debt relief for Guyana. In 2000, the IMF had occasions for proving its ability to play the role of a stabilizing lender to various countries, including Pakistan and Turkey. Pakistan was late in repaying $1 billion to foreign lenders and owed in excess of $30 billion in total foreign debts. The IMF extended a 10-month loan of $596 million and offered technical assistance in helping Pakistan secure additional loans from the World Bank. Note the nature of the IMF loan: It was short term and it was prompted by an immediate balance-of-payments crisis. The IMF approved $7 billion for Turkey to be issued over the course of a year in order to help prevent currency devaluation and assist the country in continuing its external (foreign) debt reduction.[20]

The General Agreement on Tariffs and Trade (GATT), organized in Geneva in 1947, was the forerunner of the WTO, which was formed in 1995. The announced organizational purpose during the GATT years and since 1995 has been straightforward: to promote international trade by reducing barriers (such as tariffs) to trade and to resolve trade disputes between governments. In dealing with members or potential members, WTO officials scrutinize a country's domestic laws to ascertain whether restraints of trade are encoded therein, and if so, the WTO seeks to eliminate these restraints. For example, WTO negotiators have secured commitments from China to alter its economic policies, which in the past have protected its own semiconductor and computer industries from competition with foreign companies; to join the WTO, China agreed to rescind selected restrictions on foreign companies operating in China as well as restrictions making it difficult for Chinese firms to purchase products from international suppliers. In recent years, the WTO has examined numerous trade disputes arising when one or more countries charge another country with hindering free trade and simultaneously protecting its own domestic industries, including U.S. disputes with Korea over imported stainless-steel products, U.S. disagreements with Australia and New Zealand over imported lamb, Argentine disagreements with European countries regarding leather imports, and Guatemalan disputes with Mexico over cement imports. The WTO points to increasing levels of international trade—noting, for example, that international trade levels in 1997 were 14 times higher than levels in 1950—as evidence of its success as an international organization in mediating these and other controversies. Like the Bretton Woods institutions, the WTO operates on the premises that (1) economic stability is in the interest of all member states and (2) IGOs such as the WTO are key players in achieving this stability.[21]

All three IGOs have grown beyond their original members and have adapted to economic developments not necessarily anticipated by their founders. The WTO had enlarged to 146 member states as of December 2003. The IMF and World Bank counted 184 states as members as of the same period.[22]

With respect to internal decision-making procedures, influence within the World Bank and IMF is based on the amount of the funds each member state pays into the institution. The world's most affluent countries—the United States, Germany, Japan, the United Kingdom, and France—are major powers within both Bretton Woods institutions. The WTO has often presented itself as a less hierarchical organization in that its decisions are generally made by consensus. However, a number of observers, including former South African President Nelson Mandela, have pointed out that poorer countries are often at a disadvantage in WTO discussions: Poorer countries cannot always afford to send representatives to international WTO meetings, have fewer resources with which to bargain during negotiating rounds, and may feel pressured not to threaten the consensual process for fear of economic retaliation by more powerful members.[23]

The years 1996 and 2002 were pivotal for the IMF and the World Bank. In 1996, the IMF and World Bank issued the Heavily Indebted Poor Country Initiative (HIPC), and in 2002 the institutions announced that 27 countries had enjoyed debt relief under this initiative. The HIPC was important for many reasons: It pointed out that economic development had not been even and economic affluence had skipped over many of the world's countries, despite several years of operation by the IMF, World Bank, and GATT/WTO; it acknowledged that the international debts incurred by the world's poorest countries had grown so large as to be unpayable; and it offered tangible (though limited) relief to the poorest, most indebted states. In specific terms, HIPC identified 41 developing countries with such low gross national product (GNP) per capita levels and such high external debt levels as to merit classification as countries with inordinately excessive debt. These countries were targeted by the HIPC initiative for assistance in reducing and/or rescheduling their foreign debts. To qualify for the HIPC debt reduction/rescheduling, countries had to agree to follow IMF/World Bank measures for achieving creditworthiness. Such measures are known as **structural adjustment programs (SAPs)**.[24]

The linking of SAPs with HIPC debt relief was not a surprise to IGO analysts. SAPs are part of the long-standing repertoire of IMF and World Bank lending mechanisms. That is, SAPs have not been restricted to the 41 countries identified in the HIPC initiative but have, rather, been among the general requirements imposed by the IMF and World Bank on recipients needing (according to the lenders) improved creditworthiness. SAPs typically include provisions for reducing government expenditures through cuts in social welfare programs, reductions in subsidies for local businesses, the opening up of consumer markets for imports, and a shift away from public services to fee-based provisions of social services. To accord with SAP requirements, for example, countries may be required to sell government-owned facilities (such as water delivery systems) and/or to initiate fees for using public schools and/or public health clinics. If a country refuses to introduce SAPs, it fails to get the loans.[25]

As you can imagine, SAPs have proved a controversial dimension of IMF and World Bank lending. Three criticisms are often directed against SAPs. First, if the IMF and World Bank can make a government introduce one policy rather than another, what does this say about state sovereignty? Has the IGO not undermined the sovereignty of the state in such a scenario? Second, SAPs often result in immediate economic and/or social suffering for many citizens. Critics ask, How are poor people not hurt when government-funded social welfare programs are curtailed, or when schools and/or public health clinics start charging fees? Third, SAPs may not address the long-term needs of poor countries and may not promote movement toward an eventual reduction in a country's economic dependency. SAP-based economies are generally geared toward the development of export-oriented commodity production; that is, countries are encouraged to pour investment resources into producing coffee, palm oil, peanuts, or some other item to be sold abroad. However, it is exactly this type of economic production that, according to many accounts, renders these countries economically vulnerable. Declines in world prices for exports, for example, reduce countries' abilities to pay off their loans, create the dilemma whereby countries must decide whether to take on additional loans to keep up their preexisting debt payment plans, and over time threaten to deepen the poverty burden. Moreover, domestic industries (especially if SAP requirements go into effect and eliminate government subsidies to such firms) may be unable to compete with cheaper imported goods and may go bankrupt.[26]

The impact of SAPs is more clearly seen, perhaps, when specific country examples are analyzed. The case of Kenya illustrates the potential threat to state sovereignty. In the fall of 2000, Kenya qualified for an IMF loan in the amount of $198 million on the condition that it agree to surrender financial policy decisions to the IMF. IMF observers writing for such journals as *The Economist* and *African Business* noted that this requirement seemed especially harsh, even by IMF and World Bank standards. Why would the government of Kenya agree to these terms? Well, Kenya was desperate. Drought had wiped out water supplies so that both water and power were rationed. Business activity was stifled. International prices for coffee (a major export product) were too low to spur economic recovery. Unemployment rates were rising. Sovereignty turned out to be an item exchanged for immediate economic relief.[27]

States not so desperate have sometimes said no to SAPs and IMF and World Bank lending requirements. Zambia is one example. Zambia is one of several African countries to have endured economic setbacks as well as public health crises relating to AIDS in recent years. In Zambia, conflict between the government and the World Bank became especially acute. Zambia wanted a World Bank loan to allow the country to expand its distribution of low-cost AIDS drugs to its citizens. The bank agreed to a loan, and agreed further that the loan could be used to combat AIDS-related health problems, but stipulated that the loan must be used to fund drug research and to cover consultants' fees. Zambia turned down the loan offer rather than see the money go to pharmaceutical interests and outside consultants.[28]

In response to controversies and criticisms, the World Bank, IMF, and WTO have increasingly enlisted the input of citizens' groups, especially those organized as nongovernmental organizations (NGOs). The World Bank has also recently approved loans to environmental NGOs working on developmental projects favored by the Bank. One such loan went to the World Wildlife Fund, which used the money to help equip a sawmill operation in Papua New Guinea. The sawmill met the World Wildlife Fund's standards of environmental protection, created jobs, and stimulated local market activity. Hoping to quiet recent protesters charging the Bank with undermining sovereignty and/or promoting policies ruinous of the economics of poor countries, the World Bank has staffed its regional offices with personnel whose main task is to collaborate with NGOs such as the World Wildlife Fund in formulating and implementing additional projects.[29]

Whatever the future decisions of these three powerful IGOs, their actions take place within a context of extreme economic inequality. Access to the world's riches is uneven, as indicated by the following startling equation: A handful of individuals (358 billionaires, to be exact) possess as much wealth as the poorest 45 percent of the world's entire population.[30] In many countries, the sum of the entire nation's wealth is less than that of a single multinational corporation. In fact, if one were to make a list of all the world's economic entities, ranking these entities by size, 51 of the top 100 entities would be corporations, not countries.[31]

According to the World Bank's Development Report of 2004, the average wealth of a citizen of Albania is $1,380 per year, and the average wealth of a citizen of the United States is $35,060 per year. Citizens of Afghanistan, Gambia, Liberia, Somalia, Swaziland, and Equatorial Guinea are not likely to live to be 52 years old. In 2003, only 43 percent of the women and men living in the world's poorest countries had access to sanitation services. The randomness of birth in a world of inequality gives pause—readers of this book who are approaching their early twenties would be considered middle-aged in these societies.[32]

Indeed, although the United States is one of the richest countries in the world, readers of this book are probably acutely aware that the lives of the rich and the poor hold few similarities. As just noted, the wealth of the average U.S. citizen is more than $30,000 per year. This figure is reached by dividing the GNP or gross domestic product (GDP) (market value of goods and services in the country) by population to produce a number designated as GNP or GDP per capita. GNP/GDP per capita does *not* reveal how equally or unequally wealth is distributed within a country. Therefore, although GNP per capita for the United States amounts to an impressive figure, it is also the case that the *poorest* fourth of U.S. families had, on average, only $12,000 in 1992, whereas the comparable amount for the *richest* U.S. families was in excess of $90,000. As you can see, numbers denoting "averages" (such as GNP or GDP per capita) can conceal major gaps separating those on the top from those on the bottom (just like an "average" test grade for an entire class fails to mention the gap between the highest and lowest scores).[33]

---

**BOX 12.3　Jubilee USA Network and Protesting Globalization Effects**

---

International NGOs abound. One such NGO is known as Jubilee USA Network, formerly known as Jubilee 2000. It is an NGO made up of people from across the world joining together in opposition to World Bank, IMF, and WTO policies. Jubilee USA Network takes its name from the biblical book of Leviticus, Chapter 25, which presents a theological vision of a society in which debts are to be canceled and land is to be returned to original owners every 50 years (the year of Jubilee). Drawing on this biblical teaching, Jubilee USA Network members have called on governments and international lending institutions such as the IMF and World Bank to cancel the debts owed by the world's poorest countries and to develop lending policies that address human needs, alleviate suffering, and promote economic equality. Jubilee USA Network activists have criticized SAPs, have upheld citizen participation in economic decision making, and have critiqued the Bretton Woods system that prioritizes maintaining the status quo rather than achieving a more equitable redistribution of the world's wealth. The NGO has charged the Bretton Woods system with promoting ethical bankruptcy, not just economic bankruptcy of the world's poor governments; it is ethically unjustifiable, critics charge, to maintain lending policies that perpetuate impoverishment in countries such as those identified in the HIPC initiative while other countries amass fortunes.

Indeed, Jubilee USA Network has questioned whether globalization, the process through which the economies and cultures of the world are becoming increasingly interconnected, is bringing greater costs or gains. With globalization, middle-class citizens in countries such as the United States may see their lives enriched by Internet exchanges that cross borders, consumer purchases that cross borders, cell phone transmissions that cross borders, and, perhaps, distance learning classes that cross borders. Such citizens may feel exhilarated by global linkages and cosmopolitan cultural and economic opportunities unknown by previous generations. These citizens may wonder why WTO-inspired international trade and IMF- and World Bank-supported global investment could ever become controversial.

Jubilee USA Network and similar NGOs have pointed to the other side of globalization. They note that

- Global economic development is not eliminating the vast economic or technology gap between rich and poor countries.
- Working people are not allowed to be as "global" as is investment capital. Specifically, globalization may have erased borders for Internet surfers, but it has certainly not done so for immigrant workers and refugees. In many parts of the new global system, immigration restrictions continue to throw up barriers to individual workers seeking to cross borders in search of higher paying jobs. In the same global economy that encourages international capital transfers in the name of profitable investments, immigrants from Mexico seeking to enter the United States, for example, continue to risk harassment and arrest. In other words, in many cases, it is easier for you to transfer your money to an overseas investment project if you are a stock broker than it is to transport your body from a poor country to a rich country if you are seeking a higher paying job.
- IMF lending allows multinational corporations (MNCs) to externalize their risks while maintaining their profits, but populations in poor countries have no insurance to protect themselves from cumbersome debt loads. For example, an MNC

---

**BOX 12.3** *Continued*

investing in a government (for example, an international bank extending a commercial loan to a government) can do so knowing that if the recipient government has trouble paying the money it owes to the MNC, that government can go to the IMF for a ``backup'' loan; this IMF loan can then be used to finance payments to the MNC. In this situation, the MNC gets its money, even as the government incurs increasingly more debt (from new backup loans as well as its original loans) and as the citizens of the indebted government become increasingly more vulnerable to SAP-driven austerity programs. The MNC has insurance against losses (in the form of the IMF), but citizens of the cash-poor indebted government have no such insurance.

- Decision makers in the World Bank, IMF, and WTO are not elected by citizens, nor are these decision makers held accountable to citizens.
- Decisions made by the World Bank, IMF, and WTO often lack ``transparency''; that is, these decisions are often closed to public scrutiny and genuine grassroots-level citizen participation.

- Individuals and corporations in countries such as the United States are allowed to declare bankruptcy, but governments are not allowed to do so no matter how impoverished they become.
- Citizens in heavily indebted countries often had no input into their government's decision to acquire loans because many of these governments were authoritarian, military-led, and/or corrupt.
- The most heavily indebted countries have debts so large that their debt payments exceed government expenditures on basic health and education programs.

In Seattle in 1999 and in Prague in 2000, individuals from the NGO joined with other citizens, labor, and environmental NGOs to protest the global economic logic of the World Bank, IMF, and WTO. Forgive debts; end predatory lending; empower people, not IGOs; and embrace a vision of equality rather than hierarchy. These were among the protest demands—demands inspired by the ancient book of Leviticus.

SOURCES: Jubilee USA Network (www.jubileeusa.org); Jubilee South (www.jubileesouth.net); on globalization, see also Kenneth N. Waltz, ``Globalization and Governance,'' *PS: Political Science and Politics* 32 (December 1999): 693–700.

---

In addition, in the United States the wealthiest 10 percent of all citizens own 89 percent of the country's stock.[34] Moreover, a study by the Center on Budget and Policy Priorities recently found that the gap between the U.S.'s richest and poorest families grew during the past decade in 37 states, representing 87 percent of the U.S. total population.[35] Poor Americans are less likely than their affluent counterparts to graduate from high school, less likely to enroll in colleges and universities, and, when enrolled, less likely to graduate from colleges and universities. In short, poor Americans are more likely to venture toward low-skill jobs than the high-skill jobs created by technological and economic development.[36]

Looking beyond the United States, Nafis Sadik, executive director of the United Nations Population Fund, points out that one out of five humans worldwide lives in poverty, and 2003 figures from the International Monetary Fund support his estimate.[37] This means that in some countries, such as Brazil and

Pakistan, child labor can become a vital means of supplementing family incomes. Brazilian children as young as 7 years old (the legal age for employment is 12 years old) can be found working in various industries. Pakistani child workers comprise perhaps one-fourth of that country's unskilled labor market. Impoverishment can also impose grueling work lives on adult family members. For instance, in parts of South Africa, women in low-income families may travel on foot 5 miles every 2 days to bring back to their families as much as 65 pounds of firewood.[38]

This book began with a discussion of politics as the process of deciding who gets what and how much of what the world has to offer. What does the future of politics hold in the twenty-first century? Despite the past century's scientific and technological accomplishments, as Nafis Sadik's comments make clear, politics often remains a struggle for food, shelter, secure employment, and other necessities that continue to be uncertain items in the lives of millions of women and men.

As you reflect on the material covered in this text, think about what political science has to offer in terms of analytical perspectives on the very real problems of everyday life. Consider, for instance, how idealists and realists might define the responsibilities of governments in addressing the issues of violence and poverty. What might idealists suggest as a foreign policy goal of the United States in meeting its obligations in a world characterized by economic insecurity and impoverishment? How might a realist respond to the same question? How might a critic of both realism and idealism respond? How do you begin to respond?

## SUMMING UP

- In studying the terrorist attack of 9/11, political science has offered insights drawn from comparative analysis of terrorist groups, critiques of international relations models of realism and idealism, and analyses based on the context of globalization.

- Globalization refers to an international arena in which state boundaries are increasingly penetrable; globalization has been occurring for centuries.

- Political science analyses of media relations highlight the complexity of media in relation to globalization's reach and unevenness, the media as an agent both responding to and driving events it labels newsworthy, media activities as varied in relation to government structural components, and the processing of media outputs as affected by electronic vs. print structures and quickened news cycles.

- The IMF, World Bank, and WTO are three IGOs charged with promoting economic stabilization by fostering both short-term and long-term lending to states and by reducing trade barriers; critics point to structural adjustment programs, internal hierarchies, and lending and trade decisions that threaten sovereignty and fail to alleviate economic inequality as failed legacies of these three institutions.

# STUDY QUESTIONS

1. What do studies of comparative suicide terrorism suggest, and how might such findings surprise people who exclusively recall 9/11 when they think of suicide terrorism?

2. Is globalization of recent origin?

3. What is Joseph Nye's model of understanding international relations?

4. In what manner might realism and idealism be considered to be identical, and why is this problematic when one tries to analyze the events of 9/11?

5. Compare and contrast the operations of the World Bank, IMF, and WTO. Despite their different tasks, all three share a larger philosophical/political goal—what is it?

6. What are structural adjustment programs (SAPs)? What is the relationship between a SAP and the concept of creditworthiness? What are some criticisms of SAPs?

7. What does GNP per capita measure? Does it provide a measurement of whether economic resources within a country are distributed equally or unequally within the country for which GNP per capita information is available?

8. Identify three ways in which you think your life would be different if you lived in a high-income versus a low-income country. How do you think these differences would change the way you view politics? How would these differences influence the types of governmental policies you would like to see enacted?

# FOLLOWING UP THROUGH INTERNET SOURCES

- BBC (http://www.bbc.co.uk)

- International Monetary Fund (http://www.imf.org)

- World Bank (http://www.world-bank.org)

- World Trade Organization ( http://www.wto.org)

# Notes

## Chapter 1

1. Kofi Annan is quoted in "Annan Says 2004 Should Be `Year of Kept Promises' in Fight against Global Ills." UN news, http://un.org/apps/news/ticker/, 23 December 2003; Republican Jim Gibbons is discussed in Sheryl Gay Stolberg, "Ease a Little Guilt, Provide Some Jobs; It's Pork on the Hill," New York Times (20 December 2003), http://nytimes.com.

2. Robert Dahl, *Modern Political Analysis* (Englewood Cliffs, NJ: Prentice Hall, 1963), p. vii.

3. David Easton, *The Political System: An Inquiry into the State of Political Science* (Chicago: University of Chicago Press, 1971), p. 42; see also Howard J. Wiarda, *Introduction to Comparative Politics* (Belmont, CA: Wadsworth, 1993), p. 12.

4. John McCormick, *Comparative Politics in Transition* (New York: Wadsworth, 1995), p. 3.

5. Harold D. Lasswell, *Politics: Who Gets What, When, How* (New York: Meridian Books, 1958), p. 13; see also p. 167.

6. Aristotle, *Politics of Aristotle,* trans. and introd. Ernest Barker (New York: Oxford University Press, 1973), p. 6.

7. Dahl, p. 6. See also E. E. Schattschneider, *Two Hundred Million Americans in Search of a Government* (New York: Holt, Rinehart and Winston, 1969), p. 4, for a discussion of the universality of politics and political institutions.

## Chapter 2

1. Hugh R. Slotten, "Humane Chemistry or Scientific Barbarism? American Responses to World War I Poison Gas, 1915–1930," *The Journal of American History* 77 (September 1990): 476–498.

2. See, for instance, the discussion in David Easton, *The Political System: An Inquiry into the State of Political Science* (Chicago: University of Chicago Press, 1971), p. 3.

3. Many works discuss these various historical developments. See James Farr, "Francis Lieber and the Interpretation of American Political Science," *Journal of Politics* 52 (November 1990): 1027–1049; Gabriel Almond,

"Political Theory and Political Science," *American Political Science Review* (December 1966): 869; Bernard Susser, "From Burgess to Behavioralism and Beyond," in *Approaches to the Study of Politics,* edited by Susser (New York: Macmillan, 1992), p. 3; Wilfred M. McClay, introd. by John W. Burgess, *The Foundations of Political Science* (New Brunswick, NJ: Transaction Publishers, 1994), pp. viii–ix; Albert Somit and Joseph Tanenhaus, "Trends in American Political Science: Some Analytical Notes," *American Political Science Review* 57 (December 1963): 934.

4. Somit and Tanenhaus, p. 934.

5. American Political Science Association, APSA Member Services (http://www.apsanet.org/membership/member2.html); David M. Ricci, *The Tragedy of Political Science: Politics, Scholarship, and Democracy* (New Haven, CT: Yale University Press, 1984), p. 8.

6. See the discussion of political science as a profession in Samuel P. Huntington, "One Soul at a Time: Political Science and Political Reform," *American Political Science Review* 82 (March 1988): 3.

7. Frank J. Goodnow, "The Work of the American Political Science Association," in *Proceedings of the American Political Science Association, Chicago, Ill. December 28–30, 1940* (Lancaster, PA: Wickersham Press, 1905), p. 37.

8. For discussions of the traditionalist perspective, see Alan C. Isaak, *Scope and Methods of Political Science* (Pacific Grove, CA: Brooks/Cole, 1985), pp. 34–38; Roy C. Macridis, "Major Characteristics of the Traditional Approach," in Susser, ed., pp. 16–26; Gregory M. Scott and Stephen M. Garrison, *The Political Science Student Writer's Manual* (Englewood Cliffs, NJ: Prentice Hall, 1995), pp. 9–12; Leon Hurwitz, *Introduction to Politics: Traditionalism to Postbehavioralism: Theory and Practice* (Chicago: Nelson-Hall, 1979), p. 127; Lois D. Hayes and Ronald D. Hedlund, "The Conduct of Political Inquiry: An Overview," in *The Conduct of Political Inquiry: Behavioral Political Analysis,* edited by Hayes and Hedlund (Englewood Cliffs, NJ: Prentice Hall, 1970), pp. 4–6.

9. Robert A. Dahl, "The Behavioral Approach in Political Science: Epitaph for a Monument to a Successful Protest," in Susser, ed., pp. 27–28; Avery Leiserson, "Charles Merriam, Max Weber, and the Search for Synthesis in Political Science," *American Political Science Review* 69 (March 1975): 176; and Heinz Eulau, "Political Science," in *A Reader's Guide to the Social Sciences,* edited by Bert F. Hoselitz (Glencoe, IL: Free Press, 1959), p. 107.

10. Behavioralism is one of most widely discussed areas of political science. Useful introductory surveys include Joseph Dunner, ed., *Dictionary of Political Science* (Totowa, NJ: Littlefield, Adams., 1970), pp. 46–47; Isaak, pp. 38–44; David Easton, "The Current Meaning of Behavioralism," in Susser, ed., pp. 47–48; Dennis Kavanagh, *Political Science and Political Behavior* (Boston: Allen & Unwin), Chapter 1; Hurwitz, pp. 122–233; Hayes and Hedlund, pp. 7–19. See also John Gunnell, *The Descent of Political Theory: The Genealogy of an American Vocation* (Chicago: University of Chicago, 1993), especially Chapters 1 and 10.

11. Harry Eckstein, *Regarding Politics: Essays on Political Theory, Stability, and Change* (Berkeley: University of California Press, 1992), p. 5.

12. Mary Hawkesworth, "The Science of Politics and the Politics of Science," in *Encyclopedia of Government and Politics,* edited by Hawkesworth and Maurice Kogan (New York: Routledge, 1992), p. 34.

13. See the discussion of empiricism in Carl G. Hempel, "The Empiricist Criterion of Meaning," in *Logical Positivism,* edited by A. J. Ayer (New York: Free Press, 1959), pp. 108–129.

14. See Elinor Ostrom, "Beyond Positivism," in *Strategies of Political Inquiry* (Beverly Hills, CA: Sage, 1982), p. 14, for a discussion of the historical perspective of many political science studies. See also Roger Benjamin, "The Historical Nature of Social Scientific Knowledge: The Case of Comparative Political Inquiry," pp. 69–98 in the same book.

15. Hurwitz, pp. 148–149; Dahl, pp. 40–41; Easton, "The Current Meaning of Behavioralism," p. 47.

16. David Easton, "The New Revolution in Political Science," *American Political Science Review* 63 (December 1969): 1051–1061. Students can find this essay

reprinted in abbreviated form in Susser, ed., pp. 49–50.

17. Ibid. See also Hurwitz, pp. 236–238; Hawkesworth, p. 34; Sheldon S. Wolin, "Political Theory as a Vocation," *American Political Science Review* 63 (December 1969): 1063.

18. Easton, "The New Revolution in Political Science," p. 1053.

19. Lucius J. Barker, "Limits of Political Strategy: A Systematic View of the African American Political Experience," *American Political Science Review* 88 (March 1994): 10–11.

20. David M. Ricci, *The Tragedy of Political Science* (New Haven, CT: Yale University Press, 1984), p. 24. On the variety of perspectives following the traditionalist–behavioralist–postbehavioralist debates, see Ruth Lane, "Concrete Theory: An Emerging Political Method," *American Political Science Review* 84 (September 1990): 927.

21. Albert Einstein and Leopold Infeld, *The Evolution of Physics: The Growth of Ideas from Early Concepts to Relativity and Quanta* (New York: Simon & Schuster, 1952), preface.

22. Ibid.

23. John Ziman, "What Is Science?" in *Introductory Readings in the Philosophy of Science,* edited by E. D. Klemke, Robert Hollinger, and A. David Kline (Buffalo, NY: Prometheus, 1980), p. 35.

24. Philip E. Converse, "Power and the Monopoly of Information," *American Political Science Review* 79 (March 1985): 2.

25. Students may find excellent discussions of hypothesis formulation and the scientific method in general in Louise G. White, *Political Analysis: Technique and Practice,* 3rd ed. (Belmont, CA: Wadsworth, 1994), pp. 38–39; Thomas R. Dye, *Power & Society: An Introduction to the Social Sciences,* 7th ed. (Belmont, CA: Wadsworth, 1996), Chapter 2.

26. G. David Garson, *Political Science Methods* (Boston: Holbrook, 1976), p. 118.

27. See, for example, White's discussion on p. 146.

28. See Paul S. Herrnson, "Replication, Verification, Secondary Analysis, and Data Collection in Political Science," *PS: Political Science & Politics* 28 (September 1995): 452.

For testing involving counterfactuals, see James D. Fearon, "Counterfactuals and Hypothesis Testing in Political Science," *World Politics* 43 (January 1991): 169–195.

29. George C. Homans, *The Nature of Social Science* (New York: Harbinger, 1967), p. 18.

30. Duncan MacRae, Jr., "The Science of Politics and Its Limits," in *Political Science: The Science of Politics,* edited by Herbert F. Weisberg (New York: Agathon, 1986), p. 26.

31. W. Phillips Shively, *The Craft of Political Research,* 3rd ed. (Englewood Cliffs, NJ: Prentice Hall, 1990), p. 15.

32. James N. Rosenau, *The Dramas of Politics: An Introduction to the Joys of Inquiry* (Boston: Little, Brown, 1973), pp. 164–165.

33. Thomas R. Dye, "Politics, Economics and the Public: Looking Back," in *Political Scientists at Work,* edited by Oliver Walter (Belmont, CA: Duxbury, 1971), p. 145.

34. Ibid.

35. See Maurice Cranston, "Francis Bacon," in *Encyclopedia of Philosophy,* Vol. 1, edited by Paul Edwards (New York: Macmillan and Free Press, 1972), pp. 235–240.

36. See Ida Husted Harper, *The Life and Work of Susan B. Anthony,* Vol. 1 (Indianapolis, IN: Hollenbeck, 1898), p. 90.

37. Stephen Jay Gould discusses Haeckel and other writers in *Ever since Darwin: Reflections in Natural History* (New York: Norton, 1977), pp. 217–218. See also Stephen Jay Gould, *The Mismeasure of Man* (New York: Norton, 1981), Chapter 4.

38. Students may consult a variety of works discussing case studies. See, for instance, Dunner, p. 80; Isaak, p. 35; White, p. 28; Frank L. Wilson, *Concepts and Issues in Comparative Politics: An Introduction to Comparative Analysis* (Upper Saddle River, NJ: Prentice Hall, 1996), p. 7; M. Lal Goel, *Political Science Research: A Methods Handbook* (Ames: Iowa State University Press, 1988), p. 62. On the limits of the case study approach, see Karen L. Remmer, "New Theoretical Perspectives on Democratization" [review article], *Comparative Politics* 28 (October 1995): 107.

39. See Howard Wiarda, *Introduction to Comparative Politics* (New York: Harcourt, 1993), p. 88; Howard Wiarda, *Politics in*

*Iberia: The Political System of Spain and Portugal* (New York: HarperCollins, 1993), pp. 78–79.

40. For discussions of this episode, see Barbara Ryan, *Feminism and the Women's Movement: Dynamics of Change in Social Movement, Ideology and Activism* (New York: Routledge, 1992), p. 43; Susan Gluck Mezey, *In Pursuit of Equality: Women, Public Policy, and the Federal Courts* (New York: St. Martin's, 1992), pp. 36–38.

41. This incident is discussed in Alan R. Gitelson, Robert C. Dudley, and Melvin J. Dubnick, *American Government* (Boston: Houghton Mifflin, 1993), p. 254.

42. For more detailed discussions of these and other aspects of survey research, see White, pp. 183–198; Garson, pp. 177–187; Goel, Chapter 4.

43. Denise L. Baer, "Political Parties: The Missing Variable in Women and Politics Research," *Political Research Quarterly* 46 (September 1993): 547–576.

44. Ibid.

45. White, pp. 193–194.

46. Sharon Begley with Howard Fineman and Vernon Church, "The Science of Polling," *Newsweek* (28 September 1992): 38.

47. Daniel Goleman, "Pollsters Enlist Psychologists in Quest for Unbiased Results," *New York Times* (7 September 1993), pp. B5, B8.

48. Ibid., p. B8.

49. See *The World Almanac and Book of Facts, 1994,* edited by Robert Farrighetti (Mahwah, NJ: Funk & Wagnalls, 1993), p. 975.

50. See Sam Roberts, "Private Opinions on Public Opinion: Question Is, What Is the Question," *New York Times* (21 August 1994): E7.

51. Jerry L. Yeric and John R. Todd, *Public Opinion: The Visible Politics,* 3rd ed. (Itasca, IL: Peacock, 1996), pp. 229, 232–233.

52. See the discussion in ibid., pp. 245–250.

53. Experiments and quasi-experiments are discussed in White, Chapter 5; Shiveley, pp. 86–90; Barry Anderson, "The Social Science Experiment," in Hayes and Hedlund, eds., pp. 127–132; Goel, Chapter 3.

The Zimbardo Prison Experiment is discussed in Goel, pp. 53–55. Negative campaign ads are discussed in Stephen Ansolabehere, Roy Behr, and Shanto Iyengar, *The Media Game: American Politics in the Television Age* (New York: Macmillan, 1993), pp. 180–183; see also Stephen Ansolabehere, Shanto Iyengar, Adam Simon, and Nicholas Valentino, "Does Attack Advertising Demobilize the Electorate?" *American Political Science Review* 88 (December 1994): 829–838.

54. Goal, pp. 46–48.

55. White, p. 115.

56. See White's work for a detailed discussion and explanation, pp. 182, 242–257.

57. Peter Menzel, *Material World: A Global Family Portrait,* introd. Paul Kennedy and text by Charles C. Mann (San Francisco, CA: Sierra Club Books, 1994). It is important to note that the indirect quantitative analysis was supplemented by extensive interviews with family members in the 30 countries. Kennedy's comments are found on p. 8.

58. Wilson, p. 6.

59. Stephen Jay Gould, "Asking Big Questions on Science and Meaning" [book review], *New York Times* (16 October 1995): B2.

60. Natalie Angier, "Flyspeck on a Lobster Lip Turns Biology on Its Ear," *New York Times* (14 December 1995): A1, A18.

61. William H. Honan, "Professor Writing of Aliens Is under Inquiry at Harvard," *New York Times* (4 May 1995): A9. See also Walter Goodman, "Abductions by Aliens: What People Remember," *New York Times* (27 February 1996): B3.

62. Daniel Goleman, "Brain May Tag a Value to Every Perception," *New York Times* (8 August 1995): B5, B9. See also George Johnson, "The Spies' Code and How It Broke," *New York Times* (16 July 1995): A16, on the difficulty of being random and how this has made it possible to break spy codes.

63. Morris R. Cohen, "Reason in Social Science," in *Readings in the Philosophy of Science,* edited by Herbert Feigl and May Brodbeck (New York: Appleton-Century-Crofts, 1953), pp. 663–664; Alan Wolfe, "Understanding Society: Realism and Romanticism in Sociology," *Current* 372 (May 1995): 20–27. For a statement on this problem of

nonrepeatability in the natural sciences, see Alan Lightman, "Uncertainty Principle," *Technology Review* (April 1996): 35–40.

64. "And Here Is Your Next President," *The Economist* (December 23 1995–January 5 1996): 31–33.

65. See the excellent discussion of Charles Taylor, "Neutrality in Political Science," in *Philosophy of Social Explanation,* edited by Alan Ryan (New York: Oxford University Press, 1973), p. 142.

66. Hawkesworth discusses the problems with empiricism, pp. 14–34.

67. Dye, "Politics, Economics, and the Public," p. 146.

68. Many political scientists have worried that political science has become less interesting as it has become more scientific and have argued that the discipline probably has less to say to citizens about what actually concerns them than it had before becoming so empirically oriented. See Ricci, Gunnell, and the discussion of this body of critical work in John S. Dryzek and Stephen T. Leonard, "History and Discipline in Political Science," *American Political Science Review* 82 (December 1988): especially 1250–1252.

69. See, for example, the discussion in Miriam Feldblum, "The Study of Politics: What Does Replicability Have to Do with It?" *PS: Political Science and Politics* 29 (March 1996): 7–9.

70. See the brief discussion of the secondary literature on Pasteur in Robert J. P. Hauck, "Oh Monsieur Pasteur, We Hardly Knew You!" *PS: Political Science and Politics* 28 (September 1995): 443.

71. Kuhn, *The Structure of Scientific Revolutions* (Chicago: University of Chicago, 1970), pp. 77–78, is especially helpful in discussing this point.

72. Paul Feyerabend, "How to Defend Society against Science," in *Introductory Readings in the Philosophy of Science,* edited by E. D. Klemke, Robert Hollinger, and A. David Kline (Buffalo, NY: Prometheus, 1980), pp. 55–65.

73. Larry D. Spence, *The Politics of Social Knowledge* (University Park: Pennsylvania State University Press, 1978), p. 22.

74. See, for example, the way in which the director of the National Science Foundation

poses this question in *Quotable Quotes* " … Science and Values …" NSF Director Neal Lane at National Press Club, April 22, 1997 (http://www.nsf.gov/od/lpa/news/media/ qvalues.htm, accessed 10 March 1998).

75. See Roberts.

76. This example and others like it are discussed in Christopher Hitchens, "Voting in the Passive Voice: What Polling Has Done to American Democracy," *Harper's* (April 1992): 45–52.

77. This study and the ethical questions it raises are superbly discussed in James H. Jones, *Bad Blood: The Tuskegee Syphilis Experiment* (New York: Free Press, 1993); see also Jean Heller, "Syphilis Victims in U.S. Study Went Untreated for 40 Years," *New York Times* (26 July 1972): 1, 8.

78. RealAudio: *National Public Radio's May 15, 1997 Talk of the Nation* (http://www. realaudio.com/contentp/npr/ne7M15.html, accessed 11 March 1998).

79. Keith Schneider, "Cold War Radiation Test on Humans to Undergo a Congressional Review," *New York Times* (11 April 1994): A12; Philip J. Hilts, "Secret Radioactive Experiments to Bring Compensation by U.S." *New York Times* (20 November 1996): A1, A11.

## Chapter 3

1. On the U'wa struggle, see Paul Jeffrey, "U'wa vs. 'Oxy,'" *National Catholic Reporter* (8 September 2000): 13–14.

2. See Robert A. Dahl, *Modern Political Analysis* (Englewood Cliffs, NJ: Prentice Hall, 1964), Chapter 5; W. Phillips Shively, *Power and Choice: An Introduction to Political Science,* 4th ed. (New York: McGraw-Hill, 1995), pp. 6–13.

3. Probably all definitions and discussions of power are, ultimately, less than fully adequate, capturing some of the dynamics of power while failing to articulate others. For an idea of how social scientists disagree on how best to conceptualize power, consult Steven Lukes, *Power: A Radical View* (New York: Macmillan, 1979), in which the author assesses alternative definitions of power; see also the discussion in Keith M. Dowding, *Rational Choice and Political Power* (Brookfield, VT: Elgar, 1991), Chapter 1, and the articles

in John Scott, ed., *Power: Critical Concepts,* Vol. 2 (New York: Routledge, 1994).

4. William E. Connolly, *The Terms of Political Discourse* (Lexington, MA: Heath, 1974), pp. 86–87 makes this distinction relative to the two reaches of power (obtaining an end versus influencing an agent) and elaborates on its importance. See also Dowding, who distinguishes between power as the (a) ability to produce an effect and (b) the ability to change the decision making of others, pp. 2, 47–48. See also Kenneth E. Boulding, *Three Faces of Power* (New York: Sage, 1989), Chapter 1, and Kent Brudney, "Power," in *Political Concepts: An Introduction,* edited by David A. Freeman (Dubuque, IA: Kendall/Hunt, 1994), p. 26, wherein the author distinguishes between power as obtaining something desired and power as using other people to get something desired.

5. Students may consult Brian Fay, *Critical Social Science: Liberation and Its Limits* (Ithaca, NY: Cornell University Press, 1987), p. 120, for an analysis of power conceptualizing power as what is exercised over another agent, compelling the second agent to act in a manner contrary to the second agent's choice.

6. Jeffrey Isaac discusses this point along with several other dimensions of power in "Conceptions of Power," *Encyclopedia of Government and Politics,* Vol. 1, edited by Mary Hawkesworth and Maurice Kogan (New York: Routledge, 1992), p. 56.

7. See *The Compact Edition of the Oxford English Dictionary* (1971).

8. Numerous social scientists have pointed to the importance of this dimension of power. Students may wish to read the accounts in Dahl, *Modern Political Analysis,* p. 40, as well as Dennis H. Wrong, *Power: Its Forms, Bases, and Uses* (Chicago: University of Chicago, 1988), pp. 2–5; James MacGregor Burns, "Wellsprings of Political Leadership," *American Political Science Review* 71 (March 1977): 273; and Connolly, pp. 93–94; Douglas W. Rae, "Knowing Power: A Working Paper," in *Power, Inequality, and Democratic Politics: Essays in Honor of Robert A. Dahl* (Boulder, CO: Westview, 1988), p. 40, in which Rae discusses power as knowingly bringing about a willed change. See also Kenneth B. Clark, *Pathos of Power* (New York: Harper Torchbooks, 1973), p. 77. For a contrasting view,

which denies that power exists only when it is known by and willed by the power holder, see Hugh V. McLachlan, "Is 'Power' an Evaluative Concept?" in Scott, p. 319; Lukes, *Power: A Radical View.*

9. Wrong discusses this aspect of power, pp. 6–10.

10. Wrong, pp. 92–93.

11. For discussions of force, see also Boulding, pp. 25–27, in which he discusses threats in terms of physical means of deploying power; Wrong discusses force, pp. 24–28.

12. Martin Luther King, Jr., "Letter from Birmingham Jail," in *Ideals and Ideologies: A Reader,* edited by Terrence Ball and Richard Dagger (New York: HarperCollins, 1991), see especially pp. 319–320 and 321–323.

13. See Sylvia Alicia Gonzales, *Hispanic American Voluntary Organizations* (Westport, CT: Praeger, 1985), pp. 209–214; Eugene Nelson, *Huelga: The First Hundred Days of the Great Delano Grape Strike* (Delano, CA: Farm Worker Press, 1966).

14. Margaret Rose, "Dolores Huerta," in *Notable Hispanic American Women,* edited by Diane Telgen and Jim Kamp (Detroit, MI: Gale Research, 1993), pp. 210–214.

15. *Narrative of the Life of Henry Box Brown Written by Himself,* introd. Richard Newman (New York: Oxford University Press, 2002).

16. Paul Lewis, "Nigeria's Deadly Oil War: Shell Defends Its Record," *New York Times* (13 February 1996): A1, A4; "After the Hangings," *The Economist* (18 November 1995): 41; Joshua Hammer, "Letter from Nigeria: Nigeria Crude," *Harper's Magazine* (June 1996): 58–70.

17. Saul D. Alinsky, *Rules for Radicals* (New York: Vintage, 1971), p. 138.

18. Wrong, pp. 32–34.

19. See Charles A. Madison preface to Jacob Riis, *How the Other Half Lives* (New York: Dover, 1971).

20. Lizette Alvarez, "Iranian Lawyer, Staunch Fighter for Human Rights, Wins Nobel," *New York Times* (11 October 2003): A1, A6; "She Is Very Brave," *Time* (20 October 2003): 39; Karl Vick, "Big Prize, Little Change," *Washington Post* (4 November 2003): A19.

21. See the discussion in Wrong, pp. 28–32, and Fay, p. 121.

22. Wrong, p. 30.

23. Lawrence R. Jacobs and Robert Y. Shapiro, "Presidential Manipulation of Polls and Public Opinion: The Nixon Administration and the Pollsters," *Political Science Quarterly* 110 (Winter 1995–1996): http://epu.org/psnixo.html.

24. Ibid.

25. Jeff Shear discusses the Domenici incident in "Can-Do Domenici," *National Journal* 27 (10 June 1995): 1394–1397; and the leak is discussed in Susan Welch et al., *Understanding American Government* (Los Angeles: West, 1991), p. 191.

26. Keith Bradsher, "Sugar Price Supports Survive Political Shift," *New York Times* (9 September 1995): A1, A5.

27. See, for example, Harry Allen, "Local Candidates' Announcement: Manipulation Is Avoidable," *Editor and Publisher* 126 (30 October 1993): 36, 44.

28. "Teaching Self-Image Stirs Furor," *New York Times* (13 October 1993): B8.

29. See the discussions in Adrienne Rich, "Compulsory Heterosexuality and Lesbian Existence," *Signs* 5 (1980): 631–660; Herbert G. Reid, ed., *Up the Mainstream: A Critique of Ideology in American Politics and Everyday Life* (New York: McKay, 1974); see the articles in Paula S. Rothenberg, *Race, Class, and Gender in the United States: An Integrated Study* (New York: St. Martin's, 1995) for an overview of supporters and critics of such perspectives.

30. Exchange power is discussed in Boulding, pp. 27–28; Charles E. Lindblom, *Politics and Markets: The World's Political Economic Systems* (New York: Basic Books, 1977), Chapter 3; and Lindblom, "The Market as Prison," in *Voices of Dissent: Critical Readings in American Politics* (New York: Harper-Collins, 1993), pp. 16–23.

31. Christopher Torcha, "Afghan Farmers Get Cash as Poppy Crops Destroyed," *Albuquerque Journal* (11 April 2002): A9; U.S. State Department, Fact Sheet: USAID Programs for Economic and Social development in Colombia, March 13, 2001, http://www.ciponline.org/colombia; Michael Wines, "Leasing, if not Building an Anti-Taliban Coalition," *New York Times* (18 November 2001): 3; "Six Plus Two Group Stresses Need for Broad-Based Afghan Government," *UN News Service* (12 November 2003).

32. Tony Horwitz, "Going Nowhere: Boomtowns Lure Poor with Plenty of Work–But Not Much Else," *Wall Street Journal* (16 June 1994): A1, A6.

33. Keith Schneider, "Plan for Toxic Dump Pits Blacks against Blacks," *New York Times* (13 December 1993): A7.

34. See Lindblom, "The Market as Prison," and Boulding, pp. 27–28.

35. See the analysis by Michel Foucault in Michael Walzer, *The Company of Critics* (New York: Basic Books, 1988); Timothy Lukes, *Screens of Power: Ideology, Domination, and Resistance in Informational Society* (Urbana: University of Illinois Press, 1989); Stephen David Ross, "Power, Discourse, and Technology: The Presence of the Future," in *After the Future: Postmodern Times and Places*, edited by Gary Shapiro (Albany: State University of New York Press, 1990), pp. 262–264.

36. Clifford J. Levy and William K. Rashbaum, "Bush and Top Aids Proclaim Policy of 'Ending' States That Back Terror; An Arrest Shuts New York Airports," *New York Times* (14 September 2001): A1.

37. Discussions of the concept of the state include Joseph Dunner, ed., *Dictionary of Political Science* (Totowa, NJ: Littlefield, Adams, 1970), p. 498; Dahl, *Modern Political Analysis*, pp. 12–13; Gerald C. MacCallum, *Political Philosophy* (Englewood Cliffs, NJ: Prentice Hall, 1987), pp. 37, 68; Lewis W. Snider, "Identifying the Elements of State Power: Where Do We Begin?" *Comparative Political Studies* 20 (October 1987): 319; Ted Robert Gurr, "War, Revolution, and the Growth of the Coercive State," *Comparative Political Studies* 21 (April 1988): 47–48; Bertrand Badie and Pierre Birnbaum, *The Sociology of the State*, trans. Arthur Goldhammer (Chicago: University of Chicago, 1983), pp. 135–137; Mark Juergensmeyer, "The New Religious States," *Comparative Politics* 27 (July 1995): 383; Stephen R. Graubard, ed., *The State* (New York: Norton, 1979).

38. Discussions of the three organizational types can be found in Alan R. Ball, *Modern Politics and Government*, 5th ed. (Chatham,

NJ: Chatham House, 1993), pp. 51–52; Frank L. Wilson, *Concepts and Issues in Comparative Politics: An Introduction to Comparative Analysis* (Upper Saddle River, NJ: Prentice Hall, 1996), pp. 160–164; Jurg Steiner, *European Democracies*, 4th ed. (New York: Longman, 1998), pp. 112–117.

39. John L. Allen, *Student Atlas of World Politics* (Guilford, CT: Dushkin, 1994), pp. 16–17.

40. For overviews of state formation and evolution in individual countries, students may consult William E. Leuchtenburg, "The Pertinence of Political History: Reflections on the Significance of the State in America," *Journal of American History* 73 (December 1986): 590; and Gary B. Nash et al., *The American People: Creating a Nation and a Society,* Vol. 1 (New York: Harper & Row, 1986), p. 526.

41. Robert Gilpin, *The Political Economy of International Relations* (Princeton, NJ: Princeton University Press, 1987), pp. 231–232.

42. Terry Collingsworth, J. William Goold, and Pharis J. Harvey, "Time for a Global New Deal," *Foreign Affairs* 73 (January 1994): 8–13.

43. Ibid.

44. Lindblom, *Politics and Markets,* p. 356; see also the debates outlined in Richard Newfarmer, "Multinationals and Marketplace Magic in the 1980s," in *The Political Economy of Development and Underdevelopment*, 3rd ed, edited by Charles K. Wilber (New York: Random House, 1984); Robert J. Samuelson, "The Multicultural Corporation," *Washington Post* (23 August 1989): A27; Hobart Rowen and Jodie T. Allen, "Brave New World, Inc.," *Washington Post* (19 March 1989): C1, C4; "The Shape of the World. The Nation-State Is Dead. Long Live the Nation-State," *Economist* (23 December–5 January 1996): 15–18; "The Myth of the Powerless State," *Economist* (7 October 1995): 15–16; Phillip M. Rosenzweig and Nitin Nohria, "Influences on Human Resources Management Practices in Multinational Corporations," *Journal of International Business Studies* 25 (1994): 229–251; Yao-Su Hu, "Global or Stateless Corporations Are National Firms with International Operations," *California*

*Management Review* 34 (Winter 1995): 107–126.

45. Kenneth A. Rodman, "Sanctions at Bay? Hegemonic Decline, Multinational Corporations, and U.S. Economic Sanctions since the Pipeline Case," *International Organization* 49 (Winter 1995): 122.

46. Farouk Mawlawi, "New Conflicts, New Challenges: The Evolving Role for Non-Governmental Actors," *Journal of International Affairs* 46 (Winter 1993): 391–413.

47. Paul Wapner, "Politics beyond the State: Environmental Activism and World Civic Politics," *World Politics* 47 (April 1995): 311–340.

48. United Nations Press Release SG/SM/5829, "UN-AIDS Initiative Will Strengthen, Expand Response to Pandemic, Says Secretary-General, in World Aids Day Message" (30 November 1995), available on the Internet on the UN's press release page (http://www.un.org/plweb-cgi/iopcode.pl).

49. United Nations Press Release H/2903, "World Health Organization Says Tuberculosis Deaths Reach Historic Levels" (22 March 1996), available at the press release page cited in note 52.

50. J. P. Nettl, "The State as a Conceptual Variable," in *The State: Critical Concepts,* Vol. 1, edited by John A. Hall (New York: Routledge, 1994), p. 24, discusses the difference between a state and sovereignty.

51. Robert H. Jackson and Carl G. Roseberg, "Why Africa's Weak States Persist: The Empirical and Juridical in Statehood," in *The State: Critical Concepts,* Vol. 2, edited by John A. Hall (New York: Routledge, 1994), p. 270.

52. Ibid., see the authors' conclusions regarding the absence of an effective state in territories in sub-Saharan Africa on p. 281.

53. For discussions of how culture has been defined by social scientists, see Glen Gendzel, "Political Culture: Genealogy of a Concept," *Journal of Interdisciplinary History* 28 (Autumn 1997): 225; Robert W. Jackman and Ross A. Miller, "A Renaissance of Political Culture," *American Journal of Political Science* 40 (August 1996): 653.

54. See Robert D. Putnam et al., "Explaining Institutional Success: The Case of Italian Regional Government," *American Political*

*Science Review* 77 (March 1983): 56, 65: Robert D. Putnam, *Making Democracy Work: Civic Traditions in Modern Italy* (Princeton, NJ: Princeton University Press, 1993), p. 182; Sidney Tarrow, "Making Social Science Work across Space and Time: A Critical Reflection on Robert Putnam's *Making Democracy Work*," *American Political Science Review* 90 (June 1996): 389–390; Robert W. Jackman and Ross A. Miller, "The Poverty of Political Culture," *American Journal of Political Science* 40 (August 1996): 697–716; Duane Swank, "Culture, Institutions, and Economic Growth: Theory, Recent Evidence, and the Role of Communitarian Politics," *American Journal of Political Science* 40 (August 1996): 660–679.

55. Ronald A. Inglehart and Paul R. Abramson, "Economic Security and Value Change," *American Political Science Review* 88 (June 1994): 336–354; Robert D. Brown and Edward G. Carmines, "Materialists, Postmaterialists, and the Criteria for Political Choice in U.S. Presidential Elections," *Journal of Politics* 57 (May 1995): 483–494.

56. Jeffrey W. Legro, "Culture and Preferences in the International Cooperation Two-Step," *American Political Science Review* 90 (March 1996): 118–137.

57. John S. Duffield, "Political Culture and State Behavior: Why Germany Confounds Neorealism," *International Organization* 53 (Autumn 1999): 764.

58. See the discussions by Jackman and Miller, "The Poverty of Political Culture"; Tarrow; Rodney E. Hero and Caroline J. Tolbert, "A Racial/Ethnic Diversity Interpretation of Politics and Policy in the States of the U.S.," *American Journal of Political Science* 40 (August 1996): 851–871. See also Putnam's discussion of the complexity of culture, state, and structure relations in *Making Democracy Work*, pp. 180–181, and his comments in which he distances himself from Inglehart (and others) in Alexander Stille, "An Old Key to Why Countries Get Rich," *New York Times* (13 January 2001): A19.

59. James N. Rosenau, "The Relocation of Authority in a Shrinking World," *Comparative Politics* (April 1990): 253–272.

60. In addition to Rosenau's work, see the essays in *Contending Sovereignties: Redefining Political Community,* edited by R. B. J.

Walker and Saul H. Mendlovitz (Boulder, CO: Rienner, 1990), and David Maybury-Lewis, "Tribal Wisdom," *Utne Reader* (July–August 1992): 68–79.

61. See the excellent analysis of Walker Conner, "A Nation Is a Nation, Is a State, Is an Ethnic Group, Is a ..." in *Nationalism,* edited by John Hutchinson and Anthony D. Smith (New York: Oxford University Press, 1994), pp. 36–46.

62. Terrence Ball and Richard Dagger, *Political Ideologies and the Democratic Ideal* (New York: HarperCollins, 1991), p. 18.

63. On the difficulties and ambiguities in definitions and perceptions of nation and nationalism, see Dan Smith "Reconciling Identities in Conflict," in *Europe's New Nationalism: States and Minorities in Conflict,* edited by Richard Caplan and John Feffer (New York: Oxford University Press, 1996), especially pp. 200–201.

64. Ben Halpern, "Zionism," in David Sills, ed., *International Encyclopedia of the Social Sciences,* Vol. 17 (New York: Macmillan and Free Press, 1968), pp. 593–598.

65. For a discussion of the language act, see Michael Macmillan, "Quebec," in *Contemporary Minority Nationalism,* edited by Michael Watson (New York: Routledge, 1990), pp. 117–134; developments on nationalist referendum processes are discussed by Clyde H. Farnsworth, "Canada Holds Its Breath as Quebec Votes," *New York Times* (31 October 1995): A7; Christopher S. Wren, "Quebec's Separatists Unlikely to Seek a New Vote Soon," *New York Times* (4 November 1995): A4; Clyde H. Farnsworth, "Ottawa Moves Quickly in Effort to Mollify Quebec," *New York Times* (2 November 1995): A3.

66. "The Balkan Conflict: Where Things Stand," *New York Times* (3 August 1995): A4; Leonard J. Cohen, "The Disintegration of Yugoslavia," *Current History* (November 1992): 369–375; Michael G. Roskin, *The Rebirth of East Europe,* 2nd ed. (Englewood Cliffs, NJ: Prentice Hall, 1994).

67. See the discussion in Edward Dolnick, "Deafness as Culture," *Atlantic Monthly* (September 1993): 37–53. Although some leaders in the movement use the phrase *deaf culture* (rather than deaf nation), their self-descriptions resemble those of nationalist

groups whose nationalism is rooted in ethnicity. Indeed, they repeatedly compare their position to that of Russians, Italian-Americans, African-Americans, and other nationalist subgroups. Perhaps the most striking indicator of nationalism is the response of the community to calls for cures; that they define such using the language of genocide is a compelling indicator of the nationalist identity of the deaf culture movement.

68. Phillip Gourevitch, "The Poisoned Country," *New York Review of Books* (6 June 1996): 58–64; Donatella Lorch, "Now, Rwanda's Neighbor Hovers Near the Brink," *New York Times* (3 February 1995): A3; Donatella Lorch, "Ethnic Hate Tears Pupils in Burundi," *New York Times* (13 February 1995): A6.

69. Chinua Achebe, *Things Fall Apart* (New York: Fawcett Crest, 1959), p. 162.

70. Mark R. Amstutz, *International Conflict and Cooperation: An Introduction to World Politics* (Chicago: Brown and Benchmark, 1995), pp. 30–31.

71. John McCormick, *Comparative Politics in Transition* (New York: Wadsworth, 1995), Chapter 6; Ashis Nandy, "The Politics of Secularism and the Recovery of Religious Tolerance," in *Contending Sovereignties,* edited by Walker and Mendlovitz, pp. 125–144; Juergensmeyer, pp. 385–387.

72. The pros and cons of conceptualizing gays as a nation are discussed in Charles Fernandez, "Undocumented Aliens in the Queer Nation," *OUT/LOOK* 3 (Spring 1991): 20–23.

73. African-American nationalism is examined in relation to the Nation of Islam in *The Autobiography of Malcolm X* (New York: Grove Press, 1965); Lewis Lord, Jeannye Thornton, and Alejandro Bodipo-Memba, "The Legacy of Malcolm X," *U.S. News & World Report* (23 November 1992): 76–84; see also the discussion in Errol Henderson, "Black Nationalism and Rap Music," *Journal of Black Studies* 26 (January 1996): 308–339.

74. C. Vann Woodward discusses the issue of Southern distinctiveness in "The Search for Southern Identity," in *Myth and Southern History,* edited by Patrick Gerster and Nicholas Cords (Chicago: Rand McNally, 1974), pp. 137–150.

75. Compare the conceptualizations of nations and nationalism found, for example, in W. Phillips Shively, *Power and Choice: An Introduction to Political Science,* 3rd ed. (New York: McGraw-Hill, 1993), pp. 27–33; James N. Danzinger, *Understanding the Political World: A Comparative Introduction to Political Science* (New York: Longman, 1996), pp. 135–142; Hans Kohn, *Nationalism: Its Meaning and History* (Princeton, NJ: Van Nostrand, 1955), p. 9; Michael Watson, *Introduction to Contemporary Minority Nationalism,* p. 2; Kendall W. Stiles, *Case Histories in International Politics* (New York: Harper-Collins, 1995), p. 257.

76. Andrew Bell-Fialkoff, "A Brief History of Ethnic Cleansing," *Foreign Affairs* (Summer 1993): 110–121.

77. Ibid.

## Chapter 4

1. Plato's background is discussed in William T. Bluhm, *Theories of the Political System,* 3rd ed. (Englewood Cliffs, NJ: Prentice Hall, 1978), pp. 24–39, and Gilbert Ryle, "Plato" and D. A. Rees, "Platonism and the Platonic Tradition" in *The Encyclopedia of Philosophy,* Vols. 5 and 6, edited by Paul Edwards (New York: Macmillan and Free Press, 1967), pp. 314–333, 333–341; for the allegory of the cave, see Plato, *The Republic,* trans. Desmond Lee (New York: Penguin, 1974), pp. 317–320.

2. Plato, p. 204.

3. Ibid., p. 206.

4. Ibid. Students will find a large body of work that provides discussions and commentaries on Plato's theory of justice, as recorded in *The Republic.* See, for example, Christopher Rowe, "Plato: The Search for the Ideal Form of State," in *Political Thought from Plato to NATO,* introd. Brian Redhead (Chicago: Dorsey, 1988), pp. 23–25; Wilhelm Windelband, *A History of Philosophy,* Vol. 1 (New York: Harper Torchbooks, 1958), p. 127; Alvin W. Gouldner, *Enter Plato: Classical Greece and the Origins of Social Theory* (New York: Basic Books, 1965), pp. 219–221; Robert Booth Fowler and Jeffrey R. Orenstein, *An Introduction to Political Theory: Toward the Next Century* (New York: HarperCollins,

1993), p. 67; H. A. Pritchard, "Justice in the Republic," in *Plato's Republic: Interpretation and Criticism,* edited by Alexander Seronske (Belmont, CA: Wadsworth, 1966), pp. 58–65.

5. See debates over interpretation in William T. Bluhm, *Theories of the Political System,* 3rd ed. (Englewood Cliffs, NJ: Prentice Hall, 1978), pp. 63–70; Lee Cameron MacDonald, *Western Political Theory,* Part 1 (New York: Harcourt Brace Jovanovich, 1968), pp. 33–36; Dale Hall, "The Republic" and the "Limits of Politics," and Allan Bloom, "Response to Hall," in *Political Theory: Classic Writings, Contemporary Views,* edited by Joseph Losco and Leonard Williams (New York: St. Martin's, 1992); Karl R. Popper, *The Open Society and Its Enemies,* Vol. 1 (Princeton, NJ: Princeton University Press, 1962), Chapter 6; Thomas A. Spragens, Jr., *Understanding Political Theory* (New York: St. Martin's, 1976), pp. 89–91.

6. *Aubrey's Brief Lives,* edited by Oliver Lawson Dick (London: Secker and Warburg, 1949), p. 156.

7. Thomas Hobbes, *Leviathan, Parts I and II,* introd. Herbert W. Schneider (Indianapolis, IN: Bobbs-Merrill, 1958), p. 24.

8. Ibid., pp. 104–105.

9. Ibid., p. 107.

10. Ibid., p. 152.

11. Ibid., p. 107.

12. Debates on Hobbes are found in Bluhm, pp. 271–292; James Glass, "Hobbes and Narcissism," *Political Theory* (August 1980): 335–363; Hiram Caton, "Is Leviathan a Unicorn? Varieties of Hobbes Interpretation," *Review of Politics* (Winter 1994): 101–125.

13. *The Politics of Aristotle,* edited and trans. by Ernest Barker (New York: Oxford University Press, 1973), pp. 73–91. See also the discussion in Terrence Ball and Richard Dagger, *Political Ideologies and the Democratic Ideal* (New York: HarperCollins, 1991), pp. 25–26.

14. You can read the Declaration on the Internet (gopher://ucsbuxa.ucsb.edu:3001/11/.stacks/.historical), or go to the American Political Science Association page (gopher://apsa.trenton.edu/) and find it by selecting the American Political Theory section.

15. "Tecumseh to Governor Harrison at Vincennes" (1810) in *The World's Famous Orations,* Vol. 8, edited by William Jennings Bryan (New York: Funk & Wagnalls, 1906), pp. 14–15; see also the discussion of Tecumseh within the larger context of Lockean political theory found in James P. Sterba, *Social and Political Philosophy: Classical Western Texts in Feminist and Multicultural Perspectives* (Belmont, CA: Wadsworth, 1995). See also Sharon Malinowski, ed., *Notable Native Americans* (New York: Gale Research, 1995); Carl Waldman, *Who Was Who in Native American History: Indians and Non-Indians from Early Contacts through 1900* (New York: Facts on File, 1990).

16. Julie Wheelwright, "Chico Mendes: The Pioneer Frontier Martyr," in *Political Ideologies and Political Philosophies,* edited by H. B. McCullough (Toronto: Thompson, 1995), pp. 261–262; "Assassin of Famed Rain Forest Guardian Escapes from Jail," Associated Press, 1993, available at Human Rights Watch (hrwatchdc@igc.apc.org); *Fight for the Forest: Chico Mendes in His Own Words,* with Tony Gross (London: Latin America Bureau, 1989).

17. Nietzsche, *Twilight of the Idols and the Antichrist,* trans. R. J. Hollingdale (New York: Penguin, 1968), p. 172. See Nietzsche's *On the Genealogy of Morals* and *Beyond Good and Evil* for an extended discussion of the two moralities. Students may also wish to consult some of the secondary discussions of these complex and often difficult concepts. See William E. Connolly, *Political Theory and Modernity* (New York: Blackwell, 1988), Chapter 5; Walter Kaufman, *Nietzsche: Philosopher, Psychologist, and Antichrist,* 4th ed. (Princeton, NJ: Princeton University Press, 1974), especially pp. 296–297; Mark Warren, *Nietzsche and Political Thought* (Cambridge, MA: MIT Press, 1988), pp. 211–212.

18. Debates on interpreting Nietzsche are discussed in Ferdinand Protzman, "Not a Superman, but a Titan Here," *New York Times* (10 November 1994): A4; Bluhm, pp. 491–497; "Nietzsche Is Not Dead," *Economist* (15 October 1994): 117–118; Charles Larmore, "The View from Everywhere—The Nietzsche Legacy in Germany, 1890–1990 by Steven E. Aschheim," *New Republic* (17 May 1993): 50–53.

19. Kurt Vonnegut, *Welcome to the Monkey House* (New York: Dell, 1968). Students who wish to explore some of the varied interpretations and uses of Vonnegut may find it useful to look to Robert Merrill, ed. *Critical Essays on Kurt Vonnegut* (Boston: Hall, 1990). Professor Sandord Kessler introduced me to the use of Vonnegut as a means of teaching introductory theory when I co-taught a course with him at North Carolina State University in the mid-1980s.

20. Niccolò Machiavelli, *The Prince*, trans. Christian E. Detmold (New York: Airmont, 1965), p. 11. See the useful discussion of Machiavelli in Gary Wills, *Certain Trumpets: The Call of Leaders* (New York: Simon & Schuster, 1994), pp. 228–232.

21. Ibid., p. 81.

22. Hamilton, Madison, and Jay, *The Federalist Papers* (New York: New American Library, 1961), No. 47, p. 301.

23. Ibid., Madison, No. 48, p. 308.

24. Mill, "Liberty and Individuality," in *Ideals and Ideologies: A Reader*, edited by Terrence Ball and Richard Dagger (New York: HarperCollins, 1991), pp. 110–115.

25. Ibid., p. 112.

26. Ibid., p. 113

27. Ibid., p. 112.

28. Ibid., p. 111.

29. Dwight B. Billings and Shaunna L. Scott, "Religion and Political Legitimation," *Annual Review of Sociology* 20 (1994): 173–202; Ahmed Rashid, *Taliban: Militant Islam, Oil and Fundamentalism in Central Asia* (New Haven, CT: Yale University Press, 2000), p. 94.

30. Rory McCarthy, "The Last Afghan Town Still in the Television Age: Ancient Equipment Continues to Pump out Anti-Taliban News," *The Guardian* (1 November 2000): 1; Scott Peterson, "Lives Still Restricted, Afghan Women See Hope," *Christian Science Monitor* (30 December 1999): 1.

31. Rashid, see Chapter 6.

32. Ibid., pp. 88–90.

33. Ibid., Chapter 8; Peterson.

34. RAWA (http://www.rawa.org); Katha Pollitt, "Underground against the Taliban," *The Nation* (29 May 2000): 10.

35. Patrick J. Buchanan, *Right from the Beginning* (Boston: Little, Brown, 1986), pp. 340–342.

36. Ibid., p. 359.

37. Sam Howe Verhovek, "A Klansman's Black Lawyer, and a Principle," *New York Times* (10 September 1993): B9.

38. These various incidents are discussed in Franklin G. Jennifer, "Hate Speech Is Still Free Speech," *New York Times* (13 May 1994): A15; Doreen Carvajal, "Family Photos or Pornography? A Father's Bitter Legal Odyssey," *New York Times* (30 January 1995): A1, A13; Richard L. Berke, "Red Cross Tones Down AIDS Materials," *New York Times* (13 September 1995): A14; Leslie Miller, "Parents Join Fight against On-Line Indecency Law," *USA Today* (4 March 1996): 6D; William Claiborne, "Community vs. Klan in a Contest of Rights," *Washington Post* (19 January 2001): A3.

## Chapter 5

1. For an overview of how political scientists typically conceptualize ideology, see Terence Ball and Richard Dagger, *Political Ideologies and the Democratic Ideal* (New York: HarperCollins, 1991), Chapter 1; Kenneth R. Hoover, *Ideology and Political Life,* 2nd ed. (Belmont, CA: Wadsworth, 1994), p. 4; David E. Ingersoll and Richard K. Mathews, *The Philosophic Roots of Modern Ideology,* 2nd ed. (Englewood Cliffs, NJ: Prentice Hall, 1991), pp. 7–12; Leon P. Baradat, *Political Ideologies: Their Origin and Impact,* 4th ed. (Englewood Cliffs, NJ: Prentice Hall, 1991), pp. 1–10; Lyman Tower Sargent, *Contemporary Political Ideologies: A Comparative Analysis,* 10th ed. (Belmont, CA: Wadsworth, 1996), pp. 3–4; Andrew Heywood, *Political Ideologies: An Introduction* (New York: St. Martin's, 1992), pp. 6–8; Roy C. Macridis and Mark L. Hulliung, *Contemporary Political Ideologies: Movements and Regimes,* 6th ed. (New York: HarperCollins, 1996), pp. 2–8; N. A. Kosolapov, "An Integrative Ideology for Russia: The Intellectual and Political Challenge," *Russian Social Science Review* 37 (January 1996): 60–94.

2. Ball and Dagger point to this origin of *liberalism,* p. 49.

3. For discussions of liberalism, see Charles Larmore, "Political Liberalism," *Political Theory* 18 (August 1990): 339–360; H. J. McCloskey, "Liberalism," *Philosophy* 49 (January 1974): 13–32; Sheldon Wolin, *Politics and Vision: Continuity and Innovation in Western Political Thought* (Boston: Little, Brown, 1960), Chapter 9; Andrew R. Cecil, "Moral Values of Liberalism and Conservatism: The Historical Development," *Vital Speeches of the Day* 61 (1 April 1995): 368–373.

4. Information on Locke's background is available in a wide variety of sources. Students may wish to consult James Gordon Clapp, "John Locke" in *Encyclopedia of Philosophy,* Vol. 4, edited by Paul Edwards (New York: Macmillan and Free Press, 1967), pp. 487–502; see also Peter Laslett's extensive discussion in Laslett's introduction to John Locke, *Two Treatises of Government* (New York: New American Library, 1960); Patricia Springborg, "Mary Astell (1666–1731), Critic of Locke," *American Political Science Review* 89 (September 1995): 622–623; Ball and Dagger, pp. 59–61.

5. For a discussion of Locke's dispute with Filmer, see Laslett and Gordon Schochet, *Patriarchialism in Political Thought: The Authoritarian Family and Political Speculation and Attitudes Especially in Seventeenth-Century England* (New York: Basic Books, 1975); Geriant Parry, "Individuality, Politics and the Critique of Paternalism in John Locke," *Political Studies* 32 (1964): 163–177; Mark Hulliung, "Patriarchalism and Its Early Enemies," *Political Theory* 7 (1974): 410–419.

6. R. W. K. Hinton, "Husbands, Fathers and Conquerors," *Political Studies* 15 (1967): 291–300; R. W. K. Hinton, "Husbands, Fathers and Conquerors," *Political Studies* 16 (1968): 55–62; Richard Ashcraft, "Locke's State of Nature: Historical Fact or Moral Fiction?" *American Political Science Review* 62 (September 1968): 898–915.

7. See Locke, *Two Treatises,* Chapters 2 and 5. The state of nature concept is discussed in Basil Willey, *The Seventeenth Century Background: The Thought of the Age in Relation to Religion and Poetry* (New York: Doubleday Anchor, 1953), p. 265.

8. Ibid., Chapter 2, para. 6.

9. Ibid., Chapters 3 and 8.

10. Ibid., Chapter 15.

11. Stephen G. Salkever locates these arguments within the larger context of the historical development of political theory in "Virtue, Obligation and Politics," *American Political Science Review* 68 (March 1974): 86–87.

12. Smith's background is discussed in Andrew Skinner's introduction to Adam Smith, *The Wealth of Nations,* Books 1–3 (New York: Penguin, 1974). See also George Weigel, "The Other Adam Smith," *Public Interest* (Summer 1993): 123–126; George Russell, "In Praise of Enterprise" [Review of "Adam Smith in His Time and Ours: Designing the Decent Society," by Jerry Z. Muller], *Commentary* 95 (May 1993): 60–62; G. R. Bassiry and Marc Jones, "Adam Smith and the Ethics of Contemporary Capitalism," *Journal of Business Ethics* 12 (August 1993): 621–627.

13. Smith, p.118.

14. Locke, Chapter 5. For a very well-known criticism of Locke's economic theory, students may wish to consult C. B. Macpherson, *The Political Theory of Possessive Individualism: Hobbes to Locke* (New York: Oxford University Press, 1962).

15. Smith, p. 120.

16. T. H. Green, "Liberalism and Positive Freedom," in *Ideals and Ideologies: A Reader,* edited by Terence Ball and Richard Dagger (New York: HarperCollins, 1991), p. 122.

17. Green, p. 123.

18. Jane Addams, *Twenty Years at Hull-House* (New York: New American Library, 1960), p. 127.

19. See http://www.rnc.org.

20. See http://www.conservative-party.org.uk.

21. "Conservative Contradictions," *Economist* 20 (January 1996): 14.

22. Milton Friedman, *Capitalism and Freedom* (Chicago: University of Chicago Press, 1982), pp. 5–6.

23. See the party's official literature on the Internet (http://clipper.uvic.ca/GVLA/lpcan.html).

24. Marilee Haylock, "What Is Libertarianism?" at ibid.

25. See the party's platform (http://www.lp.org/lp/lp.html).

26. See the platform (http://www.democrats.org/party/convention/platform).

27. For an excellent discussion of the various schools of conservatism, see George H. Nash, *The Conservative Intellectual Movement in America since 1945* (New York: Basic Books, 1979), especially the introduction. See also Macridis and Hulliung, Chapter 4, and Ball and Dagger, Chapter 4.

28. Edmund Burke, *Reflections on the Revolution in France,* edited by Thomas H. D. Mahoney (Indianapolis, IN: Bobbs-Merrill, 1955), p. 99. See also Maurice Cranston, "Edmund Burke," in *Encyclopedia of Philosophy,* edited by Edwards, pp. 429–431.

29. Burke, pp. 55–56.

30. Ibid., p. 68.

31. Ibid.

32. Ibid., p. 99.

33. Robert A. Nisbet discusses the importance of civil institutions in traditional conservatism in *The Quest for Community* (New York: Oxford University Press, 1953), p. 24.

34. Ibid., p. 71.

35. "Appendix on Liberalism," in *Conservatism from John Adams to Churchill,* edited by Peter Viereck (Princeton, NJ: Van Nostrand, 1956), p. 162.

36. Burke, p. 98.

37. "Programme of Principles of the Conservative Party" (http://www.hoyre.no).

38. William J. Bennett and Dan Coats, "Moving beyond Devolution," *Wall Street Journal* (5 September 1995): A14; "Broken Compass," *American Legion Magazine* 140 (January 1996): 36–37. Charles Krauthammer discusses Bennett and traditional/social conservatism generally in "A Social Conservative Credo," *Public Interest* (Fall 1995): 15–22.

39. B. Drummond Ayres, Jr., "Dornan, House Firebrand, Joins the '96 Race," *New York Times* (14 April 1995): A7.

40. B. Drummond Ayres, Jr., "Black Conservative Enters Race for G.O.P. Nomination," *New York Times* (27 March 1995): A6; Elizabeth Kolbert, "Unknown Candidate Finds a Voice," *New York Times* (9 August 1995): A11; Andy Lamey, "Odd Man In," *New Republic* (17 April 1995): 16–18.

41. Elizabeth Kohlbert, "Politicians Find a Window into the Heart of the Christian Right," *New York Times* (1 November 1995): A11; FRC positions are delineated at "FRC's Issues" (http://www.frc.org).

42. David Von Drehle and Thomas B. Edsall, "The Religious Right Returns," *Washington Post Weekly Edition* (August 29–September 4, 1994): 6–9; Sara Diamond, "How to Win a Kingdom," *New York Times* (16 September 1995): A15; Frank Rich, "Holier Than Whom?" *New York Times* (22 September 1994): A19; Richard L. Berke, "Two Top Republicans Soften Their Tone," *New York Times* (17 September 1994): 8.

43. Richard L. Berke, "Christian Coalition Is United on Morality, but Not Politics," *New York Times* (8 September 1995): A12.

44. See, for example, the following discussions of pressures contributing to the splintering of conservatism: Paul Starobin, "A Penne for Your Thoughts," *National Journal* 27 (11 November 1995): 28–32; Rich Lowry, "Republicans against the Revolution," *National Review* 2 (6 June 1995): 43–45.

45. Philip J. Hilts, "Abortion Pill Leaves Republicans with Dueling Goals," *New York Times* (1 March 1995): A10.

46. William Kristol, "The Erosion of Liberalism," *USA Today: The Magazine of the American Scene* (March 1995): 87–88.

47. Peter Steinfels, "O'Connor Links Proposed Cuts in Welfare to Increase in Abortions," *New York Times* (5 March 1995): A10; Mickey Kaus, "TRB from Washington: Life Rift," *New Republic* (13 February 1995): 6.

48. David W. Dunlap, "For Gay Republicans, the Ideological Sniping Comes from Both Camps," *New York Times* (4 October 1995): A8; Steven A. Holmes, "Reversal on Gay Donation Embroils Dole," *New York Times* (19 October 1995): A11; Log Cabin Republicans, http://www.lcr/org/press/2000/004NJournalRadio.htm; Chris Kahn, "Falwell, Robertson Lay Blame, *Albuquerque Journal* (15, September 2001): A5.

49. Timothy Egan, "Goldwater Defending Clinton; Conservatives Feeling Faint," *New York Times* (24 March 1994): A1, A11; Iver Peterson, "Gov. Whitman Strongly Endorses Programs for Affirmative Action," *New York Times* (5 December 1995): A16.

50. G. D. H. Cole, *Socialist Thought: The Forerunners, 1789–1850* (New York: Macmillan, 1962), pp. 1–6.

51. George Lichtheim, *The Origins of Socialism* (New York: Praeger, 1969), p. 10; see also Warren Lerner, *A History of Socialism and Communism in Modern Times: Theorists, Activists, and Humanists* (Englewood Cliffs, NJ: Prentice Hall, 1982), p. 60; Michael Harrington, *Socialism* (New York: Bantam, 1972), pp. 13–16; Catherine Baird, "Religious Communism? Nicolai Berdayev's Contribution to Espirits' Interpretation of Communism," *Canadian Journal of History* 30 (April 1995): 29–47.

52. See the combination of Judeo-Christian principles and socialism in the practices of the communal societies in the United States in the late 1800s, as discussed by Charles Nordhoff in *The Communistic Societies of the United States from Personal Visits and Observation* (New York: Dover, 1966), especially pp. 81–84, in which he discusses the Harmony community.

53. Classical Greek theory influenced Marx's ideas on socialism, as explained in George E. McCarthy, *Marx and the Ancients* (Savage, MD: Rowman and Littlefield, 1990).

54. See the analysis of David McLellan, *Karl Marx* (New York: Penguin, 1975), pp. 21–25; Gary Teeple, *Marx's Critique of Politics, 1842–1847* (Toronto: University of Toronto Press, 1984), pp. 186–187.

55. See Marx and Engels, "Manifesto of the Communist Party" in *The Marx-Engels Reader,* 2nd ed., edited by Robert C. Tucker (New York: Norton, 1978), p. 474.

56. Ibid., p. 473, footnote 5; McLellan, *Karl Marx,* pp. 43–44. Jon Elster points out that Marx used different descriptions of class in "Three Challenges to Class," in *Analytical Marxism,* edited by John Roemer (New York: Cambridge University Press, 1989), p. 142, and Jon Elster, *Making Sense of Marx* (New York: Cambridge University Press, 1985), p. 319.

57. Karl Marx, "The German Ideology," in Tucker, p. 187.

58. Karl Marx, "Economic and Philosophic Manuscripts of 1844," in Tucker, pp. 70–81.

59. See the discussion in Raymond Williams, *Marxism and Literature* (New York: Oxford University Press, 1977).

60. Marx and Engels, "Manifesto of the Communist Party," p. 486.

61. Marx and Engels discuss the bourgeoisie's search for markets in ibid., p. 477.

62. Ibid., p. 476; see also the discussion in Marshall Berman, *All That Is Solid Melts into Air: The Experience of Modernity* (New York: Simon & Schuster, 1982), pp. 91–129.

63. Marx and Engels, "Manifesto of the Communist Party," p. 491.

64. Karl Marx, "Speech in Amsterdam, 1872," in *Karl Marx: Selected Writings,* edited by David McLellan (New York: Oxford University Press, 1977), pp. 594–595.

65. Karl Marx, "Address of the International Workingmen's Association to the National Labor Union" (11 May 1869) in *Karl Marx and Frederick Engels, Letters to Americans, 1848–1895* (New York: International Publishers, 1953), pp. 75–76.

66. Eugene Kamenka, ed., *The Portable Karl Marx* (New York: Penguin, 1983), p. 327.

67. "Karl Marx to Laura Lafargue," in Kamenka, p. 68.

68. V. I. Lenin, "The Vanguard Party," in *Essential Works of Socialism,* edited by Irving Howe (New Haven, CT: Yale University Press, 1976), pp. 286–290.

69. For a positive assessment of Lenin's theory of the party, students may wish to consult Georg Lukacs, *Lenin: A Study on the Unity of His Thought,* trans. Nicholas Jacobs (Cambridge, MA: MIT Press, 1971), Chapter 3.

70. V. I. Lenin, "The State and Revolution," in Howe, p. 317. For a more extended discussion of the role of parties in Marxist–Leninist theory and politics, students may wish to consult Robert K. Furtak, "The Fundamentals, Characteristics and Trends of Elections in Socialist States," in *Elections in Socialist States,* edited by Robert K. Furtak

(New York: Harvester Wheatsheaf, 1990), pp. 4–19.

71. V. I. Lenin, "Imperialism: The Highest Stage of Capitalism," in *Ideals and Ideologies: A Reader,* edited by Ball and Dagger, pp. 221–223.

72. David McLellan, *Marxism after Marx* (Boston: Houghton Mifflin, 1979), pp. 199–240.

73. Frank Cunningham, *Democratic Theory and Socialism* (New York: Cambridge University Press, 1987), p. 16.

74. See Labour party documents (http://www.proptel.org.uk/labour-party). On the shift toward liberalism and away from socialism, see Detlef Jahn and Matt Henn, "The 'New' Rhetoric of New Labour in Comparative Perspective: A Three Country Discourse Analysis," *West European Politics* 23 (January 2000).

75. Thirty-Seventh Congress of the Finnish Social Democratic Party, Helsinki, June 6–9, 1996, *Statement on Domestic Politics, Starting Points* (http://www.sdp.fi).

76. "What Is the Party of Catalonia's Socialists?" (http://www.intermail.es/psc).

77. Ibid.

## Chapter 6

1. Ralph Blumenthal, "A Survivor's Legacy, To the Highest Bidder," *New York Times* (3 December 1997): B1, B8.

2. William Brustein, "The 'Red Menace' and the Rise of Italian Fascism," *American Sociological Review* 56 (October 1991): 652–664.

3. Robert O. Paxton, "The Five Stages of Fascism," *Journal of Modern History* 70 (March 1998): 1–23; William R. Keylor, *The Twentieth-Century World* (New York: Oxford University Press, 1996), Chapter 4.

4. Roberto Vivarelli, "Interpretations of the Origins of Fascism," *Journal of Modern History* 63 (March 1991): 30–32.

5. Terence Ball and Richard Dagger, *Political Ideologies and the Democratic Ideal* (New York: HarperCollins, 1991), p. 185.

6. Christopher Leeds, *Italy under Mussolini* (New York: Putnam's, 1972), p. 13.

7. Mussolini, *Fascism: Doctrine and Institutions* (Rome: Ardita, 1935), pp. 15–31.

8. Ibid.

9. Ian Kershaw, "The Essence of Nazism: Form of Fascism, Brand of Totalitarianism, or Unique Phenomenon?," in *The State: Critical Concepts,* edited by John A. Hall (New York: Routledge, 1994), p. 113; Phillip Morgan, *Italian Fascism, 1919–1945* (New York: St. Martin's, 1995), pp. 79–81; see also Ball and Dagger, p. 176. Giovanni Gentile, "Fascism as a Total Conception of Life," in *Fascism,* edited by Roger Griffin (New York: Oxford University Press, 1995), pp. 53–54; Maurice Cranston, "Fascism," in *Encyclopedia of Philosophy,* edited by Paul Edwards (New York: Macmillan, 1967), pp. 182–184.

10. Students may consult Leeds, Chapter 2, for a discussion of these and other decrees.

11. Scholars debate the extent to which the fascist ideology of totalistic control was, in practice, extended over the entire population. See Gordon A. Craig, "Man of the People?" *The New York Review of Books* (20 November 1997): 22.

12. Ian Kershaw, *Popular Opinion and Political Dissent in the Third Reich: Bavaria 1933–1945* (Oxford, UK: Clarendon, 1983), p. 42.

13. Martin Broszat, *The Hitler State,* trans. John W. Hiden (New York: Longman, 1981), p. 154.

14. Ibid.

15. Leonard B. Weinberg, *After Mussolini: Italian Neo-Fascism and the Nature of Fascism* (Washington, DC: University Press of America, 1979), p. 78; Juan J. Linz, "Some Notes toward a Comparative Study of Fascism in Sociological Historical Perspective," in *Fascism: A Reader's Guide: Analyses, Interpretations, Bibliography,* edited by Walter Laqueur (London: Wildwood House, 1976), p. 12; see also Zeev Sternhell, "Fascist Ideology," in Laqueur, pp. 315–376; Eve Rosenhaft and W. R. Lee, "State and Society in Modern Germany: Beamtenstaat, Klassenstaat, Wohlfahrtsstaat," in *The State and Social Change in Germany, 1880–1980,* edited by Lee and Rosenhaft (New York: Berg, 1990), p. 5; Benito Mussolini, "The Achievements of the Fascist Revolution," in Griffin, p. 65.

16. Ibid.

17. Edwin P. Hoyt, *Mussolini's Empire: The Rise and Fall of the Fascist Vision* (New York: Wiley, 1994), p. 102.

18. Morgan, p. 82.

19. Carl Schmitt, "The Legal Basis of the Total State," in Griffin, pp. 137–138; Tracy H. Koon, *Believe, Obey, Fight: Political Socialization of Youth in Fascist Italy, 1922–1943* (Chapel Hill: University of North Carolina Press, 1985), p. 33.

20. Hoyt, pp. 102–103. See also Morgan, pp. 92–95; Lucy S. Dawidowicz, *The War against the Jews 1933–1945* (New York: Holt, Rinehart and Winston, 1975), p. 52. See also the discussion in Broszat, pp. 90–91.

21. See Hitler's argument on this point in *Mein Kampf*, an excerpt of which is found in Hitler, "Nation and Race," in Ball and Dagger, eds., *Ideals and Ideologies: A Reader*, p. 299.

22. Benito Mussolini, "Blood-Brothers: Fascism and Nazism," in Griffin, pp. 78–79; Koon, p. 168.

23. Dawidowicz, p. 46. See also the discussion of Nazi ideology as conveyed through Nazi party propaganda in Thomas Childers, *The Nazi Voter: The Social Foundations of Fascism in Germany, 1919–1933* (Chapel Hill: University of North Carolina Press, 1983), pp. 45–46.

24. Ibid., Chapter 3; William Carr, *A History of Germany, 1815–1845*, 2nd ed. (New York: St. Martin's, 1979), pp. 338–342.

25. R. Amy Elman, "Triangles and Tribulations: The Politics of Nazi Symbols," *Journal of Homosexuality* 30 (1996): 1–11; Barbara Distel and Ruth Jakusch, eds., *Concentration Camp Dachau, 1932-1945*, trans. Jennifer Vernum (Munich: Comite International de Dachau, 1978), p. 62.

26. United States Holocaust Museum, "The Holocaust: An Historical Summary" (http://www. Ushmm.org); Anne Harrington, "Unmasking Suffering's Masks: Reflections on Old and New Memories of Nazi Medicine," *Daedalus* 125 (Winter 1996): 121–205; Karen J. Winkler, "Debating the Role of Anti-Semitism in the Holocaust," *Chronicle of Higher Education* 42 (22 September 1995): A17–A18.

27. Daniel Jonah Goldhagen, *Hitler's Willing Executioners: Ordinary Germans and the Holocaust* (New York: Vintage, 1997), pp. 137–171; Deborah Dwork and Robert Jan Van Pelt, *Auschwitz: 1270 to the Present*

(New York: Norton, 1996), p. 172; Reinhard Rurup, *Topography of Terror: Gestapo, SS an Reichssicherheitshauptamt on the Prinz-Albrecht-Terrain: A Documentation* (Berlin: Arenhovel, 1989), pp. 90–106.

28. Peter Heigl, *Guide to the Flossenbürg Concentration Camp* (Lichtung: Viechtach, 1994).

29. For a discussion of the laws regarding such parties, see Geoffrey Hand, Jacques Georgel, and Christoph Sasse, eds., *European Electoral Systems Handbook* (London: Butterworth, 1979), pp. 74, 159; Ferdinand Protzman, "Germany Moves to Ban a Second Neo-Nazi Party," *New York Times* (11 December 1992): A9.

30. James O. Jackson, "Fascism Lives 50 Years Later, the Legacy of Hitler and Mussolini Still Bedevils Europe," *Time* (6 June 1994): 50–51; Daniel Singer, "Forza's Destiny in Italy," *Nation* (11 April 1994): 480–484; Peter Morris, *French Politics Today* (New York: Manchester University Press, 1994), pp. 147–151; Nonna Mayer, "Ethnocentrism, Racism, and Intolerance," in *The French Voter Decides*, edited by Daniel Boy and Nonna Mayer (Ann Arbor: University of Michigan Press, 1993), pp. 21–43; Maxim Silverman, *Deconstructing the Nation: Immigration, Racism and Citizenship in Modern France* (New York: Routledge, 1992), p. 167; Paul Hockenos, *Free to Hate: The Rise of the Right in Post-Communist Eastern Europe* (New York: Routledge, 1993), pp. 46–51; Michael Minkenberg, "What's Left of the Right? The New Right and the Superwahljahr 1994 in Perspective," in *Germany's New Politics: Parties and Issues in the 1990s*, edited by David P. Contradt, Gerald R. Kleinfeld, George K. Romoger, and Christian Soel (Providence, RI: Berghahn, 1995), pp. 255–271; William Drozdiak, "Austria's Haider Resigns as Head of Freedom Party; Far-Right Leader Blasts EU 'Exorcism,'" *Washington Post* (2 May 2000): A17; Rick Kuhn, "The Threat of Fascism in Austria," *Monthly Review* 52 (June 2000): 21–35; Patrick Smyth, "French Presidency of EU Announces End to Sanctions on Austria," *Irish Times* 13 (September 2000): 13.

31. "Asylstreit Entscheidet Wahl," *Der Spiegel* 44 (October 1992): 58–65.

32. Hockenos, pp. 29–31; Roger Cohen, "Young Asian Knifed by German

Neo-Nazis," *New York Times* (27 December 2000): A8.

33. Stephen Silver, "Music of Hate," *New York Times* (8 February 1994): A17; Ferdinand Protzman, "Music of Hate Raises the Volume in Germany," *New York Times* (2 December 1992): A1, A6. See also the discussion of neo-Nazism as a phenomenon of pop culture in Janet Kramer, "Neo-Nazis: A Chaos in the Head," *New Yorker* (14 June 1993): 52–70.

34. R. G. Butler, "This Is Aryan Nations," pp. 147–149, and R. G. Butler, "Twelve Foundation Stones to Establish a State for Our Aryan Racial Nation," pp. 149–159, both of which are found in *Extremism in America,* edited by Lyman Tower Sargent (New York: New York University Press, 1995); David Van Biema and David S. Jackson, "When White Makes Right," *Time* (9 August 1993): 40–42.

## Chapter 7

1. Center for American Women and Politics, Eagleton Institute of Politics—Rutgers, The State University of New Jersey, "Women in Elected Office 2003. Fact Sheet Summaries" (http://www.rci.rutgers.edu/~cawp/facts/officeholders/cawpfs.html).

2. Audre Lord, "Age, Race, Class, and Sex: Women Redefining Difference," in *Race, Class, and Gender in the United States: An Integrated Study,* 3rd ed., edited by Paula S. Rothenberg (New York: St. Martin's, 1995): 445–451.

3. A number of scholars have noted that despite the competing definitions of feminism, equality/egalitarianism is a central concept in feminist discourse. This egalitarian orientation underlies feminism's opposition to forces that would impose a subordinate status on women. See M. E. Hawkesworth, *Beyond Oppression: Feminist Theory and Political Strategy* (New York: Continuum, 1990), p. 11, and Jean Bethke Elshtain's explication of how feminism's commitment to equality leads it to advocate bringing women fully and equally into public life, in *Public Man, Private Woman: Women in Social and Political Thought* (Princeton, NJ: Princeton University Press, 1981), p. 202.

4. The connection between liberalism and feminism has been discussed by Zillah Eisenstein in *The Radical Future of Liberal Feminism* (New York: Longman, 1981), p. 4. See also Zillah Eisenstein, *Feminism and Sexual Equality: Crisis in Liberal America* (New York: Monthly Review Press, 1984), pp. 12–13. It is one of the ironies of history that the very classical liberals (such as John Locke) making these arguments about natural freedom and natural equality excluded women from their claims; that is, Locke could simultaneously proclaim the existence of natural equality of all (men) and assert the existence of natural inequality or differences relative to women and men. For a discussion of this point, students may consult of number of works, including Teresa Brennan and Carole Pateman, "Mere Auxiliaries to the Commonwealth: Women and the Origins of Liberalism," *Political Studies* 27 (1979): 183–200; Carole Pateman, "Women and Consent," *Political Theory* 8 (May 1980): 149–168; Lorenne M. G. Clark, "Women and John Locke; or, Who Owns the Apples in the Garden of Eden?" *Canadian Journal of Philosophy* 7 (December 1977): 699–724.

5. Anne Phillips analyzes the complex relationship between feminism and democracy in *Engendering Democracy* (University Park: Pennsylvania State University Press, 1991), Chapter 1.

6. Rosemarie Tong, *Feminist Thought: A Comprehensive Introduction* (Boulder, CO: Westview, 1989), p. 1. See also Karen Green, *The Woman of Reason: Feminism, Humanism, and Political Thought* (New York: Continuum, 1995), p. 2. The preceding definition of feminism is influenced also by the analysis of Marlene LeGates, who has attempted to define feminism broadly enough to be inclusive of varied feminist perspectives while also avoiding *essentializing* (rigid/fixed notions) categories. See LeGates, "Feminists before Feminism: Origins and Varieties of Women's Protest in Europe and North America before the Twentieth Century," in *Women: A Feminist Perspective,* 5th ed., edited by Jo Freeman (Mountain View, CA: Mayfield), p. 494.

7. See the discussion of patriarchy in Kathy E. Ferguson, "Patriarchy," in *Women's Studies Encyclopedia,* edited by Helen Tierney (New York: Peter Bedrick Books, 1991), pp. 265–267.

8. Emily MacFarquhar, "The War against Women," *US News & World Report* (28 March 1994): 42–48.

9. Meena Poudel, "Poverty, Prostitution and Women," *World Health* (November 1994): 10–11.

10. Nancy Seufert-Barr, "Seeking Action for Equality, Development, Peace," *UN Chronicle* (June 1995): 39–43; see also the analysis in the case study of women in South Korea found in Kyung Ae Park, "Women Workers in South Korea: The Impact of Export-Led Industrialization," *Asian Survey* 35 (August 1995): 740–756.

11. Carl Hartman, "Women Still Earn Less Than Men," *Albuquerque Journal* (30 July 1996): D6.

12. Helen Rodriguez-Trias, "Topics for Our Times: From Cairo to Beijing— Women's Agenda for Equality," *American Journal of Public Health* (March 1996): 305–306.

13. United Nations, Economic and Social Council, Thirty-Ninth Session, *Commission on the Status of Women, Participation of Women in Political Life and Decision-Making. Report of the Secretary-General* (New York: 15 March–4 April 1995), p. 23.

14. Jill Petty, "Only 5 of 190 World Leaders Are Women. How Are They Doing?" *Ms.* (March 1996): 20–23.

15. Seufert-Barr.

16. Ibid.

17. *Economist* (18 September 1993): 38.

18. Jo Richardson and Gene Feder, "Domestic Violence against Women," *British Medical Journal (International)* 311 (14 October 1995): 964–965.

19. Seufert-Barr; MacFarquhar.

20. Saba Bahar, "Human Rights Are Women's Rights: Amnesty International and the Family," *Hypatia* 11 (Winter 1996): 105–134.

21. J. W. Peltason, *Corwin & Peltason's Understanding the Constitution*, 7th ed. (Hinsdale, IL: Dryden, 1976), p. 196.

22. See the controversy raised by this issue, as discussed in Maryanne Cline Horowitz, "The Image of God in Man—Is Woman Included?" *Harvard Theological Review* 72 (July–October 1979): 175–206.

23. Azadeh Kian, "Gendered Occupation and Women's Status in Post-Revolutionary Iran," *Middle Eastern Studies* 31 (July 1995): 407–421.

24. Souad Dajani, "The Struggle of Palestinian Women in the Occupied Territories: Between National and Social Liberation," *Arab Studies Quarterly* 16 (Spring 1994): 13–26.

25. Laura M. Markowitz, "Buddhist Nuns Buck the System," *Ms.* 6 (July 1995): 10–12.

26. Kathleen B. Jones, "Citizenship in a Woman-Friendly Polity," *Signs* 15 (Summer 1990): 781–812; see also Susan Moller Okin, *Women in Western Political Thought* (Princeton, NJ: Princeton University Press, 1979), pp. 79–83.

27. Okin offers a thorough discussion of Rousseau's theory, ibid., see especially her conclusions on pp. 153–160.

28. These and other incidences of sexism through popular culture in the United States are discussed in Stephanie Coontz, *The Way We Never Were: American Families and the Nostalgia Trap* (New York: Basic Books, 1992), pp. 31–32.

29. Claire Robertson, "Grassroots in Kenya: Women, Genital Mutilation, and Collective Action, 1920–1990," *Signs* 21 (Spring 1996): 615–642. See also the discussions in Hamid Rushwan, "Female Circumcision," *World Health* 48 (September 1995): 16–17; Barbara Reynolds, "The Move to Outlaw Female Genital Mutilation," *Ms.* 5 (July 1994): 92–93. FGM is an issue that often divides family members in regions of Africa where the tradition persists, as discussed in Celia W. Dugger, "A Refugee's Body Is Intact but Her Family Is Torn," *New York Times* (11 September 1996): A1, A8–A9.

30. Laura DeLuca and Shadrack Kamenya call on readers to think about these issues when assessing FGM in "Representation of Female Circumcision in Finzan, a Dance for the Heroes," *Research in African Literatures* 26 (Fall 1995): 83–87.

31. Moira Ferguson, introduction to *Maria, Or the Wrongs of Woman*, by Mary Wollstonecraft (New York: Norton, 1975), pp. 5–6.

32. Mary Wollstonecraft, *A Vindication of the Rights of Woman,* edited by Carol H. Poston (New York: Norton, 1975), pp. 3–31. See also the discussion of Wollstonecraft's philosophy in Carolyn W. Korsmeyer, "Reason and Morals in the Early Feminist Movement: Mary Wollstonecraft," in *Women and Philosophy: Toward a Theory of Liberation,* edited by Carol C. Gould and Marx W. Wartofsky (New York: Perigree Books, 1976), pp. 97–111.

33. Mary Wollstonecraft, *A Vindication of the Rights of Woman,* edited by Carol H. Poston (New York: Norton, 1975), pp. 3–31. See also the discussion of Wollstonecraft's philosophy in Carolyn W. Korsmeyer, "Reason and Morals in the Early Feminist Movement: Mary Wollstonecraft," in *Women and Philosophy: Toward a Theory of Liberation,* edited by Carol C. Gould and Marx W. Wartofsky (New York: Perigree Books, 1976), pp. 97–111.

34. Wollstonecraft, *Vindication,* p. 33.

35. Ibid., pp. 16–52.

36. Ibid., p. 73.

37. Betty Friedan, *The Second Stage* (New York: Summit, 1981); Barbara Ryan, *Feminism and the Women's Movement: Dynamics of Change in Social Movement Ideology and Activism* (New York: Routledge, 1992), p. 54; Elshtain, pp. 228–255; Myra Marx Ferree and Beth B. Hess, *Controversy and Coalition: The New Feminist Movement* (Boston: Twayne, 1985), pp. 149–150; Jean E. Friedman, "Contemporary Feminism: Theories and Practice," in *Our American Sisters: Women in American Life and Thought,* 2nd ed., edited by Jean E. Friedman and William G. Shade (Boston: Allyn and Bacon, 1976), pp. 430–444; Judith Stacey, "The New Conservative Feminism," *Feminist Studies* 9 (Fall 1983): 559–583.

38. See also the contemporary discussion of the politics of love, romance, autonomy, and liberty in Shulamith Firestone, "The Culture of Romance," in *Feminist Frameworks: Alternative Theoretical Accounts of the Relations Between Women and Men,* 3rd ed., edited by Alison M. Jagger and Paula S. Rothenberg (New York: McGraw-Hill, 1993), pp. 448–453.

39. This study is discussed in the larger context of household labor in Theodore N. Greenstein, "Gender Ideology and Perceptions of the Fairness of the Division of Household Labor: Effects on Marital Quality," *Social Forces* 74 (March 1996): 1029–1042.

40. See the essays in *Women and Revolution: A Discussion of the Unhappy Marriage of Marxism and Feminism,* edited by Lydia Sargent (Boston: South End Press, 1981); *Capitalist Patriarchy and the Case for Socialist Feminism,* edited by Zillah R. Eisenstein (New York: Monthly Review Press, 1979); Ryan, p. 55; Elshtain, pp. 256–284; Ferree and Hess, pp. 154–159.

41. Elshtain, pp. 204–228; Ferree and Hess, pp. 160–165; Ryan, p. 55; Catherine MacKinnon, "Sex Equality: Difference and Dominance," in Jagger and Rothenberg, pp. 182–186.

42. I combine Jagger and Rothenberg's classifications of "multicultural feminism" and "global feminism" in the category of diversity feminism.

43. See the discussions in M. Rivka Polatnick, "Diversity in Women's Liberation Ideology: How a Black and a White Group of the 1960s Viewed Motherhood," *Signs* 21 (Spring 1996): 679–706; Elizabeth Martinez, "In Pursuit of Latina Liberation," *Signs* 20 (Summer 1995): 1019–1028.

44. Aparna Basu, "Feminism and Nationalism in India, 1917–1947," *Journal of Women's History* 7 (Winter 1995): 95–107.

45. Rodriguez-Trias.

46. Students may wish to read Gerda Lerner's analysis of the concept of diversity in feminist works in her essay "Reconceptualizing Differences among Women," in Jagger and Rothenberg, especially pp. 237–238. See also Ofelia Schutte, "Philosophical Feminism in Latin America and Spain: An Introduction," *Hypatia* 9 (Winter 1994): 142–146; Carolle Charles, "Gender and Politics in Contemporary Haiti: The Duvalierist State, Transnationalism, and the Emergence of a New Feminism, 1980–1990," *Feminist Studies* 21 (Spring 1995): 135–164. Charles points out that in authoritarian systems and societies engulfed in civil conflict, violence may be the primary feminist issue for women.

47. Susan L. Flader, *Thinking Like a Mountain: Aldo Leopold and the Evolution of an Ecological Attitude toward Deer, Wolves and Forests* (Lincoln: University of Nebraska Press, 1974), p. 5.

48. Paul R. Ehrlich, *The Machinery of Nature: The Living World around Us and How It Works* (New York: Simon & Schuster, 1986), p. 13.

49. These discoveries are analyzed in Michael E. Kowalok, "Common Threads: Research Lessons from Acid Rain, Ozone Depletion, and Global Warming," *Environment* 35 (July 1993): 12–20.

50. Russell J. Dalton discusses the politics and history of these associations in "The Environmental Movement in Western Europe," in *Environmental Politics in the International Arena: Movements, Parties, Organizations, and Policy,* edited by Sheldon Kamieniecki (Albany: State University of New York Press, 1993), pp. 41–68.

51. Lester W. Milbrath discusses environmental principles as constituting a specific "paradigm"/model of viewing the world in "The World Is Relearning Its Story about How the World Works," in Kamieniecki, pp. 21–39.

52. Aldo Leopold, *A Sand County Almanac, with Essays on Conservation from Round River* (New York: Ballantine, 1966), p. 239.

53. Wendell Berry, "The Obligation of Care," *Sierra* (September–October 1995): 62–67, 101. Berry also discusses these issues in his collection of essays in *Home Economics* (San Francisco: North Point Press, 1987), p. 139.

54. Jane Kay, "Native Frog Is Listed as Threatened," *San Francisco Examiner* (20 May 1996): A4.

55. T. H. Watkins, "What's Wrong with the Endangered Species Act?" *Audubon* (January–February 1996): 37–41.

56. Mark Kurlansky, "Europe's Threatened Catch," *Audubon* (January–February 1996): 18–20.

57. See Berry's discussion of using and owning in "The Obligation of Care," especially pp. 66–67; see also Berry, *Home Economics,* p. 139.

58. Sue Hubbell, *A Country Year: Living the Questions* (New York: Random House, 1986), pp. 6–7.

59. E. O. Wilson, "The Current State of Biological Diversity," in *Learning to Listen to the Land,* edited by Bill Willers (Washington, DC: Island Press, 1991), p. 18.

60. *The Wilderness World of John Muir,* introd. Edwin Way Teale (Boston: Houghton Mifflin, 1954), pp. 316–317. Students will also find Muir discussing this point in *My First Summer in the Sierra* (San Francisco: Sierra Club Books, 1988), p. 17. See also the example of David Ehrenfeld, "From the Arrogance of Humanism," in Willers, pp. 74–104, for a critique of the human mastery perspective.

61. Details of the Green Revolution's environmental and health costs are discussed in Douglas L. Murray, *Cultivating Crisis: The Human Cost of Pesticides in Latin America* (Austin: University of Texas Press, 1994).

62. This problem is discussed briefly in Stephen Mink, "Poverty and the Environment," *Finance and Development* 30 (December 1993): 8–9.

63. Timothy E. Wirth, "The Human Factor," *Sierra* (September–October 1995): 76–79.

64. Harvey A. Feit, "James Bay Cree Self-Governance and Land Management," in *We Are Here: Politics of Aboriginal Land Tenure,* edited by Edwin N. Wilmsen (Berkeley: University of California Press, 1989), pp. 68–98.

65. The European examples are examined in Barbara Jancar-Webster, "Eastern Europe and the Former Soviet Union," in Kamieniecki, pp. 199–221.

66. Frank Graham, Jr., "Unnatural Predation," *Audubon* (November–December 1995): 84–89.

67. Leopold, pp. 137–141.

68. Scott Alan Lewis, "Trouble on Tap," *Sierra* (July–August 1995): 54–58.

69. D. L. Skole, W. H. Chomentowski, W. A. Salas, and A. D. Nobre, "Physical and Human Dimensions of Deforestation in Amazonia," *Bioscience* 44 (May 1994): 314–322.

70. Richard Evans Schultes, "Burning the Library of Amazonia," *Sciences* 34 (March 1994): 24–31.

71. Ibid.

72. Henry David Thoreau, *Walden and Civil Disobedience* (New York: Signet Classic, 1960), pp. 8, 10, 19, 66.

73. Edward Abbey, *The Journey Home: Some Words in Defense of the American West* (New York: Dutton, 1977), p. 230.

74. Ibid., p. 229.

75. Ed Abbey, "Why Wilderness?," in *The Best of the West: An Anthology of Classic Writing from the American West,* edited by Tony Hillerman (New York: HarperPerennial, 1991), pp. 466–469. Students may wish to consult Wendell Berry's discussion of Abbey, Thoreau, and environmentalism in "A Few Words in Favor of Edward Abbey," in *Resist Much, Obey Little: Remembering Ed Abbey,* edited by James R. Hepworth and Gregory McNamee (San Francisco: Sierra Club Books, 1996), pp. 1–14.

76. Le Anne Schreiber, "The Long Light," in *Uncommon Waters: Women Write about Fishing,* edited by Holly Morris (Seattle, WA: Seal Press, 1991), p. 3.

77. Leopold, pp. 246–247.

78. Ibid., pp. 228–229.

79. This debate is analyzed in Paul Rauber, "What Price a Walk in the Woods?" *Sierra* 78 (May 1993): 46–49.

80. Sandra Hackman, "After Rio: Our Forests, Ourselves," *Technology Review* 95 (October 1992): 32–40.

81. "Green Justice: The Facts," *Global Issues* 93/94, 9th ed., edited by Robert M. Jackson (Guilford, CT: Dushkin, 1993), pp. 68–69.

82. Jean-Franois Lyotard, "The Postmodern Condition," in *Culture and Society: Contemporary Debates,* edited by Jeffrey C. Alexander and Steven Seidman (New York: Cambridge University Press, 1993), pp. 330–341. Lyotard's contributions are discussed in Steven Connor's very readable overview titled *Postmodernist Culture: An Introduction to Theories of the Contemporary,* 2nd ed. (Cambridge, MA: Blackwell, 1997), pp. 23–43. See also the analysis of metanarratives and postmodernism in

Stephen K. White, *Political Theory and Postmodernism* (New York: Cambridge University Press, 1991), pp. 4–7; Fred Dallmayr, *Margins of Political Discourse* (Albany: State University of New York Press, 1989), p. 96; Norman K. Denzin, "Postmodern Social Theory," *Sociological Theory* 4 (1986): 194–195; Richard Wolin, "Modernism vs. Postmodernism," *Telos* (Winter 1984–1985): 26–27.

83. Students may wish to consult Harland G. Bloland's essay for a very well-written overview of postmodernism; see Bloland, "Postmodernism and Higher Education," *Journal of Higher Education* 66 (September 1995): 521–559. In addition, useful and readable overviews of postmodernism's themes are found in Stanley Aronowitz, *The Politics of Identity: Class, Culture, Social Movements* (New York: Routledge, 1992), Chapter 8; Kerwin Lee Klein, "In Search of Narrative Mastery: Postmodernism and the People without History," *History & Theory* 34 (December 1995).

84. Discussions of feminism's relation to postmodernism are found in *Feminism/Postmodernism,* ed. and introd. Linda J. Nicholson (New York: Routledge, 1990); Iris Marion Young, "Gender as Seriality: Thinking about Women as a Social Collective," *Signs* 19 (Spring 1994): 713–738; Tong, *Feminist Thought,* Chapter 8; Suzanna Danuta Walters, "From Here to Queer: Radical Feminism, Postmodernism, and the Lesbian Menace (Or, Why Can't a Woman Be More Like a Fag?)," *Signs* 21 (Summer 1996): 830–869.

85. See the discussions found in Brenda K. Marshall, *Teaching the Postmodern: Fiction and Theory* (New York: Routledge, 1992), pp. 3–4; Horace L. Fairlamb, *Critical Conditions: Postmodernity and the Question of Foundations* (New York: Cambridge University Press, 1994), pp. 57–58.

86. Judith Butler, "A Skeptical Feminist Postscript to the Postmodern," in *Postmodernism across the Ages,* edited by Bill Readings and Bennet Schaber (Syracuse, NY: Syracuse University Press, 1993), p. 235.

87. John McGowan writes of this theme in *Postmodernism and Its Critics* (Ithaca, NY: Cornell University Press, 1991), pp. 29, 183.

88. Carol A. Stabile, "Postmodernism, Feminism, and Marx: Notes from the Abyss," *Monthly Review* 47 (July 1995): 89–107.

## Chapter 8

1. Information on both countries is found in *Political Handbook of the World: 1995–1996,* edited by Arthur S. Banks et al. (Binghamton: CSA Publications State University of New York, 1996); *The Statesman's Year-Book: Statistical and Historical Annual of the States of the World for the Year 1995–1996,* edited by Brian Hunter (New York: St. Martin's, 1995); *The World Almanac and Book of Facts 1994,* edited by Robert Famighetti (Mahwah, NJ: Funk & Wagnalls, 1993), p. 772.

2. Terrence Ball and Richard Dagger, *Political Ideologies and the Democratic Ideal,* 2nd ed. (New York: HarperCollins, 1995), p. 24.

3. Frank Cunningham, *Democratic Theory and Socialism* (New York: Cambridge University Press, 1987), p. 5 and Chapter 3. See also Larry Diamond, Juan L. Linz, and Seymour Martin Lipset, "Introduction: Comparing Experiences with Democracy," in *Politics in Developing Countries: Comparing Experiences with Democracy,* edited by Diamond, Linz, and Lipset (Boulder, CO: Rienner, 1991), p. 7; Robert Dahl, "Justifying Democracy," *Society* 32 (March–April 1995): 47; Ross E. Burkhart and Michael S. Lewis-Beck, "Comparative Democracy: The Economic Development Thesis," *American Political Science Review* 88 (December 1994): 904.

4. Ian Shapiro notes that democracy's elements sometimes create counterpressures and contradictions in "Three Ways to Be a Democrat," *Political Theory* 22 (February 1994): 147. Students may also wish to consult Anthony Downs, whose writings have long noted the tensions in democracy. See, for instance, Downs, "The Evolution of Democracy: How Its Axioms and Institution Forms Have Been Adapted to Changing Social Forces," *Daedalus* (Summer 1987): 119–148.

5. See the discussion of the identification, conceptualization, definition, and analysis of protective, developmental, pluralist, and participatory democracy in William E. Hudson, *American Democracy in Peril: Seven Challenges to America's Future* (Chatham, NJ: Chatham House, 1995), Chapter 1. See the analysis of performance as an element of assessing systems in a comparative sense as discussed in John D. Nagle, *Introduction to Comparative Government: Political System Performance in Three Worlds* (Chicago: Nelson-Hall, 1992), pp. 11–17.

6. For a discussion of democracy's relation to equality, see Thomas Christian, *The Rule of the Many: Fundamental Issues in Democratic Theory* (Boulder, CO: Westview, 1996), p. 3.

7. Ian Budge comments on this dimension of democracy in "Comparative Politics and Reflexive Democracy," in *Developing Democracy,* edited by Ian Budge and David McKay (Thousand Oaks, CA: Sage, 1994), p. 1.

8. Michael Lienesch discusses democracy's requirement of civic commitment in "Wo(e)begon(e) Democracy," *American Journal of Political Science* 36 (November 1992): 1009–1011. See also Robert Dahl, "A Democratic Dilemma: System Effectiveness versus Citizen Participation," *Political Science Quarterly* 109 (Spring 1994): 23–34; James David Barber, *The Book of Democracy* (Englewood Cliffs, NJ: Prentice Hall, 1995), p. 6.

9. Pericles, "Funeral Oration," in *Ideals and Ideologies: A Reader,* 2nd ed., edited by Terence Ball and Richard Dagger (New York: HarperCollins, 1995), pp. 20–21.

10. Jan-Erik Lane and Svante Ersson, *Comparative Politics: An Introduction and New Approach* (Cambridge, MA: Polity Press, 1994), p. 82; Evelyne Huber, Dietrich Rueschemeyer, and John D. Stephens, "The Paradoxes of Contemporary Democracy: Formal, Participatory, and Social Dimensions," *Comparative Politics* 29 (April 1997): 324. This discussion also draws on Mark E. Warren's argument that democratic politics should encompass challenges to public officials about how those officials disperse goods within their respective systems; see Warren, "Deliberative Democracy and Authority," *American Political Science Review* 90 (March 1996): 46–60. Clearly, measuring the effects of policy and linking specific policies to performance outcomes is very difficult, as discussed at length in Kevin Neuhouser, "Limits on Authoritarian Imposition of Policy: Failed Ecuadoran Military Populism in Comparative Perspective," *Comparative Political Studies* 29 (December 1996): 635–659.

11. Students who peruse the political science literature on democracy and democratization will find that despite their best efforts to achieve clarity and precision in their use of terminology, political scientists are at odds over definitions, concepts, and classifications of democracy, as outlined in the observations of David Collier and Steven Levitsky, "Democracy with Adjectives: Conceptual Innovation in Comparative Research," *World Politics* 49 (April 1997): 430–451.

12. See the essays in Craig R. Smith, *Silencing the Opposition: Government Strategies of Suppression of Freedom of Expression* (Albany: State University of New York Press, 1996).

13. Rhodes Cook, "Clinton's Easy Second-Term Win Riddles GOP Electoral Map," *Congressional Quarterly Weekly Reports* (9 November 1996): 3194; Curtis Gans, "Pollyanna's America," *Washington Post* (6 August 1997): A19; "Report Gore Won Popular Vote by 539,897," *Washington Post* (21 December 2000): A9.

14. Susan J. Tolchin, *The Angry American: How Voter Rage Is Changing the Nation* (Boulder, CO: Westview, 1996), p. 9. See also Charles C. Euchner, *Extraordinary Politics: How Protest and Dissent Are Changing American Democracy* (Boulder, CO: Westview, 1996), p. 30.

15. Jean Bethke Elshtain, *Democracy on Trial* (New York: Basic Books, 1995), p. 2.

16. Wilson Carey McWilliams, *The Politics of Disappointment: American Elections 1976–1994* (Chatham, NJ: Chatham House, 1995), p. 3.

17. Christopher Flavin, "Facing Up to the Risks of Climate Change" in *State of the World 1996,* edited by Lester Brown et al. (New York: Norton, 1996), pp. 32-33. See also John H. Cushman, Jr., "Why the U.S. Fell Short of Ambitious Goals for Reducing Greenhouse Gases," *New York Times* (20 October 1997): A9.

18. John Keane, *Democracy and Civil Society* (New York: Verso, 1988), p. x. On a related point, it is difficult to discern whether democracy outside of government—i.e., within society—is more likely to be a cause or effect of democracy within government. This point is discussed in Edward N. Muller

and Mitchell A. Seligson, "Civic Culture and Democracy: The Question of Causal Relationships," *American Political Science Review* 88 (September 1994): 635–652.

19. John S. Dryzek, *Democracy in Capitalist Times: Ideals, Limits, and Struggles* (Cambridge, MA: Oxford University Press, 1996), p. 61.

20. Sanford Lakoff, *Democracy: History, Theory, Practice* (Boulder, CO: Westview, 1996), p. 243; Sara Meiklejohn Terry, "Poland: A Troubled Transition," in *Establishing Democracies,* edited by Mary Ellen Fischer (Boulder, CO: Westview, 1996), p. 214; Michael G. Roskin, *The Rebirth of East Europe* (Englewood Cliffs, NJ: Prentice Hall, 1991), p. 171; Michael Walzer, "The Civil Society Argument," in *Dimensions of Radical Democracy: Pluralism, Citizenship, Community,* edited by Chantal Mouffe (New York: Verso, 1992), pp. 89–90; Mehran Kamrava, *Understanding Comparative Politics: A Framework for Analysis* (New York: Routledge, 1996), pp. 159–162. In contrast to the preceding Eastern European examples, the absence of a strong civil society in many countries of Africa has been associated with lower levels of democracy within government, as explained by Henry Bienent and Jeffrey Herbst, "The Relationship between Political and Economic Reform in Africa," *Comparative Politics* 29 (October 1996): 28–30.

21. This distinction is informed by classifications found in John McCormick, "A Post Cold-War Approach," *PS: Political Science and Politics* (March 1995): 81–82; John McCormick, *Comparative Politics in Transition* (Belmont, CA: Wadsworth, 1995), pp. 8–16; Kamrava, pp. 81–96; Robert J. Jackson and Doreen Jackson, *A Comparative Introduction to Political Science* (Upper Saddle River, NJ: Prentice Hall, 1997), pp. 79–80; Richard Rose, "Where Are Postcommunist Countries Going?" *Journal of Democracy* 8 (July 1997): 96.

22. See, for example, the discussion in Kurt Weyland, "Obstacles to Social Reform in Brazil's New Democracy," *Comparative Politics* 29 (October 1996): 1–22.

23. See, for example, James Eisenstein et al., *The Play of Power: An Introduction to American Government* (New York: St. Martin's, 1996), p. 396.

24. Gordon S. Wood, *The Radicalism of the American Revolution* (New York: Vintage, 1991), p. 56.

25. V. O. Key, Jr., *Southern Politics in State and Nation* (Knoxville: University of Tennessee Press, 1984), Chapters 26 and 27. Daniel Hellinger and Dennis R. Judd, *The Democratic Facade,* 2nd ed. (Belmont, CA: Wadsworth, 1994), pp. 128–129. Eisenstein et al., p. 413.

26. Anastatia Sims, "Armageddon in Tennessee: The Final Battle over the Nineteenth Amendment," in *One Woman, One Vote: Rediscovering the Woman Suffrage Movement,* edited by Marjorie Spruill Wheeler (Troutdale, OR: New Sage Press, 1995), p. 350.

27. Jurg Steiner, *European Democracies,* 2nd ed. (New York: Longman, 1991), p. 173.

28. *The Statesman's Year-Book, 1995–1996,* 132nd ed., edited by Brian Hunter (New York: St. Martin's, 1995), p. 1242.

29. On the immigration referendum, see *Financial Times* (25 September 2000). The referenda and initiative processes are discussed in Steiner, pp. 152–153; Hanspeter Kriesi, "Political Power and Decision Making in Switzerland," in *Switzerland in Perspective,* edited by Janet Eve Hilowitz (New York: Greenwood, 1990), pp. 40–41, 45–49; Wolf Linder, *Swiss Democracy: Possible Solutions to Conflict in Multicultural Societies* (New York: St. Martin's, 1994), pp. 85–91, 97–114; Hanspeter Kriesi and Dominique Wisler, "Social Movements and Direct Democracy in Switzerland," *European Journal of Political Research* 30 (July 1996): 20–21.

30. *The Statesman's Year-Book, 1995–1996,* 132nd ed., p. 1243; *Political Handbook of the World: 1995–1996,* p. 913; Steiner, p. 174.

31. *The Political Handbook of the World: 1995–1996,* pp. 913–916; Linder, p. 97.

32. Dryzek distinguishes between active and passive state policies on the matter of interest inclusion and representation, pp. 64–70.

33. John Mack Faragher, *The Encyclopedia of Colonial and Revolutionary America* (New York: Facts on File, 1990), pp. 123–124; *Dictionary of American Biography,* Vol. 3, edited by Allen Johnson and Dumas Malone (New York: Scribner's, 1959), p. 584.

34. The U.S. approach to pluralism through church–state separation is discussed in Kenneth D. Wald, *Religion and Politics in the United States* (New York: St. Martin's, 1987), pp. 103–107.

35. German Embassy, Washington, DC, Background Papers, Church and State in Germany, http://www.germany-info-org *The German Polity,* 5th ed. (New York: Longman, 1993), p. 40; Russell J. Dalton, *Politics in Germany,* 2nd ed. (New York: HarperCollins, 1993), p. 255; Evangelical Church in Berlin-Brandenburg, "Church Tax" (http://www.ekibb.com/english/tasks/tax.htm, accessed 6 August 1997); William E. Downey, "Church Taxes in Germany: Not Taking the Pledge," *Christian Century* 114 (13 August 1997): 731–734.

36. Evangelical Church in Berlin-Brandenburg.

37. Wald, pp. 106–107.

38. Quoted in Craig R. Whitney, "Scientology and Its German Foes: A Bitter Conflict," *New York Times* (7 November 1994): A6.

39. U.S. Department of State, *Germany Country Report on Human Rights Practices for 1996.* Released by the Bureau of Democracy, Human Rights, and Labor (30 January 1997); Heber C. Jentzsch, "Feature Release: Even Hitler Paid the Church Tax" (http://hatewatch.freedommag.org/press/eng/major/05/97000501.htm, accessed 7 August 1997); Teresa Malcolm, "Church Tax Proposed," *National Catholic Reporter* 33 (8 November 1996): 10–11; "Germany Is Focus of Scientology Dispute," *Christian Century* 114 (5–12 February 1997): 123–124; "A German Eye on Scientology," *Economist* (1 February 1995): 50.

40. For a succinct overview of how political scientists have conceptualized, operationalized, and researched political socialization, students may wish to consult Ronald H. Chilcote, *Theories of Comparative Politics: The Search for a Paradigm* (Boulder, CO: Westview, 1981), pp. 231–234; Roberta S. Sigel, "Introduction: Persistence and Change," in *Political Learning in Adulthood: A Sourcebook of Theory and Research,* edited by Roberta S. Sigel (Chicago: University of Chicago Press, 1989), pp. vii–xvi.

41. William J. Clinton, "Proclamation 6937—National Character Counts Week, 1996," *Weekly Compilation of Presidential Documents* 32 (21 October 1996): 2047; William F. Buckley, Jr., "School Uniforms?!" *National Review* (26 February 1996): 71.

42. Ken Schroeder, "In Brief ... Character Counts," *Education Digest* 60 (January 1995): 75.

43. Velma LaPoint, Lillian O. Holloman, and Sylvan I. Alleyne, "Dress Codes and Uniforms in Urban Schools," *Education Digest* 58 (March 1993): 32–34.

44. M. Sue Stanley, "School Uniforms and Safety," *Education and Urban Society* 28 (August 1996): 424–435.

45. The process of democratization in Argentina is discussed in Aldo C. Vacs, "Argentina: The Melancholy of Liberal Democracy," in *Establishing Democracies,* edited by Mary Ellen Fischer (Boulder, CO: Westview, 1996), pp. 149–177; Peter G. Snow, "Argentina: Politics in a Conflict Society," in *Latin American Politics and Development* (Boulder, CO: Westview, 1985), pp. 135–136; Gerardo L. Munck and Carol Skalnik Leff, "Modes of Transition and Democratization: South America and Eastern Europe in Comparative Perspective," *Comparative Politics* 29 (April 1997): 353–354.

46. Roxana Morduchowicz, Edgardo Catterberg, Richard G. Niemi, and Frank Bell, "Teaching Political Information and Democratic Values in a New Democracy: An Argentine Experiment," *Comparative Politics* 28 (July 1996): 465–476. The state's role in the political socialization process and in the educational system is discussed generally in Robert F. Arnove, Alberto Torres, Stephen Franz, and Kimberly Morse, "A Political Sociology of Education and Development in Latin America: The Conditioned State, Neoliberalism, and Educational Policy," *International Journal of Comparative Sociology* 37 (June 1996): 140–158. This article focuses on Argentina, Nicaragua, Chile, and Brazil.

47. Morduchowicz et al., pp. 471–472.

48. Ibid., p. 467; Arnove et al., pp. 143–144.

49. Students who go on to study U.S. law will discover that political scientists disagree as to whether it is most appropriate to consider the first 10 or the first 8 amendments as constituting the Bill of Rights proper. The debate centers around the fact that the first 8 amendments possess content that is more precisely oriented toward rights, even though the Ninth and Tenth Amendments have also been used by the courts to promote policies protective of rights and were ratified at the same time as the first 8 amendments.

50. The original Constitution did include three rights: protections against bills of attainder and ex post facto laws, as well as provisions for writs of habeas corpus. Tadahisa Kuroda and Erwin L. Levine, "The United States: Creating the Republic," in *Establishing Democracies,* edited by Fischer, pp. 56–86; Lee Epstein and Thomas G. Walker, *Constitutional Law for a Changing America: Rights, Liberties, and Justice* (Washington, DC: Congressional Quarterly Press, 1992), pp. 3–7.

51. Jane Mansbridge analyzes democracy's need to be regulative and coercive in "Using Power/Fighting Power: The Polity," in *Democracy and Difference: Contesting the Boundaries of the Political,* edited by Seyla Benhabib (Princeton, NJ: Princeton University Press, 1996), pp. 46–66. On the Patriot Act, see ACLU, Surveillance Under the Patriot Act, http://www.aclu.org; Alison Beard, "Patriot Act Puts on Compliance Pressure", *Ft.com* (26 June 2002): 1; Mike Allen, "Bush Faces Sustained Dissension on the Right: A Sense of Disappointment Is Spreading," *Washington Post* (22 April 2002): A1.

52. Thomas G. West discusses various limitations on speech in "Freedom of Speech," *Current* (July 1996): 28–31.

53. *Griswold and Roe* are discussed in Epstein and Walker, pp. 267–273, 294–313; see also Susan C. Wawrose, *Griswold v. Connecticut: Contraception and the Right to Privacy* (Danbury, CT: Franklin Watts, 1996). Epstein and Walker point out that various provisions of the Constitution were used in the privacy cases of recent years. See also Susan Gluck Mezey, *In Pursuit of Equality: Women, Public Policy, and the Federal Courts* (New York: St. Martin's, 1992), pp. 214–216.

54. Lawrence S. Graham, Richard P. Farkas, Robert C. Grady, Jorgen Rasmussen,

Taketsugu Tsurutani, *Politics and Government*, 3rd ed. (Chatham, NJ: Chatham House, 1994), pp. 80–82; Alexander MacLeod, "Britain's Constitutional Question," *Comparative Politics 94/95*, 12th ed., edited by Christian Soe (Guilford, CT: Dushkin, 1994), pp. 18–19.

55. Jorgen S. Rasmussen, *The British Political Process: Concentrated Power versus Accountability* (Belmont, CA: Wadsworth, 1993), pp. 46–51; Philip Norton, *The British Polity*, 2nd ed. (New York: Longman, 1991), pp. 72–77. David Pannick, "What Could Be More British," *The London Times* (3 October 2000); Sarah Lyall, "209 Years Later, the English Get American-Style Bill of Rights," *New York Times* (2 October 2000): A3.

56. Major is quoted in "The Tug for the Flag," *Economist* (29 June 1996): 51.

57. MacLeod discusses Charter 88, pp. 18–19.

58. World Bank, *World Development Report 1996* (New York: Oxford University Press, 1996), pp. 194–195.

59. Ibid., p. 189.

60. Ibid., pp. 198–199.

61. World Bank, 1996, p. 197; "The Wealth Divide," *Multinational Monitor* (May 2003): 11–15.

62. Frank Newport, "Americans Upbeat, but Not Extraordinarily So," Gallup Organization (http://www.gallup.com/poll/news/970516~1.htm, accessed 13 August 1997).

63. Marie Arana-Ward, "For Children of the Fields, Education Is Elusive," *Washington Post* (4 August 1997): A1.

64. McCormick, *Comparative Politics in Transition*, pp. 320–322; *The Statesman's Yearbook, 1996–1997*, 133rd ed., edited by Brian Hunter (New York: St. Martin's, 1996), pp. 644–645; Shashi Tharoor, "India, Poised to Become an Economic Superpower," *Washington Post* (10 August 1997): C1.

65. The Gallup India Survey (http://www.gallup.com/poll/special/india/report, accessed August 21, 1997).

66. World Bank, *World Development Report, 1996*, pp. 188, 198.

67. *Political Handbook of the World 1997*, pp. 366–367; *The Statesman's Yearbook, 1996–1997*, p. 642; McCormick, *Comparative Politics in Transition*, pp. 319–322.

68. *The Statesman's Yearbook, 1996–1997*, p. 642; *Political Handbook of the World, 1997*, pp. 366–367; McCormick, *Comparative Politics in Transition*, p. 323.

69. For an assessment of India's democracy, students may wish to consult the general discussion found in Arend Lijphart, "The Puzzle of Indian Democracy: A Consociational Interpretation," *American Political Science Review* 90 (June 1996): 258.

70. Students may wish to examine the discussion of nondemocratic government found in Martin C. Needler, *Identity, Interest, and Ideology: An Introduction to Politics* (Westport, CT: Praeger, 1996), p. 25. Although he does not explicitly mention the five components of democracy discussed here in his analysis of dictatorships, his definition does implicitly draw attention to the fact that numerous processes are involved in authoritarian politics; these processes, he notes, relate to the denial of participation, the use of government as an instrument of popular control, and the suppression of the development of pluralistic viewpoints. See also Daniel A. Bell, "A Communitarian Critique of Authoritarianism: The Case of Singapore," *Political Theory* 25 (February 1997): 6–32.

71. W. Phillips Shively, *Power and Choice: An Introduction to Political Science*, 4th ed. (New York: McGraw-Hill, 1995), p. 140.

72. Students may find further discussions of these cases in J. Samuel Valenzuela and Arturo Valenzuela, "Chile and the Breakdown of Democracy," in *Latin American Politics and Development*, edited by Wiarda and Kline, pp. 241–247; Kendall W. Stiles, *Case Histories in International Politics* (New York: HarperCollins, 1995), pp. 220–230; Lawrence C. Mayer et al., *Comparative Politics: Nations and Theories in a Changing World*, pp. 218–219.

73. Neuhouser, p. 645.

74. Bill Keller, "African Ruler Finds Himself an Anachronism," *New York Times* (1 June 1993): A1, A6; Bill Keller, "Foes Gather to Jeer Fallen African Founding Father," *New*

*York Times* (26 January 95): A5; "After Banda," *The Economist* (21 May 1994): 46; Andrew Meldrum, "Legacy of a Dictator," *Africa Report* 40 (March 1995): 56–59.

75. Lara Marlowe, "Revolutionary Disintegration," *Time* (26 June 1995): 42–43.

76. Gretchen Casper, *Fragile Democracies: The Legacies of Authoritarian Rule* (Pittsburgh, PA: University of Pittsburgh Press, 1995), pp. 40–47.

77. David Wurfel, *Filipino Politics: Development and Decay* (Ithaca, NY: Cornell University Press, 1988), p. 120.

78. Jose V. Abueva, "Philippine Ideologies and National Development," in *Government and Politics of the Philippines,* edited by Raul P. De Guzman and Mila A. Reforma (New York: Oxford University Press, 1988), p. 56.

79. Wurfel, pp. 165–166.

80. Ibid., p. 166.

81. Madeleine Albright's characterization of the government is found in Dennis Bernstein and Leslie Kean, "People of the Opiate," *The Nation* (16 December 1996): 18; "A SLORC by Any Other Name," *Washington Post* (6 March 1998): A24 (http://www.washingtonpost.com/wp-srv/Wplate/1998-03/06/0001-030698-idx.html); "Myanmar Leader Says Military Will Not Rule Forever," *Reuters* (13 April 1998): (http://www.infoseek.com/Content?arn=a0035…+Kyi,Soros,UNOCAL&col=NX&kt=A&ak=news 1486).

82. Ibid.

83. Ibid., p. 12.

84. Shively breaks nondemocratic regimes down into three categories: military, party, and individual leaders (pp. 142–148).

85. *Political Handbook of the World: 1994–1995,* edited by Arthur S. Banks (Binghamton: State University of New York/CSA Publications, 1995), p. 333. On the matter of instability and nondemocratic government, see Karen Remmer's discussion of the viability and stability of democracies versus authoritarian governments in "The Sustainability of Political Democracy: Lessons from South America," *Comparative Political Studies* 29 (December 1996): 611–634.

86. McCormick, *Comparative Politics in Transition,* p. 159.

87. F. Gregory Gausse III, *Oil Monarchies: Domestic and Security Challenges in the Arab Gulf States* (New York: Council on Foreign Relations), pp. 8–9, 115–116; *Political Handbook of the World, 1994–1995,* pp. 718–719; Andrew Rathmell and Kirsten Schulze, "Political Reform in the Gulf: The Case of Qatar," *Middle Eastern Studies* 36 (October 2000): 47.

88. Shively, *Power and Choice,* p. 147.

89. Brantly Womack and James R. Townsend, "Politics in China," in *Comparative Politics Today: A World View,* 5th ed., edited by Gabriel A. Almond and G. Bingham Powell, Jr. (New York: HarperCollins, 1992), pp. 420–422; Maurice Meisner, *Mao's China: A History of the People's Republic* (New York: Free Press, 1977), pp. 217–225; Patrick E. Tyler, "Deng Xiaoping, Architect of Modern China, Dies at 92," *New York Times* (20 February 1997): A1, A8; McCormick, *Comparative Politics in Transition,* pp. 188–191.

90. McCormick, *Comparative Politics in Transition,* pp. 190–191; Patrick E. Tyler, "Deng Xiaoping: A Political Wizard Who Put China on the Capitalist Road," *New York Times* (20 February 1997): A10–A12; William H. Overholt, "China after Deng," *Foreign Affairs* 75 (May–June 1996): 63–78; Robert A. Scalapino, "The End of Communism in Asia: What Next?" *Current* (September 1995): 16–22; "China: A Funny-Looking Tiger," *Economist* (17 August 1996): 17–19.

91. BBC News, "Profile: Hu Jintao" (5 March 2003): bbc.co.uk.

92. Patrick E. Tyler, "Deng Xiaoping: A Political Wizard," p. A10; Tony Carnes, "Smack Down," *Christianity Today* (23 October 2000), p. 22; Melanie Manion, "The Electoral Connection in the Chinese Countryside," *American Political Science Review* 90 (1996): 736–813.

## Chapter 9

1. For a discussion of the political fights over measuring time, see Freeman J. Byson, "Clockwork Science," *New York Review of Books* 50 (6 November 2003), www.nybook.com/archives/16739; on vilifying gays, see Michael Moore, "What You Can't Get Away with on TV," *The Nation* (18 November 1996): 10.

2. Frank Rich, "Bashing to Victory," *New York Times* (14 February 1996): A15.

3. "The G.O.P. Hones Its Message," *Harper's* (January 1996): 23.

4. Caroline Fraser, "The Raid at Silver Spring," *The New Yorker* (19 April 1993): 77.

5. Neal D. Barnard and Stephen R. Kaufman, "Animal Research Is Wasteful and Misleading," *Scientific American* (February 1997): 80–82; James M. Jasper and Jane D. Poulsen, "Recruiting Strangers and Friends: Moral Shocks and Social Networks in Animal Rights and AntiNuclear Protests," *Social Problems* 42 (November 1995): 493–512.

6. This definition is informed by the analyses of Mark P. Petracca, "The Rediscovery of Interest Group Politics," in *The Politics of Interests: Interest Groups Transformed*, edited by Mark P. Petracca (Boulder, CO: Westview, 1992), pp. 6–7; Martin C. Needler, *Identity, Interest, and Ideology: An Introduction to Politics* (Westport, CT: Praeger, 1996), p. 96; Jeffrey M. Berry, *The Interest Group Society*, 2nd ed. (Glenview, IL: Scott Foresman/Little, Brown, 1989), p. 4.

7. Frist is quoted in "Broad Bills Stuffed with Lawmakers' Pet Items," *New York Times* (27 November 2003): A26; Clifford Krauss, "Lobbyists of Every Stripe on Health Care Proposal," *New York Times* (24 September 1993): A1, A12.

8. "From the K Street Corridor," *National Journal* (9 August 1997): 1607.

9. Peter H. Stone, "Lobbyists Come out Smokin'," *National Journal* (2 August 1997): 1555.

10. Keith Bradsher, "Sugar Price Supports Survive Political Shift," *New York Times* (9 September 1995): A1, A12.

11. "Big Airlines' Lobbying Efforts ... Produce Unwelcome Turbulence," *Congressional Quarterly* (12 July 1997): 1610–1611; "Another Front in the Air War," *Congressional Quarterly* (26 July 1997): 1768.

12. Details on this case are outlined in David E. Rosenbaum, "For Every Bill There Is the Perfect Lobbyist," *New York Times* (7 May 1993): A1, A12.

13. Stephen Engelberg, "Business Leaves the Lobby and Sits at Congress's Table," *New York Times* (31 March 1995): A1, A11.

14. Jonathan Weisman, "Documents Offer a Closer Look at Tobacco's Clout in Congress," *Congressional Quarterly* (16 August 1997): 1960.

15. "How a Bill Becomes a Law: The New Approach," *Harper's* (July 1995): 9.

16. These cases are discussed in Rick Wartzman, "In Washington, Groups with Conflicting Views Hire Same Lobbyists without Creating Problems," *Wall Street Journal* (4 October 1993): A14; Burt Solomon, "Forever Unclean," *National Journal* (March 18, 2000): 858–860.

17. David E. Rosenbaum, "Well, Yes, Being an Ex-Congressman Helps," *New York Times* (20 October 1993): A11.

18. Louis Jacobson, "Young Guns," *National Journal* (13 September 1997): 1775.

19. Dean Baquet, "Ex-Aide Is Now Lobbyist with White House Ties," *New York Times* (12 May 1994): A1, A12.

20. Joel Brinkley, "Lobbying Rule of the 1990s: Show the Most Vulnerable," *New York Times* (16 June 1993): A1, A12. Students can read about another grassroots campaign directed toward scaring the public as a means of generating donations to the interest group conducting the campaign in Erik Eckholm, "Alarmed by Fund Raisers, the Elderly Give Millions," *New York Times* (12 November 1992): A1, A11.

21. Jane Fritsch, "The Grass Roots, Just a Free Phone Call Away," *New York Times* (23 June 1995): A1, A11.

22. Jane Fritsch, "Sometimes, Lobbyists Strive to Keep Public in the Dark," *New York Times* (19 March 1996): A1, A14.

23. Daniel Hellinger and Dennis R. Judd, *The Democratic Facade*, 2nd ed. (Belmont, CA: Wadsworth, 1994), pp. 75–77; Peter Stone, "Starting Over," *National Journal* (February 26, 2000): 604–609.

24. Steven A. Holmes, "N.A.A.C.P. Tries to Build Political Power for 1996," *New York Times* (2 October 1995): A6.

25. John P. Heinz et al., *The Hollow Core: Private Interests in National Policy Making* (Cambridge, MA: Harvard University Press, 1993), p. 387.

26. Jason DeParle, "A Fundamental Problem," *New York Times Magazine* (14 July 1996): Section 6, p. 22.

27. DeParle, p. 32; Kim A. Lawton, "Christian Coalition Moves ahead Despite Political Growing Pains," *Christianity Today* (28 October 1996): 84–85. See also Jill Abramson and Leslie Wayne, "Nonprofit Groups Were Partners to Both Parties in Last Election," *New York Times* (24 October 1997): A1, A13.

28. Seth Mydans, "Evangelicals Gain with Covert Candidates," *New York Times* (27 October 1992): A1, A9.

29. Eliza Newlin Carney, "Stealth Bombers," *National Journal* (16 September 1997): 1642.

30. See, for example, the information provided in Jonathan S. Krasno, Donald Philip Green, and Jonathan A. Cowden, "The Dynamics of Campaign Fundraising in House Elections," *Journal of Politics* 56 (May 1994): 459–474; Peter H. Stone, "The GOP's New Gold Mine," *National Journal* 26 (3 December 1994): 2869.

31. Specific examples can be found in Peter H. Stone, "PACs Giving Republicans a Second Look," *National Journal* 26 (29 October 1994), pp. 2523–2525.

32. Ibid., p. 1640.

33. Leslie Wayne, "Congress Uses Leadership PACs to Wield Power," *New York Times* (13 March 1997): A1. Students may find more extensive discussions of the politician-affiliated PACs in Eliza Newlin Carney, "PAC Men," *National Journal* 26 (1 October 1994): 2268–2273; Eric Moses, "Leader of the PAC," *National Journal* 28 (16 March 1996): 587–590.

34. Richard L. Berke, "Health Debate Is Filling Campaign Coffers," *New York Times* (19 April 1994): A1, A10.

35. Leslie Wayne, "Loopholes Allow Presidential Race to Set a Record," *New York Times* (8 September 1996): A19.

36. Jonathan Weisman, "Documents Offer a Closer Look at Tobacco's Clout in Congress," *Congressional Quarterly* (16 August 1997): 1960.

37. See, for example, the discussion in George Hager, "Amid Cries for Reform, Parties and Politicians Pack Coffers," *Congressional Quarterly* (9 August 1997): 1911–1912.

38. Wayne, "Loopholes," p. A19.

39. Alan Greenblatt, "Politics and Marketing Merge in Parties' Bid for Relevance," *Congressional Quarterly* (16 August 1997): 1967; Wayne, "Loopholes," p. A19.

40. James M. Perry, "Senate Republicans Plan Independent Ad Expenditures," *Wall Street Journal* (23 September 1996): A22.

41. Terry M. Neal, "RNC Invests Heavily in `Issue' Attack Ads," *Washington Post* (22 October 1997): A1.

42. Greenblatt, p. 1969; FEC (www.fecweb1.fec.gov/press).

43. FECA, FAQ on the BCRA and Other New Rules, September 2003, www.fec.gov; Thomas Edson, ington Post *(21 June 2002): A1.

44. Richard L. Berke, "Before Asking for Votes, Candidates Ask for Cash," *New York Times* (10 May 1994): A11.

45. See the discussion of this strategy within the context of comparative politics in Susan M. Olson, "Comparing Women's Rights Litigation in the Netherlands and the United States," *Polity* 38 (Winter 1995): 199–200, 209, 215.

46. Schlozman and Tierney, Chapter 14; Gregg Ivers, "Religious Organizations as Constitutional Litigants," *Polity* 25 (Winter 1992): 243–266.

47. For a more complete discussion of these events, see Lee Epstein and C. K. Rowland, "Interest Groups in the Courts: Do Groups Fare Better?," in *Interest Group Politics,* edited by Cigler and Loomis, pp. 278–279.

48. Joe Taylor, "Group Fights for Religious Free Speech in Schools," *Albuquerque Journal* (22 December 1992): A8.

49. Nick Alexander, "Sweatshop Activism: Missing Pieces," *Z Magazine* (September 1977): 14.

50. Jurg Steiner, *European Democracies,* 4th ed. (New York: Longman, 1998), pp. 131–132.

51. Jonas Pontusson, "Sweden," in *European Politics in Transition,* 2nd ed. (Lexington, MA: Heath, 1992), pp. 492–493.

52. W. Lance Bennett and Erik Asard, "The Marketplace of Ideas: The Rhetoric

and Politics of Tax Reform in Sweden and the United States," *Polity* 38 (Fall 1995): 4.

53. Corporatism in Sweden, Denmark, and Scandinavia generally is analyzed in Jan-Erik Lane and Svante Ersson, "The Nordic Countries: Contention, Compromise and Corporatism," in *Political Institutions in Europe,* edited by Joseph M. Colomer (New York: Routledge, 1996), pp. 254–281.

54. Definitions and examples of interest group pluralism and democratic corporatism are found in Steiner, Chapter 6; Almond and Powell, pp. 74–76; Martin J. Smith, *Pressure, Power and Policy: State Autonomy and Policy Networks in Britain and the United States* (Pittsburgh, PA: University of Pittsburgh Press, 1993), pp. 15–37; Jane J. Mansbridge, "A Deliberative Theory of Interest Representation," in Petracca, pp. 38–47; Pepper D. Culpepper, "Organisational Competition and the Neo-Corporatist Fallacy in French Agriculture," *West European Politics* 16 (July 1993): 295–315; William D. Coleman, "Reforming Corporatism: The French Banking Policy Community, 1941–1990," *West European Politics* 16 (April 1993): 122–143; Razeen Sally, "The Basel Chemical Multinationals: Corporate Action within Structures of Corporatism in Switzerland," *West European Politics* 16 (October 1993): 561–580; Wyn Grant, *Pressure Groups, Politics and Democracy in Britain,* 2nd ed. (New York: Harvester Wheatsheaf, 1995), pp. 28–39; Frank L. Wilson, *Concepts and Issues in Comparative Politics: An Introduction to Comparative Analysis* (Upper Saddle River, NJ: Prentice Hall, 1996), pp. 102–105.

55. Peter A. Hall, "Policy Paradigms, Social Learning, and the State: The Case of Economic Policymaking in Britain," *Comparative Politics* 25 (April 1993): 281. Useful comparisons of state autonomy, corporatism, and pluralism are also found in Sylvia Bashevkin, "Interest Groups and Social Movements," in *Comparing Democracies: Elections and Voting in Global Perspective,* edited by Lawrence LeDuc, Richard G. Niemi, and Pippa Norris (Thousand Oaks, CA: Sage, 1996), pp. 145–152.

56. Ibid., pp. 290–291.

57. Kay Lehman Schlozman and John T. Tierney, *Organized Interests and American*

*Democracy* (New York: Harper & Row, 1986), p. 10.

58. Virginia Gray and David Lowery, *The Population Ecology of Interest Representation: Lobbying Communities in the American States* (Ann Arbor: University of Michigan Press, 1996), p. 12.

59. See, for example, the discussion in Gabriel A. Almond and G. Bingham Powell, Jr., eds., *Comparative Politics Today: A World View,* 6th ed. (New York: HarperCollins, 1996), pp. 71–73.

60. Ibid.

61. Virginia Foster Durr, *Outside the Magic Circle: The Autobiography of Virginia Foster Durr* (New York: Touchstone, 1985), pp. 280–283.

62. Almond and Powell, pp. 71–73.

63. George T. Crane, "Collective Identity, Symbolic Mobilization, and Student Protest in Nanjing, China, 1988–1989," *Comparative Politics* 26 (July 1994): 397.

64. Marcia A. Weigle and Jim Butterfield, "Civil Society in Reforming Communist Regimes: The Logic of Emergence," *Comparative Politics* 25 (October 1992): 14–15.

65. Michael G. Roskin, *The Rebirth of East Europe* (Englewood Cliffs, NJ: Prentice Hall, 1991), p. 124.

66. Almond and Powell, pp. 75–76.

67. Wayne A. Cornelius, "Politics in Mexico," in Almond and Powell, pp. 517–520.

68. Sam Dillon, "Union Vote in Mexico Illustrates Abuses," *New York Times* (13 October 1997): A6.

69. Ibid.

70. This discussion is based on Kenneth Janda, "Comparative Political Parties: Research and Theory," in *Political Science: The State of the Discipline II,* edited by Ada W. Finifter (Washington, DC: American Political Science Association, 1993), p. 166.

71. Janet M. Box-Steffensmeier, Laura W. Arnold, and Christopher J. W. Zorn, "The Strategic Timing of Position Taking in Congress: A Study of the North American Free Trade Agreement," *American Political Science Review* 91 (June 1997): 324–338.

72. David Corn, "Dick Gephardt: Working-Class Hero, On-the-Make Pol or Both?" *The Nation* (7 July 1997): 11–12.

73. Lawrence C. Dodd and Bruce I. Oppenheimer, "Revolution in the House: Testing the Limits of Party Government," in *Congress Reconsidered,* 6th ed., edited by Dodd and Oppenheimer (Washington, DC: Congressional Quarterly Press, 1997), p. 47.

74. See Jackie Koszczuk, "Party Stalwarts Will Determine Gingrich's Long Term Survival," *Congressional Quarterly* (26 July 1997): 1751.

75. For a fuller discussion of the different Republican attacks, see E. J. Dionne, Jr., "The Republicans' Fine Mess," *Washington Post Weekly Edition* (4 August 1997): 2; attacks on Gingrich for being "soft" on gay issues are discussed in "Gingrich Upsets Pro-Family Advocates," *Human Events* (10 May 1996): 5.

76. "Two Are Two, and All Alone," *Economist* (18 May 1996): 23–25.

77. Janda, pp. 171–172; Frank J. Sorauf, *Party Politics in America,* 5th ed. (Boston: Little, Brown, 1984), Chapter 3; Everett Carl Ladd, "Of Political Parties Great and Small: Democracy and Political Parties," *Current* (December 1994): 33–39. See also the discussion in David W. Rohde, *Parties and Leaders in the Postreform House* (Chicago: University of Chicago Press, 1991), in which the author points out that the election focus may not always preclude party unity.

78. Sorauf, pp. 295–296; David Cantor and Paul S. Herrnson, "Party Campaign Activity and Party Unity in the U.S. House of Representatives," *Legislative Studies Quarterly* 22 (August 1997): 400–405; Paul S. Herrnson and Kelly D. Patterson, "Toward a More Programmatic Democratic Party? Agenda-Setting and Coalition-Building in the House of Representatives," *Polity* 27 (Summer 1995): 625, 628; Richard Herrera, "Cohesion at the Party Conventions: 1980–1988," *Polity* 26 (Fall 1993): 75–89; Terry J. Royed and Stephen A. Borrelli, "Political Parties and Public Policy: Social Welfare Policy from Carter to Bush," *Polity* 29 (Summer 1997): 561.

79. This characteristic has prompted observers to describe U.S. parties and campaigns as candidate driven or oriented, as noted in David M. Farrell "Campaign Strategies and Tactics," in *Comparing Democracies,* edited by LeDuc, Niemi, and Norris.

80. Tanya Melich, "The Silent Republicans," *New York Times* (7 March 1996): A23; Alan Greenblatt, "GOP's Conservative Camp Makes Its Voice Heard," *Congressional Quarterly* (10 August 1996): 2267–2268.

81. Cantor and Herrnson, p. 410; Stephen E. Frantzich, *Political Parties in the Technological Age* (New York: Longman, 1989), p. 231.

82. Dan Balz, "GOP's Five Warring Factions Help Democrats, Pollster Says," *Washington Post* (26 February 1997): A2.

83. Alan Greenblatt, "Politics and Marketing Merge in Parties' Bid for Relevance," *Congressional Quarterly* (16 August 1997): 1969.

84. Sarah Widoff, "Alaska's 'Fringe': The Parties' Future?" *Congressional Quarterly* (16 August 1997): 1974.

85. Bruce E. Keith, David B. Magleby, Candice J. Nelson, Elizabeth Orr, Mark C. Westlye, and Raymond E. Wolfinger, *The Myth of the Independent Voter* (Berkeley: University of California Press, 1992), pp. 198–199; A. James Reichley, "The Future of the American Two-Party System after 1994," in *The State of the Parties: The Changing Role of Contemporary American Parties,* 2nd ed., edited by John C. Green and Daniel M. Shea (Lanham, MD: Rowman & Littlefield, 1996), p. 11.

86. Students may wish to consult John C. Coleman, "Resurgent or Just Busy? Party Organizations in Contemporary America," pp. 367–384 in Green and Shea (see preceding note). Coleman offers a more complete overview of the debate in political science over whether declining party loyalty signals overall party decline in *Party Decline in America: Policy, Politics, and the Fiscal State* (Princeton, NJ: Princeton University Press, 1996), pp. 5–9; Howard L. Reiter and Julie M. Walsh, "Who Votes for Non-Major-Party Candidates? The Cases of Longley, Sanders, and Weicker," *Polity* (Summer 1995): 651–663.

87. Alan Greenblatt, "Politics and Marketing Merge in Parties' Bid for Relevance," *Congressional Quarterly* (16 August 1997): 1967.

88. Michael Nelson, "The Election: Turbulence and Tranquility in Contemporary American Politics," in *The Elections of 1996,* edited by Michael Nelson (Washington, DC: Congressional Quarterly, 1997), pp. 55–56; Marjorie Connelly, "Who Voted: A Portrait of American Politics, 1976-2000," *New York Times* (12 November 2000): Section 4, p. 4.

89. Frantzich, p. 158. The New Deal Coalition is, of course, a general pattern, with the coalition exhibiting stronger staying power in some states and localities than others; see Peter F. Nardulli for a discussion of how electoral coalitions in general display surprisingly large variations when viewed from a subnational perspective, "The Concept of Critical Realignment, Electoral Behavior, and Political Change," *American Political Science Review* 89 (March 1995): 10–22. See also Rhodes Cook, "Cities: Decidedly Democratic Declining in Population," *Congressional Quarterly* (12 July 1997): 1645.

90. Frantzich, p. 5.

91. Parties share this process with interest groups; see Frantzich, p. 5, and, especially, Jeremy Richardson, "The Market for Political Activism: Interest Groups as a Challenge to Political Parties," *West European Politics* 18 (January 1995): 116–139.

92. J. David Gillespie, *Politics at the Periphery: Third Parties in Two-Party America* (Columbia: University of South Carolina Press, 1993), p. 13.

93. Micah L. Sifry, "Crashing the Parties," *The Nation* (10 February 1997): 23.

94. These examples are discussed in Gillespie, pp. 9–12, 122–127. On the Minnesota Democratic Farmer Labor Party, see James M. Perry, "Politics in Minnesota Offer a Look at Woes Facing the Democrats," *Wall Street Journal* (25 September 1995): A1, A7. The results of the 2000 elections are analyzed in "Report: Gore Won Popular Vote by 539,897," *Washington Post* (21 December 2000): A9; Michael Powell, "Seared but Unwilted; Democrats See Red, but Green Party Faithful Say They Made Their Point," *Washington Post* (27 December 2000): C1.

95. Steiner, p. 29.

96. These categories and propositions are found in Almond and Powell, pp. 94–96.

97. Ibid.

98. Ibid.

99. *Political Handbook of the World, 1994–1995,* edited by Arthur S. Banks (Binghamton: State University of New York/CSA Publications, 1995), pp. 432–433.

100. This paragraph is based on Almond and Powell, pp. 94–95; Arend Lijphart, "The Puzzle of Indian Democracy: A Consociational Interpretation," *American Political Science Review* 90 (June 1996): 258.

101. John Ross, "After Elections, Apocalypse?" *The Nation* (8–15 August 1994): 157.

102. Wayne A. Cornelius, "Politics in Mexico" identifies and explains these five processes in Almond and Powell, pp. 520–522; see also Monica Serrano, "The End of Hegemonic Rule? Political Parties and the Transformation of the Mexican Party System," in *Party Politics in "An Uncommon Democracy": Political Parties and Elections in Mexico,* edited by Neil Harvey and Monica Serrano (London: Institute of Latin American Studies, 1994), pp. 1–4; Jose Antonio Crespo, "Governments of the Opposition: The Official Response," in *Opposition Government in Mexico,* edited by Victoria E. Rodriguez and Peter M. Ward (Albuquerque: University of New Mexico Press, 1995), p. 32. See also the discussions of the PRI's violations of human rights as part of its antiopposition strategy, as discussed in Scott Sherman, "Mexico's Morning After," *The Nation* (July 28–August 4, 1997): 20–23. Government programs as tools of protecting PRI dominance are analyzed in Anthony DePalma, "Anti-Poverty Program under Fire in Mexico," *New York Times* (3 July 1995): 5.

103. Jorge I. Dominguez and James A. McCann, "Shaping Mexico's Electoral Arena: The Construction of Partisan Cleavages in the 1988 and 1991 National Elections," *American Political Science Review* 89 (March 1995): 35; Tim Golden, "Governing Party in Mexico Suffers Big State Defeat," *New York Times* (14 February 1995): A1, A5.

104. Sam Dillon, "Newly Elected Mexican Opposition to Fight President's Economic Plan," *New York Times* (10 November 1997): A8.

105. See the observations of Cornelius, pp. 523, 529; Jorge Alcocer V., "Recent Electoral Reforms in Mexico: Prospects for a Real Multiparty Democracy," in *The Challenge of Institutional Reform in Mexico,* edited by Riordan Roett (Boulder, CO: Rienner, 1995), pp. 57–75; and Robert R. Bezdek's discussion of scholarly debates on democratization in Mexico in "Democratic Changes in an Authoritarian System: Navismo and Opposition Development in San Luis Potosi," in Rodriguez and Ward, p. 33 (see note 102); Mary Beth Sheridan, "Zedillo Leaves behind Great Achievements—and Significant Failures," *Los Angeles Times* (1 December 2000): A8; Sam Dillon, "Whoever Wins, Vote in Mexico Will Be Fateful," *New York Times* (2 July 2000): 1, 8.

106. Quoted in Cornelius, p. 496.

107. Quoted in Robert J. Dinkin, *Voting in Provincial America: A Study of Elections in the Thirteen Colonies, 1689–1776* (Westport, CT: Greenwood, 1977), p. 99; see Dinkin, p. 4, Chapter 2, p. 93, on the general nature of colonial elections.

108. Details are documented and discussed in Theodore J. Lowi and Benjamin Ginsberg, *Embattled Democracy: Politics and Policy in the Clinton Era* (New York: Norton, 1995), pp. 9–14; Gloria Borger with Kenneth Walsh, Matthew Cooper, and Michael Barone, "Clinton Breaks Out," *U.S. News & World Report* (27 July 1992): 26; George J. Church, "The Long Road," *Time* (2 November 1992): 28–43; Eleanor Clift, "Testing Ground," *Newsweek* (30 March 1992): 34–36; John Leland, "Rap and Race," *Newsweek* (29 June 1992): 47–52; Jonathan Alter, "Perot's Last Casting Call," *Newsweek* (12 October 1992): 44; Wick Allison, "How Bush Can Win," *National Review* (6 July 1992): 36–37; Maureen Dowd, "On the Trail, the Contradictory Sides of Bush," *New York Times* (2 November 1992): A1, A10; "'Manhattan Project,' 1992," *Newsweek* (November–December 1992): 40–56; "Face to Face in Prime Time," *Newsweek* (November–December 1992): 88–91.

109. Gwen Ifill, "Off-the-Books Advisers Giving Clinton a Big Lift," *New York Times* (1 April 1993): A10.

110. R. W. Apple, Jr., "Clinton's Refocusing," *New York Times* (5 May 1993): A10.

111. Richard L. Berke, "Dole Takes First Real Steps toward '96 Presidential Race," *New York Times* (15 June 1994): A1, A10.

112. Alison Mitchell, "Stung by Defeats in '94, Clinton Regrouped and Co-opted G.O.P.'s Strategies," *New York Times* (7 November 1996): B5.

113. Ibid., and James Bennet, "Liberal Use of 'Extremist' Is the Winning Strategy," *New York Times* (7 November 1997): B1, B7.

114. R. W. Apple, Jr., "The Economy, Again, Helps Clinton," *New York Times* (6 November 1996): A1, A13.

115. James Bennet, "Voter Interviews Suggest Clinton Was Persuasive on Path of U.S.," *New York Times* (7 November 1996): A11.

116. Eric Schmitt, "Half the Electorate, Perhaps Satisfied or Bored, Sat out Voting," *New York Times* (7 November 1996): B6.

117. On the Clinton contests, see ibid. For information on the 2000 elections, see "The Calendar of the Count," *New York Times* (14 December 2000): A23; Raja Mishra, "Bush Suit Eyes Military Votes Wants 13 Counties to Revisit Hundreds Deemed Invalid," *Boston Globe* (23 November 2000): A7; "Decision 2000/America Waits; Hundreds of Felons Cast Illegal Votes in Florida," *Los Angeles Times* (2 December 2000): 23; Albert R. Hunt, "The Disaffected Minority," *Wall Street Journal* (14 December 2000): A27; Tom Hamburger and Joni James, "Its Role in Question, Electoral College Picks Bush," *Wall Street Journal* (19 December 2000): A22; Don Van Natta, Jr., "Gore Lawyers Focus on Ballot in Palm Beach County," *New York Times* (16 November 2000): A25; Mike Downey, "California and the West: Is This Any Way to Pick a President?" *Los Angeles Times* (15 December 2000): A3; "Report: Gore Won Popular Vote by 539,897."

118. Matthew Hoffman, "Electoral College Dropouts," *The Nation* (17 June 1996): 15–16.

119. See the analysis by George Brown Tindall, *America: A Narrative History* (New York: Norton, 1984), pp. 381–383, 701–705, 844–845.

120. "An Order on Fairness" [editorial], *The Chattanooga Times* (10 July 1996): A6; Judy Walton, "Ruling Makes Judges' Re-Election Tougher," *The Chattanooga Times* (2 December 1997) (http://www.chattimes.com/news/today/ Tuesday/december21997/CTStoryaljdg122.html; 12/05/97); Michael E. Lewyn, "When Is Cumulative Voting Preferable to Single-Member Districting?" *New Mexico Law Review* 25 (Winter 1995): 197–215; Joseph F. Zimmerman, "Fair Representation for Minorities and Women," in *United States Electoral Systems: Their Impact on Women and Minorities,* edited by Wilma Rule and Joseph Zimmerman (New York: Greenwood, 1992), p. 4; Edward Still, "Cumulative Voting and Limited Voting in Alabama," in Rule and Zimmerman, pp. 183–196; Malcolm Jewell and David Olson, *American State Political Parties and Elections* (Homewood, IL: Dorsey, 1978), p. 5.

121. Zimmerman, p. 4; Douglas J. Amy, *Real Choices/New Voices: The Case for Proportional Representation Elections in the United States* (New York: Columbia University Press, 1993), pp. 18–20.

122. Russell J. Dalton and Martin P. Wattenberg discuss various models of voting choice in "The Not So Simple Act of Voting," *Political Science: The State of the Discipline II,* edited by Ada W. Finifter (Washington, DC: American Political Science Association, 1993), pp. 196–202; see also Dalton's analysis of the decline of sociological cleavages as a shaper of voter choice in Dalton, "Political Cleavages, Issues, and Electoral Change," in *Comparing Democracies,* edited by LeDuc, Niemi, and Norris, pp. 319–342.

123. Helmut Norpoth, "Presidents and the Prospective Voter," *Journal of Politics* 58 (August 1996): 778–779; Helmut Norpoth, "The Economy," in *Comparing Democracies,* edited by LeDuc, Niemi, and Norris, p. 317; Lonna Rae Atkeson and Randall W. Partin, "Economic and Referendum Voting: A Comparison of Gubernatorial and Senatorial Elections," *American Political Science*

*Review* 89 (March 1995): 99–100; David Sanders, "Economic Influences on the Vote: Modelling Electoral Decisions," in *Developing Democracy: Comparative Research in Honour of J. F. P. Blondel,* edited by Ian Budge and David McKay (Thousand Oaks, CA: Sage, 1994), especially pp. 80–82.

124. Norpoth, pp. 776–777.

125. See Arend Lijphart, "Unequal Participation: Democracy's Unresolved Dilemma. Presidential Address, American Political Science Association, 1996," *American Political Science Review* 91 (March 1997): 1, 5–6, for quote and for turnout figures.

126. Arend Lijphart, *Electoral Systems and Party Systems: A Study of Twenty-Seven Democracies, 1945–1990* (New York: Oxford University Press, 1994), p. 148.

127. See, for example, the discussions of these tendencies (as well as an analysis of why no single means of measuring the vote absolutely guarantees a fixed number of parties) in Steiner, Chapter 2; Almond and Powell, pp. 89–90; Lijphart, "Unequal Participation," pp. 7–8; Matthew Soberg Shugart, "Electoral Reform in Systems of Proportional Representation," *European Journal of Political Research* 21 (1992): 207–224; Giovanni Sartori, "The Influence of Electoral Systems: Faulty Laws or Faulty Method?" in *Electoral Laws and Their Consequences,* edited by B. Grofman and Arend Lijphart (New York: Agathon, 1986), p. 58; Ande Blais and Louis Massicotte, "Electoral Systems," in *Comparing Democracies: Elections and Voting in Global Perspective,* edited by Lawrence LeDuc, Richard G. Niemi, and Pippa Norris (Thousand Oaks, CA: Sage, 1996), pp. 49–81; Gary W. Cox, *Making Votes Count: Strategic Coordination in the World's Electoral Systems* (New York: Cambridge University Press, 1997), especially Chapter 3.

128. Steiner, pp. 42–44; Giovanni Sartori, *Comparative Constitutional Engineering: An Inquiry into Structures, Incentives and Outcomes,* 2nd ed. (London: Macmillan, 1997), p. 8.

129. Dalton and Wattenberg, pp. 210–211; John T. Ishiyama, "Electoral Systems Experimentation in the New Eastern Europe: The Single Transferable Vote and

the Additional Member System in Estonia and Hungary," *East European Quarterly* 29 (Winter 1995): 487–507; David M. Farrell, Malcolm Mackerras, and Ian McAllister, "Designing Electoral Institutions: STV Systems and Their Consequences," *Political Studies* (1996): 24–43.

130. Dalton and Wattenberg, p. 210; Mark N. Franklin, "Electoral Participation," in *Comparing Democracies,* edited by LeDuc, Niemi, and Norris, pp. 226–227.

131. Dalton and Wattenberg, p. 210; Lijphart, "Unequal Participation," p. 7; Franklin, pp. 226–227.

132. Dalton and Wattenberg, p. 210; Lijphart, "Unequal Participation," pp. 7–8.

133. Lijphart, "Unequal Participation," pp. 3, 8–10; Franklin, pp. 226–227.

134. *The Political Handbook of the World, 1994–1995,* edited by Arthur S. Banks (Binghamton: State University of New York, 1995), pp. 601–602.

## Chapter 10

1. See Giovanni Sartori, *Comparative Constitutional Engineering,* 2nd ed. (London: Macmillan, 1997), Chapters 5–6; Douglas V. Verney, "Parliamentary Government and Presidential Government," in *Parliamentary versus Presidential Government,* edited by Arend Lijphart (New York: Oxford University Press, 1992), pp. 32–46; Juan J. Linz, "The Perils of Presidentialism," in *The Global Resurgence of Democracy,* edited by Larry Diamond and Marc F. Plattner (Baltimore, MD: Johns Hopkins University Press, 1993), pp. 109, 111.

2. See Article II of the U.S. Constitution.

3. Richard E. Neustadt, "The Power to Persuade," in *The American Presidency: Historical and Contemporary Perspectives,* edited by Harry A. Bailey, Jr., and Jay M. Shafritz (Chicago: Dorsey, 1988), pp. 421–438.

4. Carl M. Cannon, "What Bush Said," *National Journal* (July 26, 2003); DHS, http://www.dhs.gov; Greg Hitt and David S. Cloud, „Bush Security Plan Faces Obstacles", *Wall Street Journal* (10 June 2002): A4.

5. Details in this paragraph are found in James Bennet and Robert Pear, "A Presidency Largely Defined by the Many Parts of Its Sum," *New York Times* (8 December

1997): A1, A14. See also Roger H. Davidson and Walter J. Oleszek, *Congress and Its Members,* 6th ed. (Washington, DC: Congressional Quarterly Press, 1998), p. 282; Jackie Koszczuk, "The `Comeback Kid': Down but Not Out," *Congressional Quarterly Weekly Reports* (15 November 1997): 2822–2823.

6. Larry Berman, *The New American Presidency* (Boston: Little, Brown, 1987), pp. 53, 69–70, 106, 224; Raymond Tatalovich and Byron W. Daynes, "Toward a Framework to Explain Presidential Power," in Bailey, Jr., and Shafritz, p. 441.

7. Davidson and Oleszek, p. 278.

8. Davidson and Oleszek, pp. 278–296.

9. Aaron Wildavsky, "The Two Presidencies," in Bailey, Jr., and Shafritz, pp. 235–237.

10. Davidson and Oleszek, pp. 296–298; see also Richard Rose, *The Postmodern President: The White House Meets the World* (Chatham, NJ: Chatham House, 1988), p. 2; Seymour Martin Lipset, "The Centrality of Political Culture," in Diamond and Plattner, p. 135; Carl M. Cannon, "Judging Clinton," *National Journal* 1 (January 2001): 23.

11. Martin Harrop, "An Apathetic Landslide: The British Election of 2001," *Government and Opposition* 36 (Summer 2001): 308.

12. Warren Hoge, "To Counter His Critics, Blair Focuses on the Poor," *New York Times* (11 December 1997): A6; see also Jill Sherman, "Labour Rebels Keep Harman under Pressure," *London Times* (16 December 1997) (http://www.the-times.co.uk/news/pages/Tuesday-Times/frontpage.html? 2149730, accessed 19 December 1997).

13. The preceding discussion of the structures and processes associated with the executive is based on information in Steiner, pp. 61–71; Jorgen S. Rasmussen, *The British Political Process: Concentrated Power versus Accountability* (Belmont, CA: Wadsworth, 1993), pp. 75–83; Martin Burch and Ian Holliday, *The British Cabinet System* (New York: Prentice Hall/Harvester Wheatsheaf, 1996), p. 51; Simon James, "The Cabinet System since 1945: Fragmentation and Integration," *Parliamentary Affairs* 47 (October 1994): 619–629; Martin Burch, "The British Cabinet: A Residual Executive," *Parliamentary Affairs* 41 (January 1988): 51.

14. Richard Rose, "British MPs: More Bark than Bite?" in *Parliaments and Parliamentarians in Democratic Politics* (New York: Holmes & Meier, 1986), pp. 8–40; Anthony Mughan and Roger M. Scully, "Accounting for Change in Free Vote Outcomes in the House of Commons," *British Journal of Political Science* (27 October 1997): 640.

15. For a particularly compelling discussion of just how much U.S. parties are not oriented toward platform and how this affects congressional–legislative relations, see David R. Mayhew, *Divided We Govern: Party Control, Lawmaking, and Investigations, 1946–1990* (New Haven, CT: Yale University Press, 1991), especially pp. 125–127.

16. Executive dominance in Britain is discussed in Rasmussen, pp. 75–79; Dawn Oliver, "Parliament, Ministers and the Law," *Parliamentary Affairs* 47 (October 1994): 643; Philip Norton, *The British Polity,* 2nd ed. (New York: Longman, 1991), pp. 197–205. Executive dominance in parliamentary democracy generally is analyzed in Michael Laver and Kenneth A. Shepsle, *Making and Breaking Governments* (New York: Cambridge University Press, 1996), pp. 3–5, 280–281.

17. Terry J. Royed, "Testing the Mandate Model in Britain and the United States: Evidence from the Reagan and Thatcher Eras," *British Journal of Political Science* 26 (January 1996): 47, 60, 66, 76.

18. R. A. W. Rhodes, "Introducing the Core Executive," in *Prime Minister, Cabinet and Core Executive,* edited by R. A. W. Rhodes and Patrick Dunleavy (New York: St. Martin's, 1995), p. 13.

19. Students can find more extensive discussions of the preceding and other features of the French, German, and Japanese cases in Steiner, Chapter 3; John McCormick, *Comparative Politics in Transition* (Belmont, CA: Wadsworth, 1995), Chapter 2; Almond and Powell, eds., Chapters 10–12; Thomas Saalfeld, "The West German Bundestag after 40 Years: The Role of Parliament in a Party Democracy," in *Parliaments in Western Europe,* edited by Phillip Norton (London: Cass, 1990): 68–89; Nicholas D. Kristof, "Japanese Election's Outcome Strengthens Premier's Position," *New York Times* (22 October 1996): A6.

20. "First Session Highlights," *Congressional Quarterly Weekly Reports* (6 December 1997): 3012.

21. Information on the legislative process and the procedures of both houses is found in Davidson and Oleszek, pp. 204–205, 227–248; Fred R. Harris, *Deadlock or Decision: The U.S. Senate and the Rise of National Politics* (New York: Oxford University Press, 1993), Chapter 5; Barbara Sinclair, *Unorthodox Lawmaking: New Legislative Processes in the U.S. Congress* (Washington, DC: Congressional Quarterly, 1997), Chapters 2–4; John B. Bader, *Taking the Initiative: Leadership Agendas in Congress and the "Contract with America"* (Washington, DC: Georgetown University Press, 1996), pp. 3–7; C. Lawrence Evans and Walter J. Oleszek, "Congressional Tsunami? The Politics of Committee Reform," in *Congress Reconsidered,* 6th ed. (Washington, DC: Congressional Quarterly, 1997), pp. 193–211; U.S. House of Representatives, "The U.S. House of Representatives. The Legislative Process—Tying It All Together" (http://www.house.gov/ Tying_it_all.html, accessed 16 December 1997); U.S. Senate, "Senate Committees. About the Senate Committee System" (http://www.senate. gov/committee/about.html, accessed 16 December 1997).

22. "The Vapors of Filibustering," *Newsweek* (19 August 1963): 31.

23. Davidson and Oleszek, p. 228.

24. Richard F. Fenno, Jr., *The Emergence of a Senate Leader: Pete Domenici and the Reagan Budget* (Washington, DC: Congressional Quarterly, 1991), p. 20.

25. Davidson and Oleszek, pp. 130, 143–144; Harris, pp. 134–137.

26. Tim Weiner, "Sending Money to Home District: Earmarking and the Pork Barrel," *New York Times* (13 July 1994): A1, C18.

27. Harris, pp. 260–261; Jonathan Weisman, "Domenici Dug Deep for State's Ditches," *Congressional Quarterly Weekly Reports* (12 July 1997): 1620.

28. House of Lords, "Brief Introduction to the House of Lords and Some Statistics" (http://www.parliament.the-stationary-office.co.uk/pa/ld199697/ldinfo/ld14info/ld14info.htm, accessed 16 December 1997);

"Time to Put This House in Order," *The Observer* (2 April 2000): 28; Joan Smith, "Everyone Wants to Be a Lady: The New House of Lords Is as Undemocratic as the Old One, but Women Especially Are Keen to Partake of This Blairite Patronage," *The Independent* (7 May 2000): 29.

29. Nevil Johnson, "Opposition in the British Political System," *Government and Opposition* 32 (Autumn 1997): 487–510.

30. Philip Cowley and David Melhuish, "Peers' Careers: Ministers in the House of Lords, 1964–95," *Political Studies* 45 (1997): 22.

31. An analysis of the distinctive choices, strategies, and actions of members of the House of Lords, given the fact that the House of Lords is a unique chamber, is found in Anthony Mughan and Jonathan P. Swarts, "The Coming of Parliamentary Television: The Lords and the Senate Compared," *Political Studies* 45 (1997): 36–48.

32. These numbers are provided by House of Lords, "The House of Lords at Work: Continued. The Work in the House. Primary Legislation" (http://www.parliament. the-stationary-office.co.uk/pa/ld199697/ ldinfo/ido2work/workhse.htm#p55, accessed 16 December 1997). See also Anthony Lewis, "Champions of Liberty," *New York Times* (31 January 1997): A19.

33. This discussion of British parliamentary structure and process is based on The United Kingdom Parliament, http://www. parliament.uk/works; Nevil Johnson, "Taking Stock Constitutional Reform," *Government and Opposition* 36 (Summer 2001): 331–354; Michael Cole, "Local Government in Britain, 1997–2001: National Forces and International Trends," *Government and Opposition* 38 (Spring 2003): 181–202; Rasmussen, pp. 93–104; Norton, pp. 287–298; Brian Hunter, ed., *The Statesman's Year-Book*, 1995–1996 (New York: St. Martin's, 1995), pp. 1313–1314; House of Lords, "The House of Lords at Work: Continued. The Work of the House. Primary Legislation" (http://www.parliament. the-stationary-office.co.uk/pa/ld199697/ ldinfo/ld02work/workhse.htm#p55, accessed 16 December 1997); Philip Norton, "The United Kingdom: Restoring Confidence?" *Parliamentary Affairs* 50 (July 1997): 357–372; Philip Norton and David Wood, "Constituency Service by Members of Parliament: Does It Contribute to a Personal Vote?" *Parliamentary Affairs* 43 (April 1990): 196–208.

34. Henry J. Abraham, *The Judicial Process*, 6th ed. (New York: Oxford University Press, 1993), pp. 271–288, 306–310; Jerome R. Corsi, *Judicial Politics: An Introduction* (Englewood Cliffs, NJ: Prentice Hall, 1984), pp. 284–285.

35. Abrahamson, p. 272.

36. Limitations on the use of judicial review and Court powers generally are analyzed in Abrahamson, pp. 323–324; Corsi, Chapter 7; Robert A. Carp and Ronald Stidham, *Judicial Process in America*, 3rd ed. (Washington, DC: Congressional Quarterly Press, 1996), Chapter 11.

37. Students will find expanded discussions of the various arguments over judicial review in Abraham, pp. 312–327; J. W. Peltason, *Corwin & Peltason's Understanding the Constitution*, 7th ed. (Hinsdale, IL: Dryden, 1976), pp. 26–28.

38. Abrahamson, p. 288.

39. Abrahamson, pp. 270–271; Steiner, pp. 96–98.

40. Abrahamson, pp. 288–289; Steiner, pp. 98–100; Norton, p. 344; Rasmussen, p. 131; Francesca Klug, Keir Starmer, and Stuart Weir, "Civil Liberties and the Parliamentary Watchdog: The Passage of the Criminal Justice and Public Order Act 1994," *Parliamentary Affairs* 49 (October 1996): 537; G. W. Jones, "The British Bill of Rights," *Parliamentary Affairs* 43 (January 1990): 36.

## Chapter 11

1. See M. J. Peterson, "The Use of Analogies in Developing Outer Space Law," *International Organization* 51 (Spring 1997): 245–274, for an analysis of the preceding details and for a discussion of additional aspects of this case, including its use in critiquing realism.

2. This point is made in Charles W. Kegley, Jr., and Eugene R. Wittkopf, *World Politics: Trend and Transformation*, 6th ed. (New York: St. Martin's, 1997), p. 19.

3. This analysis of idealism—defined broadly to include both early idealists and

contemporary idealist-inspired neoliberals and institutionalists—is based on John T. Rourke, *International Politics on the World Stage,* 4th ed. (Guilford, CT: Dushkin, 1993), pp. 144–149; Scott Burchill, "Introduction" and "Liberal Internationalism," in *Theories of International Relations,* edited by Scott Burchill and Andrew Linklater (New York: St. Martin's, 1996), pp. 4–5, 61–63; Mel Gurtov, *Global Politics in the Human Interest,* 3rd ed. (Boulder, CO: Rienner, 1994), p. 54; Mark R. Amstutz, *International Conflict and Cooperation: An Introduction to World Politics* (Madison, WI: Brown & Benchmark, 1995), pp. 16–19; Joseph M. Grieco, "Anarchy and the Limits of Cooperation: A Realist Critique of the Newest Liberal Institutionalism," in *Neorealism and Neoliberalism: The Contemporary Debate,* edited by David A. Baldwin (New York: Columbia University Press, 1993), pp. 116–140.

4. See, for example, the arguments of Vaclav Havel, "A Call for Sacrifice: The Co-Responsibility of the West," *Foreign Affairs* 73 (March–April 1994): 2–7.

5. The concept of human security versus state security is presented in Ken Booth and Peter Vale, "Security in Southern Africa: After Apartheid, beyond Realism," *International Affairs* 71 (1995): 291–298; Michael Renner, "Transforming Security," in *The State of the World 1997,* edited by Linda Starke (New York: Norton, 1997), pp. 128–131.

6. Ibid.

7. Grieco, pp. 119–120; Amstutz, p. 17; Gurtov, pp. 54, 227–228.

8. Neta C. Crawford discusses the league and its support for idealist perspectives in "A Security Regime among Democracies: Cooperation among Iroquois Nations," *International Organization* 48 (Summer 1994): 345–385.

9. This section's discussion of realism is guided by the observations in Rourke, pp. 142–144; Amstutz, pp. 15–16; Stephen G. Brooks, "Dueling Realisms," *International Organization* 51 (Summer 1997): 445–477; Frances A. Beer and Robert Hariman, "Realism and Rhetoric in International Relations," in *Post-Realism: The Rhetorical Turn in International Relations,* edited by Francis A. Beer and Robert Hariman (East Lansing: Michigan State University Press, 1996), pp. 1–30; Scott Burchill, "Realism and Neorealism," in Burchill and Linklater, pp. 67–92; David A. Baldwin, "Neoliberalism, Neorealism, and World Politics," in Baldwin, pp. 3–25; Kenneth A. Oye, "Explaining the End of the Cold War: Morphological and Behavioral Adaptions to the Nuclear Peace?" in *International Relations Theory and the End of the Cold War,* edited by Richard Ned Lebow and Thomas Risse-Kappen (New York: Columbia University Press, 1995), pp. 57–83; John Spanier and Steven W. Hook, *American Foreign Policy since World War II,* 14th ed. (Washington, DC: Congressional Quarterly Press, 1998), p. 332; Robert O. Keohane and Joseph S. Nye, *Power and Interdependence: World Politics in Transition* (Boston: Little, Brown, 1977), Chapter 2; Jim George, *Discourses of Global Politics: A Critical (Re)Introduction to International Relations* (Boulder, CO: Rienner, 1994), especially pp. 118–134; Andrew Linklater, "Neo-Realism in Theory and Practice," in *International Relations Theory Today,* edited by Ken Booth and Steve Smith (University Park: Pennsylvania State University Press, 1995), pp. 241–261; Joel H. Rosenthal, *Righteous Realists: Political Realism, Responsible Power, and American Culture in the Nuclear Age* (Baton Rouge: Louisiana State University Press, 1991), pp. 1–12; Richard Ned Lebow, "The Long Peace, the End of the Cold War, and the Failure of Realism," *International Organization* 48 (Spring 1994): 249–277; Rey Koslowski and Friedrich V. Kratochwil, "Understanding Change in International Politics: The Soviet Empire's Demise and the International System," *International Organization* 48 (Spring 1994): 215–247.

10. Information on U.S. intervention is found in Mi Yung Moon, "Explaining U.S. Intervention in Third World Internal Wars, 1945–1989," *Journal of Conflict Resolution* 41 (August 1997): 580–602.

11. See the extended analysis in Barnett R. Rubin, "Women and Pipelines: Afghanistan's Proxy Wars," *International Affairs* 73 (1997): 283–296.

12. This proposition is associated most closely with the neorealism of Kenneth Waltz, as discussed in Burchill, "Realism and Neo-Realism," p. 85.

13. George F. Kennan and John Lukacs, "From World War to Cold War," *American Heritage* (December 1995): 42–67; Spanier and Hook, pp. 36–41; William R. Keylor, *The Twentieth-Century World: An International History* (New York: Oxford University Press, 1996), pp. 261–262; George Brown Tindall, *America: A Narrative History* (New York: Norton, 1984), pp. 1191–1192; Frederick H. Hartmann and Robert L. Wendzel, *America's Foreign Policy in a Changing World* (New York: HarperCollins, 1994), pp. 206–212.

14. Keylor, pp. 262–263; David W. Ellwood, *Rebuilding Europe: Western Europe, America and Postwar Reconstruction* (New York: Longman, 1992), Chapters 4–6 and p. 155.

15. Spanier and Hook, pp. 63–64.

16. Students can find extended discussions of the Cold War tensions and the easing of tensions in Tindall, pp. 1191–1308; Rourke, pp. 42–48; Hartmann and Wendzel, p. 210.

17. Numbers of refugees, including internally displaced persons, are found in UN High Commissioner for Refugees, *What Is UNHCR?* (http://www.unhcr.ch/un&ref/what/what.htm, accessed 15 January 1998).

18. CNN Balkan Conflict News, *Roots of the Balkan Troubles: A History of Ethnic Skirmishes* (http://www.cnn.com/World/Bosnia/history/index/html, accessed 13 January 1998); CNN Balkan Conflict: Timeline, *With Independence Came War: Recent Events in the Balkans* (http://www.cnn.com/WORLD/Bosnia/time/time6.html, accessed 13 January 1998).

19. U.S. Department of State, *Safe and Secure Dismantlement of Nuclear Weapons in the New Independent States.* Fact Sheet released by the Bureau of Public Affairs, March 20, 1996 (http://www.state.gov/regions/nis/russia_nuclear_weapons.html, accessed 13 January 1998); Nuclear Regulatory Commission, *TIP05—Assistance to Regulatory Bodies of Russia and Ukraine* (http://www.nrc.gov/OPA/gmo/tip/tip9705.htm, accessed 14 January 1998).

20. Spanier and Hook, pp. 294–300; *SIPRI Yearbook 2002* (New York: Oxford University Press, 2002), pp. 63–66.

21. Charter of the United Nations: Chapter 1 (http://www.un.org/aboutun/charter/chapter1.htm, accessed 15 January 1998).

22. Ibid.

23. These five divisions are discussed in United Nations, *The UN in Brief* (http://www.un.org/Overview/brief.html, accessed 15 January 1998). One of the original major divisions—the Trusteeship Council—has suspended operations.

24. *U.N. Peacekeeping Operations, Frequently Asked Questions* (http://www.un.org/Depts/dpko/faq.htm, accessed 15 January 1998).

25. U.N. Economic and Social Council (http://www.un.org/Overview/Organs/ecosoc.html, accessed 15 January 1998).

26. United Nations, The International Court of Justice (http://www.un.org/Overview/Organs/icj.html, accessed 15 January 1998).

27. United Nations, The World Health Organization; *Headquarters' Major Programmes* (http://www.who.ch, accessed 15 January 1998).

28. United Nations, *Major Achievements of the United Nations* (http://www.un.org/Overview/achieve.html, accessed 14 January 1998).

29. Bice Maiguashca, "The Transnational Indigenous Movement in a Changing World Order," pp. 356–382, and Chadwick F. Alger, "Citizens and the UN System in a Changing World," pp. 301–329, in *Global Transformation: Challenges to the State System,* edited by Yoshikazu Sakamoto (New York: United Nations University Press, 1994).

30. *UN Peacekeeping Operations, Frequently Asked Questions;* UN Report, "More International Troops and Equipment Needed in Liberia" (18 December 2003): http://www.un.org/apps/news.

31. International Court of Justice, *Statement of the President of the Court. The Limitations on the Contribution by the International Court of Justice to the Maintenance of Peace,* statement by Judge Mohammed Bedjaoui, President of the International Court of Justice, made in plenary meeting of the General Assembly at its 51st session on 15 October 1996 (http://www.icj-cij.org/Presscom/SpeechPresidentGA1996e.htm, accessed 15 January 1998).

32. Maurice Bertrand, "The Role of the United Nations in the Context of the

Changing World Order," pp. 462–474. On Annan and Iraq, see "20 March 2003 Statement by the Secretary-General on Iraq" and "Iraq Statements: Annan" at http://www. un.org/news.

33. NATO Fact Sheets, NATO Basic Fact Sheet Nr. 12, *What Is NATO?* (http:// www.nato.int).

34). NATO Communiques, *The Alliance's New Strategic Concept* (http://www.nato. int.docu/comm/c911107a.htm, accessed 14 January 1998).

35. NATO Fact Sheets, NATO Basic Fact Sheet Nr. 2, *The North Atlantic Cooperation Council (NACC)* (http://www.nato.int/ docu/facts/nacc.htm, accessed 14 January 1998).

36. NATO Fact Sheets, NATO Basic Fact Sheet Nr. 18, *The Development of NATO's Partnership with Ukraine June 1997* (http:// www.nato-int/docu/facts/ukr.htm, accessed 14 January 1998).

37. NATO Fact Sheets, NATO Basic Fact Sheet Nr. 9, *Partnership for Peace (PFP)* (March 1996).

38. For arguments in support of and against NATO enlargement, students may wish to read NATO Fact Sheets, NATO Basic Fact Sheet Nr. 13, *NATO's Enlargement* (June 1997) (http://www.nato.int/docu/ facts/enl.htm, accessed 13 January 1998); Sherle R. Schwenninger, "The Case against NATO Enlargement: Clinton's Fateful Gamble," *The Nation* (20 October 1997): 21–31; Ronald Steel, "Instead of NATO," *New York Review of Books* (15 January 1998): 21–24; Howard Baker, Jr., Sam Nunn, Brent Scowcroft, and Alton Frye, "NATO: A Debate Recast," *New York Times* (4 February 1998): A23. For updated information, see the NATO Fact Sheets at http://www. nato.int.

## Chapter 12

1. *SIPRI Yearbook 2002* (New York: Oxford University Press, 2002), pp. 39–44, 67–68; Loch K. Johnson, "Introduction—A New Foreign Policy for a Fragmented World," *PS* 36 (January 2003): 3; Robert A. Pape, "The Strategic Logic of Suicide Terrorism," *American Political Science Review 97* (August 2003): 356; David E. Sanger, "bin Laden Is Wanted in Attacks, `Dead or Alive,' President Says," *New York Times* (18 September 2001): A1, B4; John F. Burns, "Taliban Refuse Quick decision over bin Laden," *New York Times* (18 September 2001): A1, B2; Douglas Frantz, "Taliban Say They Want to Negotiate with the U.S. over bin Laden," *New York Times* (3 October 2001): B1; John F. Burns, "New Push to Get bin Laden to Agree to Quit Afghanistan," *New York Times* (8 September 2001): A1, B3; R. W. Aple, Jr, "A Clear Message: `I Will Not Relent,'" *New York Times* (21 September 2001): A1.

2. Pape, pp. 343–361.

3. Daniel Philpott, "The Challenge of September 11 to Secularism in International Relations," *World Politics* 55 (2002): 66–95.

4. Joseph S. Nye, Jr., *The Paradox of American Power* (New York: Oxford University Press, 2002), pp. 38–39. On hyperstatism as a response, see Walter LaFeber, "The Post September 11 Debate over Empire, Globalization, and Fragmentation," *Political Science Quarterly* 117 (2002): 2.

5. LaFeber, p. 2; Nye, Chapter 3. For the number of articles on globalization appearing in the *New York Times* and *Washington Post*, see Doug Henwood, "Beyond Globophobia," *The Nation* (1 December 2003): 17.

6. Susan Carruthers, "Media and Communications Technology," in *Issues in World Politics,* ed. Brian White et al., 2nd ed (New York: Palgrave, 2001), p. 214.

7. Brigitte L. Nacos, "Terrorism as Breaking News: Attack on America," *Political Science Quarterly* 118 (2003): 23–52. On CNN's response, see Larry J. Sabato, "Sobering Up: The Media World Remade," in *American Government in a Changed World: The Effects of September 11, 2001* (New York: Longman, 2003), p. 35.

8. Holli A. Semetko, "The Media," in *Comparing Democracies: Elections and Voting in Global Perspective,* edited by LeDuc, Niemi, and Norris, pp. 254–279.

9. Brian T. Evans, "United Kingdom," in Gross, ed., pp. 99–122; Semetko, p. 259.

10. Wolfgang Hastert, "Germany," in Gross, ed., pp. 127–128.

11. Joseph S. Johnson, "China," in Gross, ed., pp. 277–298.

12. Brigitte L. Nacos, "Terrorism as Breaking News: Attack on America," *Political Science Quarterly* 118 (2003): 23–52.

13. Robert J. Donovan and Ray Scherer, "Politics Transformed," *Wilson Quarterly* (Spring 1992): 1992; Desmond Smith, "TV News Did Not Just Happen—It Had to Invent Itself," *Smithsonian* (June 1989): 77. Michael Dukakis made this comment about the succinct quote, as discussed in Daniel C. Hallin, "Sound Bite Democracy," *Wilson Quarterly* (Spring 1992): 34.

14. Rowland Lorimer with Paddy Scannell, *Mass Communications: A Comparative Introduction* (New York: Manchester University Press, 1994), p. 15 discusses the visual dimension of electronic media. Doris Graber, "Political Communication: Scope, Progress, Promise," in Ada Finifter, *Political Science: The State of the Discipline II* (Washington, DC: American Political Science Association, 1993), p. 313.

15. Public broadcasting and public radio stations also feel commercial pressures, as analyzed in James Ledbetter, "Public Broadcasting Sells (Out?)," *The Nation* (1 December 1997): 11–14. See Ian Ward, *Politics of the Media* (New York: Macmillan, 1995), pp. 108–109, and W. Lance Bennett, *News: The Politics of Illusion,* 3rd ed. (White Plains, NY: Longman, 1996), pp. 9–10, for a discussion of the commercial and structural pressures on the creation of news. Graber, p. 313.

16. Walter Karp, "Who Decides What Is News? (Hint: It's Not Journalists)," *Utne Reader* (November–December 1989): 60–68. Bennett, p. 1

17. David D. Driscoll, "The IMF and the World Bank: How Do They Differ?" at IMF (http://www.imf.org); Raymond F. Mikesell, "Bretton Woods: Original Intentions and Current Problems," *Contemporary Economic Policy* (October 2000): 404–414; Joaquina Pires-O'Brien, "The Misgivings of Globalisation," *Contemporary Review* (November 2000): 264–272.

18. "World Bank Aid Falls in FY 2000," *ENR* (2 October 2000): 13.

19. See the sources in note 17.

20. IMF reports (December 2003), http://www.imf.org. "Asiawweek: Business Briefs: Pakistan Wins a Breather," *Asiaweek* (15 December 2000): 1; "Asia: Pakistan's Cash," *The Economist* (9 December 2000): 48.

21. "The WTO in Brief, Part I: The Multilateral Trading System—Past, Present, Future" (http://www.wto.org/english/thewto_e/whatis_e/inbrief_e/inbr01_e.htm); "WTO Dispute Settlement: List of Panel and Appellate Body Reports" (http://www.wto.org/english/tratop_e/dispu_e/distab_e.htm); Jack Robertson, "China Shows Pockets of Progress: A Few Local Electronics Manufacturers Prove They Can Hold Their Own against Global Competition," *Electronic Buyers'* News (4 December 2000): 69.

22. IMF, World Bank, and WTO reports at http://www.imf.org, http://worldbank.org, and http://www.wto.org, respectively

23. The World Bank Group, "Who Runs the World Bank" and "Membership in the World Bank" (http://www.worldbank.org). Driscoll; Mandela is quoted in Aileen Kwa, "In Focus: WTO and Developing Countries," *Foreign Policy in Focus* 3 (November 1998), p. 2.

24. IMF, "Debt Initiative for the Heavily Indebted Poor Countries (HIPCs)" (http:www.imf.org, accessed 5 September 1999). See also Regina JereMalanda, "The Economic Gains of Debt," *New African* (November 2000): 21; "Finance and Economics: Can Debt Relief Make a Difference," *The Economist* (18 November 2000), pp. 85–86. Reports for 2003 are available at IMF, ww.imf.org.

25. Ibid. See also Biplab Dasgupta, *Structural Adjustment, Global Trade, and the New Political Economy* (New York: Zed Books, 1998), especially Chapter 3.

26. See Dasgupta, Chapter 3. See also Soren Ambrose, "Multilateral Debt," *Foreign Policy in Focus* 21 (August 1999), n.p.

27. Anver Versi, "The New Fight for Independence," *African Business* (September 2000): 9; Milan Vesely, "Kenya: IMF to Call the Tune," *African Business* (September 2000): 27–28; "International: Dancing in Kenya to the Donors' Tune," *The Economist* (5 August 2000): 43.

28. "AIDS Loan Rejected," *New Africa* (November 2000): 12.

29. Robert Lenzer, "Power without Fire-bombs," *Forbes* (27 November 2000): 156; Anja Helk, "The Bosses Have Gone International, Now It's Our Turn," *Euromoney* (September 2000): 17–18; James H. Smalhout, "The World Bank's New Clients," *Barron's* (25 September 2000): 59.

30. Richard J. Barnett, "Stateless Corporations: Lords of the Global Economy," *The Nation* (19 December 1994): 754; see also the data analyzed in Paul Rogers, "Reviewing Britain's Security," *International Affairs* 73 (1997): 660–661.

31. Robert D. Kaplan, "Was Democracy Just a Moment?" *The Atlantic Monthly* 280 (December 1997): 71.

32. World Bank development report 2004 at http://www.worldbank.org.

33. For an excellent discussion of the drawbacks and limitations of using GNP/ GDP indicators, see Clifford Cobb, Ted Halstead, and Jonathan Rowe, "If the GDP Is Up, Why Is America Down?" *The Atlantic Monthly* 276 (October 1995): 59–78. On U.S. figures, see Aaron Bernstein, "Inequality: How the Gap between Rich and Poor Hurts the Economy," *Business Week* (15 August 1994): 78–79.

34. "Forum: Does America Still Work?" *Harper's Magazine* (May 1996): 44.

35. Richard Perez-Pena, "New York's Income Gap Largest in Nation," *New York Times* (17 December 1997): A14; see also the related data discussed in Paulette Thomas, "Poverty Spread in 1992 to Total of 36.9 Million," *Wall Street Journal* (5 October 1993): A2, A6.

36. Benjamin Schwarz, "American Inequality: Its History and Scary Future," *New York Times* (19 December 1995): A19.

37. Nafis Sadik, "Poverty, Population, Pollution," in *Global Issues 93/94,* 9th ed., edited by Robert M. Jackson (Guilford, CT: Dushkin, 1993), p. 135. This is reprinted from *The UNESCO Courier* (January 1992): 18–21. Projections on global poverty levels are also discussed in James H. Mittelman, *Out from Underdevelopment: Prospects for the Third World* (New York: St. Martin's, 1988), p. 11.

38. Daphne Topousiz, "The Feminization of Poverty," in Jackson, ed., p. 133; this article is reprinted from *Africa Report* (July–August 1990): 60–63.

# Glossary

**allegory of the cave**  A discussion in Plato's *Republic,* often read as an exploration of the processes, difficulties, and rewards of seeking enlightenment, which presents enlightenment as liberating

**amicus curiae briefs**  Legal documents known as "friend of the court" briefs; often filed by U.S. interest groups as part of a larger strategy of **judicial involvement**

**anarchy**  Absence of government, emphasized by realism in explaining the nonexistence of any overarching governing power in international politics

**anomic interest groups**  Groups exhibiting the lowest level of organizational identity

**associational groups**  Highly organized interest groups possessing formal rules of operation, designated leaders, official structures, and an official name

**behavioralism**  A perspective in political science presenting itself as an alternative to **traditionalism;** behavioralism emphasizes empirical analysis of the actual behavior of politically involved individuals and groups, as opposed to historical/textual analysis of institutions and laws

**Bill of Rights**  The first 10 amendments to the U.S. Constitution

**bipolar system**  An international system in which two superpower governments exist

**bundling**  A way of making direct contributions to candidates running for U.S. office; the process of combining numerous individual contributions together to make a single large contribution

**campaign involvement**  A U.S. interest group strategy that can include such activity as registering voters, working on behalf of certain candidates, convincing candidates to support certain positions, joining political parties and shaping party decisions from the inside, or making campaign contributions

**case study**  An investigation of a particular process, phenomenon, or entity

**classical liberalism**   Liberalism drawing on the teachings of such theorists as John Locke and Adam Smith and emphasizing limited government, capitalism, human rationality, and a wide range of personal liberty beyond the scope of government regulation

**cloture**   Procedure requiring a three-fifths majority vote through which the Senate can terminate a **filibuster**

**collective responsibility**   The cabinet's custom of publicly upholding positions taken by the executive in Britain

**comparative politics**   The study of governments and/or political processes across countries and/or time periods

**confederalism**   An organization with power decentralized and held primarily or exclusively by local offices

**conference committee**   Used in U.S. Congress to settle differences when the two chambers of the Congress disagree on the wording of a bill; consists of members from both the House and the Senate

**conflictual party relations**   Party relations in democracies wherein political parties are divided by extreme ideological disagreements and lack established moderating routines through which parties soften their disagreements

**consensual party relations**   Party relations in democracies wherein political parties are in agreement on fundamental ideological issues

**conservatism**   Includes **classical liberal conservatism** and **traditional conservatism**

**consociational party relations**   Party relations in democracies wherein parties differ radically on fundamental issues (as in conflictual systems) but possess established routines of bargaining and compromise

**constituency relations**   Services performed by government officials on behalf of voters

**constructive vote of no confidence**   A process in Germany wherein rules state that the German legislature cannot cast a no-confidence vote unless it also agrees on whom to name as a new chancellor

**containment**   The name given to U.S. foreign policy objective of limiting Soviet expansionism in the years immediately after World War II; George F. Kennan spelled out the logic of containment policy in 1946 and 1947

**correlation**   A relationship in which changes in one variable are found when there are changes in another variable

**cumulative voting**   A type of election in which voters cast as many votes as there are offices to be filled; voters can combine their votes for a single candidate or split their votes among two or more candidates; among the candidates, the top vote recipients are the winners

**democratic corporatism**   Found in democracies and involving patterns of government coordination of interest groups, government incorporation of interest groups into the actual governing process, and the presence of peak interest group associations; that is, democratic corporatist societies are ones in which interest groups are not outsiders relative to democratic government but, rather, are partners with democratic government

**democratic government**   Government in which the people and the government are connected; in other words, the people are self-governed in terms of inputs and outputs. Democratic government may be viewed as consisting of five components: **participation, pluralism, developmentalism, protection,** and **performance**

**dependent variable**   Something that is being affected; that which is being explained

**developmentalism**   A component of democracy describing the process involving people developing their human potential sufficient to possess an awareness of their actions so that those actions are self-directed and self-governing

**direct contributions**   Campaign contributions given to candidates themselves

**direct lobbying**   A strategy whereby U.S. interest groups make personal contact with political officials and try to persuade officials to support the aims of the interest group

**discharge petition**   A device used in the U.S. House to bring a bill out of committee and to the House for a vote; requires 218 votes

**double day**   The workday during which women work for wages (as employees at factories, offices, etc.) but also work for no wages as members of families

**electoral college**   A system, as required by U.S. Constitution, for electing U.S. presidents and vice presidents; to win the presidency, a candidate must receive a majority (270) of electoral college votes

**electorate**   Eligible voters

**empirical**   Observable, factual

**environmentalism**   Ideology asserting the importance of viewing natural resources from an ecological perspective emphasizing stewardship and ecosystem integrity

**epistemology**   A branch of philosophy that examines evaluations of what constitutes truth

**exchange**   A type of power involving incentives

**expansive liberty**   A form of liberty promoted by interventionist government when government acts to promote conditions in which human potential can be maximized; advocated by modern liberalism

**experiment**   Investigates hypotheses through the use of a test group and a control group

**fascism**   An ideology advocating the creation of the totalistic (totalitarian) state

**federalism**   Organization of government into different levels with power divided among the levels (local, state, and national)

**feminism**   An ideology that opposes the political, economic, and/or cultural relegation of women to positions of inferiority and advocates gender equality

**filibuster**   A process in the U.S. Senate of "talking a bill to death"

**force**   Power by physical means

**globalization**   Both a condition and a process in which state boundaries become increasingly penetrable; globalization has been occurring for centuries

**grassroots lobbying**   A U.S. interest group strategy of trying to convince voters and members of the public to support the interest group's positions

**Hawthorne effect**   Effect produced when members of a test group modify their behavior because they know they are in an **experiment**

**hold**   A practice in the U.S. Senate whereby a senator can request that a bill not be scheduled for consideration

**hypothesis**   A statement proposing a specific relationship between phenomena

**idealism**   A model of analysis in international relations stressing the capacity of states to coexist and interact peacefully and harmoniously; an alternative to **realism**

**impeachment**   A provision in the U.S. Constitution allowing the removal of public officials from office; U.S. presidents may be impeached by the House of Representatives and either acquitted or convicted by the Senate

**independent expenditures**   Campaign spending in U.S. politics, which takes the form of spending on behalf of candidates for office but not of giving the expenditures directly to candidates for office

**independent variable** Something that acts on or affects something else

**indirect quantitative analysis** A research approach that is indirect in the sense that it uses data already compiled and assesses quantitative (that is, mathematical, statistical) information to discover **empirically** verifiable patterns

**interest group** A group of individuals or institutions sharing interests or opinions and united enough to work together to seek to influence political outcomes

**interest group pluralism** A pattern found in democracies in which interest groups operate as entities outside of government, pursue their choices of strategies independently of government directions or coordination, and compete with a variety of other interest groups to influence democratic politics

**intergovernmental organizations (IGOs)** Political organizations in which membership is held exclusively by states

**interventionist government** Regulatory government advocated by modern liberalism

**judicial involvement** U.S. interest group strategy that may include filing **amicus curiae briefs** and interest group decisions to file civil (noncriminal) suits, to offer legal assistance to individuals in court cases, to try to shape judicial appointments, and to try to influence judicial opinions by publicizing the interest group's viewpoints

**judicial review** Power of a court to overturn laws and actions of government officials on the grounds that such laws and actions violate constitutional principles

**legitimacy** The property states possess when their citizens view their **sovereignty** as appropriate, proper, or acceptable

**liberal institutionalism** A form of **idealism** focusing on the concepts of economic interdependence of states and the importance of international organizations

**liberalism** Includes **classical liberalism** and **modern liberalism**

**libertarianism** A contemporary application of classical liberalism

**Magna Carta** A document signed in 1215 by King John that provided that England's king would acknowledge the rights of his subjects and would recognize the feudal rights of the nobility

**majoritarian outcomes** Outcomes in which major parties control national legislatures over time by holding majorities in these legislatures

**manipulation** A type of power in which the agent using power conceals the objective

**markup** The process of revising a bill in the U.S. Congress

**Marshall Plan** A policy, beginning in 1948, that provided U.S. economic aid to Europe, consistent with the **containment** philosophy

**Marxism–Leninism** A form of socialism that combines the teachings of Marx with those of Lenin and draws on Lenin's advocacy of a centralized party, his use of imperialism as an analytical construct, and his advocacy of violence as a means of bringing about socialism

**membership organizations** Interest groups that have official members

**model of analysis** A worldview or set of assumptions associated with a certain perspective or outlook

**modern liberalism** A form of liberalism, associated with the teachings of theorists such as T. H. Green, that stresses the need for an active, interventionist state to advance expansive liberty and to correct such problems as economic inequality

**multinational corporations (MNCs)** International businesses that have operations, transactions, and assets in the territories of different states and have the potential to act as rivals to states

**multinational states**   States in which two or more nations exist

**multiparty outcomes**   Outcomes in which no single party controls a national legislature

**nation**   A group of people with a sense of unity based on the importance the group attributes to a shared trait, attribute, or custom

**New Deal Coalition**   A voting group consisting of lower income, minority, and Southern voters that emerged in the United States in the 1930s in support of President Franklin Roosevelt's New Deal

**nonassociational groups**   Groups exhibiting low levels of organization but possessing a more enduring organization than that characterizing **anomic interest groups**

**nondemocratic government**   Government in which the people are not self-governing and are not directing government policy toward the expression of their interests

**nongovernmental organizations (NGOs)**   Nonstate, voluntary groups that pursue political objectives

**nonmembership organizations**   Groups such as universities, corporations, and hospitals that possess a formal organizational structure but do not have members who have officially "joined"; however, insofar as the staff, stockholders, and/or clients have shared interests and act to shape political events in a manner consistent with those interests, the nonmembership organization acts as an interest group

**normative**   Pertaining to value judgments and ethics

**North Atlantic Treaty Organization (NATO)**   An alliance formed in 1949 to create a common defense of member countries; the United States, Canada, Denmark, Iceland, Italy, Norway, Portugal, Britain, France, Belgium, The Netherlands, and Luxembourg were the original members. Members pledged to defend any other member attacked; under these terms, NATO was intended to provide a deterrence against Soviet military expansion

**operational definition**   A definition so precise that it allows for empirical testing

**parliamentary sovereignty**   The authority of Parliament—not a separate judicial branch—to exercise ultimate authority in deciding the soundness of laws and governmental actions; alternative to **judicial review**

**parliamentary systems**   Governmental arrangements in which (1) legislatures select executive leadership; (2) executives can be removed by votes of no confidence and new elections may be necessitated; and (3) executive and legislative powers are combined, not separated, in order to forge a working partnership between the two branches of government

**participation**   A component of democracy referring to the processes whereby people act in political ways to connect themselves to government and thus become self-governing

**performance**   A component of democracy referring to outputs reflective of a self-governing population's pursuit of well-being

**persuasion**   A nonphysical type of power in which the agent using power makes its intentions and desires known to the agent over whom power is exercised

**pluralism**   A component of democracy that refers to the multiplicity, diversity, or plurality of opinions and groups free to express themselves within a political system

**pocket veto**   A type of veto exercised when the following occurs: If a bill is sent by Congress for the president to sign into law, and if the president simply does nothing with the bill—provided that Congress is adjourned within 10 days—the bill is killed (vetoed)

**political action committees (PACs)**   Organizations that raise and distribute campaign contributions in the United States

**political party**   An organization that puts forward proposed leaders for positions in government

**political socialization**   A process of political learning that results in the formation of an individual's political attitudes, values, and behaviors

**pork barrel legislation**   U.S. laws that are narrow in terms of benefits and are passed to help a congressperson's district or state

**postbehavioralism**   A political science perspective that offers an alternative to both **traditionalism** and **behavioralism;** postbehavioralists argue that political science should be relevant as well as empirically reliable

**postmodernism**   A philosophical outlook positing that any ideology putting forward absolute statements as truths is to be viewed with profound skepticism

**power**   An ability to act in order to (1) influence an outcome that allows for the achievement of an objective and/or (2) influence another agent to act in a manner in which the agent, on its own, would not choose to act

**presidential systems**   Governmental arrangements in which executive–legislative relations operate as follows: (1) Executives and legislatures are elected in distinct, separate elections for fixed terms of office; (2) executives cannot be removed by votes of no confidence; and (3) executive power is separated from legislative power

**proportional representation**   Types of election procedures under which parties (and their candidates) receive a percentage of offices based on the percentage of votes won in an election

**prospective voting**   Voting on the basis of a rational assessment of probable future benefits

**protection**   A component of democracy that refers to democracy's commitment to limiting governmental power so that governments do not become tyrannical

**protest**   Interest group strategy that may be used to publicize an interest group's viewpoints and sway public opinion

**quasi-experiments**   Experiments "in the real world" that do not fully meet the conditions used in experiments

**realism**   A model of analysis in international relations that emphasizes the power component in international affairs and focuses on the likelihood of conflict between states existing in anarchic international conditions; an alternative to **idealism**

**referendum**   A measure submitted for a popular vote

**retrospective voting**   A voting decision in which a voter makes up his or her mind by looking at the present and/or past performance of candidates or parties and then either rewards or penalizes those candidates or parties on the basis of this performance

**Rosenthal effect**   Effect produced when investigators convey their expectations to the subjects in an **experiment**

**scientific method**   A set of procedures for gathering information, characterized by epistemological **empiricism** insofar as it is based on the assumption that what is true is that which is observable

**single-member plurality (SMP) elections**   Elections in which the winner is the candidate who receives more votes than anyone else even if the winner does not gain a majority of votes

**single transferable vote (STV) elections**   Elections in which voters can rank candidates on the ballot as first, second, third, etc. choices; when all votes are counted, second, third, etc. choices are taken into account to reward candidates other than first-place winners

**social democracy**   A form of **socialism** that combines socialist and democratic principles and asserts that socialism must be pursued and implemented peacefully and with respect for democratic freedoms

**socialism**   An ideology that argues that citizens are best served by policies focusing on meeting the basic needs of the entire society rather than by policies focusing on serving the needs of individuals as individuals; socialism draws on diverse traditions and can be applied in a **Marxist–Leninist** fashion as well as in a **social democratic** fashion

**sociological cleavages**   A process in which voting decisions are affected by membership in certain groups

**Socratic method**   Critical, analytical questioning of fundamental philosophical issues

**sovereignty**   The property a state has when it has the actual capacity to carry out the ultimate rule making and rule enforcement in society, including the provision of security, the extraction of revenues, and the formation of rules for resolving disputes and allocating resources within the boundaries of the territory in which the state exercises jurisdiction

**state**   A set of offices with security, extractive, allocative, and final rule-defining authority

**state autonomy**   A pattern of government–interest group relations in which governments originate policy on their own, rather than responding to interest group pressures

**state corporatism**   Government coordination of interest groups and governmental inclusion of interest groups into the formal governing process in such a manner as to facilitate government control over interest groups to such an extent that the groups serve the government

**Structural Adjustment Programs (SAPs)**   Programs designed to establish creditworthiness as defined by International Monetary Fund/World Bank lending criteria

**survey research**   The use of surveys (questionnaires and/or interviews) to gather data

**third parties**   Minor parties; parties lacking the capacity to capture a plurality of votes

**traditional conservatism**   Conservatism drawing on the teachings of Edmund Burke and emphasizing the importance of civil institutions, the dangers of political change, and the value of following traditional morality

**traditionalism**   A perspective in political science that seeks to understand politics by examining laws, governmental offices, constitutions, and other official institutions associated with politics and to describe how institutions operate through formal rules and publicly sanctioned procedures; an alternative to **behavioralism** and **postbehavioralism**

**Truman Doctrine**   A policy announced by President Truman in 1947 claiming that the interest of the United States was served by providing economic assistance to countries that might otherwise come under Soviet influence

**unitary states**   States that concentrate power at the central, or national, level of government

**variable**   Something that varies, changes, or manifests itself differently from one case to another

**veto**   Process in which U.S. presidents negate bills passed by Congress; includes regular and **pocket vetos**

**volition**   Will or choice

# Index

# Credits

This page constitutes an extension of the copyright page. We have made every effort to trace the ownership of all copyrighted material and to secure permission from copyright holders. In the event of any question arising as to the use of any material, we will be pleased to make the necessary corrections in future printings. Thanks are due to the following authors, publishers, and agents for permission to use the material indicated.

**Chapter 1. 4:** © Suzanne De Chillo/The New York Times **6:** AP/Wide World **6:** © Paul Boisvert/The New York Times
**Chapter 5. 106:** © Alan S. Weiner
**Chapter 6. 128:** Ellen Grigsby
**Chapter 8. 177:** © Dominique Aubert/Sygma/CORBIS
**Chapter 9. 207:** AP/Wide World **211:** © James Estrin/The New York Times **211:** © Jeff Mitchell/Reuters/CORBIS
**Chapter 11. 245:** © Chang W. Lee/The New York Times